Edmund Ruffin

Edmund Ruffin

A Biography

BETTY L. MITCHELL

INDIANA UNIVERSITY PRESS · BLOOMINGTON

Manufactured in the United States of America

Library of Congress Cataloging in Publication Data

Mitchell, Betty L
Edmund Ruffin.

Bibliography: p.288
Includes index.
1. Ruffin, Edmund, 1794–1865.   2. Secession.
3. United States—Politics and government—1857–1861.
4. Virginia—Biography.   I. Title.
F230.R932M57   973.7'13'0924 [B]   80–8381
ISBN 0-253-03876-3   AACR1
1 2 3 4 5 85 84 83 82 81

For
Mark,
with love

Biography represents imagination limited by truth, facts raised to the power of revelation.

The biographer must be a sort of bifurcated animal, digger and dreamer; for biography is an impossible amalgam: half rainbow, half stone. To exist at all, it must feed upon the truth of facts, and yet to exist on its highest level, it must pursue the truth of interpretation.

Paul Murray Kendall

CONTENTS

PREFACE

Over the past twenty years or so, much has been done in the way of Civil War scholarship concerning slavery and the abolitionists. The works of Kenneth M. Stampp, John Blassingame, Eugene Genovese, Herbert Gutman, Stephen B. Oates, Fawn M. Brodie, and others have contributed new insights to our understanding of both these important topics. Very little, by way of comparison, has been written about Southern whites and specifically those extreme Southern nationalists commonly called fire-eaters.

This is the first full-scale biography of Edmund Ruffin based on original research to appear in almost half a century. I believe it is time to take a fresh look at a man whose life is in so many ways indicative of Southern temperament during the antebellum and Civil War period of United States history. If the philosopher George Santayana is right and those who do not learn the lessons of the past are doomed to repeat its mistakes, then studying the people on the losing side is as important as studying the winners.

In no sense has it been my purpose or intention to write an apologia or justification of Edmund Ruffin and what he stood for. Nor have I tried to psychoanalyze him. Instead I have endeavored to understand this complex human being, this complicated and essentially tragic figure, and to let my readers draw their own conclusions about him. Wherever possible, I have allowed Ruffin to speak in his own words. As a biographer must do, I tried to remain "invisible," to let Ruffin occupy center stage, for this is his story, of course. Mainly, I hoped, in the words of Paul Murray Kendall, "to elicit, from the coldness of paper, the warmth of a life being lived."[1]

I would like to express my thanks to all the people who kindly helped me during the research and writing of this biography. I am grateful to the library staff at the University of Massachusetts at Amherst, particularly the Interlibrary Loan Department, which assisted me in locating and obtaining some obscure documents. The Library of Congress and the University of North Carolina were also of great help. Special acknowledgment goes to the archivists at the Virginia Historical Society in Richmond. In addition to being most hospitable, they did everything possible to make their considerable resources accessible to me.

While I was in Virginia doing research, I visited one of the Edmund Ruffin plantations, Marlbourne. The family members still living there were gracious and flattered me by their interest in my work. I would particularly like to thank Mr. and Mrs. Sterling P. Anderson, Jr. of Mechanicsville, who furnished me with valuable information pertaining to family genealogy.

My sincere appreciation goes to Professors Leonard L. Richards and Frederick W. Turner of the University of Massachusetts, who read the book in manuscript and offered valuable criticisms and advice.

But I owe my greatest debt of gratitude to Professor Stephen B. Oates of the University of Massachusetts, who gave unstintingly of his time and encouragement in helping me at every stage of this project. By word and example, he taught me that biography is indeed an art.

Not least of all, I would like to thank my husband, Mark Gerstein, who patiently read each chapter, calmed my writer's insecurities, and kept his sense of humor.

Edmund Ruffin

1

The Prophet of Marl

1

THE FOURTH OF OCTOBER, 1859, was a bright day, perfect for an autumn wedding. Guests from every part of Virginia's Tidewater region had been arriving at the Marlbourne mansion all morning. At twelve o'clock, Mildred Ruffin would marry Burwell B. Sayre. The bridegroom, whose brother William had married the bride's older sister Elizabeth, was delighted to be thus connected with one of Virginia's oldest, wealthiest, and most respected planter families. And Mildred, age thirty-two, was delighted to be finally wed. The only one decidedly out of place on this joyous occasion was the bride's father, Edmund Ruffin, who felt wretched.

Mildred was Ruffin's last unmarried daughter; and the old man, now sixty-five and a widower for over ten years, had secretly harbored the selfish hope that she would remain his companion until his death. Only the evening before they had shared a last tender moment together when Mildred sat at the melodeon, playing her father's favorite tunes. Never again, Ruffin despaired, would he and his beloved Mildred share "the same intimate & exclusive relation." Sons-in-law were almost impossible to "assimilate," and already the jealous father suspected that he saw "seeds of alienation" planted between the Sayre and Ruffin families. Seven years before, when Elizabeth Ruffin married William Sayre, Ruffin pointedly expressed his disapproval by conspicuously absenting himself from the wedding ceremony. Today, however, he glumly tried to reconcile himself to his loss and "put the best face on things" for Mildred's sake. But it was "a painful duty," he admitted, and try as he might to hide his true feelings, he knew he looked like "a miserable & desolate old man" from the time the guests arrived to the moment they were finally gone.[1]

Alone in his room that night, Ruffin pulled out his diary and poured onto its pages all his pent-up grief and self-pity. In less than five years, death had taken away three daughters and one cherished daughter-in-law, while his last daughter, his favorite "child," was lost to him through her marriage bonds. "If I had died five years ago," he mourned, "how much of unhappiness would have been escaped."[2]

For the next couple of weeks, Ruffin moped around the plantation, missing Mildred terribly. Conversational topics with Elizabeth and William Sayre, Marlbourne's only other residents, quickly ran dry; and besides, they only aggravated his resentment over Mildred's marriage. This left him with nothing to say, nothing to do, nothing to write. He was idle, and he hated it.

Added to these family problems was a sense of personal failure. Ruffin had given up active management of his Marlbourne estate in 1855 and sold it outright to his children two years later in the hopes of becoming, as he put it, "an itinerant missionary of disunion of the south & north." But now in the autumn of 1859, after years of zealous agitation, he could not count a single Virginia convert. The enormity of his tribulations overwhelmed him, and on October 18, 1859, he longed for death and may even have contemplated suicide. "I have lived long enough," he confided in his diary, "& a little more time of such unused & wearisome passage of time will make my life too long."[3]

2

Unknown to Ruffin, an event had already taken place in a different part of Virginia that would radically change his present despondent mood and fully revive his will to live. On Monday morning, October 17, the citizens of a little town in northwestern Virginia called Harper's Ferry awoke to the sounds of church bells tolling the alarm of servile insurrection. A band of eighteen men, led by the notorious Kansas Free-Soiler and abolitionist, John Brown, had marched into town under cover of darkness, seized the federal armory, and waited for Virginia's slaves to join them in an all-out race war.[4]

"If God be for us, who can be against us?" Brown had demanded of his followers. But with or without God's approval, Brown's ill-conceived and badly executed plans to stir up a general slave revolt were doomed almost from the start. Not a single slave voluntarily joined his would-be liberators, and in less than thirty-six hours, the raid was over. Brown was captured and imprisoned, and the rest of his band were either dead or in jail.

But John Brown's pathetic attempt to incite a slave rebellion had hit a raw Southern nerve. Every Southern white carried the fear of slave insurrection in his heart, if not on his tongue, and the panic generated by the desperate and futile raid at Harper's Ferry quickly spread from Virginia throughout the South. Rumors of similar raids became so common that many frightened Southerners expected at any moment to see an army of John Browns marching down from the North, stirring up Negro slaves and filling rivers and lakes with white men's blood.[5]

News of the Harper's Ferry fiasco reached the brooding Ruffin on Wednesday, October 19. Like his fellow white Southerners, he reacted with shock and moral outrage, but his deep depression lifted. He felt almost cheerful. The idea of a Northern abolitionist invasion seemed "incredible" but also afforded him a kind of grim satisfaction. "I earnestly hope that such may be the truth of the case," wrote the buoyant secessionist. "Such a practical exercise of abolition principles is needed to stir the sluggish blood of the south."[6]

3

Ruffin had spent the better part of his sixty-five years trying, in one way or another, "to stir the sluggish blood of the south," without much success. Certainly no one who had known him from boyhood could have predicted his abilities for such activity or such longevity. Born on January 5, 1794, at the Evergreen mansion in Prince George County, Virginia, Edmund had come into this world a squalling and puny baby. His young mother, Jane Lucas Ruffin, like so many other women, had precious little time to know her firstborn before she died, and her husband, George Ruffin, feared that their weak infant son would soon follow his mother to the grave.

George Ruffin represented the sixth generation of Ruffins in the Old Dominion. The first Ruffin in the New World was William Ruffin, who had emigrated from Scotland to France to Virginia's Tidewater region and finally settled in Isle of Wight County in 1666. Since then, William and succeeding generations of Ruffins had acquired more and more valuable property holdings in land and slaves and had insured their wealth and status with a series of wisely arranged marriages into Virginia's best families. When his first son was born, George was a prosperous planter who owned more than 140 slaves, making him the second largest slaveholder in Prince George County. The baby, Edmund Ruffin, had only to live to claim his rightful place among the Old Dominion's established planter aristocracy.[7]

Relatives and friends took one look at the scrawny infant, shook their heads sadly, and predicted he would soon die. Despite their dire predictions, though, Ruffin survived. But he was such a delicate, sickly child that no one expected he would live past the age of fifteen. Not long after his mother's death, his father remarried. His new stepmother, Rebecca Cocke, pampered him as much as possible, but the arrival of six more children in almost as many years left her few spare moments to lavish on him the personal attention he craved. The bouts of illness which would plague him all his life must have kept the youngster from enjoying the usual childhood games and engaging in playtime roughhousing, and his father probably refused to endanger his eldest son's life by allowing him to participate in work around the plantation.

Ruffin's relationship with his father undoubtedly left a lot to be desired, for not once in all his future writing and voluminous correspondence would he refer to his father or to his childhood family experiences. The memories were so painful, perhaps, and evoked such strong feelings of hostility, that he repressed them. George Ruffin, an active man with several plantations to run, might have been too busy and too fault-finding to spend much time with a son whose poor health was surely a disappointment. Then too, he could have been afraid to let himself get attached to a boy whose chances for survival seemed so slim. But Ruffin, a sensitive child who was eager for love and approval, did not understand this detachment, and criticism always made him feel inadequate and put him on the defensive. Sensing his father's disappointment, he probably interpreted it as a personal rejection. He reacted in all likelihood as he would as an adult. Meeting with rejection, real or fancied, he sulked. He withdrew.

Retreating to his father's large library, young Ruffin found that books helped to assuage his feelings of loneliness and resentment, and soon he developed a voracious appetite for reading, especially fiction. Before he reached his eleventh birthday, he had finished all of Shakespeare's plays. But the works of the immortal bard did not entirely suit him. Plain and simple prose "divested of the beauties of poetry, which I could not appreciate, & of the dramatic action & form, which I did not understand," would have been far preferable, he later explained. And with a prudishness surprising in one so young, he found Shakespeare's occasional bawdiness so offensive that he developed censorship habits that he carried over into all his other readings, skipping over those passages he considered inappropriate or "unattractive."[8]

In truth, he found the romantic medieval tales of Sir Walter Scott more suitable and pleasing to his refined young tastes. Scott's exciting and dependable heroes were always men of wealth, family, and aristocratic bearing, knights unswervingly loyal and devoted to exalted principles, fighting with unparalleled bravery and courage. From them Ruffin would learn to exaggerate the importance of honor and pride. Seated in his father's library or underneath a favorite tree with one of Scott's Waverly novels tucked in his lap, the Virginia planter's weakling child escaped the confines of body, place, and time. Transported back over the centuries, Ruffin could easily imagine himself transformed into a properly chivalric and dashing Scottish knight. Did he not have noble blood flowing through his own veins? On his grandmother's side, he could trace his bloodlines back to Charlemagne. Another of his ancestors was Lord Ruthven, Earl of Gowrie, a Scottish Protestant nobleman whose well-known enmity toward the Catholic ruler, Mary, Queen of Scots, earned him a swift execution. His son, William Ruthven, who later changed his name to Ruffin, barely escaped the same fate at the hands of Mary's son, James I of England, by his timely emigration to the royal colony of Virginia. This romantic blend of fictional and familial adventures fascinated young Ruffin, and later, as an adult, he wrote a short story recounting the Revolutionary War exploits of his namesake grandfather, Edmund Ruffin, entitling the piece "The Blackwater Guerilla."[9]

4

Still, this kind of sheltered reverie could not continue indefinitely, and when Ruffin reached the unexpected age of sixteen, his parents decided he must leave his tutors at Evergreen and receive a proper gentleman's education. So, in 1810, he left home for the first time in his life. He was a skinny, gray-eyed youth, with preposterously long dark brown hair falling well below his shoulders and cheeks alternately pale or rosy depending on his state of health. His spindly legs barely supporting his five-foot eight-inch frame, he presented himself at William and Mary College.

The College of William and Mary, located at Virginia's old capital, Williamsburg, was not known for its rigorous course work, which generally overlapped academy and even grammar school instruction. Despite these lax academic standards, Ruffin proved a singularly erratic student and a disappointing scholar. Ironically, it may have been his fondness for books which was his undoing. He did occasionally apply himself diligently to his studies, but more often than not, he found them tiresome. On a typical day, his textbooks would lie unopened while he unsparingly devoted himself to his own pleasure and amusement, which included reading works of history, literature, and especially fiction.[10]

If the youth who would grow up to be a shy, serious, and sober adult ever had any wild oats to sow, he sowed them during his college days. Drawn increasingly to the dissipated habits of his rowdier classmates, Ruffin, according to his own recollections, began to drink daily "to the extent of intemperance." The "habit" of alcoholic overindulgence was "universal" in Virginia, partly because of the notorious lack of safe drinking water. A consequent fondness for the julep left many a planter and his sons staggering about in a stupor. Compared to that of his peers, Ruffin had to admit that his own indulgence in spirits was "temperate & moderate." But he feared that had he not imposed almost superhuman restraints upon his appetites, he surely would have "died a drunkard's death."[11]

When not befuddled by liquor, Ruffin's impressionable young mind appears to have been intoxicated with love. In Williamsburg, Ruffin seems to have put down his novels long enough to seek a successful romance of his own for the first time, wooing and winning the attractive Susan Hutchings Travis. Susan, a petite, doe-eyed brunette, came from a prominent Williamsburg family. Her father, Champion Travis, had been a Jamestown Burgess for six years, attended the Virginia Conventions of 1775–1776, and served as Virginia's Naval Commissioner during the Revolutionary War. Evidently neither Susan nor her family found anything objectionable about her rich young suitor, so the match between the two young people was concluded a short time afterwards at the old Travis House.[12]

5

Affairs of the head and the heart rarely mix, and after only one term at William and Mary, Ruffin's student days came to an abrupt end. The college authorities suspended Ruffin for continuous neglect of his studies, so he packed his bags, bid a temporary farewell to his fiancée, and returned to the family plantation. While he was away at school, his father, George Ruffin, only forty-five years old, had suffered a premature death. As part of his inheritance, Edmund received a modest-looking mansion with extensive farmlands, located along the James River at Coggin's Point in Prince George County.[13]

But the young Ruffin was by no means decided on his future as a planter. An unidentified "easy" guardian did not press him for a definite commitment, allowing him instead all the time he wanted to indulge his own "tastes and disposition." First he satisfied his taste for romance by marrying Susan Travis. Then when war broke out with Great Britain in 1812, he gave in to his latent need for adventure. Barely eighteen years old, this frail young man hungered after a soldier's life and enlisted at the first muster as a private in a local volunteer company. In August, 1812, he kissed his new bride good-by and marched with the first regiment called out from Virginia. Whatever hopes he had had for military adventure went unfulfilled, for his company saw no action. But Ruffin liked to remember his six-month stint at Norfolk fondly as a time of great suffering and terrible privation, a time in which he had acquitted himself quite nobly. He believed that gentlemen made naturally superior soldiers. "Young people of 'gentle blood' or used to daily comforts," he would later insist, "could undergo necessary hardships with more contentment & cheerfulness than other persons of lower origin, & less accustomed to the indulgences & the training that wealth & high position afford."[14]

Out of uniform in February, 1813, the ex-soldier found that even a man of gentle blood must find some way to earn a living, if he wishes to maintain his "wealth & high position." He could no longer put off the choice of a career. Lacking the skills and training for any other gentlemanly vocation, Ruffin made the obvious decision. He took immediate charge of his Coggin's Point estate. He brought to his task a total inexperience with plantation management and a thorough ignorance of agricultural methods and procedures. Thus armed with "gentle blood," good intentions, and some not inconsiderable handicaps, nineteen-year-old Ruffin determined to make his mark as a successful Virginia planter.

6

A novice to the farming business, Ruffin found himself saddled with a troublesome inheritance. The soil on his Coggin's Point plantation was played out. Walking about his estate, he watched his slaves at work and wondered how long he could afford to feed and clothe them. Glumly, he eyed the fields of stunted grain and the barren patches of ground. His overseer could barely wring ten bushels of corn per acre from the larger portion of his farmland, while the "better half" averaged a scant six bushels of wheat per acre. It was a sorry state of affairs, not one designed to give a young man and expectant father much cheer.[15]

But if misery loved company, Ruffin had plenty of that; his neighbors were in the same desperate situation. The effects of over two centuries of exhaustive tobacco cropping had robbed much of Virginia's arable land of its original fertility. "The Virginians of the lower country are very easy and negligent husbandmen," observed Johann D. Schopf, a European traveler visiting the Old Dominion in 1783. "New land is taken up, the best to be had, tobacco is grown on it for three or four years, and then Indian corn as long as any will come. And in the end, if the soil is thoroughly impoverished, they begin again with a new piece and go through the rotation." Sixteen years later, in 1799, John H. Craven arrived in Albemarle County, in Virginia's Piedmont district. A new settler, Craven surveyed the "butchered" land of the surrounding countryside and reported a "scene of desolation that baffles description—farm after farm . . . worn out, washed and gullied, so that scarcely an acre could be found in a place fit for cultivation."[16]

The depressed economic condition of eastern Virginia, particularly the Tidewater, continued throughout the early national period and into the first three decades of the nineteenth century. From 1800 to 1830, various travel-

ers wrote unhappily of the "absolute desolation in the lower parts" of
Virginia, the "red-gullied and turned-out lands," and the rivers full of mud.
The apparent determination of his countrymen not to quit their ruinous
farming habits greatly distressed the elderly Thomas Jefferson, who feared
that the impoverished lands would force Virginians to abandon their plantations and seek homes in the more lucrative fields of the new southwestern
states. John Randolph of Roanoke, whose dry ascerbic wit never failed him,
especially in times of crisis, predicted that the day was not far off when
Negro slaves would take out paid advertisements in the public newspapers
for the recovery of runaway masters![17]

The very seriousness of their predicament seemed to render all who
should have been the most concerned immobile. "Nowhere else in the U.S."
had the visiting Philadelphia editor Robert Walsh encountered such a
feeling: "something like despair of amelioration." The worn-out, unkempt
Virginia plantations with their once proud but now dilapidated mansions;
sagging fences; and abandoned, weed-infested fields contrasted sharply with
the green and neatly tilled farms of English country squires, whom the
planters desperately tried to emulate in every other way. Virginia's sloppy
agriculture and the abuse of the land and the farm animals so shocked and
outraged one European visitor that he exclaimed disgustedly, "The whole
compass of the Virginian husbandry consists in first, raising a good supply
of maize for the planter's family, his Negroes, and his cattle; then tobacco
and a little wheat for keeping up appearances; and, for the rest of the year,
doing nothing at all."[18]

This assessment was not quite accurate. Most of the planter elite did
not let the run-down condition of their family estates or thoughts of almost
certain poverty looming in the not too distant future distract them from
present enjoyments or from concentrating on the pursuit of an aristocratic
lifestyle. In addition to "doing nothing at all," they engaged in a fairly
constant round of foxhunts, fishing expeditions, barbecues, dinners, lavish
balls, and drinking parties. The planters of Prince George County were no
exception, and Ruffin, suddenly serious under the pressures of manhood,
condemned his neighbors for their feckless, spendthrift ways. "Like the
inhabitants of a city ravaged by the plague," he marveled, "they thought
more of present enjoyment than of providing for future wants; and there
prevailed generally habits of idleness and improvidence, of pleasure seeking
and neglect of business."[19]

Ruffin, though, refused to give in to self-indulgence or self-pity. Nor
would he heed the well-meaning friends and neighbors who advised him to
salvage what he could, leave his native state, and head westward to find his
fortune in healthy virgin soils. Conditions in Virginia were appalling, but
no less so, Ruffin insisted, than the defeatism of his fellow planters. Some-

where there must be a remedy less drastic than emigration, something to rejuvenate and restore Virginia's ailing soil to its original vitality, and Ruffin would not relinquish the land of his forefathers until he had at least made a thorough search.

7

This was serious business, realized young Ruffin, leaving no room for frivolity. But critical as he was of his neighbors' dissipation, he feared that deep down he was as much of a pleasure seeker as any of them. He dealt with these fears in ways that became characteristic. Vulnerabilities that shamed Ruffin, that he loathed and suspected in himself, he either repressed, denied, or attributed to others. Self-control became almost an obsession. So, exercising almost ruthless self-denial, he cut from his life any pleasurable activity, even one so innocent as chess playing, which he judged to be "a mere amusement that is engrossing of time & attention, & . . . entirely unproductive of any good effect, except present amusement." A bit reluctantly, Ruffin even gave up the "comfort" of tobacco, but he did not hesitate a moment on the subject of intoxicants. Liquor, the consumption of which had constituted his most pleasurable pastime and which he sincerely believed to be his worst vice, was all but banished from the Ruffin household. Rather than succumb to the evils of alcoholism, Ruffin preferred total abstinence; to shield his children from temptation and to control their habits also, he never permitted the serving of intoxicating beverages at his table. He did keep a small quantity of spirits on hand to offer elderly guests whose regular moderate imbibing he deemed medicinal, but he never gave a drink to a stranger, a youth, or a person who had a reputation for liking liquor. Any visitor to Coggin's Point who hoped for something strong in the way of liquid refreshment almost always left disappointed.[20]

Faced with the near herculean task of saving his plantation, Ruffin knew that he needed his wits about him. First, he had to overcome his own ignorance and learn all he could about agricultural operations. Day-to-day planting procedures were simple enough to master quickly, but their evident lack of past success convinced Ruffin that there was much more to know. So when this inexperienced planter was not bending over his own fields learning practical farming from firsthand experience, he was closeted in his library, hungrily devouring the contents of every book and article on the subject that he could unearth. Most of the agricultural writings available at the time were geared to conditions in Great Britain and largely inapplicable to Virginia's peculiar ailments. But Ruffin liked these British works, because they offered valuable insights into the latest scientific methods in vogue in countries outside the United States. Such a sharp contrast to

Virginia's slipshod habits! Ruffin decided that he would imitate their careful planning and investigative methods as he carried out his own experiments to restore his depleted soil and save his patrimony.[21]

To begin with, he considered the 300 acres of tide marsh alongside the James River that bordered the Coggin's Point plantation. At high tide, the river waters hid this entire area from view. As one of his first experiments, Ruffin decided to reclaim thirty-two acres of the marsh and bring the land under cultivation. After five years of hard work, he successfully drained the section, but the ensuing rewards were hardly commensurate with the effort. The new lands yielded three large corn crops followed by three of progressively declining quantity and quality. Finally, the day came when Ruffin admitted failure and directed his fieldhands to abandon the project. The river then "reclaimed" the freshly exhausted soil.[22]

Ruffin plainly needed advice, but he could not expect much help from Virginia's husbandmen, who, with a few rare exceptions, had developed a "morbid aversion" to writing on agricultural subjects. John Taylor, an agriculturalist and statesman from Caroline County, Virginia, was one of these rare exceptions. An early advocate of scientific agriculture, Taylor had conducted experiments at Hazlewood, his Rappahannock River plantation, and published the results in 1803 in a series of agricultural articles. Ten years later, in 1813, these same articles were published in a book, *Arator: Being a Series of Agricultural Essays, Practical and Political.* That same year, nineteen-year-old Ruffin took control of the Coggin's Point plantation. *Arator* created quite a stir in the South, particularly in Tidewater Virginia. "When the great agricultural patriarch of Virginia first published his *Arator,*" recalled one planter, "his opinion was in the mouths of everybody; and I was then young enough to believe confidently all Virginia would soon be a perfect garden." Nearly forty years after first reading *Arator,* Ruffin, who considered himself "one of the thousands" of Taylor's "devoted disciples," spoke to a crowd of Caroline County farmers, praising their native son as "the first, & a great enlightener & benefactor of agriculture" and the "first great teacher, & earliest pioneer of a then untrodden track." "His voice, when first heard," Ruffin told his audience, "was to us as the sound of the trumpet in the struggle for life & death in the field of battle."[23]

Ruffin enjoyed *Arator* immensely, for Taylor made an effort to boost the cause of agricultural reform by appealing to the pride and vanity of his readers. The pursuit of agriculture, he promised farmers, guaranteed vigorous health to both body and mind, encouraged morality, and thus became "the best architect of a complete man." These inspiring words were like music to the ears of a young man still a bit shaky and insecure about his present vocation.[24]

8

Taylor's advice, although faulty at times, helped his earnest young pupil over some initial rough spots, not the least of which was the moral dilemma presented by the sudden ownership of other human beings. Like so many idealistic Virginians of the post-Revolutionary era, Ruffin considered himself a "speculative abolitionist," agreeing in principle that slavery was indeed an evil that must end someday, but in fact unable to devise any practical scheme for emancipation. Before Ruffin inherited his father's plantation and his slaves, he had had the detachment, leisure time, and cultivated education to agonize over the moral paradox of a "free" society which held millions of black human beings in perpetual bondage. Once he became actively involved in planting at Coggin's Point, however, he was less inclined to stand back and question the means he employed in the day-to-day building of his economic fortune. Also, his personal supervision of plantation activities provided him with numerous opportunities for friendly relationships with his fieldhands, relationships which helped to obscure the harsher, exploitative side of slavery. And truthfully, though he was no tyrant, he enjoyed exercising the absolute power and control over human beings that the slave system allowed him. Besides, what real choice did he have? Freeing his slaves would have left Ruffin economically and socially bereft in a plantation society based on slave labor.

Turning to his mentor, John Taylor, Ruffin searched the pages of *Arator* for a solution to his problem. At first he found little comfort. "Negro slavery," began the author in essay 14, "is a misfortune to agriculture, incapable of removal, and only within the reach of palliation." But as Ruffin read on, it became clear that Taylor was not referring to slavery's moral burdens or economic drawbacks but to the dangerous presence of free Negroes and mulattoes in a slave society. Certainly, guilt-ridden slaveowners should not trouble themselves over the ownership of their human chattels. Individual slavery, its harshness tempered by the master's self-interest and humanity, argued Taylor, was after all infinitely preferable to slavery to an interest or faction incapable of such feelings. And while scolding status-seeking planters for greedily overstocking their plantations with slaves beyond the limits of efficient labor management, he soothed their consciences with the assurance that if well managed, "slaves are docile, useful and happy" creatures.

For another opinion, Ruffin turned to Thomas Jefferson, who, in his *Notes on Virginia,* had deplored what he believed was slavery's greatest evil, the arousal of tyrannical despotic passions in the planter, who transmitted them to his children. Taylor refuted Jefferson in his *Arator* essay 14, countering, "It seems that slaves are too far below, and too much in the power of the master to inspire furious passions; that such are nearly as rare towards slaves as towards horses; that slaves are more frequently the objects of benevolence than of rage; that children . . . are . . . hardly ever suffered to tyrannize over them . . . , and that fewer good public or private characters have been raised in countries enslaved by some faction or particular interest, than in those where personal slavery existed." A forthright apologist for the South's "peculiar institution," John Taylor anticipated the arguments of later pro-slavery defenders like Thomas R. Dew, George Fitzhugh, and Edmund Ruffin himself.[25]

9

Ruffin embraced John Taylor's proslavery principles almost without question, but his advice on agricultural reforms was more difficult to accept. Taylor urged planters to use better farm implements; rotate crops; adopt a system of deep horizontal plowing; and forbid cattle from grazing in the fields, through the enclosure method. The real key to agricultural success, insisted Taylor, lay in returning manures of all descriptions, animal and particularly vegetable, to the infertile soil. Crops raised on former grazing lands should be fed without delay to the cattle, whose manure could then be plowed under to enrich the soil. Fields of clover, cowpeas, or other legumes must also be plowed under to add the necessary putrescent vegetable manure. These reforms seemed easy, and Taylor's "devoted disciple," Edmund Ruffin, confidently anticipated great and profitable results.

But if he had expected an agricultural renaissance, Ruffin must have suffered bitter disillusionment. Taylor's enclosure system was an "utter disappointment," for clover would not grow in Ruffin's exhausted fields, and deep plowing subjected the shallow Coggin's Point soil to serious erosion. Nor did the land respond as expected to the application of vegetable manures. After a few years, the decaying manure disappeared, and the land became sterile again. Ruffin gave Taylor's precepts a fair trial for close to six years, but in the end he discarded them as "either profitless, entirely useless, or absolutely, and in some cases greatly injurious." No part of his poor land was more productive than it had been before he began his labors, and his only reward was "a tenfold increase . . . of the previously large space of galled and gullied hillsides and slopes."[26]

Faced with still another disappointing harvest in the fall of 1817, Ruffin made up his mind to accept defeat and move on. Like the older planters of lower Virginia, he finally concluded that these wretched lands were incapable of revitalization and enrichment, a theory he had hitherto rejected as "monstrous agricultural heresy." Perhaps in "the rich western wilderness" the support of his growing family would not demand his "whole income and more." But as he readied his family and slaves for the trek westward, he discovered, to his chagrin, that the initial step of procuring a buyer for his estate was no easier than trying to raise a decent crop of wheat or corn. "There was scarcely a proprietor in my neighborhood," Ruffin lamented, "who did not desire to sell his land, and who was prevented only by the impossibility of finding a purchaser, unless at half the then very low estimated value. All wished to sell, none to buy."[27]

10

At this critical and desperate juncture in his career, Ruffin chanced upon a copy of Sir Humphrey Davy's *Elements of Agricultural Chemistry,* which had recently been published in the United States. Although Ruffin knew nothing of chemistry, one passage in the book held him riveted. An English country squire named Sir Joseph Banks had complained to Davy about the sterile soils on his Lincolnshire farm. Davy had obligingly analyzed soil samples from the estate and found them rich in iron sulphates, a mineral acid. The great soil chemist had a sure remedy for his client. "If on washing a sterile soil it is found to contain the salt of iron, or any other acid matter," he directed, "it may be ameliorated by the application of quick-lime."[28]

Could it be, Ruffin wondered, that these same mineral acids "poisoned" his own worn-out soil and therefore most of Virginia's Tidewater? Excited, he began testing clumsily for the presence of salts of iron at Coggin's Point, but he found none. Another dead end. But before discarding Davy's theories, Ruffin took another inquisitive look at his farmlands. He noticed that sheep sorrel and pine as well as other plants known to contain vegetable acids grew with great vigor and in abundance in fields no longer fit for crop cultivation. Ruffin tested these soils and discovered that they were lime-free. Pine and sorrel were conspicuously absent, though, from small portions of shelly land, obviously calcareous, long noted for their exceptionally lasting fertility. Their fossil shells, commonly called marl, were chemically a mixture of clay and carbonate of lime. Beds of marl were plentiful throughout Tidewater Virginia and much of the Upper South, but Davy's use of lime had only been as a corrective for the presence of mineral acids. Still, on the basis of his observations, crude experimentation, and an intuitive scientific feeling, Ruffin separately concluded that organic vegetable acids were the villains sucking the lifeblood from his lands. Perhaps marl, an as yet untapped natural resource, was the calcareous "medicine" which would neutralize these poisonous acids and restore the soil to its original fertility. Lime, he knew, had been used in Europe for centuries and had even been tried in the New World, but never before had there been a logical rationale behind its application. This idea so intrigued Ruffin that although he was never able to confirm his theories with direct evidence of vegetable acids, he decided to proceed on the assumption that they were present in his soil.[29]

Planting season had hardly begun in February, 1818, before Ruffin began seeking tangible proof of his new theories on vegetable acidity and lime or calcareous manures. First he sectioned off 2½ acres of newly cleared but sterile fields for his experiment. His fieldhands then hauled cartload after cartload of calcareous manures, newly excavated from one of the plantation's extensive marl pits. Finally Ruffin directed his slaves to cover the earth with 125–200 bushels of marl per acre and plant one crop of corn and another of wheat. For comparative purposes, Ruffin scientifically set aside an equal plot of unmarled ground of like soil quality and planted similar crops of corn and wheat. Then he waited impatiently to see if any good would come of his toil.

11

The results went beyond even Ruffin's most sanguine expectations. The corn and wheat production on the marled lands exceeded the yields on the untreated fields by at least 40 percent. Since his lands were similar to those of all Tidewater planters, Ruffin believed his discoveries would raise him from obscure planter to agricultural savior of the Old Dominion. Hastily he wrote up his theories and the results of his experiments and hurried off to share his good fortune with his fellow Virginians. In October, 1818, Ruffin, then twenty-four, feeling shy and nervous, stood before the Prince George Agricultural Society, where he haltingly but earnestly delivered his paper on the marvelous nature of calcareous manures.[30]

If he expected instant thanks or immediate recognition as a public benefactor, Ruffin was badly mistaken. The audience heard his message and was singularly unimpressed. Although Ruffin's words forecast a bright, sunny future for Virginia's agriculturalists, they had no impact on his unbelieving audience. The older planters rejected Ruffin's scientific theories as mere "book farming." Who was this young upstart anyway, they asked one another, this meddlesome crackpot who talked of organic acids and carbonate of lime and tried to tamper with the established farming practices of centuries with his library reforms? These men did not comprehend Ruffin's advanced notions of dynamic rather than static soil chemistry. It was sheer folly, Ruffin insisted, for cultivators to try to enrich their barren soils with barnyard or organic vegetable manures until generous doses of marl had neutralized the harmful vegetable acidity. Once marled, the earth would be ready to accept and retain other manures and benefit from better plowing, crop rotation, the growing of clover and cowpeas, the building of covered drains, an intelligent reduction in the slave force, and the other good farming techniques that John Taylor had first advocated. But his words fell on skeptical ears. Tidewater planters insisted that the soil contained only a fixed amount of nutritious chemical ingredients. Crop cultivation removed these nutrients one by one until the land was sterile, and nothing available to man could replace what was forever lost. When Ruffin tried to spread the gospel of marl and explain its long-term benefits, most of his neighbors were hard put to contain their laughter. Others sneered at him. Few willingly imitated his example, while the two Prince George County planters who did attempt to follow their young neighbor's methods executed their marling operations so badly that they too abandoned any further trials. Thereafter, one man liked to point out his marl pit to visitors, scornfully referring to the shelly hole as "Ruffin's Folly." Stung by their ingratitude, Ruffin retorted that most farmers were too determinedly block-headed to understand even the simplest ideas if they related to chemistry.[31]

12

This unanticipated burst of public ridicule and derision hurt Ruffin deeply. Feeling that both he and his efforts had been rejected, he retreated to the sanctuary of Coggin's Point. Still, despite the indifference of his unenlightened planter colleagues, this budding soil chemist did not lose faith in his scientific procedures or conclusions. The rebuff he met only rekindled his enthusiasm and determination to prove the truth of his new theories. He would turn his Coggin's Point estate into a showplace, a shining example of a model plantation.

Aware that he still possessed only a rudimentary knowledge of soil chemistry, Ruffin painstakingly built up his library and searched through all the available scientific literature of the ages as well as current publications, from home and abroad, for any mention of marl and its historical use in agriculture. Besides Davy's study, he read the works of Darwin, Dickson, Morveau, Grisenthwaite, and Dundonald. He even taught himself enough French so that he could extract and translate foreign material possibly meriting future reexamination.

Feeling the need for more conclusive findings, Ruffin built the necessary laboratory apparatus and began running and carefully recording scientific soil analyses. In order to test a more representative sampling, Ruffin gathered soil deposits from all over Coggin's Point, neighboring plantations, and once even sent for samples from as far away as Huntsville, Alabama. The results only confirmed his belief in the regenerative qualities of calcareous manures, so he started collecting detailed information on the character and extent of Virginia's marl deposits. Carefully weighing the estimated costs of marling against its projected financial returns, he devoted a great deal of time to figuring the best and cheapest means for its exploitation.

By no means was all this scientific experimentation done indoors in bottles and test tubes. The bountiful results of his 1818 harvest encouraged Ruffin to extend his marling operations more and more each year. Ruffin devised different tests for his marl. He treated one field with animal and vegetable manures, another with marl alone, and a third with a combination of organic and calcareous manures. Ruffin studied and analyzed the results, then lovingly recorded them in accurate and minute detail. His labors were not in vain. Increases in crop yields and quality were remarkable, as production rose in some cases by 200 percent. A glimpse of the luxuriant fields of corn and wheat grown at Coggin's Point should stifle the snickers and jeers of his less fortunate neighbors, reasoned Ruffin. They would be sorry they had maligned his genius. Even "doubting Thomases" could no longer deny with their eyes what their ears had refused to believe.[32]

2

Dogma and Demagogues

1

RUFFIN'S BATTLES with his land and his fellow planters revealed a man with a critical mind and a stubborn, independent spirit. Not surprisingly, he applied both of these characteristics to religious matters as well. His skepticism of the prevailing agricultural orthodoxy spilled over to his attitude toward accepted religious dogma. Imbued with eighteenth-century enlightenment ideals, he placed his faith in scientific reason, logic, and rationalism. Reason convinced him that God existed, but that same rationalism made him insist on his right as an individual Christian to interpret and judge the authenticity of the Bible and the Scriptures for himself.

Blind submission to clerical dogma was anathema to Ruffin's strongly individualistic nature, and he declared more than once that "theology is the science of misconstruction—to teach as the meaning of the scriptures . . . what no unprejudiced reader . . . would have inferred—& often what is entirely opposed *to the plain & obvious sense.*" Ruffin wanted no one—lay or clergy—to tell him what to think or what to do. Priests and theologians, claiming divine revelation, exercised such a powerful influence over their congregations, Ruffin discovered, that many of his staunchly religious friends held beliefs which had in fact no biblical basis. Where in Genesis, he asked in his diary, was there any evidence that the serpent who tempted Eve was really Satan in disguise? He combed the pages of the Old Testament but found no mention of a heaven or hell or even an immortal soul. Nor did the Gospel of Matthew in the New Testament offer any plain or even inferential statement of the later all-important doctrine of God the Father, the Son, and the Holy Ghost—the Divine Trinity.[1]

Ruffin was just as quick to challenge those who insisted on a literal interpretation of the Bible's stories, and he argued that the Bible and the Scriptures needed an editor to expurgate all the objectionable and "unworthy" sections. Among the first selections to go should be "The Book of Esther," which he contemptuously dismissed as a mere piece of Eastern or Jewish folklore, and especially the "Song of Solomon," which struck him as "a lascivious & indecent amatory poem." The Book of Judges, he laughed, had as much to do with religion and morality as the legend of King Arthur and his Knights of the Round Table or the fable of Jack the Giant Killer.[2]

Brought up as an Episcopalian, Ruffin was nonetheless tolerant of other religious faiths. He considered religious persecution repugnant, except against those he labeled "consistent fanatics." "With ... sincere & honest fanatics, intolerance is a necessary principle," Ruffin asserted, "& persecution of heretics is not only right, but is a duty which it would be a sin & crime against God to neglect to enforce."[3]

Still, in his estimation, not all faiths were of equal worth. The ancient Hebrews he wrote off as a "base & contemptible people" whose lives were so petty and insignificant that the Greek historian Herodotus could not be bothered to mention them. Mormonism, he sneered, was nothing but a "bare-faced imposture." But especially in his later years, Ruffin enjoyed attending different church services. In Charleston, South Carolina, in 1857 and 1858, he described a synagogue as "a noble & beautiful edifice" and found the extremely secularized services "impressive & solemn" but admitted avoiding Charleston's two other synagogues, which were orthodox and were attended by "foreign," non–Charleston-born Jews of the "ignorant class." Ruffin felt that he also had to forgo Catholic worship. Pews in the church were all privately owned, and he refused to sit in the only available public seats, which were next to "decent negroes," for fear of being mistaken for an abolitionist.[4]

Although he occasionally attended Presbyterian services, Ruffin detested the harsh Calvinism of the Pilgrim fathers because of what he called its "hell-flavored doctrines" and "diabolical creed." Ruffin condemned as "shocking & horrible" the Calvinist belief that salvation was predestined to only a few "elect" and that damnation and everlasting torment were the lot of the masses, no matter how pure and virtuous their lives. What bothered him most—what he simply refused to accept—was the philosophy that men and women had no control over their destinies. The grim, sour New England Pilgrims, thought Ruffin, must have been "hard & ferocious bigots" who, whether sincere Calvinists or "compulsory hypocrites," served a "cruel & hateful deity" through their own "intolerant & bloody worship." Ruffin could not accept their malevolent deity, and after conducting his own characteristically thorough investigations of biblical literature, he concluded that "all the evidences, citations of passages of scripture, & reasoning & deductions therefrom ... would never make me believe that the all-beneficent & benevolent & merciful creator of mankind should have doomed the greater number, from & because of the first offense & fall of Adam & irrespective of their acts in life, to misery & tortures from which the most cruel monsters among mankind would have shrunk from inflicting ... on their worst & most hated enemies." Nor could he swallow the worshippers' professions of piety and sincere devotion to this ferocious God who seemed to love injustice and cruelty and exercised His mighty wrath against the innocent and unborn. "I would as soon believe that the victims of the most bloody, unjust, & cruel persecutors could be loved and reverenced by their victims," Ruffin mocked. "There is nothing of iniquity ascribed to Satan, in my opinion, that is worse than the Calvinistic creed ascribes to ... God."[5]

Believing that his own salvation was at stake, Ruffin gave much time and thought to refuting the proposition that the keys to heaven were the exclusive property of any one faith or sect. Since accidents of parentage, native country, rearing, education, and personal acquaintance, instead of more substantial factors, like truth and reason, determined a person's religious creed, Ruffin's logical mind rejected the idea that a wise and merciful supreme being would pronounce everlasting and irrevocable sentence on such a flimsy basis. A change of native land and early childhood associates, he argued, might have transformed such well-known evangelical Protestants as William Wilberforce and John Wesley into Hindu idolators or Tibetan worshippers of the Grand Lama. Surely if the most devout Christian martyrs had been born and raised in non-Christian countries, Ruffin reasoned, they would have held beliefs damnable in the eyes of orthodox Christians.[6]

Rejecting any creed's particular orthodoxy, Ruffin based his own beliefs on Jesus' teachings in the "Sermon on the Mount." Clergymen might threaten members of their flock with eternal hellfire and damnation unless they accepted certain articles of faith as God's word, but Ruffin was immune to such bullying. There was no evidence in the "Sermon on the Mount" that such articles were necessary for salvation or that they were man's only avenue of escape from excruciating torment in the afterlife. The only reasonable requirements for salvation that Ruffin could discover were a belief in one supreme being, obedience to God's ten commandments, and a life filled with good deeds founded on good intentions.[7]

2

Although he normally prided himself on being an outspoken man, Ruffin took great care to hide his practical religion from his family and friends.

His wife, Susan, was a practicing and believing Christian, and their nine surviving children—three others died in infancy—were all devoted members of the Church. "My children," complained Ruffin, "like all other Christians, hold to the erroneous constructions of the theologians & preachers, & submit their judgment & understanding entirely to their dictates— & all their respect for me would not prevent their confounding my opposing the false and unsupported constructions of the bible, with opposition to the bible itself, & to the religion it teaches."[8]

Ruffin placed only one restriction on his growing children as far as religion was concerned. He insisted that they wait until adulthood before publicly announcing an allegiance to any faith or joining any church. Otherwise, Ruffin feared, their innocent "childish enthusiasm & delusion" might later condemn them to shameful lives of apostasy or hypocrisy. Later, his grown children did join the Church and became firm believers. Their father was sincerely pleased, but he still thought that their faith was embellished with myths and founded upon a mountain of errors.[9]

Christianity's main attraction, maintained Ruffin, was fear and terror —fear and terror that all those who did not embrace the Christian religion and all its tenets would be cast into hell. So to spare his children any worry over their father's certain damnation and to prevent their having to shield their own children from their grandfather's wicked influence, Ruffin tried to remain silent about his religious doubts and heterodox opinions. But this silence was a painful restraint on both his patience and his impetuous tongue, which Ruffin found a bit easier to bear only when he had reached what he termed "the years of discretion."[10]

For the sake of his children also, Ruffin refused their entreaties to debate what he considered the "essential" Christian questions and always joined in the regular family prayers, taking part in all that concurred with his private beliefs and quietly passing over the rest. Sundays found him seated next to his wife and children in the neighborhood Episcopal church, listening politely, if irreverently, to the service and the sermon that followed. But he never compromised himself by professing himself a Christian or by becoming a church member.

The Ruffin children, though, were not completely fooled by their father's outward conformity to Christian practices. Despite his almost superhuman efforts at self-control, occasionally the dam would burst. Ruffin's sporadic outbursts at such times over what he felt were "theological misconstructions" or downright "pious fraud" were a source of exasperation and possible embarrassment to his family. When, every so often, the Episcopal bishop or some other church official paid a visit to the Ruffin plantation, the entire household tensed for fear their eldest member would forget himself, disgrace them, and seal his own doom.[11]

But despite his own doubts over what he thought was a "contaminated Christianity," Ruffin had no quarrel with pure religion and no desire to shake the confidence of any individual in his or her religious creed by exposing factual mistakes in theological dogma. Ironically, for all his faith in science and mathematics, Ruffin accepted the Bible's account of the earth's creation rather than the newer geological theories, arguing that evidence from fossil remains proved rather than disproved scriptural accounts of man's history. And many times, when saddened by some personal loss, Ruffin envied the true believer his religious consolation, no matter how deluded the comfort. For even an erroneous Christianity, admitted Ruffin, because of its promises of future rewards, served a useful social purpose, helping to make individuals more virtuous, communities less vicious, and all elements of society—especially slaves and lower-class whites—more content under their present afflictions.[12]

Ruffin knew that it was up to the better sort of people, the gentlemen and their families, to set a good example for the community. So, because his station in life demanded certain proprieties, Ruffin squirmed but held his tongue, regularly attended church, and for all unsuspecting observers appeared a model Christian.

3

Ruffin realized that membership in the South's exclusive planter aristocracy carried with it important duties as well as certain privileges. Duty required at least the outward appearance of a moral Christian life. But along with this obligation came the right and privilege to exert political leadership, and Ruffin particularly looked forward to exercising this responsibility.

Ruffin had no need of politics for personal enrichment. His agricultural reforms and marling operations at Coggin's Point had made him a prosperous planter; he owned more than fifty slaves and was not above joining them in their farm labors. But agricultural success did not satisfy all his ambitions; and Ruffin probably agreed with George Fitzhugh, a fellow Virginian and an unsuccessful planter, who wrote, "Farming is the recreation of great men, the proper pursuit of dull men." Ruffin still longed for the wider acceptance and recognition denied him as a youngster. Besides, the Ruffin family had a tradition of public service. Ruffin's namesake grandfather had spent four years in the Virginia House of Delegates, attended the Virginia Constitutional Convention of 1789, and served as county lieutenant in 1789 and as sheriff in 1797. Edmund's father, George Ruffin, whose premature death had cut off any future political hopes, had also served four years as a member of the state's House of Delegates. Given his family background, social position, and his own private inclinations, Ruffin naturally expected that one day he too would enter the political arena.[13]

But it was not rough-and-tumble politics—the kind that would later characterize the Jacksonian era—that Ruffin desired. He found his ideal state in books describing the ancient Greek and Roman civilizations, where all the members of a highly stratified and slave-based society recognized the right of natural-born aristocrats—men of superior breeding, intellect, and morality—to govern.

As his political hero, Ruffin chose the Roman patrician Cincinnatus. Like Ruffin, Cincinnatus was an agriculturalist and a slaveowner, and like Ruffin, he was not too proud to work occasionally out in his fields under the broiling sun at the head of his slaves. Cincinnatus, as Ruffin pictured him, was a plain and simple aristocrat, never seeking honors or high office, desiring nothing more than to be let alone to enjoy the basic pleasures of rural life. But when war threatened the safety of Rome, he humbly allowed his countrymen to press him into service, first as a military leader, then as absolute dictator. Once his nation's grave danger had passed, Cincinnatus voluntarily relinquished the reins of power and returned gratefully to his plow, only to accept public office again at the age of eighty. No doubt, fancied Ruffin, if this were ancient Rome and not nineteenth-century America, he would himself be honored in similar fashion. Although Ruffin was, in fact, anything but reluctant to give up the rewards of agriculture for the rewards of office, he never shook the feeling that his own identity and that of this Roman farmer–statesman were somehow linked; in the future, he would often sign anonymous newspaper articles "Cincinnatus" or "Virginius."[14]

4

If Cincinnatus provided Ruffin with his model of the disinterested but patriotic public servant, John Taylor of Caroline taught him his political catechism. Taylor, who prided himself on being truer to the states' rights and strict construction tenets of Jeffersonian republicanism than Thomas Jefferson, had once informed the Sage of Monticello that he was fanatical about only two subjects—agriculture and republicanism.[15]

In Taylor's view, a true republican had no use for a national bank, federally sponsored internal improvements, or a protective tariff system. This so-called American System, he argued, benefited only northeastern manufacturing interests at the expense of southern agriculturalists. Protective duties, in particular, robbed planters and farmers of money desperately needed to make agricultural improvements and used it instead to line the pockets of rich northern industrialists.[16]

Taylor's political arguments held special appeal for the planters of eastern Virginia. Tired of cursing their poor land, they welcomed the opportunity to blame their agricultural misfortunes on the federal tariff policy. Even Ruffin, who must have known that the protective duties alone were not responsible for Virginia's agrarian plight, sided with the antitariffites. Part of his zeal in advocating agricultural reform stemmed from the hope that once prosperity was restored to the South, its commensurate political influence could abolish harmful and discriminatory federal legislation. And when several local agricultural societies banded together in 1818 to form the United Agricultural Societies of Virginia, the membership chose its secretary, Edmund Ruffin, to draft a collective tariff protest, the first such petition that Congress ever entertained.[17]

Although Ruffin had found some serious laws in John Taylor's agricultural bible, *Arator,* he found nothing wanting in his teacher's political dogma. So while he generally held himself aloof from party affiliation, Ruffin embraced Taylor's republican orthodoxy and used it to test every candidate for political office. The test was particularly stringent, and that is why, in the summer of 1823, Ruffin rejected all five of the leading prospective candidates for President—John Adams, Andrew Jackson, Henry Clay, John C. Calhoun, and William H. Crawford.

In an anonymous article in the Richmond *Enquirer,* Ruffin charged that Adams was nothing more than a political opportunist, "an apostate federalist, who deserted his party at precisely the most convenient time, for his own interest." Jackson had "openly trampled on the constitution"; while Clay, Calhoun, and Crawford had sold their republican souls to the detestable American System. Such political turncoatism disgusted Ruffin, who preferred that Virginia's vote go to John Marshall, chief justice of the Supreme Court, who had honestly and consistently advocated principles Ruffin abhorred, rather than to a Federalist disguised in republican's clothing![18]

The United States government, contended Ruffin, needed a President who combined the simple agrarian virtues of Cincinnatus with the republican purity of John Taylor. Taylor was seriously ill, so he could not be considered for the position. Instead, Ruffin offered the name of one of Taylor's closest allies, Nathaniel Macon, a senator and planter from North Carolina, whom Ruffin had met once in his life and then only for a few minutes.[19]

Although their acquaintance was all too brief, Macon had impressed Ruffin with his simple dignity and impeccable integrity. Macon was an old-fashioned planter–aristocrat who, despite his Princeton education, was a plainspoken man, who habitually referred to himself as "Meekins." A soldier and statesman like Cincinnatus, Macon had fought for his country

during the Revolutionary War and then served it for twenty-six years in the
House of Representatives and eight years in the Senate. Patriotism, not love
of power or profit, assured Ruffin, had pushed Macon into politics. As
proof, Ruffin pointed out that after each congressional adjournment, Macon
always hurried back eagerly to his plantation and, like the noble Cincinnatus, was never too proud to toil like a fieldhand. Macon, he thought,
would have preferred to stay at home and relish the tranquil enjoyments of
agrarian life, but out of a sense of noblesse oblige, he bowed to the people's
urgent need for his political guidance. Even more importantly, as a legislator, Macon had maintained his pristine republicanism and compiled one of
the most remarkable records for no-votes in congressional history.[20]

In the rather obscure Macon, Ruffin believed he had found another
model of unsullied statesmanship, a man with whom he could personally
identify and whose fine qualities he knew he himself possessed. Ruffin
awaited only the public's clamor for his own services.

5

Notwithstanding his self-proclaimed resemblance to Cincinnatus and Nathaniel Macon, Ruffin had only a remote chance of being elected to any
public office after the debacle of his 1818 speech to the Prince George
Agricultural Society. Who would vote for such a crackpot planter? Yet five
years later, in 1823, the district of Sussex, Surry, Southampton, Isle of
Wight, Prince George, and Greenesville counties elected Ruffin to represent
them for four years in the Virginia Senate.

This remarkable turnabout in local public opinion was due in large part
to the very agricultural address which had shamed him in 1818. Three years
after his initial presentation, *The American Farmer,* a new agricultural
journal in Baltimore, decided to publish the speech in essay form. "On the
Composition of Soils, And Their Improvement by Calcareous Manures,"
proclaimed editor John Skinner, represented "the first systematic attempt
. . . wherein a plain, practical, unpretending farmer, has undertaken to
examine the real composition of the soils which he possesses and has to
cultivate." Skinner insisted that every farmer, indeed "every intelligent
cultivator of the soil," must study Ruffin's essay. If anyone questioned the
sincerity of his endorsement, Skinner removed all doubts by printing extra
copies of the article and distributing them free of charge to all his subscribers.[21]

This time, instead of mockery and derision, Ruffin's words earned a
modest amount of fame for their author. Public response to the article was
overwhelmingly favorable, especially from readers outside Prince George
County and Virginia. Interested planters wrote letters begging for more

information about calcareous manures and soliciting Ruffin's personal advice on just how to begin marling operations. Delightedly, Ruffin answered their requests and wrote back warm words of encouragement.

Not satisfied with letters, some curious planters and farmers made special trips to Coggin's Point to see the effects of marl for themselves. These visitors never went away unimpressed, for just as he had pledged in 1818, Ruffin had marled his plantation into an agricultural showplace, a healthy green oasis contrasting with a land sore with waste and devastation.[22]

Ruffin's undeniable agricultural achievements and his growing reputation as one of the South's most progressive planters impressed not only strangers. One by one, even his most skeptical neighbors had to admit a new respect for marl and the man they had jeered as a mere book farmer. Ruffin basked in their grudging admiration, confident that an appreciative public was now ready for his leadership. So in the fall of 1823, at the age of twenty-nine, he offered his name in nomination for the state Senate.

Although he willingly offered himself to the citizens of his district, Ruffin could not bring himself to ask for their vote. Never had a man so eager for political office been so reluctant to campaign. Ruffin felt ill at ease speaking before crowds, and besides, he believed that the office should seek the man and not vice versa. Let demagogues court the masses, cajoling and pleading for their support; Ruffin haughtily disdained the art of electioneering. Would Cincinnatus or Nathaniel Macon stoop so low as to bribe their constituents, buying public office with liquor, barbecues, and other common treats? Would either of these great but plainspoken statesmen cater to the people's baser instincts through popular but dangerous appeals to political and social egalitarianism? The answer, Ruffin believed, was no. The public must recognize and defer to the right of gentlemen—men of substantial property, breeding, education, and ability—to govern them without popular interference.

A thorough elitist, Ruffin would have no truck with democratic notions of popular government based on equal rights and universal manhood suffrage. Largely, he blamed one of Virginia's most beloved sons, Thomas Jefferson, for the spreading acceptance of these "corrupting" ideas. Ruffin accused the great "Commoner" of being *"par excellence,* the apostle of the most extreme democratic doctrines." "Jefferson," he stated regretfully, "by his great influence in proposing his most dangerous & abominable principles of government, & by their contaminating & poisoning every one of the constitutions of his country . . . has done more harm to his countrymen than perhaps any other politician." Jefferson's foolish democratic ideals, Ruffin contended, made people equal in theory but really meant "the supremacy of the lowest & basest class, led & directed by baser & mercenary demagogues, seeking exclusively their own selfish benefit." Instead of elevating those best fit for office, democratic tools like universal suffrage only insured "a government by & for the *worst* of the people."[23]

Fortunately for Ruffin, whose unspectacular campaign for office lacked the common touch, Virginia had not yet translated its democratic ideals into democratic realities. The state constitution restricted the franchise to those men with property to guard, and, through provisions which ignored or discounted the growing white population west of the Blue Ridge Mountains, gave disproportionate representation and influence to slaveholding interests in eastern Virginia. Thus well protected from the machinery of democracy, Ruffin won his first election.

6

Once in office, State Senator Ruffin, according to his own testimony, worked zealously and diligently for the public good. Not a single deviation from conservative republican principles tarnished his voting record, and for a time, he rivaled even Nathaniel Macon in his reputation for chronic obstructionism. The Committee on Internal Improvements learned that it had at least one member keeping a watchful eye out for needless expenditures, while bankers soon discovered that in Ruffin they had an implacable foe who opposed every motion to recharter the Farmer's Bank of Virginia. Mindful, too, of the dangers of democracy and of the best interests of his own class, Ruffin labored long and hard to thwart the continual effforts of nonslaveowning western Virginians to gain fairer legislative representation and increased suffrage.[24]

But Ruffin soon found out that hard work and a clean republican conscience alone earned him low marks and little glory in the world of politics. Noble sentiments and ideals counted almost for nothing unless nobly expressed, and here Ruffin encountered his greatest single obstacle, his own artless tongue. Public speaking was agonizing for him; he knew he was a poor speaker, nervous and unconvincing. Among colleagues who valued grand oratorical flourishes, Ruffin's plain, rustic speech was a political handicap and a personal embarrassment.

Toward those whose ringing eloquence could arouse rapt audiences to tears or laughter and bring a crowd to its feet, cheering and applauding, Ruffin evinced outright suspicion and even contempt, dismissing such talents as pure demagoguery. But his true feelings revealed a deep envy and a disappointment that he had not been so gifted. "I felt sour that I had no talent for oratory, or to influence popular assemblies," he later admitted to his old friend, former President John Tyler, "and I was too proud to be willing to be deemed below any station in which I might be placed."[25]

Failing as an effective public speaker, Ruffin only compounded his problem in private conversation. The art of diplomatic persuasion escaped him. Blunt, even tactless, his words drove wedges between men when they should have been forging compromises. When in earshot of those having opposing viewpoints, Ruffin feared above all else that a politic silence on his part might be misconstrued as assent. So, despite dozens of resolves to the contrary, Ruffin threw caution to the wind and repeatedly gave in to what he called his "besetting sin"—his "incurable propensity" to speak out freely and candidly on any topic, invoking as much censure and sarcasm as he felt the subject deserved. He discovered, too, that he possessed "some talent . . . for sharp & biting satire" and a flair for verbally painting "ludicrous caricatures" of well-known personalities. His favorite targets, he later recalled, were "base villains" in public office who had used their fortune, family, or political position to gain the popularity of "sycophants & of the public"— men, in other words, who had received the respect and acceptance Ruffin relished for himself. As listeners repeated his "ludicrous caricatures," embellishing them, complained Ruffin, with distortions and exaggerations, his own popularity decreased precipitously with the public around him and even with the more remote public outside the capital.[26]

Ruffin stated repeatedly that he could never "tolerate base conduct" in any individual, and most of his unguarded remarks were meant to be light and jocular and were spoken in innocence and entirely without malice. He was extremely sensitive to any insult, real or imagined, to his own person but was remarkably insensitive to the feelings of others. Most times his frank, brutally honest speech was unintentionally offensive, and he was genuinely amazed when a lampooned character, formerly a friend or an "indifferent," turned into a bitter enemy.[27]

While Ruffin busied himself alienating those around him, the people back home began to complain about their senator's effectiveness as a legislator. He had entered politics ready to exercise his high ideals and lofty principles, but his constituents demanded more mundane and tangible benefits. Friends and political supporters plagued the freshman senator with requests for personal favors. Could Ruffin please use his influence and position to promote this piece of private legislation? Would he pull the appropriate strings to have that man appointed to a lucrative public job? Every member of the legislature received similar requests, and many considered such favors part of their official duties, but Ruffin was highly insulted. Although he regretted that he was not always strong enough to resist these personal pressures, his whole being recoiled at such unstatesmanlike conduct. Compromise, even on such trivial matters, was unthinkable moral hypocrisy. Cincinnatus would surely never bend his principles for mere popularity and neither, vowed Ruffin, would he.

But Ruffin's constituents had no idea that they had elected a high-minded Roman statesman, and they continued to nag their Cincinnatus with demands he deemed petty and demeaning. When he continued to ignore or even oppose their wishes as selfish and narrow, Ruffin kept his self-respect but lost the last shred of his waning public esteem.[28]

Finally, in 1826, after three years in the Senate, having accrued more private enemies than public glory, Ruffin resigned his seat, "tired & disgusted," he said, "with being 'a servant of the people.' " After this, in his writing and even in ordinary conversation, Ruffin spat out the word "politician" as an expletive, using it interchangeably with "demagogue." Embittered by his personal shortcomings and the public's failure to recognize and reward his true worth, Ruffin decided what to do next. He would teach those who rejected him a lesson. He would punish them with his absence by withdrawing himself entirely from the public arena. Retiring to his plantation and the simpler joys of a bucolic existence, he waited, perhaps like Cincinnatus, for the time when a more discerning and grateful country would beg for his services.[29]

3

Prophet without Honor

1

"YOU, LIKE ME & almost all Virginia boys, first turned your attention to politics," John Tyler complimented his friend Edmund Ruffin. "But you soon gave up the pursuit, & devoted yourself to agriculture—& in that pursuit you have done more good to the country than all our political great men put together. . . . How much better was it for you to have seen at first, & to refuse to pursue, the empty rewards of political life!"

Tyler's flattering words, spoken over thirty years after Ruffin had resigned his Senate seat, were inaccurate, and Ruffin was too doggedly honest to accept false praise. "I perceive that you, like many other friends who have known me more intimately, have mistaken me in this respect," he informed Tyler. "It was not because I was devoid of ambition, or of the desire to wield political power, that I have not sought political stations. On the contrary, few persons would have been more gratified by being so placed —& very few young men read more, or felt more interest, in the subjects of government & political economy." But he lacked winning eloquence; his political oratory was artless and abrasive. "Even if I could have obtained popular favor," claimed Ruffin, "& political eminence as its reward, I never knew the time that I would have been willing to purchase the honor, at the cost of paying the necessary price for popularity."[1]

But Ruffin did pay a heavy price for the failure of his political ambitions. Cincinnatus and Nathaniel Macon may have preferred the affairs of agriculture to the affairs of state, but they had never been forced to make that choice. When Ruffin left the Virginia Senate in 1826 and returned to

29

his James River plantation, he experienced increasing discontent with his prospects as nothing more than another gentleman planter. Suffering from the same boredom with rustic life, the same fantasies of political power that afflicted other Southern intellectuals like James Henry Hammond, William Gilmore Simms, and Nathaniel Beverley Tucker, Ruffin began to neglect his crops. His plantation management became sloppy and negligent. Disappointing wheat, corn, and cotton crops and low prices in 1827 further depressed Ruffin, rendering him, he wrote in his farm journal, "incapable of making proper efforts." Finally, admitted Ruffin, he lapsed into "almost total withdrawal of my personal attention from my farming."[2]

Compounding his alienation from farming, Ruffin moved his family in 1828 from their riverfront house, several miles inland to a mansion he called Shellbanks. Shellbanks was removed from the malaria-infested swamps along the James River and also distanced the master of the plantation from his fields. The house was located three miles from the middle of his farmlands, and though Ruffin could easily cover the distance on horseback in thirty minutes, he did so less and less frequently. Plantation operations, he complained, were "distasteful" and no longer "interesting or attractive to engage my continued attention." "Every little obstacle of weather, of indisposition, & of aversion to effort, or attraction of amusement," Ruffin said, "was soon sufficient to induce me to decline my ride of half an hour to see my work."[3]

For a while, Ruffin isolated himself completely from any personal contact with field work. He tried employing white overseers to do the job in his absence, but this scheme proved unsuccessful. Ruffin fired three men in succession for cruelly abusing his slaves. Besides, he found that the presence of an overseer "operated the more to make me indulge myself in withholding my personal attention" from plantation management. He became so despondent that he ceased keeping a regular farm journal.[4]

Ruffin's sudden disenchantment with the practical side of planting did not extend to the theoretical aspects of agricultural reform, however. Unfortunately, the publication in 1821 of his article on calcareous manures in the *American Farmer* had not signaled the beginning of an agricultural revival in Virginia. The planters and farmers of Lower Virginia were so slow and cautious in adopting Ruffin's methods that while his production had doubled between 1818 and 1828, that of his marling neighbors had risen one-tenth or less. The majority of husbandmen in Prince George County—indeed throughout Virginia—had not even begun to use marl.[5]

When Ruffin moved to Shellbanks, Virginia was in a terrible agricultural slump. Plantation profits had never been lower, and many planters suffered unexpected bankruptcies. Yet despite this general depression and his own loud complaints about bad crops and worse prices, Ruffin had reason to be thankful for his comparative prosperity. Because of his marling operations, his income exceeded his expenditures, and he was able to brag that he had more than doubled his inheritance.[6]

But Ruffin got no special satisfaction from gloating over his own success and his neighbors' misfortunes. Compelled by a need for approval, he wished to save them from financial ruin and, in so doing, reinstate himself in the public's estimation. The question was how. Only two years before, in 1826, he had thought he had the perfect answer. He remembered the article in the *American Farmer* that had lifted him from obscurity to some small measure of fame and began making tentative plans to issue a revised, enlarged, and updated version of his original essay. But the counsel and warning of Ruffin's neighbor and confidant, Thomas Cocke, scotched these plans and prevented the book's immediate publication.[7]

Thomas Cocke, although nearly twenty years Ruffin's senior, was perhaps the closest friend Ruffin had in Prince George County. An eccentric recluse, Cocke, like Ruffin, had spent his youth mainly in the society of books. He married in middle age and endured company only for his wife's sake. A man of great intellect, he loved humanity in the abstract but avoided it in the flesh. "If not a misanthrope," Ruffin said of Cocke, "at least [he] heartily despised his fellow man." "He saw very few persons & wished to see yet fewer." But Cocke found welcome companionship in Ruffin, whose mind, literary tastes, and brooding spirit were similar to his own. Cocke showed considerable interest in Ruffin and his agricultural experiments and even became a slow convert and then a disciple of Ruffin's doctrine of soil fertility. Ruffin, in turn, relied greatly on the older man's perception and friendly criticism. So, in 1826, when an embittered Ruffin returned to Prince George County after a short career in politics and confided his plans to publish a book about calcareous manures, it was easy for the misanthropic Cocke to convince him that the public was not ready properly to appreciate such a bold work. Disappointed, Ruffin heeded his friend's advice and put his manuscript away for six years.[8]

2

An Essay on Calcareous Manures finally appeared in print in January, 1832, just as Virginia's General Assembly began its debate over manumission. The impetus for this historic occasion, which marked the end of free and open discussion of slavery in the antebellum South, came from an event that had occurred almost five months earlier in Southampton County.

On Monday, August 22, 1831, shortly after midnight, the Southampton slave preacher, Nat Turner, sure that he was acting as God's own terrible instrument, led a handful of black insurrectionists on a bloody mission to free themselves and their people from bondage. As they zig-zagged through the countryside to avoid detection, Turner and his men stopped systematically at farm after farm, recruiting blacks and maiming or killing the white occupants. The black conspirators slaughtered some sixty white men, women, and children before Tuesday morning, when militia and troops rallied and Turner and his band scattered in all directions.

By the following Sunday, all the insurgents except Turner were either dead or in jail. Turner remained at large for eight weeks, but even after his capture, traumatized and hysterical whites in Virginia and North Carolina continued to wreak bloody vengeance. Driven by terror and a mob spirit, white vigilantes executed scores of slaves, women and children included, most of whom had had nothing to do with the revolt. As a horrible warning to all potentially rebellious slaves, white Virginians lined the roads with the gory heads of murdered blacks fixed atop long poles.[9]

Throughout the South, news of the Turner rebellion engendered panic and fear that this fiendish slave plot extended beyond Virginia's borders. Wild rumors circulated until some Southerners were convinced that the uprising had spread to all the slave states. In North Carolina, whose northern counties were located only twenty miles from Southampton County, reports informed the governor that three citizens had literally been scared to death by false alarms since the Virginia rebellion. And in the Old Dominion, particularly in the black-belt Tidewater region, where blacks outnumbered whites, the fear of continued violence and bloodshed lingered. Frightened people all over Virginia bombarded Governor John Floyd with petitions insisting that he send them arms and troops for protection. In front of their slaves, Virginians tried to appear calm and unworried, but a sympathetic Northern visitor easily saw through this bravado. "The horrors of Southampton have aroused them," he informed friends and family in the North. "They lie down to sleep with fear. They hardly venture out on nights. A lady told me that for weeks after the tragedy, she had quivered at every blast of wind, and every blow of the shutter. Bolts and bars were tried, but the horrid fear haunted the whole population day and night."[10]

Ruffin's reaction at Shellbanks was an exception to the general hysteria which followed Turner's insurrection. The facts of the Southampton slave uprising were enough to "inspire terror," Ruffin agreed, but he could not condone the ensuing vicious bloodbath and cowardly atrocities unleashed on innocent backs. Unlike most of his terrified neighbors, Ruffin regarded the Southampton conspiracy as no more than an unfortunate local incident with no widespread implications of impending racial holocaust. The majority of slaves, he contended, were content with their servitude and harbored no feelings of hatred or ill will toward their kind masters and mistresses.

When fear and panic in the South magnified the Turner affair into a nation-wide conspiracy, Ruffin clucked and accused his neighbors of indulging in "community insanity." And when a slave in Ruffin's own Prince George County was tried, convicted, and sentenced to hang for participation in the Turner rebellion, Ruffin, who believed the man falsely charged, circulated a petition to Governor Floyd demanding a full pardon.

Dozens of other slaves, some as far as one hundred miles away from the actual uprising, were similarly accused and condemned on the weight of testimony, Ruffin contended, "which at any sober time would not have been deemed sufficient to convict a dog suspected of killing a sheep." As for the condemned slave in Prince George County, the evidence against him had come from a disreputable lower-class white man whose words were "not worthy of belief." But according to Ruffin, the attorneys who prosecuted such cases and the judges who tried them "dared not do justice" or suffered the same "fits of insanity" that were shaking most of the Southern white community.[11]

Ruffin, though, was never a man to bridle his own free speech, even if his stance on an issue was unpopular, and he continued to defend the local slave. Riding through Prince George County, he stopped at plantation after plantation, arguing the innocence of the condemned black man and imploring residents to affix their names to the petition to prevent a terrible miscarriage of justice. He was pleased when most of his neighbors confessed their sincere belief that the convicted black man was guiltless. But when he brought out his petition, the same gentlemen refused to sign and turned away, explaining that they had no wish to "meddle in the matter." In all, Ruffin collected only eleven signatures besides his own.

With these dozen names, Ruffin proceeded to Richmond, where he presented his unimpressive petition to Governor Floyd. The governor himself was hardly immune to the prevailing public hysteria, however, and refused to grant the pardon. But Floyd had already taken steps to save condemned blacks who were manifestly innocent by commuting their sentences to sale and transportation outside United States boundaries, which, in effect, meant removing them from the Old Dominion.

Ruffin begged in vain for a full pardon. But later on, he was glad that Governor Floyd had yielded somewhat to political pressures and "community insanity." Had Floyd granted the pardon and returned the absolved slave to his Prince George master, foul play would have been the inevitable result. Ruffin thought the released prisoner would have been murdered, swiftly and secretly, by "fellows of the baser sort, who in times like these always rise in power & influence—& who could then have committed such a murder, even openly, with impunity, under the claim of patriotism & protection of the vital interests of the community."[12]

In all the hysteria that followed the Turner revolt, Ruffin's honest and bold efforts on behalf of a slave convicted of insurrection placed him under public suspicion as a possible abolitionist collaborator and a traitor to the South. His sane and moderate pleas for justice, Ruffin complained, branded him as a "favorer, if not approver, of murderous insurgents, & midnight slayers of sleeping men, women & children." Throughout Prince George County, the Ruffin name acquired odium, until even those men who had secretly admitted the justice of Ruffin's petition were vying with each other to condemn his actions the most loudly. And from some quarters came threats of personal violence and suggestions—never acted upon—that the master of Shellbanks deserved a good thrashing.[13]

3

Publication of *An Essay on Calcareous Manures* several months after the Turner rebellion did much to raise the author in the public's esteem and dissipate some lingering local anger and resentment. The original seven-page article had grown into a 242-page book, which was destined to appear in four subsequent editions; a fifth edition—thickened with appendices to 493 pages—appeared in 1852.

Praise for Ruffin's *Essay* poured in from all parts of the United States and even Great Britain, as readers scrambled to buy the 750 available copies. Reviewers hailed Ruffin as a hero of agricultural reform. *An Essay on Calcareous Manures* was a "masterpiece," proclaimed one writer, "an original work of merit," declared another. An English reviewer congratulated the author on performing a "very important service to the scientific agriculturalist in this country, as well as America." "Your little book on Calcareous Manures, in its valuable consequences," John Tyler later assured Ruffin, "will be worth more to the country than all the state papers that have been the most celebrated in our time."[14]

Basking once more in the unexpected limelight of public approval, Ruffin determined this time to hold onto his new popularity and also to rescue himself from the boring life of an ordinary planter, which had grown completely unbearable. The success of his book proved, he believed, that it was through the written and not the spoken word that he could best achieve the eminence he desired, leading Virginia and the South in a true agricultural revolution. Still, Ruffin was dissatisfied with the success of his book, because his admirers seemed "too easily convinced." His reservations stemmed perhaps from his own self-doubts and deep-seated feelings of inferiority and unworthiness. Did he really deserve such praise? he wondered. For as much as he wanted public favor, he was suspicious, almost unnerved, whenever it came his way. Then too his love–hate relationship with the rest of society practically forced him to hold the public—and the people it honored—in contempt. So, for a variety of personal reasons, most of which he never admitted, even to himself, Ruffin felt flattered but not a little uneasy when the public smiled at him. "Few [readers] carefully followed or strictly scrutinized the train of argument, or disputed any of the steps," he now complained. "They were content to receive the results as fully proved truths." Southern planters and farmers obviously needed his constant prodding and advice. Convinced that his future lay in this direction, Ruffin made plans to edit his own agricultural journal, the *Farmers' Register.* "With this publication," Ruffin remembered, "was begun a new & distinct era of my life."[15]

In order to solicit subscribers, Ruffin first sent out a prospectus. The purpose of the *Farmers' Register,* he explained, was to improve the present miserable economic condition of Virginia by disseminating important and up-to-date information about agricultural reforms. For a subscription rate of five dollars per year, readers would receive a monthly publication consisting of approximately sixty-four pages devoted solely to agricultural subjects. No mere "puffs" or dishonest advertisements would disgrace the *Register's* pages, Ruffin promised. Nor would the journal contain articles on purely political, and therefore potentially controversial, subjects. As editor, Ruffin pledged to draw not only from his own writings but also from the best selections that American, English, and French agricultural journals had to offer. He especially encouraged "practical farmers" like himself to use the *Farmers' Register* as a medium for agricultural dialogue and exchange by contributing their own letters and articles.[16]

In June, 1833, Ruffin launched the first issue of the *Farmers' Register.* "And he gave it for his opinion," boasted the frontispiece, "that whoever could make two ears of corn, or two blades of grass to grow upon a spot of ground where only one grew before, would deserve better of mankind, and do more essential service to his country, than the whole race of politicians put together." Ruffin, who protested too much, in view of his own frustrated political dreams, was fond of this quote from Dean Swift. He hoped that the political "demagogues" at the state capital would read his paper and squirm.

Readers liked the *Farmers' Register,* frontispiece and all; and the new periodical was instantly successful. John Skinner, former editor of the *American Farmer,* a rival agricultural journal, enthusiastically endorsed the newcomer as the "best publication on agriculture which this country or Europe has ever produced," while the Richmond *Enquirer* heralded the dawning of a new era in Virginia's agricultural history. In the ensuing year, the *Register* acquired over one thousand regular subscribers in Virginia and almost two hundred from fifteen other states and the District of Columbia.

Theodorick McRoberts, publisher of Virginia's only other agricultural paper, the *Virginia Farmer,* quickly recognized that he could not compete with this bright new rival and that his little paper must "drop like the harebell before the sun." After a few months, the *Virginia Farmer* quietly folded, leaving the field entirely to the *Farmers' Register.* [17]

Ruffin worked hard to make the *Farmers' Register* worthy of its reputation for high quality. The articles he chose for the *Register* treated topics of every possible interest to farmers and planters. The entire magazine was devoted to the improvement of agriculture. In any issue, a reader could expect to find a wealth of practical information and advice on such diverse subjects as how to build a better drain, choose a reliable overseer, care for a slave, rotate crops, or spread manure. Or, if he were interested, the reader might catch up on the latest foreign and domestic advancements in agricultural physics and chemistry. He was certainly not likely to put down the paper before reading at least one article or letter testifying to the effectiveness of the editor's pet reform, marl. And with special editions of the *Farmers' Register,* the lucky subscriber would also receive a reprint of John Taylor's *Arator,* the *Westover Manuscripts,* the *Bland Papers,* or Ruffin's *Essay on Calcareous Manures*—valuable agricultural works, which the editor thoughtfully appended free of charge.[18]

The first few editions of the *Farmers' Register* came from the printing presses of J. W. Campbell in Petersburg. But early in 1834, in order to cut down on expenses, Ruffin moved the entire operation to his Shellbanks plantation, where he personally took over the jobs of proprietor and publisher as well as editor. Ruffin was also the journal's chief contributor. Since, despite his urgings, the "practical farmers" of the Old Dominion did not make reliable correspondents, Ruffin had to write nearly half of every issue himself, including most of the anonymous articles.[19]

All this extra work demanded most of Ruffin's time and attention, but he did not complain. The business of editing and publishing, he gushed, was so "engrossing and delightful" that by 1835, he had made up his mind to abandon the tiresome life of a planter, sell all his property, and devote himself completely to his satisfying new career. Writing for "practical farmers" seemed much more attractive than actually being one. So, with scarcely a backward glance at the county where he was born, Ruffin left Prince George and moved with his family to the town of Petersburg. There he set up shop at the corner of High and Market streets.[20]

Still, Ruffin could not detach himself entirely from his former agrarian life. Although he tried to sell all his Coggin's Point property and landholdings when he moved to Petersburg, he was unable to sell his largest plantation, Beechwood. This obstacle only increased his aversion to country life. Eventually he would sell Beechwood to his oldest son, Edmund, but in the meantime, he visited Prince George County only to see his married children or to talk with his former neighbor, Thomas Cocke.[21]

4

It was on just such a rare occasion in February, 1840, that Ruffin last spoke with his trusted old friend. Cocke was sixty-four years old and a widower. An apoplectic attack a few years earlier had enfeebled him, making breathing difficult for him and preventing him from pursuing his former active plantation management. The few contemporaries he had associated with were now dead, and according to Ruffin, Cocke felt like "the last remaining individual of the preceding generation." His children were either away at school or were too young to be suitable companions, so Cocke reverted to his previous hermit-like existence, rarely leaving his room even for meals. "Thus he was almost entirely alone," Ruffin recalled sadly, "& his mind permitted to be continually brooding over his real & imaginary causes of unhappiness." Although books were still some comfort, age and infirmity had dulled the old man's memory to such an extent that he scarcely recalled what he had read. Such an obvious sign of mental decay, Ruffin knew, "was a matter of mortification to his pride" and robbed Cocke of his one remaining source of distraction.[22]

Sick, lonely, and feeling himself a burden to his family, Cocke confided to Ruffin that he longed for death to take him quickly. But despite his many ailments, Cocke had no serious illness and thus seemed doomed to a long and useless life. "I cannot bear it," Cocke muttered over and over during their long conversation, "& I *will not* bear it." When he began to discuss the question of suicide, Ruffin tried to change the subject at once. "I could not bring myself to acknowledge to him, to let him know fully, that I comprehended the drift of his dark expressions, & suspected his design," Ruffin remembered. "It seemed to me, that to do this, would have removed [the] one obstacle in his way." Hoping to delay his friend from acting impulsively, Ruffin argued that suicide was always an act of temporary insanity; but Cocke simply replied, "In that, you are *altogether* mistaken."[23]

But when it was time for Ruffin to leave, Cocke was in a cheerful mood and assured Ruffin that he appreciated his company and conversation. Three days later, Saturday morning, February 22, Thomas Cocke committed suicide. Waiting until the rest of the family had eaten breakfast and left the house, the old man slipped out unnoticed and made his way to a secluded thicket on the edge of a deep ravine. In happier days, this spot had been a favorite retreat. Now, seated beneath a hugh old oak tree, Cocke propped the muzzle of a rifle in his mouth, checked his pocket for the razor he had brought in case the gun refused to fire, and then pulled the trigger with his big toe.[24]

At eight o'clock that evening at his Petersburg home, Ruffin received a message from his son Edmund that Cocke had taken his own life. Ruffin left for Beechwood immediately, and the next morning, at the Cocke plantation, he helped gather the blackened fragments of his friend's skull and brains scattered under the ancient oak.

The funeral was an especially sad affair, as mourners grieved the loss of Cocke even more because of the horrible manner of his death. Although orthodox Christianity condemned suicide as a major sin against God, Ruffin refused to sit in judgment. "I venture no comment upon this awful deed," he decided. "It is not for men to judge, but for God—and God judges it in mercy! But while I cannot attempt to justify & will not try even to offer excuses in mitigation of the last & greatest offense of his life, neither will I in any manner join in the universal cry of condemnation." "When death calls me from this world," he stated humbly, "may my dread account of sins over-balancing virtues, be not greater than that of my self-slaughtered friend."[25]

Although he never blamed Cocke for committing suicide, Ruffin was overcome by remorse and self-reproach when he recalled their last conversation together. Cocke's words had been a warning, a call for help. Why, Ruffin asked himself, had he done nothing to dissuade his friend and prevent this bloody tragedy?[26]

Finally, in an effort to exorcise his guilt and express his feelings of regret, Ruffin sat down and composed an eleven-page "Statement of the Closing Scenes of the Life of Thomas Cocke," recording each step of the gory suicide in vivid and minute detail. But even as he wrote, the presence of Cocke's headless corpse seemed to fill the room. "I am as perfectly free from all belief in supernatural visitations, or appearances, as is any man on earth," insisted Ruffin, "nor has my reason treated such fears as otherwise than too absurd & ridiculous for serious thought. But it is not reasoning, nor even any distant approach to belief, but my painful feeling & shattered nerves, that make me, as I write, alone & in the depth of night, feel almost afraid to look around, lest the object which so dwells on my mind's eye should be more palpably present, & thus demand of me more strongly & sternly than does my own heart, 'Why did you make no effort to prevent this deed?' "[27]

5

While visions of his mangled friend continued to haunt Ruffin's dreams, his waking hours were increasingly preoccupied with a struggle against more tangible demons—the state banks. Ruffin had never liked banks, but personal losses incurred after the Panic of 1837 whipped his dislike into a fury and a desire for revenge.

Back in 1835, when Ruffin sold his Shellbanks and Coggin's Point plantations, he had no idea what to do with his surplus capital. For years, the high price of cotton had encouraged Americans to indulge feverishly in financial investments, and Ruffin was ready to join in the general speculative mania. First he tried becoming a money-lender. But although he lent money only to people he considered friends and gave them generous repayment terms at legal interest rates, he soon discovered that no one likes a creditor; his loans often cost him both money and friends.[28]

Then "friendly" financial advisors took him into their confidence and assured him that investments in public bonds and private stocks yielded high interest with no bother and little risk. Without troubling himself to investigate their claims of easy money, Ruffin plunged into the financial market. Following what he thought were valuable tips, he purchased ten thousand dollars worth of stock in the Greensville Railway and, in the space of a few months, cleared fifteen hundred dollars in dividends. Then the boom days were over. The stock had been oversubscribed. Ruffin did not see another cent from his investment in the next fifteen years.[29]

Stubbornly, he kept investing in railroads. He spent another ten thousand dollars for stock in the Raleigh and Gaston Railroad and then bought twenty more shares before learning that the railroad had been bankrupt almost from the beginning. The Raleigh and Gaston never paid a single dividend and finally had to be mortgaged and sold to pay off its debts.[30]

Although Ruffin made his largest financial investments in railroads, he also dabbled in cotton textile factories, water power, and tenement houses. The factories were never even built. Ruffin sold what he could at a loss and was stuck with the remaining worthless stock. Nor was he more successful as a landlord. He kept his three tenements for three to nine years but collected next to nothing in rent and finally sold the buildings at much less than the purchase price.[31]

Early in 1837, the bubble of speculation burst and the good times ended. Cotton prices began to fall and a financial crisis in Great Britain precipitated a chain of bank failures in the United States. Just before the economy dived and the banks suspended specie payment, Ruffin had estimated the value of his property at one hundred thousand dollars. During the Panic of 1837, when prices began to fall drastically, Ruffin went to his former financial advisors for help. These "advisors" had long since unloaded their worthless securities, leaving unsuspecting investors like Ruffin to take the brunt of the depression. Ruffin suffered losses amounting to thirty thousand dollars.[32]

At first, Ruffin berated himself, moaning that his own "credulity and trust" had blinded him to "things which would be noticed by even ignorant

& dull minds." But he was not the kind of man to accept blame or examine what were probably the true reasons for his misfortunes: vanity, greed, and poor judgment. Criticism in any form made him feel uncomfortable and ashamed. So even when he admitted mistakes, he managed to turn his faults into virtues: he was too trusting, too honorable. Then he looked for a scapegoat, choosing for his target a person, group, or institution to which he attributed excessive powers—figures of authority not unlike his own father. This time, banks were the culprits. The banks, he charged erroneously, had encouraged gullible speculators like himself by issuing paper money far in excess of their cash reserves. The ultimate effect of the expanded currency, complained a sadder but wiser Ruffin, was "to reward the first and cunning operators at the expense of the more tardy & ignorant followers, who made later investments & have nearly all the final losses. I belonged to the latter class."

Ruffin was convinced that banking abuses were chiefly responsible for his financial difficulties. When banks could not redeem their notes in gold and silver and the Virginia legislature made it a crime for creditors to refuse paper money and insist on payment in specie, he accused politicians and bankers of collusion to impair the legal obligation of contracts. Both federal and state banking systems, he said, were engaged in "fraud & pillage." His countrymen might cravenly submit to such abuses, Ruffin fumed, but "I determined to resist."[33]

In 1841, Ruffin launched his campaign for bank reform, using the columns of the *Farmers' Register* as his main forum. He called for laws to restrict excessive loans, check speculative financial ventures, and curb wildly fluctuating currency values by paying hard cash on demand. These basic reform measures were in every planter's and farmer's own interest. Virginia's bankers had grown so mighty, Ruffin warned his readers, that they controlled the state legislature and blocked vital agricultural reforms.

At first, Ruffin's articles and editorials on banking were calm and judicious. But when his warnings elicited no positive response and his readership appeared content to submit quietly to banking "inequities," Ruffin's pen grew less cautious and more impassioned. Besides the *Farmers' Register,* he used other friendly papers to lash out at banking "evils" and attack his banking "enemies." Thinly disguising his authorship, Ruffin liked to sign his articles with the name of some ancient Roman statesman or warrior well known for his resistance to tyranny and injustice. In Petersburg, moreover, Ruffin organized the Association for Promoting Currency and Banking Reform. The Association's main function was to flood the state legislature with petitions demanding an end to bank fraud. The cause of bank reform had turned from a low-key campaign into an almost obsessive one-man crusade.

Virginians did not have to wait for the slow and cumbersome machinery of state government to move before taking action against banks, Ruffin contended. Since banks had suspended redemption of their paper money in honest hard currency, Ruffin stopped endorsing bank notes with his signature. Instead he would write, "The promise on the face of this note is FALSE; and the issue of such notes is both a banking and a governmental FRAUD, committed on the rights and interests of labor and of honestly acquired capital." Or alternatively, "The object, as well as the effect of the paper money system is to enable those who have earned or accumulated nothing by labor, to exchanged their *nothing* for *something,* and often the *everything,* earned by the labor of others."[34]

Until the banks ceased their dishonest practices, Ruffin admonished his readers, no person should sign a "cheating" bank note or send a letter without attaching some instructive antibanking message. Hoping to encourage others to follow his own forthright example, Ruffin set his presses to work printing out sheet after sheet of sample bank endorsements and then distributed them free to all who promised to paste them on the backs of bank notes and envelopes.

When he could not think of something original to write, Ruffin quoted famous antibanking statements from George Washington, John Adams, Thomas Jefferson, James Madison, Daniel Webster, Henry Clay, and of course, John Taylor of Caroline. "Of all the contrivances for cheating the labouring classes of mankind," he quoted from Webster, "none is so essential as that which deludes them with paper money. It is the most perfect expedient ever invented for fertilising the rich man's fields by the sweat of the poor man's brow." And from Adams, "There will never be . . . any settled confidence in public men or measures until paper money is done away." To insure that his hard work did not go unnoticed, Ruffin took the time to write special letters to the governor and the attorney general of Virginia and to the attorney general of the United States. Each missive was conspicuously enclosed in an envelope bearing some provocative statement.[35]

These bank reform activities naturally made Ruffin very unpopular in powerful financial and political circles. But as his banking enemies multiplied, Ruffin seemed surprisingly buoyant. For without having to acknowledge the real sources of his rage, he was able to vent some of his pent-up anger and personal frustrations. "This printing endorsements may seem to be a petty and impotent mode of attack," Ruffin told a friend. "But it puts truth before hundreds who never otherwise would have an idea of its existence. And the banking gentry are more annoyed by these small shot than by the heaviest artillery. The falling of drops of water in time wears away the hardest stone." "At any rate," he said philosophically, "it amuses me; and though the game is . . . very costly to me, I cannot expect to amuse myself free of cost." He pointed out that "other men spend their money or time & labor in hunting, shooting, fishing etc. or in pursuit of office and honours." "I have no fancy for any of these very common pleasures," Ruffin insisted—a self-deception rather than a deliberate lie—"& therefore can the better afford to amuse myself with hunting banks & bank directors, & in enjoying their anger & malignity . . . much more than dreading their revenge."[36]

But Ruffin aroused the "anger & malignity" of more than just hunted bank directors. "My cause," complained a perplexed Ruffin, "was denounced by not only the people of towns but also by many of the country, as violently as if my conduct had been that of their plunderers, instead of one striving to protect them from being plundered." Few men besides Ruffin wanted to antagonize the banking interests. Soft-money Democrats like Ruffin's "enemy" William C. Rives as well as most Virginia Whigs believed that banks and banking capital were needed to develop the Old Dominion's commercial, industrial, and agricultural resources. Even many hard-money advocates were reluctant to take strong measures against the banks. Merchants and townspeople depended on banks as their main source of loans, and planters and farmers needed bankers' easy credit for growing and selling crops and purchasing slaves.[37]

So when Ruffin began using the *Farmers' Register* to attack the country's financial institutions, frightened readers berated him as editor for breaking his promise to avoid all subjects involving politics. Ruffin protested that he had never meant to exclude topics of political economy that touched so vitally on agrarian interests, but his readers would not listen. "Now I am one of those," wrote a sarcastic subscriber, "who believe banks have done, are doing, and are destined to do more good, morally, politically, commercially, and agriculturally, than all the *marl banks* between the ocean and the mountains." Other angry letters followed, threatening to cancel subscriptions unless Ruffin returned to his original neutral editorial policy. Even formerly friendly newspaper and journal editors, like John Skinner of the *American Farmer,* turned against Ruffin and publicly defended the paper money system.[38]

Disregarding all threats and pleas to cease his private war, Ruffin denounced his critics as "schemers," "self-seekers," "knaves," "politicians," and "tools of the banking interests" and stubbornly decided to step up his attack. Articles in the *Farmers' Register* were not enough. So, in September, 1841, Ruffin started publishing another periodical, *The Bank Reformer.*[39]

"Nil Utile Quod Non Honestum," blazed the *Reformer*'s masthead. Hoping to use the monthly sixteen-page pamphlet to expose fraudulent banking practices and to attract other zealots to his cause, Ruffin designed *The Bank Reformer* for a limited six-month run and personally shouldered most of the paper's expenses. He sent free issues to all known enemies of the paper money system, reminding them that for only five dollars, they could purchase and distribute 200 additional copies of *The Bank Reformer,* thereby helping to widen the paper's appeal and further the cause of bank reform. Ruffin did not rest here. In all parts of Virginia, astonished postmasters received unsolicited bundles of *The Bank Reformer* with instructions from the editor to deliver copies to any person willing to pay the cost of postage.[40]

Despite all of Ruffin's best efforts, *The Bank Reformer* was a failure. He won no new friends for the cause, only more ferocious enemies. When Ruffin first set up shop in Petersburg, the townspeople had welcomed him as a valuable and respected addition to the community. Members of the Petersburg Benevolent Mechanic Association had wasted no time in admitting Ruffin as a printer and even selected him to deliver the Association's anniversary address. But after Ruffin's fierce antibanking crusade in the *Farmers' Register* and *The Bank Reformer,* the members withdrew their support and used their own newspapers and periodicals to print vicious attacks on his editorial policy. Ruffin claimed that town rowdies even tried to silence him permanently through "cowardly" and "assassin-like" violence, while the good citizens of Petersburg not only condoned such outrages but "openly applauded" them.[41]

In the end, hunting banks and making bank directors howl proved too dangerous and costly an amusement, no matter how cathartic. The *Farmers' Register* was no longer considered a respectable journal, and readers withdrew their names one by one from the subscription list. Moreover, Julian Ruffin, co-editor of the *Farmers' Register* since his college graduation in 1838, tired of his father's crusade and returned to Prince George County and the more peaceful life of a planter. Ruffin could no longer afford to operate alone and at a loss. In February, 1842, he stopped publishing *The Bank Reformer.* Two months later, he closed down the *Farmers' Register* as well. Feeling rejected once again, Ruffin withdrew, punishing with his absence those who had wounded his pride and failed to appreciate his worth. Bitterly he bid his readers good-by, announcing that "with the close of this volume will end the editor's labors for ten of the best years of his life; and he will no longer obtrude, on the agricultural public, services which seem to be so little aided by the sympathy of the great body of the members of the interest designated to be served."[42]

Ruffin truly believed that in the ten years he edited the *Farmers' Register,* "ten of the best years of his life," as he said, he had helped the farmers and planters of Virginia and enhanced his own reputation. Yet they were also years of great personal and financial loss, of public vituperation and ingratitude. He had given so much and gained so little. "It is more disagreeable for me to recur to & reflect upon this," Ruffin admitted, "than any other time of my life."[43]

For months after the *Register* closed, Ruffin brooded about the unfairness, the injustice, of his fate. Then in December, 1842, his fortunes changed. A letter arrived from James Henry Hammond, the newly elected governor of South Carolina, informing Ruffin that the people of the Palmetto state, through their legislature, would be honored if he would accept the position of State Agricultural Surveyor. Somewhat soothed, Ruffin replied that he would be "highly gratified" to offer his services. But the invitation and his acceptance had a bittersweet quality. Ruffin had labored diligently for his native Virginia, yet honors had come not from the Old Dominion but from a "foreign" state. It reminded him of a line from the Bible: "A prophet is not without honour, save in his own country."[44]

4

Master of Marlbourne

1

BEFORE RUFFIN BEGAN his agricultural survey of South Carolina in 1843, Governor Hammond warned him, "You will find our people . . . polite & hospitable, but even in these their most prominent qualities they evince much of that want of *enterprise* which I fear is characteristic of our state in the main. They will receive you cordially everywhere, but I cannot promise that many of them will go far to *meet* you . . . . You must have expected in your task to meet with much indifference, much obstinacy & some opposition. It will not be your least difficult part to keep your temper & press forward over all these obstacles with unabating perseverance."[1]

But no number of threatened obstacles in South Carolina could have kept Ruffin in Petersburg, "a place," he explained, "which I heartily disliked & despised & was determined to leave." So, a few weeks after receiving his appointment, Ruffin arrived in Charleston. He had visited there only once before, in 1840, and evidently liked what he saw. "Charleston may be likened to a gentleman born and bred," he had told the readers of the *Farmers' Register.* "It seemed to me that the population contained a larger proportion of gentlemen than I had ever seen in any other city."[2]

Charleston was indeed impressive, but the city and the rest of South Carolina's Tidewater region were on the decline economically. The many decaying and desolated coastal plantations reminded Ruffin of earlier agricultural conditions in eastern Virginia. Armed with five hundred copies of

45

the third edition of his *Essay on Calcareous Manures* and his own seemingly inexhaustible enthusiasm for agricultural reform, he set out to spread the gospel of marl and scientific farming throughout South Carolina, in order, he admitted candidly, "to enrich the state & thereby exalt my own reputation."[3]

Ruffin had entertained warm feelings toward South Carolina for more than ten years. When South Carolina nullified the federal tariff in 1832 and almost dared President Andrew Jackson to force her into submission, most of the other states branded its actions rash and impulsive and its politicians as hotheads and extremists. Ruffin, though, applauded the nullifiers' stand and praised South Carolina as the last great bastion of states' rights principles.

And of all the "gentlemen" he met in the Palmetto state, Ruffin most admired the present governor, James Henry Hammond. Hammond had endeared himself to the former editor of *The Bank Reformer* when, in his first annual message to the state legislature, he launched into a vicious attack against the State Bank of South Carolina. Ruffin sent Hammond a printing press, and the two men began a lively personal correspondence, swapping antibanking endorsements for use in both Virginia and South Carolina. Although Hammond's antibanking motives may have been partly political, Ruffin never questioned the sincerity of anyone sympathetic to the cause, and he and the Governor became close friends.[4]

Unlike Ruffin, Hammond was not born into upper-class planter society. But despite his rather humble upcountry origins, Hammond was no leveler, and he enthusiastically shared Ruffin's conservative and elitist notions on the proper arrangement of the social and political order. He pronounced "ridiculously absurd" Thomas Jefferson's philosophy of the natural rights of all men to life, liberty, and the pursuit of happiness. "I repudiate that much lauded but nowhere accredited dogma of Mr. Jefferson, that 'all men are born equal,' " he declared. As much as Ruffin, he deprecated "the influx of demagogism" and democracy, which, he maintained, had polluted national and local elections and had even the best and eldest Southern families practicing "their gross fawning on the vulgar." An advantageous marriage in 1831 to a wealthy Charleston heiress gave Hammond his own plantation and slaves, further cementing his allegiance to the ruling class. Afterwards even his friends called him "purse-proud," and no voice was louder than his own in the defense of an aristocratic, planter-dominated form of government.[5]

Hammond's extreme political conservatism had drawn him to the side of South Carolina's nullifiers during the nullification crisis of 1831–1832. As the bold and hot-tempered newspaper editor of the Columbia *Southern Times,* he had not only championed the extremists' position but had also seen fit to horsewhip one critic and to challenge another to a duel. As his reward, Hammond had gained favor with John C. Calhoun, Robert Hayne, James Hamilton, and other leading state politicians, and in 1834, with their support, he was elected to Congress.[6]

On the floor of the House of Representatives, in 1836, Hammond further distinguished himself as a secessionist hotspur. During the Gag Rule debates over whether or not to consider future antislavery petitions, he defended the peculiar institution as a "blessing" and threatened to return personally to South Carolina to preach secession if Northern antislavery criticism continued. Unless these dangerous abolitionist attacks stopped at once, he had warned congressional colleagues, "we may have to dissolve this Union."[7]

When Hammond resigned from Congress shortly after the debates, he was convinced that someday the slave states would have to carry out his threat of disunion and form their own separate nation. But the depressed state of agriculture, particularly in the Upper South, and Southern dependence on Northern manufacturers troubled him. Somehow, the South must be readied for eventual independence by being made economically strong.

For these reasons, he was especially concerned about agricultural reform. As the master of Silver Bluff, his wife's magnificent Savannah River plantation, Hammond worried constantly about the poverty of his own thin acres and practiced the most modern agricultural methods in the region. In 1839, he organized the State Agricultural Society, and in November, 1841, he delivered a ringing address to the Society's membership. Southern economy must cease its dependence on one-crop cotton cultivation, he insisted. To become self-sufficient, planters and farmers must learn to diversify their agriculture and recognize that industry, even with Negro slavery, must and should play a role in the South's economic future. He envisioned that manufacturing would become the special province of the Old South, which would replace the Northeast as the chief supplier of goods to the New "Cotton" South. Organically and harmoniously linked, the Old South and the New South would no longer be in fierce economic competition but would supply each other's agricultural and industrial needs for mutual profit and benefit.[8]

Hammond realized that soil revitalization was crucial to his plan for an independent South. Although skeptical at first of Ruffin's theories about marl's miraculous restorative powers, he had tried using calcareous manures at Silver Bluff. The results were so convincing that Hammond dubbed himself Ruffin's "apostle." "It is a little amusing to consider that I was once such a denouncer of Marl," he later confessed to Ruffin. "If this was a political matter how I should be reviled for inconsistency."[9]

Elected to the governorship of South Carolina in 1842, Hammond immediately called on Ruffin's agricultural services. But he had no illusions when he advised Ruffin that his job as agricultural surveyor would be difficult and exasperating. Hammond, a man of frustrated intellect like Ruffin, knew from personal experience that many of South Carolina's planters would be wary of advice from a "Book-farmer." How many times had he complained of his neighbors' ignorance, declaring contemptuously that "poor bred country gentlemen" would never read books, even if books grew like fruit on trees?[10]

Undaunted, Ruffin determined to convince South Carolina's obstinate gentlemen of the wonders of calcareous manures. For over half a year he surveyed the state, examining swamplands, clambering down rock quarries, searching for hidden beds of marl. His services to agricultural improvement met with much respect and at least an outward show of gratitude wherever he went. But Ruffin rode his marling "hobby" with such intense fervor that occasionally even the most polite and deferential Carolinian had to suppress a smile. "Mr. Ruffin is an enthusiast," joked the Richmond *Examiner* afterwards. "During his late exploration of soil through South Carolina, it was remarked of him, that he was so full of calcareous manures, that if you poured any sort of acid, acetic, or nitric, on his head he would effervesce, and indicate the presence of lime."[11]

At the end of the year, Ruffin sent Hammond the *Report of the Commencement and Progress of the Agricultural Survey of South Carolina for 1843*. The Governor thanked him profusely and praised him as South Carolina's greatest benefactor. Still, Ruffin was disappointed. The planters and farmers of South Carolina had been cordial, as Hammond had promised, but they were no more receptive to his new agrarian theories than the skeptics he had left in the Old Dominion. Not one man in a hundred, Ruffin estimated, had followed his marling instructions. Hammond, whose own efforts to enlighten his fellow planters had often proved frustrating, tried to comfort him. "You must not suppose that your labours were not appreciated here because there were some who carped," he wrote shortly after Ruffin completed his survey. "The fact is all real benefits to mankind are always spurned. You have to cram them like physic down men's throats."[12]

But Ruffin no longer had the physical strength or energy to force marl on reluctant Carolinians. Despite his initial enthusiasm for his project, Ruffin's always feeble constitution was unable to withstand the constant exposure to the hot sun and malaria that his work entailed. Even a much-needed rest in the mountains could not reverse the effects of two severe attacks of "swamp fever" and, before the year was over, he had to resign his office. Leaving his son Julian to finish the last few weeks of field work, Ruffin returned to his wife and children in Petersburg.[13]

2

Ruffin was unhappy living in Petersburg. Even before the *Farmers' Register* went out of business, he had looked in vain for a way to resume his former life as a plantation owner. Viewed in the light of many years and from the perspective of Petersburg, the life of a planter no longer seemed so dreary and unattractive. The years had also dimmed his bitterness toward his old neighborhood, so he tried to buy a plantation in Prince George County and return to the scene of his earliest agricultural labors.

Ironically, Ruffin's success as an agrarian reformer made this purchase impossible. So many of his Prince George neighbors had become converts to marl that few were willing to sell their now valuable estates, and those whose land was on the market attached extravagant price tags. In 1835, before moving to Petersburg, Ruffin had sold his plantation Shellbanks for ten dollars an acre. Five years later, the new owner refused to part with the same property for less than sixteen dollars an acre. Technically, Ruffin still owned half of the Beechwood plantation in Prince George. But his son Edmund and his family occupied the mansion, and Ruffin had no desire to share their quarters or to ask them to leave.[14]

When his publishing business folded in 1842, Ruffin was still without a plantation. He ached to leave Petersburg, and the appointment in South Carolina must have seemed like a perfectly timed godsend. Before he left for Charleston, though, Ruffin instructed Edmund to find him another suitable Tidewater estate, outside Prince George County if necessary. That autumn, just before Ruffin returned to Petersburg, Edmund wrote that his search had been successful. His father was the new owner of an approximately one-thousand-acre Pamunkey River plantation, located about sixteen miles from Richmond, in the old aristocratic neighborhood of Hanover County.

When Ruffin's former Prince George neighbors learned of his decision to move permanently to another county, they insisted on giving a testimonial dinner in his honor. The guests and guest of honor gathered for the occasion at Garysville on December 28, 1843. After presenting Ruffin with a gift of silver plate, his neighbors—friends as well as some he considered enemies—drank a toast to "Edmund Ruffin, the Pioneer of Marling, the Author of the *Essay on Calcareous Manures* and Editor of the *Farmers' Register*—Imperishable Works of genius and industry—We deeply regret his intention to leave us; he carries with him our highest respect for his character and gratitude for his services." In his after-dinner speech, Ruffin modestly and graciously accepted their thanks. Then protesting that he spoke without any exaggeration, he cast modesty aside and gave himself the credit he felt he deserved for what he called his great "social, moral & political, as well as agricultural" contributions to his native state.[15]

After the Garysville dinner, Ruffin combed the newspapers for mention of the event. His friends in South Carolina, he noted happily, had covered the occasion fully in the Charleston *Mercury.* But South Carolina's attention provided a bitter contrast when he learned that the Petersburg *Republican,* a new paper with a limited circulation, was the only newspaper in Virginia to report the dinner. The planters and farmers of Prince George had specifically invited the Richmond *Whig* and the Richmond *Enquirer,* Virginia's two principal newspapers, to publicize the proceedings, but neither had paid their request the slightest attention. And to Ruffin being ignored was the greatest insult. More than anything else, he needed notice —to know that he counted. "If any such complimentary dinner had been given to any political personage, though noted only for the unscrupulous promoting of his own private interest, his altogether selfish ambition—or to any worthless vagabond of military life—some foreign traveller of no account at home—or even if a presentation of plate had been made to a very ordinary stage player," whined Ruffin, "any of these proceedings would have been published in every paper in Virginia, none of which noticed the only such honors ever offered to me."[16]

Though "deeply mortified," Ruffin pretended not to be the least surprised at what he referred to as Virginia's "general neglect" of his great services. This recent episode of ill-treatment, he said, was "in accordance with the general slighting & ungrateful conduct which I have long experienced from the public in my native state." Hoping to find solace at his new plantation, which he appropriately named Marlbourne, Ruffin again resolved "to withdraw into the most perfect seclusion." "Further service to the public," he vowed, "I determined carefully to avoid."[17]

3

Marlbourne was the perfect hiding place. Situated on the banks of the Pamunkey River in the northwestern section of the Tidewater, the plantation was "distant" from the unfriendly environs of Prince George County and, according to Ruffin, a place "almost unknown" to others.

On New Year's day, 1844, Ruffin began the "wretched business" of moving his family and property from Petersburg northward to their new "seating" in Hanover County. All the goods had to be transported overland in carriages, but heavy rains and snowstorms had rutted roads and made travel slow and difficult. Even with three teams of horses, the move took nearly half of January to complete.

When Ruffin and his family, along with thirty slaves taken from Beechwood, finally reached Marlbourne on January 18, they were exhausted. Half of the teams were broken down, and even the mules needed two weeks' rest before they could begin work again. But once the wearisome journey was over and everyone was more comfortably settled, Ruffin took a good look at his new property and wrote his assessment in his plantation journal.[18]

He reported that the buildings on his estate included one "large and valuable" mansion with nearby kitchen, laundry, meathouse, icehouse, barn, overseer's house, and slave quarters. Aside from needing a few minor repairs, all of these structures were in very good condition.

The mansion was particularly impressive. A two-story rectangular building, painted completely white, the main house was probably built during the late Federal period and was of a common style that architects called Adamsesque. In the front and rear, tall and stately white-pillared porticos supported equally stiking white-columned covered balconies.

Inside, a wide wooden staircase, which led to the upstairs sleeping quarters, cut the downstairs into two parts. To the right of the stairs was a large dining room with high wooden ceilings and to the left a spacious family room. Adjacent to these main living areas, additional chambers for sitting, guests, and a library for the master "rambled off" in either direction.

Outdoors, mammoth oak and pine trees shaded the manicured lawns which carpeted the ground both in front and in back of the house, and gardens of brightly-colored flowers added variety to a naturally magnificent view. The Marlbourne mansion, Ruffin noted in his journal, sat on the brow of a hill overlooking the extreme bottomlands of the Pamunkey and "offers even now a prospect of rare beauty." He predicted that "when the land is improved by marl and made to bear rich crops of grain and grass," the breathtaking combination of landscape and riverscape "will be inferior to no view which does not embrace either water or mountains."[19]

There was no doubt, though, that the land was going to need a lot of improvement before the Ruffins could fully enjoy Marlbourne's beautiful view. The estate stretched over nearly a thousand acres, but most of the soil was poor, sandy, and worn-out from years of unscientific cultivation. "The last proprietor," complained Ruffin, "was a wretched farmer & manager of his business."

Before Edmund purchased Marlbourne for his father, the land's estimated value had been no more than ten to fifteen dollars an acre. The owner would have considered himself lucky to receive the latter figure as an offer. But Edmund, knowing how his father loathed Petersburg and realizing that he would soon be returning from South Carolina, was desperate to buy a plantation. So in October, 1843, exceeding his father's money limit of sixteen dollars an acre, he bid almost seventeen thousand dollars for the run-down, neglected Pamunkey River estate. Delighted with the unexpected windfall, the owner quickly closed the deal. Neighboring planters shook their heads in amazement. No one doubted that Ruffin had been bested in the bargain.[20]

But Ruffin never showed even a trace of disappointment in his son's judgment. Instead, he regarded Marlbourne, with all of its problems, as a challenge and as an exciting testing ground for his agricultural theories. He became so busy with this new agrarian adventure that he had no time to remember that his recent fever in South Carolina had "permanently impaired" his health. In fact, he admitted sheepishly, restoring Marlbourne's soil fertility engrossed him in such "new & interesting labors" that he "neglected & soon forgot" his illness, even before all the symptoms had disappeared. His emotional well-being was always a reliable indicator of his physical health, and vice versa. When he was depressed, feeling useless, he became ill; when he was happy and busy, his health improved dramatically. Now, working tirelessly on his plantation "under every exposure," Ruffin soon recovered his health.[21]

There was only one potential difficulty at Marlbourne. Despite its name, the plantation was almost destitute of marl. But the adjoining estate, New Castle, had an inexhaustible supply of calcareous manures. New Castle's trustee and proprietor, William Carter Braxton, hoped to benefit from Ruffin's agricultural advice and was thus only too glad to offer his new neighbor the unlimited use of his marl.

Ruffin was eager to get started, and on January 20—only two days after he moved to Marlbourne—he directed "all hands, except five ditchers and one carter" to begin uncovering beds of marl on Braxton's land. In less than two weeks, his slaves had completed a road connecting the two plantations and commenced hauling cartloads of calcareous manures back to Marlbourne.[22]

Wanting to make the most out of his marling opportunities that first winter, Ruffin sent every spare fieldhand and team of horses and mules to New Castle daily to bring back their precious cargo. The rest of the slave force stayed behind at Marlbourne, where they spread approximately two hundred bushels of marl a day per three acres of manure-starved soil.

That winter, Ruffin was so preoccupied with the "engrossing" marling operations that he completely forgot to fill his icehouse before the spring thaw. When an unexpected freeze came late in February, several concerned neighbors each thoughtfully sent a cart and Negro driver to Malbourne to help the Ruffins replenish their ice supply. But the temptation of extra carts and hands was too much for the master of the house, and he sent every one to the marl pits. That evening, his icehouse still empty, a satisfied Ruffin gratefully returned the carts to their bemused owners.[23]

4

But marling was only one part of the daily regimen of scientific farming that Ruffin practiced at Marlbourne. A typical day might find him out in the fields, shortly after breakfast, experimenting with new manures and possible improved fertilizers like Peruvian guano or "greensands," a combination of potash, phosphoric acid, and plain marl.

He always had a few words for his fieldhands, especially his particular favorite, Jem Sykes. Ruffin wanted to know how Jem and the other hands were adjusting to the newfangled farm machines, like the McCormick plow and reaper and the Haw thresher, which he had recently purchased for Marlbourne. After a few minutes of conversation, Ruffin was likely to seek out his white overseer to discuss the advanced and careful system of crop rotation and try to learn if the man was mistreating his slaves.

Since slaves performed all of the manual labor at Marlbourne, Ruffin was understandably concerned about the welfare of his human chattels. Besides handling sophisticated modern farm equipment, the slaves carried out a variety of agricultural and domestic tasks. Fieldhands, both male and female, applied and spread marl and other fertilizers to ready the soil for crop cultivation; planted the corn and oats; bound the wheat; cared for the horses, mules, and oxen; and butchered the hogs. Children too young for heavier work cleaned up the yards, herded livestock, and fetched water for their elders in the fields. Four female houseservants cooked, cleaned, and generally catered to the needs of the master's family in the main house, while outside, a dairy woman collected eggs, milked cows, and churned butter; a gardener devoted himself to Marlbourne's lush landscape; and a carriage driver tended to the stables.[24]

Regarding himself as a humane and paternalistic master, Ruffin always saw to his slaves' material and spiritual needs. He provided them with neat, clean living quarters behind his mansion, professional medical care that could amount to forty dollars a year per slave, and a diet as healthy and varied as the crops and livestock Marlbourne produced. Nor did he ever deny his blacks their religion, because he believed that Christianity, for all of its faults, civilized "heathen" Africans and made them better slaves. So, whenever a white minister happened by the plantation on a Sunday afternoon, Ruffin invited all his slaves to offer their children for baptism and listen to the sermon—usually some carefully selected biblical lesson that preached slave obedience.[25]

Ruffin also tried to respect his slaves' family ties, but sometimes business needs made separation of husbands and wives, brothers and sisters, or parents and children a necessity. During the move to Marlbourne, in Janu-

ary, 1844, Ruffin had split the slave force at Beechwood with his son
Edmund, thus separating many close blood relatives. Ruffin never relished
this aspect of slave ownership but rationalized that family ties between
blacks were much looser than those between "refined" upper-class whites.
Besides, he insisted that he and his wife and children were actually much
more grief-stricken by these occasional breakups than were the separated
slaves.

Ruffin refused to acknowledge the cruelty of the South's peculiar institution of slavery and strove personally to be an enlightened paternalist.
Virginians in general thought theirs the most progressive slave state, where
the system was not nearly as harsh as in the Deep South. While an occasional incident of sadism or unwarranted brutality might occur, Ruffin and
the other slaveholders of the Old Dominion saw an overall pattern of
harmony and benevolence in master–slave relations.

Though he listed his slaves in his farm journal among his mules, horses,
and other livestock, Ruffin often showed consideration and genuine affection for his "people," as he liked to call them. He even buried one beloved
black mammy, Lucy Lockett, next to his own children in the family cemetery at Petersburg and inscribed on her tombstone, "In remembrance of
Lucy Lockett, a slave, yet not less the friend of her master's family."[26]

Ruffin seemed to have less trouble with unruly or disobedient slaves
than with harsh white overseers. Although every overseer's contract contained a clause forbidding the inhumane treatment of slaves, Ruffin repeatedly hired and then had to fire overseers whose cruelty toward blacks
cancelled out whatever ability they might have possessed as plantation
managers.

Ruffin never denied that a disobedient or impudent slave might benefit from a few "stripes." He relied on the whip—or the threat of it—to control unruly slaves and to instill discipline. But he preferred to rule
lightly whenever possible, believing that slave discipline tempered by kindness and simple justice served both humanity and business. He reasoned
that a slave who was well fed and well cared for would perform his duties
willingly and carefully and thus to his owner's greatest financial profit.
Marlbourne's farm journal, sprinkled with Ruffin's praises for his slaves'
hard work and efficiency, indicates that Ruffin thought his benevolent
policies a success.

Finally, after several unhappy years of searching for the proper overseer, Ruffin decided not to employ any more whites and turned over most
of the duties of plantation management and slave discipline to Jem Sykes,
whom he made foreman of Marlbourne. Ruffin considered Sykes "my most
trustworthy negro" and proved this by letting Sykes live in the overseer's
house and by handing over to him the keys to every other building on the

plantation. "If this trust be abused and my people make use of their opportunities for an unusual amount of pilfering," remarked Ruffin, "I shall continue to prefer, as now, having no overseer." So confident was he of his black foreman's loyalty and capability that whenever Ruffin left Marlbourne, even for absences of up to two months, he put Sykes in complete charge of plantation operations. During these absences, there was no adult white male at Marlbourne except when one of Ruffin's grown sons, Edmund or Julian, came for brief and infrequent visits. The protection of Ruffin's property and the lives of family members depended entirely on the faithful services of a slave.[27]

Most times, though, Ruffin was at home and actively involved in Marlbourne's agricultural management. After he had finished his field work, he usually went to check on the construction of the new covered drains and ditches that he had personally designed for use there. Ruffin's drainage system, which eventually covered 800 acres of Pamunkey lowlands, represented another of his pioneer agricultural efforts and not only added to Marlbourne's soil fertility but also protected its residents from the autumnal ravages of malaria so common and so costly to other Pamunkey River plantations.[28]

In the evening after dinner, Ruffin might retire to his library to work on his fossil shell collection, write up the results of the day's soil experiments, or do some quiet reading. More than likely, he would join his wife and children in the living room later on for some spirited conversation or a special reading from Bowdler's family edition of Shakespeare. He especially enjoyed those evenings devoted to music. With daughter Elizabeth at the piano, daughter Mildred at the melodeon, and their father playing the harmonicon, the whole family formed a chorus to sing the plain and simple tunes that Ruffin favored.[29]

Frequently, Marlbourne housed one or more guests—friends and relatives who loved to participate in that universal Southern pastime, coming to visit. These visits could last a few days to several months; Mrs. Lorraine, the widow of a distant cousin, seems even to have turned a visit to Marlbourne into a permanent residency.

While Ruffin welcomed company, he did not go out of his way to entertain. He preferred his quiet family circle. When he was editor of the *Farmers' Register,* he charged that one of the main causes of the Tidewater's degraded agricultural condition was the pride of the Old Dominion—Virginia's reputation for lavish hospitality. Not only was a host obliged to waste his food, liquor, and precious work time entertaining friends and relatives, Ruffin chided his readers, but he must perform the same rites for "every individual of the despicable race of loungers and spongers which our custom of universal hospitality had created—*gentlemen* ... who spend their lives in feasting at the expense of other people, and who are content to live despised, provided they can live without labor."

Only in Virginia could such "spongers" thrive, Ruffin maintained. Such "gentlemen" could never exist in the frugal East or enterprising West, where they would surely either work for their food and clothing or starve. "Would to heaven they could meet the same fate here," was Ruffin's fervent prayer. "One hundred of such honorable and gentlemenly vagrants are more fatal to the district they prey upon, than would be periodic visits of Asiatic locusts, accompanied by the Asiatic cholera." At Marlbourne, at least, visitors were always treated with what Ruffin called "*true* hospitality" —plain food, lodgings, and an opportunity to join their host in his work. Certainly no time was ever taken away from business because of an excess of hospitality.[30]

5

Despite all of Ruffin's precautions, the business of planting did not seem very promising at first. The low-quality Pamunkey lands could grow a little corn and some oats, Ruffin's Hanover County neighbors asserted, but not wheat. Certainly they could never hope to equal the productivity of James River soils. But Ruffin paid their warnings no heed. He had heard this kind of gloomy agrarian pessimism before—from the same James River planters whose prosperity his new neighbors now envied. Proper drainage and marling, boasted Ruffin in reply, would make Marlbourne the rival of any James River plantation.[31]

Within four years, his boast had become reality. After predictable first-year losses, business flourished. Wheat and corn yields at Marlbourne more than doubled, and the profits for one year on wheat alone amounted to nearly six thousand dollars. And Ruffin, unlike so many of his neighbors, did not depend solely on one cash crop. Wheat, corn, oats, melons, eggs, sheep, cattle, and hogs all added variety to the marketplace as well as to the family dinner table. And with each succeeding year, the soil fertility, crop production, and resulting profits climbed steadily.[32]

Incredulous and admiring, planters and farmers from Hanover County and beyond flocked to gape at the agrarian miracle Ruffin had wrought at Marlbourne. Once again, as he had done as a young man at Coggin's Point, Ruffin had used the principles of modern scientific research to turn an agricultural ruin into a planter's paradise.

But the admiration of his fellow planters did little to convince the still brooding Ruffin that he had not been ill-treated by the citizens of his native state. He was not yet finished punishing them. Virginians had scorned him, and now he was giving the public a taste of its own medicine. So, in May,

1845, when a group of planters and farmers met in Richmond, only sixteen miles from his home, to form a State Agricultural Society, Ruffin refused to join them. In 1841, he had served as Corresponding Secretary for the then newly created State Board of Agriculture, but he had resigned after one year because of what he judged the "niggardly support & contemptuous treatment" of the Virginia legislature. He had no intention of coming out of seclusion now. Anyway, he predicted a bit maliciously, the present Society would meet to accomplish "nothing but wrong procedure" and its own "speedy extinction."[33]

Nevertheless, a surprised Ruffin later learned through the newspapers that the group that had gathered in Richmond had forgiven his absence and elected him their first president. Protesting that any honors offered now came "too late," Ruffin immediately penned a curt refusal to the Society's Executive Committee.

Although he later admitted that "the act was ungracious," Ruffin felt that in order to be consistent, he had to decline the office. "This was in accordance with my previous determination to have no further or renewed connexion with the public," he wrote his friend Hammond. "My business as well as my pleasure keep me at home," he insisted, "& I rarely leave it for more than a day, & only to visit my children."[34]

5

The Mad Dog Cry of Disunion

1

SHORTLY AFTER RUFFIN refused the presidency of the new Virginia Agricultural Society, Hammond wrote urging him to withdraw his resignation. Even his children begged him to reconsider. "That your efforts for the improvement of our race are not duly appreciated . . . by the public I have always felt," sympathized his eldest son Edmund. "But pray let not that deter you from doing that which would benefit our country & rebound to your own fame." He admitted that Virginia's ingratitude was deplorable. But "when was it ever otherwise?" he asked his father. "The greatest benefactors of the human family rarely live to see themselves acknowledged as such. The greatest worth, like the purest ore, is not always found on the surface, and of course not so immediately valued by the public at large."[1]

But that spring, personal misfortunes only confirmed Ruffin's decision to avoid all dealings with the public. His wife, Susan, became gravely ill. A slight wrist pain, diagnosed as neuralgic rheumatism, spread slowly throughout the rest of her body. Having lost the use of her limbs and, according to Ruffin, "every bodily power," Susan remained a pitiful and helpless invalid for almost a year. In February, 1846, her suffering ended, and she was buried in the family graveyard at Marlbourne.

Grief-stricken over the loss of his wife, Ruffin became even more of a recluse. Only his plantation work and the affectionate attentions of his nine children, he later recalled, kept him from "sinking into a positive state of wretchedness." The awful nature of his wife's illness recalled his worst phobias: a body painfully ravaged, out of control. Ruffin's thoughts turned increasingly morbid, and he frightened his children with his constant talk of sickness and his gloomy predictions that his own death was fast approaching.[2]

Perhaps Ruffin remembered the late Thomas Cocke—old, widowed, lonely, unappreciated, and plagued by physical and mental infirmities. Ruffin was only fifty-two when his wife died, but he was convinced that his early childhood illnesses had aged his mind and body an extra twelve to fifteen years. He complained of frequent sore throats, bronchitis, chronic dyspepsia, and a host of minor ailments. Frequent bouts of constipation—a physical manifestation perhaps of his emotional struggle to bottle up his true feelings—made him miserable and cranky. Then, too, he noticed that ever since he returned from his agricultural survey of South Carolina, his blood would suddenly and unexpectedly rush to his head. Surely, he reasoned, this symptom meant that like his friend Cocke, he would someday suffer from and possibly succumb to apoplexy. But even more disturbing, Ruffin imagined he detected early signs of senility, and loss of control over his intellect shamed and terrified him the most. "My power of memory has long been lessening," he worried, "& now scarcely at all retains the minute details of *recent* occurrences. . . . May God protect me, even if early death be the means, from my living through an old age of body & imbecility of mind."[3]

Alarmed by his melancholia, and maybe even suspecting his death wish, Ruffin's children tried to comfort and reassure him. "In all Candor & sincerity," Edmund told him, "you are the only one that has discovered any decay of your mental powers." "It gives me very much pain, my dear father, to hear you speak so often now of the decay of your mental powers, of dotage, etc.," added Julian. "I do wish you would cheer up & not allow your mind to touch upon such an idea. . . . I can honestly say that I've seen no grounds for such fears."[4]

Hammond, too, worried about Ruffin's despondency, his bitterness, and his total seclusion from the public. Even before Susan's death, Hammond had tried to rekindle his friend's interest in agricultural and political affairs. He wrote long, flattering letters cataloging his own efforts to promote marl and passing on the compliments of others who had tried marl successfully. If Virginia did not appreciate such a great public benefactor, said Hammond, why not come to South Carolina and establish another agricultural journal on friendlier soil? At the very least, he pleaded, Ruffin should continue his agricultural writings.[5]

2

Hammond's motives, while sincere, were not entirely apolitical. As governor of South Carolina, in 1844, he had attempted to lead his state out of the Union. This so-called Bluffton Movement failed, but Hammond remained a committed secessionist. Convinced, though, that cooperation rather than separate state action was the key to Southern independence, he knew that the South needed men like Ruffin to prepare it economically for disunion. So, in his efforts to return his friend to a productive public life, Hammond tried to redirect Ruffin's hostility away from Virginia and his fellow Southerners and toward the real enemy—the North.

The North, Hammond argued, with its fanatic abolitionists, so-called free laborers, hordes of ignorant immigrants, and all its "radical" movements like that for universal manhood suffrage, was the true enemy which undermined conservative Southern society. Slavery was the linchpin of that society, and Northern politicians and abolitionists seemed to be constantly trying to undermine that security. Hammond feared that time and numbers were both on the side of the "swinish multitude" of European immigrants who flooded the free states and the corrupt Northern "demagogues" who manipulated their votes. The dictatorship of the "rabble" could not be held back indefinitely, he believed. But an independent South, supported by Negro slavery and free from Northern influence would be the best kind of republican nation, a society where all white men would hold power in proportion to their unequal endowments, a society which would appreciate a Cincinnatus, an Edmund Ruffin.[6]

Ruffin was not an instant convert to Southern nationalism. But as he considered the words of his friend Hammond and others like him, Ruffin found the idea of disunion more and more alluring. That independence would mean the collapse of the present national party system did not disturb him. Always a political maverick, he had never developed strong ties to any party.

Ruffin came of political age during a period of one-party politics dubbed the Era of Good Feelings. Like most Americans, he voted for the National Republican ticket, although he was likely, as in the election of 1824, to support a rather obscure candidate like Nathaniel Macon, rather than the popular party choice. And after the Democrats won the White House in 1828, he voted Whig mainly because he wished to oust Presidents Andrew Jackson and Martin Van Buren, men he detested politically. It was for this reason only that in 1840, he voted for William Henry Harrison, even though he was unimpressed by Harrison's ability and his principles.

When Harrison died shortly after his inauguration, Ruffin wasted no time in letting others know his true feelings. I "publickly expressed my gratification at hearing the news, & pronounced that 'his dying then was the only important service he had ever rendered to his country in all his long career of public life,' " he remembered. The new President, John Tyler of

Virginia, was also a Whig, and until he disavowed any allegiance to Henry Clay's nationalist principles, Ruffin viewed him "with some dislike & more suspicion."[7]

Despite his reservations about Tyler, Ruffin undertook the task of giving the new President some unsolicited advice. First through the columns of the *Farmers' Register* and then through private correspondence, he lectured his fellow Virginian on how to proceed according to true republican principles. "You stated to me your intended firm & noble stand in maintenance of states-rights principles, 'even if you should be left alone,' " wrote Ruffin in June, 1841. "This is precisely what is demanded by patriotism, & devotion to your principles."[8]

In 1841, to help guide Tyler and other politicians along the true path to republicanism and states' rights, Ruffin began publishing a new periodical called *The Southern Magazine.* Lamenting the loss of principles in both national parties, *The Southern Magazine* promised to expose political abuses and corruption wherever it found them. The magazine would oppose both parties and adhere to none, thereby living up to its nonpartisan motto, "Party Spirit, The Madness Of The Many, For The Gain Of The Few."[9]

Ruffin dedicated his first issue "to many of the intelligent and reflecting men" who believed in free trade and states' rights, "in which the interests of the southern states . . . are so deeply involved." But *The Southern Magazine* quickly disavowed any anti-Northern sentiments. Ruffin insisted that "from these expressions of especial care for the south, it should not be inferred that we are actuated by sentiments inimical to the north. We disclaim all such feelings." "On the contrary," he admitted, "we readily testify to, and heartily applaud, the many admirable points of character and conduct, and the excellent works, of our intelligent, industrious and indefatigable fellow-citizens of the northern states." Humbly, he confessed the South's "comparative inferiority . . . for the improvement of our own southern country, for building up our own literature and science, and for sustaining our own doctrines, principles and institutions." "How immediately superior would have been the present condition of the states, from Maryland to Georgia inclusive," he reproached his fellow Southerners, "if their sons made efforts for their improvement equal to those which have been bestowed on Massachusetts."[10]

After sending out a prospectus and a second issue at his own expense, Ruffin failed to attract the necessary 200 subscribers, so he abandoned the magazine. Perhaps in his very efforts to remain nonpartisan, Ruffin had offended prospective Southern readers who preferred not to hear of Northern superiority or of Southern "comparative inferiority" on any point.

3

Although he wrote with apparent authority when he compared the North and the South, Ruffin had almost no firsthand information about the free states. He rarely traveled outside Virginia and probably left the slave states only once, from August to September, 1828, when he enrolled his son Edmund in a newly established gymnasium in New Haven, Connecticut. Edmund was only fourteen years old, and Ruffin wanted to send him to a good preparatory school. Since few such institutions existed in the South, a New England education was a common choice of many prominent Southern families.

Ruffin's first impressions of the North, though unrecorded, probably were not very pleasant. Damp Northern weather aggravated his poor health, and he felt sick the entire trip. To make matters worse, after he spent an evening at the theater in New York City, a hack accidentally drove off with all his luggage.[11]

Whatever Ruffin's initial reactions to the North, he was soon displeased when his son adjusted too favorably to his new surroundings. At first he probably chuckled when, after only three months in Connecticut, Edmund reported a number of fistfights which came about when Northern students teased Southern classmates about their strange accents. Edmund requested his mother to warn him "the first time you see any Yankeeisms in my letters." But Ruffin was not amused when, after a little more than a semester, Edmund wrote again to say, "I think the people in this part of our country are enlightened and polished. . . . They are all industrious and hardworking, a sober and religious people. I like their manners very well indeed." "I do not mean," he hastened to add, "that I like every custom." But "in general I think they are much better than those of Virginia. When you go out in the county . . . all the lands are well cultivated, and you see all around you everything pleasant and gay. I wished that Virginia was as well cultivated and the manners of its inhabitants as polished as those of . . . Connecticut. You do not see here such very rich men or such poor ones, but all seem to have enough to support them. Here the carpenter if he is honest is as much respected as the merchants."

But sensing he might have gone too far, Edmund begged his father not to let this praise of Northerners upset him. Even though Virginians had less polish and enlightenment than Northerners, Edmund assured Ruffin, he preferred his native state. And he had to admit, "The Yankees sometimes cheat if they can." If he had hoped that these last words would avert his father's anger, Edmund was mistaken. No matter how personally critical Ruffin was of his fellow Virginians, he would consistently defend them as well as all Southerners against "outsiders." Any implications of Virginia's inferiority reflected on his own honor. So, when the school year ended, Ruffin immediately removed his son from New England's radical leveling forces and enrolled him at the University of Virginia. Never again would any of his sons or daughters leave the Old Dominion for their schooling.[12]

4

Still, Ruffin's attitude toward the North had not yet hardened. Then in 1841, *The Southern Magazine* folded. A year later, partly because of competition from cheaper Northern agricultural journals, the *Farmers' Register* also failed. And his survey of South Carolina in 1843 brought Ruffin into contact with James Hammond and other anti-Northern firebrands. As a result, he became increasingly suspicious of all Northerners. In 1845, after sending a simple soil specimen to a Northern chemist for analysis, Ruffin agonized over the decision. *"Entre nous,"* he confided to Hammond, "I greatly doubt the professor. He is an able chemist, but a true trading Yankee withal. I do not suspect him of reporting his actual analysis falsely . . . but I *do* suspect him of being very willing to select & test unfair specimens."[13]

Encouraged by his friend's growing distrust of Northerners, Hammond directed Ruffin's hostility towards the most heinous Yankees of all —the abolitionists. Hammond argued that despite the relatively small number of avowed abolitionists, an accursed antislavery spirit tainted every Northern man, woman, and child. Led by fanatics like William Lloyd Garrison of Massachusetts, abolitionists conspired to shame Southerners and rob them of their wealth, their political rights, their honor. Hammond completely disregarded the fact that the Garrisonians were Christian pacifists, who, despite their emotionally charged criticisms of slavery, had repeatedly emphasized their nonviolent tactics of peaceful moral suasion. Above all, Hammond insisted, the abolitionists were out to incite slave rebellions and engulf the South in a racial holocaust like that in Santo Domingo, where, in the 1790s, the Negro slaves had risen up in bloody insurrection, driven the whites from the island, and established the independent black republic of Haiti.

Ruffin listened attentively. His own attitudes about slavery had undergone several changes during his life. Once he became a slaveowner, his youthful flirtation with theoretical abolitionism had turned quickly to a practical proslavery stance. Like most planters during the Jeffersonian period and throughout the 1820s, he believed that slavery was a "necessary evil" forced on unwilling Southerners by greedy British, Dutch, and Yankee slave traders in colonial times, an evil which Southerners now were stuck with and could do nothing to eradicate. Still, slavery was an embarrassment, a blatant and ugly contradiction of enlightenment ideals, an insult to republican institutions, and Ruffin later admitted that "it would have been difficult to find, in Virginia, a man of education who did not deem slavery both a public and private evil."[14]

Most Southerners clung to the "necessary evil" defense of slavery until after the Nat Turner rebellion in 1831. The Southampton County uprising, so reminiscent of the horrors of Santo Domingo, had again smashed the widespread myth that slaves were childlike, docile happyjacks, who felt only affection for their masters and were content with their lives in bondage. It also seemed to be the dread fulfillment of Northern abolitionist aims. To save themselves and their posterity from future black insurrections, frightened Virginians then hotly debated the question of whether or not to abolish slavery and colonize the freed blacks somewhere outside the United States. In the end, the delegates in the State House rejected colonization as too expensive. And emancipation without colonization was an unthinkable challenge, they believed, to continued white supremacy. So, instead, Virginia and other Southern state legislatures enacted new, more stringent slave codes, restricted the rights of free blacks, beefed up the old slave patrols and militia systems, and tried to protect Southern whites in every possible way against another attack from the sable enemy within.[15]

Ironically, at the same time that frightened Southerners moved to fasten the chains of bondage more securely around their blacks and the slave system itself became harsher and more oppressive than ever, they abandoned their former apologetic stance toward slavery and adopted a strident, militant vindication of their peculiar institution as an outright good. A legion of proslavery writers and orators sprang up to buttress this "positive good" theory and to glorify slavery as a "blessing" and a great "national benefit" to both blacks and whites. Slavery was not a curse, not a necessary evil, cried John C. Calhoun. It was "a good—a positive good" and "the most safe and stable basis for free institutions in the world." Dismissing the equal rights philosophy contained in the Declaration of Independence as so much "sentimental rubbish," Calhoun dug into history for examples of similar "superior" civilizations based on slave labor and pointed to the glory that was ancient Greece, the grandeur that was Rome. Others searched the Bible and the Scriptures for evidence that God had created the Negro expressly for bondage and had sanctioned and ordained the institution of slavery since man's earliest beginnings.

Over the years, Southerners augmented, polished, and refined these arguments, but whatever the justification used, they maintained the unequivocal righteousness and benevolence of Negro slavery. The greater their feelings of guilt and insecurity, the louder they protested that theirs was the best of all possible systems. To betray even the tiniest doubt, to admit even a single flaw, they feared, would endanger their society and topple their whole way of life. So in the 1830s the positive good theory became Southern orthodoxy, and slavery's defense was "the *sine qua non* of southern patriotism."[16]

5

Given Southern racial phobias, particularly in the wake of the Turner insurrection, it was small wonder that Virginians failed to uproot slavery by themselves and instead embraced a positive view of their domestic institution. But Ruffin felt that the people of the Old Dominion had taken sides and made up their minds too quickly about a serious issue, and in 1833, as editor of the *Farmers' Register,* he reminded his readers that "the question of slavery in Virginia requires . . . the exercise of cautious and sound judgment, a deliberate and clear view of the whole ground of the argument, and a disposition to arrive at the truth, wherever it may be found, and not to support particular tenets in a partizan spirit." Hesitant to launch the *Register's* "frail bark" on a "stormy ocean of controversy," Ruffin nevertheless offered his readers extracts from two opposing articles—Thomas R. Dew's proslavery "Review of the Debates of the Virginia Legislature of 1831 and 1832" and a Mr. Harrison's antislavery, "Review of the Slave Question"— so they could decide the slavery issue for themselves in a "spirit of toleration and compromise." "If we can ever settle beneficially this distracting question," he said, "it will be only by giving due consideration to the opinions of our antagonists, as well as to those on our own side."[17]

But Virginians, and Southerners in general, were in no mood for fairness or impartiality when their peculiar institution was involved. Were northern abolitionists fair or impartial? Had they demonstrated a "spirit of toleration and compromise?" demanded Southerners. Hadn't Nat Turner's revolt occurred less than eight months after that devil Garrison began publishing his fiendish abolitionist paper, *The Liberator?* Wasn't this proof enough of diabolical abolitionist intent? Thus having linked the Northern antislavery movement in their own minds with servile insurrection, Southerners feared for the very existence of their slave-based society. So, during the period, known as the Great Southern Reaction, following the Virginia debates, they militantly closed ranks around the institution of slavery and sought to insulate themselves and their blacks from all contact with abolitionists and their incendiary literature. Extremely sensitive to the dangers of abolitionism in their own midst, Southerners subdued, silenced, or drove out all those who dared to question the slave system.

Thus, despite its first-edition plea for tolerance and moderation on that controversial topic, the *Farmers' Register* quickly and wisely conformed to the limits the Great Reaction imposed. Never again, as an editor, did Ruffin make the mistake of asking his readers to consider with open minds the relative merits and demerits of manumission. Instead, he bolstered the prevailing "positive good" orthodoxy with eyewitness accounts about the failure of African colonization in Liberia, woeful tales of former slaves who were forcibly emancipated by the British during the War of 1812 and now wished to be reenslaved and returned to "their former well-fed life of slavery," and parliamentary reports of the misery and suffering of British working-class "wage slaves." Banished from the *Register's* pages were any more impartial extracts from proslavery and antislavery publications. Ruffin printed only favorable reviews of proslavery works like J. R. Pauldings's *Slavery in the United States,* which boasted of the many benefits of slavery and its particular mildness in the Old Dominion.[18]

6

As the years passed, Ruffin's own initial broad-minded feelings about slavery receded and then vanished. He resented Northern antislavery criticism. "The detestation of slavery in the abstract," he conceded, "is a feeling almost inseparable from man's best feelings." But whatever else slavery might be, it was eminently and exclusively the South's private affair.

Yet Northern abolitionists, it seemed to Ruffin, would not mind their own business. In the spring and summer of 1835, the American Anti-Slavery Society initiated a "pamphlet campaign" aimed at flooding the country with abolitionist literature. Propaganda in the form of newspapers, booklets, scarves, kerchiefs, medals, and even candy wrappers reached the South in late July. This coincided almost exactly with a recent slave insurrection scare in Mississippi, and again frightened Southerners thought they had tangible evidence connecting Yankee abolitionism with Southern servile unrest. In almost every major city and town throughout Dixie, including Petersburg, where Ruffin was living at the time, angry citizens marched in torchlight parades and held raucous antiabolitionist rallies to protest this latest antislavery onslaught. Several states even put a price on the heads of prominent abolitionists like Garrison and Arthur Tappan. And many Southerners who had managed to stay calm about slavery after the Turner uprising in 1831 now reacted strongly. So it was, in this troubled and agitated atmosphere, that Ruffin picked up his pen and for the first time lashed out at Northern abolitionists.

Addressing himself "to the great majority of the citizens of the northern states—who declare themselves friends to the south, and utterly opposed to the schemes of the abolitionists," Ruffin warned that on the subject of slavery, the South would "act as one man." "There are no party divisions to distract our views, and to prevent a united effort to maintain our interests and rights," he advised them. Southerners like Ruffin would not permit Northerners to belittle their honor or control their domestic institutions. "Whatever may be the evils of our system of slavery, and," he admitted, "we deny not that they are many for the slaves, and still more for their master, the matter is *our own concern*—and we will not consent to its regulation being touched by the people of the north."

But the North would not leave the South alone to deal with its peculiar institution, Ruffin complained. A cowardly sect of Northern abolitionists "composed of bigoted and reckless zealots" were "striving to put fire to a train of gunpowder, because they are in perfect safety from the awful and destructive explosion that may follow."

Incendiary abolitionist agitation had already taken its toll in the South with several aborted slave conspiracies like the one just discovered in Mississippi and the "partial massacre" of whites during the Turner insurrection. But, Ruffin observed, the effects of such "philanthropic" efforts were always ten times worse for blacks than whites, as anxious slaveowners acted swiftly to impose new shackles and limitations on their unfortunate bondsmen. "The efforts of the mad Abolitionists of the north," predicted Ruffin, "will only serve to destroy whatever amount of happiness and contentment is now enjoyed by our slaves." Northern troublemakers only made the slaves' plight worse than before. "If anyone desired the greatest possible amount of misery to be inflicted on the slaves of the south," he insisted, "he ought to wish for the increase of the numbers, strength, and power of the abolitionists."

How would most Northerners feel, wondered Ruffin, if the tables were turned? Suppose a few thousand southern free trade fanatics tried to ruin Northerners who favored protection. Suppose they provided materials and employed agents to burn Northern factories and poison industrialists and then tried to seduce the working classes into plundering their employers' property. Suppose that they used provocative incendiary publications and held public meetings in order to gain "proselytes to the hellish design" and that the leaders of this diabolical legion were well known and proud of their notoriety. "Would such a state of things, . . . be patiently borne by the north, and the southern states be held as friendly?" he demanded angrily.

After pleading with the bulk of the Northern population to "put down" these dangerous antislavery "fanatics," Ruffin addressed his fellow Southerners. Although he agreed with the Southern criticism levelled at Northern abolitionists and shared the determination to resist "at the bayonet's point" the practical execution of their theories, still he doubted "the propriety and the policy of giving so much importance to the ravings of the abolitionists, and to their circulation through the press and the mails."

Southern postmasters were confiscating and refusing to deliver any abolitionist literature sent from the North, while other proslavery zealots seized
and burned any publications deemed antislavery or anti-Southern. Ruffin
objected to what he saw as the excesses of the Great Reaction and worried
that "the violence of effort openly exhibited in endeavoring to suppress these
publications . . . may have as ill effects on those for whom these publications
were designed, as their circulation." "Perhaps," he cautioned, "we may be
thereby increasing the apparent importance of these societies, and possibly
their influence and power, far more than their own labors could as yet have
effected."[19]

Following his own prudent advice, editor Ruffin never again brought
up the controversial slavery issue. Besides, after the financial panic of 1837,
he was much too busy hunting banks to concern himself over what he
believed were the exaggerated dangers of Northern abolitionism. So, except
for an occasional piece offering helpful hints to slaveowners on the proper
care and maintenance of blacks, the entire ten volumes of the *Farmers'
Register* contained very few articles dealing with slavery.

7

Ruffin spoke in a voice of relative moderation on slavery, Northerners, and
abolitionism while he was an editor and while his economic and social status
were no longer visibly linked with the plantation system and slave ownership. But in 1842, his publishing business folded, and in a little more than
a year, he had rejoined the planter class. Encouraged by friendly South
Carolina political extremists like James Hammond, Ruffin turned most of
his own personal frustrations and bitterness toward the North. It was easy
for Ruffin, who felt persecuted by "enemies" in Virginia—political enemies,
banking enemies, personal enemies—who in fact needed "enemies" to
blame for his own disappointments and shortcomings, to transfer his persecution phobia to the North and see powerful enemies there too. Once rid
of these Yankee "enemies," he began to reason, the South could return to
a bygone era, a time when men like himself exercised moral and political
leadership and received the honors they rightly merited. And so, cautiously
at first, he embraced the cause of Southern nationalism. "We shall have to
defend our rights, by the strong hand, against the northern abolitionists, &
perhaps against the tariffites," he conceded to Hammond in autumn, 1845.
"I certainly hope it will be done if necessary."[20]

That the "strong hand" would be necessary became more and more
apparent to Ruffin with the increasing sectional controversy of the 1840s.
First, Texas's annexation in 1845 led to war with Mexico, and Northerners
who opposed the war claimed that it was a Southern plot to extend slave

territory. Then, in 1846, David Wilmot, a Pennsylvania Democrat, offered a proviso to Congress which prohibited slavery in any lands gained from Mexico. Southerners were furious at this new act of Northern treachery, which they feared was an abolitionist conspiracy to exclude slaveowners from their rightful share of the federal territories. "I hope you will keep Virginia *in the lead* on the Slave Question," Hammond urged Ruffin. "The safety of the South depends on it." But on this issue, even ordinarily conservative Virginians needed no prompting. If Congress dared pass the Wilmot Proviso, warned Governor William Smith in his annual message to the state legislature, "then indeed the day of compromise will have passed, and the dissolution of our great and glorious Union will become inevitable."[21]

Most Southerners agreed. In addition to hating the Proviso, Southerners objected to Northern interference with the effective capture and return of runaway slaves. And, as a further insult, antislavery Whigs in Congress were proposing to prohibit the slave trade and slavery in the nation's capital. In response to these and other provocations, the state of Mississippi, in October, 1849, issued a call to all the slave states to meet in convention at Nashville, Tennessee, the following June, in order to plan the proper mode of resistance to Northern aggression.

Then, as if to add yet another stick to the smoldering sectional fires, the newly acquired territory of California quickly organized its government and applied for admission into the Union as a free state, a move that would upset the balance of fifteen free and fifteen slave states. Southerners tensed. If Congress enacted the Wilmot Proviso in California, denying them access to that territory's rich lands and mineral resources, the Nashville Convention might well lead the entire South out of the Union. Led by the sick and aging John C. Calhoun, Southerners insisted that the North grant the South the protection and rights it needed as a numerical minority. "All we ask is to be let alone, but if trampled on it will be idle to expect that we will not resist," threatened Calhoun. "The alienation between the sections," had, he feared, "already gone too far to save the union."[22]

As the convention drew closer, Ruffin and Hammond continued their regular correspondence. In January, Hammond announced excitedly that South Carolina had appointed him to be one of its delegates. He hoped to see Ruffin at Nashville too. "The only interest I feel in public affairs," he declared, "is to see the south clear of this . . . Union." He urged Ruffin to agitate proslavery feelings in Virginia.[23]

But a month later, feelings of sectional animosity had already begun to cool, especially in the Old Dominion. Democratic and Whig party leaders agreed to support the Compromise of 1850, consisting of various proposals that Henry Clay had presented to Congress. Clay asked Congress to admit

California as a free state but to organize the Utah and New Mexico territories without any mention of slavery. When the time came for each of these territories to enter the Union, it would be entirely up to the territorial legislature whether to come in as a free or slave state. The Compromise also included measures to strengthen the Fugitive Slave Act and abolish the slave trade, but not slavery, in the District of Columbia. Hammond was worried. Neither he nor Ruffin favored any kind of compromise. "Now if the Convention does not open the way to dissolution of the Union," he wrote Ruffin, "I hope it may never meet." "I cannot perceive how any man can have any hope of saving ourselves from the fate of Jamaica," he despaired, "but by cutting loose from the Union as speedily as possible."[24]

8

Until this time, Ruffin, though sympathetic with the aims of the Southern nationalists, had not involved himself actively in their campaign. He was still nursing his own grievances against an unappreciative public, so he placed his faith in the people of South Carolina and left the fight for Southern rights to activists like Hammond and Calhoun. But by 1850, he could no longer hold himself back. A combination of men and events had convinced him that Southerners like himself had been made " 'hewers of wood and drawers of water' to minister to the grasping avarice and lust of power of the Northern states." The North, in his eyes, had become the supreme symbol of malevolent authority, a place peopled with mighty abolitionist "enemies" bent on using antislavery as a weapon to shame, control, and victimize the South—to shame, control, and victimize Edmund Ruffin. So, when the Compromise of 1850 threatened to jeopardize the outcome of the Nashville Convention, he finally shook off his melancholia, ceased complaining of his many illnesses, and joined the crusade for Southern nationalism.[25]

Choosing what he always believed to be his most persuasive and effective tool, Ruffin started writing again. Signing himself simply "A Virginian," he submitted a series of three articles for publication that March to newspapers in Virginia, South Carolina, and Georgia, in which he posed and answered the question, "What Will Be the Results of the Northern Abolition Action?"

"The earliest, important and successful aggression made by the Northern States on the Southern, in regard to slavery," Ruffin informed his readers, had begun in 1820 with the enactment of the Missouri Compromise. This "unjust and unconstitutional restriction," which divided free and slave states along the line 36°30', "ought to have been resisted by the South to the last extremity." By yielding then, the South had set a dangerous precedent for further restrictions, which had culminated in the North's latest attempt to exclude slavery from the new territories through the infamous Wilmot Proviso. The present compromise bills facing Congress represented "measures of fraud & triumph of the north, & grievous wrong and humiliation of the south." Ruffin begged Southerners not to let themselves be fooled again. "Concession to fanatics," he prophesied, "never satisfies fanaticism."

Ruffin conceded that the South had its share of fanatics too. But Southern fanaticism was only a defensive and therefore excusable reaction to the aggressive and pernicious fanaticism of Northern abolitionists, he argued. Ruffin had once dismissed these abolitionists as a small, despised, and impotent sect of troublemakers. But the Great Southern Reaction, combined with his own persecution complex, had had an effect on him. After more than fifteen years of living under the influence of a hostile anti-Northern climate, he too succumbed to a form of "community insanity," and he now characterized abolitionists as so numerous and powerful that not a single Northern political hopeful dared oppose their wishes.

Ruffin charged that antislavery forces were so influential in the North that they forced state legislatures to pass personal liberty laws which impeded slaveowners in the effective recovery of fugitive slaves. In the South, abolitionist agents craftily disguised themselves as preachers, teachers, tradesmen, and ordinary residents and scattered incendiary publications by the millions, so as to seduce and aid potential slave runaways. Distributing disgusting pictures like the popular engraving of a beautiful white woman, her hair tousled, in the lustful embrace of a black man, these agents tried to excite illiterate slaves and foment "insurrection and crimes so horrible that none but an Abolitionist could think of them without shuddering."

If the South accepted the terms of the present Compromise, Ruffin warned, the results would further the cause of Northern abolitionists. First, he predicted, Congress would immediately pass the Wilmot Proviso. Then Congress would abolish slavery in Washington, D.C., and follow this by excluding slaves from all federal forts, dockyards, and grounds for defense. Such places, even in the South, would become abolitionist arsenals. Consequently, the abolitionist party would become so powerful that it could easily summon the necessary votes to enact a federal abolition law. With emancipation, the number of blacks would soon outstrip the white population. Before long, the Southern states would sink to the condition of Jamaica and then the "deeper degradation" of Guadeloupe.[26] Finally the South would witness "the bloody horrors of St. Domingo," which would result in "the extinction of the white race and the brutal barbarism of the black." Those few whites who were spared, Ruffin shuddered, would "of necessity un-

dergo, . . . a moral and physical absorption, which will cause [them] to lose
. . . the fair type and beauty of intelligence which God has assigned to the
Caucasian family." "For these effects to be produced," he advised Southerners, "there is no difference of operation . . . between the action of the rabid
abolitionists of the Garrison and Giddings school, and the great body of the
Northern people and their representatives, who *profess* at least to respect
the constitutional rights of the South." The only difference was that "the
first class openly and honestly avow their wish to destroy us. The others aid
and give the needed force to the same deadly blow, while they hypocritically
pray God that it may so fall as not to kill the victim!"

After painting his frightful picture of race war and its terrible, apoca-
lyptic results, Ruffin advised the South "TO SUBMIT NO LONGER." If
Congress abolished slavery in Washington, D.C., or adopted the Wilmot
Proviso, the South must secede from the Union and declare its independence. For Ruffin, the political had become personal. Passage of either of
the two previous pieces of legislation would imply Northern criticism of the
South and of himself by extension. Criticism meant dishonor, shame, and
rejection, and rejection had to be punished by withdrawal.

And how the North would suffer when the South left the Union! In
glowing terms, Ruffin described the advantages of independence: free trade
with Europe, the growth of home manufacturing, shipping, and industry
and increased wealth and power for Southern cities. Should Southerners
decide to institute their own protective tariff system, he bragged, they could
virtually shut out Northern goods from Southern markets. Obviously rel-
ishing the thought, he predicted that "so heavy a blow" would deplete the
North's wealth and ruin its prosperity. Best of all, an independent South
could seal itself off from outside enemies and thus guarantee its own permanent internal safety. Northerners would become foreigners and, as such,
could be screened carefully before being allowed to set foot on Southern soil.
No longer could abolitionists enter the South and roam freely through the
slave states disguised as innocent fellow countrymen. In this way, Ruffin
declared, the new confederacy could effectively thwart the "mischievous
design" of Northern abolitionists to incite servile insurrection.

To those who objected that secession might lead to civil war, Ruffin
scoffed, "This opinion is the fruit of antiquated ideas." Money-grubbing
Yankees would not willingly sacrifice millions of dollars and thousands of
lives merely "to glut the hatred of the Abolitionists, or to attempt to excite
insurrection of the slaves," he contended. Besides, in the unlikely event that
war did break out, the South would clearly be the victor. War was expensive, and the South's valuable raw materials, particularly its rich cotton
crop, would pay for the costs. And slavery would also work to the South's
benefit. As in ancient Sparta, the large slave labor force would free citizens
from work in the fields and make every able-bodied white man a soldier.

Ruffin had only one practical suggestion for saving the Union for the present. Congress should admit California as a free state but redraw her southern boundary along the old Missouri Compromise line. The land below 36°30' would thus be guaranteed to slavery. If California rejected this boundary compromise and refused to join the Union, he argued, the South would not be the loser. The California territory north of 36°30' was immense, and nothing prevented Congress from later carving up the land into eight to ten free states, all sympathetic to Northern abolitionist interests. And if, as that "political Judas" William Seward of New York warned, California declared her independence and Oregon followed suit, so much the better. In the event of civil war, the North could not use the manpower and natural resources of these territories against the slave states.

Though his strong words would surely raise the "mad dog" cry that he was a "disunionist," Ruffin denied that this was so. He reminded his readers that Judge Baldwin, a Pennsylvania jurist, had once said that the right to recover fugitive slaves was the "corner-stone of the Federal Constitution." The abolitionists, Ruffin claimed, were "the true and only disunionists," because "they have destroyed the corner-stone on which the Constitution so safely rested."[27]

9

Ruffin then temporarily rested his case against the North, but Southerners refused to bring in a guilty verdict. Support for the congressional compromise bills gathered momentum with each passing day, while enthusiasm for the upcoming Southern convention rapidly waned. In Virginia, only a few die-hard extremists like Ruffin still urged the sending of state delegates. West of the Alleghenies, where sentiments were more allied to the free states of Pennsylvania and Ohio than to the South, the editor of the Whig *Leesburg Washingtonian* declared, "The proposed southern convention we look upon as a dangerous movement fraught with more serious danger to the prosperity of our glorious Union than almost anything now agitating our country." And from the East, the Democratic Richmond *Enquirer* echoed, "There are no disunionists at the South."[28]

That April, Hammond promised Ruffin that if the delegates at Nashville were ready for secession, he would fan every spark of resistance and join the disunion movement heart and soul. But only a few weeks later, he had no illusions left concerning the convention's likely success. "An immense deal of gas will be let off, I suppose," he grumbled.[29]

Delegates from only nine Southern states showed up at Nashville in June. As Hammond had predicted, they spent their fury in a few windy speeches and passed a series of empty-sounding resolutions listing Southern grievances. A few hotspurs like Robert Barnwell Rhett of South Carolina,

William Lowndes Yancey of Alabama, and Judge Beverley Tucker of Virginia were willing to take immediate steps toward dissolution of the Union, but the other delegates largely ignored them. Instead, they adopted a watchful attitude, agreeing to await the congressional decision on the pending compromise. They would reconvene in Nashville for a second meeting six weeks after Congress had adjourned.

That summer, Congress enacted all of the compromise measures. One by one, some willingly and others with marked reluctance, each of the slave states accepted the fact of sectional reconciliation. Southern unionists who favored the compromise won impressive victories in the state and local elections that fall, thus defeating secessionism in 1850. For the moment at least, the fires of Southern nationalism had been extinguished. South Carolina tried to rekindle secessionist sentiment by issuing a call for still another Southern convention, this time to convene in Montgomery, Alabama. Ruffin was hopeful that Southerners there would translate their fiery rhetoric into disunion. But the Virginia Assembly turned down the invitation and flatly asserted that the people of the Old Dominion were unwilling to jeopardize "the integrity of this Union." "Treason can find no foothold here," announced the Richmond *Whig.* "No man can rise in a public assembly, avow himself a Disunionist, and live, politically, one moment after it."[30]

Not so in the Palmetto state. Always in the lead on the secession question, it was the last to give in to the 1850 Compromise. In February, 1851, a thoroughly shocked and dismayed Hammond informed Ruffin that some of his fellow South Carolinians had denounced him as a "Traitor" and a "Submissionist." "My offenses are that I did not attend the second Nashville Convention, which I felt no disposition to do when I saw that the first was a farce & knew the next would be an abortion," he explained sarcastically. Also, extremists like Rhett had condemned him for favoring Southern cooperation and opposing their scheme that South Carolina withdraw from the Union alone. "The fact is, I am only a Girondist," he despaired, "& the Dantonists have I fear got possession of the state. I am happy in having escaped the guillotine."[31]

10

Ruffin would have spared his friend's head, but his own sympathies lay with the Dantonists. Disappointed by the ineffectiveness of both Nashville conventions and humiliated by what he believed was Virginia's craven submission to the "so-called Compromise measures," he longed for South Carolina to lead the way out of the Union, even if she acted alone.

It took all of Hammond's logical and persuasive talents to calm Ruffin and convince him that separate state action, for the present at least, was a desperate and unworkable solution. What would happen, he argued, if South Carolina seceded but none of the other Southern states followed? If South Carolina failed, this might forever spoil the South's future chances for unity and independence. For now, there must be some alternative mode of resistance.[32]

Reason, this time, prevailed over passion. And when in October, 1851, the election in South Carolina for delegates to the Montgomery Convention resulted in a Cooperationist triumph over Immediatists, Ruffin did not despair. He had a plan.

First, pretending to be a South Carolinian, he hurriedly dispatched an article to the Richmond papers insisting that no division existed in the Palmetto state over disunion. The Immediatists and the Cooperationists were all *secessionists;* they differed only on the best means of achieving their common goal.[33]

Then, as a Virginian, Ruffin wrote to the Charleston papers begging Carolinians to clarify their stand. "I . . . do not need to be told that much the greater number of Cooperationists are true and strenuous sustainers of Southern rights, and as much in favor of secession as are the immediate Secessionists," he declared. But Northern abolitionist enemies and Southern friends alike might misinterpret South Carolina's recent election results and conclude that it had submitted to "the (so-called) Compromise measures." "I speak of the opinions of others," he added quickly, "not of mine."[34]

Towards the victorious Cooperationists, Ruffin adopted a friendly, even diplomatic, tone. "The question of immediate secession was merely one of expediency. That question has been settled, and is no longer before us," he conceded. "The next question is what measure can be adopted instead which will come nearest to avoiding the dangers and evils imputed to immediate secession by its opposers, and which shall be nearest to securing the benefits which were expected by its friends." Generously, Ruffin proposed just such a measure, "A Plan for State Action," which he and Hammond had devised months before.[35]

Under this plan, South Carolina would cut almost every tie with the federal government—withdraw her senators and representatives from Congress and refuse to participate in presidential elections—but still pay her taxes and otherwise obey federal laws, thus affording the North no pretext to open hostilities. This way South Carolina could remain "with one foot out of the Union" until a sufficient number of other states joined her. Together, these disaffected states would then declare their independence and establish a separate Southern confederacy.[36]

If the Palmetto state moved swiftly and boldly to adopt this "armed truce," promised Ruffin, the rest of the South would rally behind her. "We look to South Carolina as our leader in this holy war," he wrote passion-

ately. "So long as she shall contend with success, we, her allies will fight
for the same cause." But he cautioned, "if she submits or even appears to
submit, her allies will lose all moral power and cannot longer continue a
hopeless struggle."[37]

11

But South Carolina was not ready to begin a holy war. She ignored Ruffin's
suggestions and did not adopt his plan. When it became evident that his best
efforts had proved fruitless, Ruffin again vowed that this was "my last
meddling with political matters—except as always, to express my opinions
. . . in the strongest terms, & without the least reserve."[38]

"I am as sick of politics as you are," Hammond agreed. "It has become
everywhere . . . a small game played by small men with the keenness of
desperation." He suggested that, for some relief from the pettiness of politics, Ruffin read the late Calhoun's *Disquisition on Government,* a brilliant
defense of the constitutional rights of minorities. "I have just devoured it,"
Hammond enthused. "Since Aristotle there has been nothing like it. . . . It
will be the Text Book of the coming ages."[39]

Hammond's future looked less enduring. South Carolinians had not
forgiven their ex-governor for boycotting the second Nashville Convention.
Twice since then, when vacancies occurred in the United States Senate, the
state legislature had passed over the hopeful expectant Hammond and
awarded the prize to one of his political rivals. Complaining bitterly of his
"undeserved infamy," Hammond then retired from politics, moved to a
faraway plantation near Augusta, Georgia, and, like Ruffin, vowed to "have
done with the public forever in every form & shape." "I am as you only
laughed at," he wailed in self-pity. "I have no assistant, no sympathizer, no
consoler." "It is outrageous," he ranted to other friends. "I wish that South
Carolina stood upon the Cliffe of Hell & I had the power to cast her into
the flaming gulf below. I would do it before you could cross a t."[40]

Ruffin understood this kind of sulking and bitterness only too well. "If
it be any consolation to you to know of others suffering like yourself," he
had commiserated in the past, "I can afford you some of it." How often had
he himself felt ridiculed, despised, alone. How many times would he have
joined his friend at the abyss and gladly pushed Virginia over the brink. But
ironically, it was now he who comforted Hammond and tried to coax him
out of retirement and back into public service. Ruffin's entire outlook had
changed. For, suddenly and quite unexpectedly, Ruffin's public had begun
to appreciate him.[41]

6

A Time of Triumph

1

A FEW WEEKS BEFORE Christmas, 1853, a happy and excited Ruffin wrote
Hammond that he felt like a different person. The unhappy and persecuted
misanthrope Hammond had known had changed, it appeared, into a happy,
confident, popular person with an uncharacteristically sunny disposition.
"You may remember some of my former letters, in which my wrongs and
resentful feelings were strongly . . . referred to," he reminded Hammond.
"My consequent entire seclusion you then opposed." Well, Hammond had
been right and "I was wrong," he admitted, "in construing the hostility or
ingratitude of the *many* to be the like feelings of *all*. I know now that when
I was most separated from my fellows, fancying that I was slighted, if not
disliked by all, that I retained numerous approvers and friends! The occurrences of the last few years . . . have shown me that . . . with the better and
larger portion of my countrymen, I hold a place in their esteem, regard, and
gratitude more exhalted than my own self-love had ever designated as my
deserved rank and portion."[1]

The source of all this public esteem and gratitude had nothing to do
with Ruffin's secessionist politics, of which most Southerners disapproved.
Instead, as in the past, Ruffin won acclaim for his many contributions to
Southern agricultural reform.

Nor was this acclaim quite as sudden and unexpected as it seemed at
first. Ruffin's promise to retire and shut himself off from the public had
always been difficult for him to keep. He wanted to say and do so many
things that he considered important; he wanted public recognition so des-

77

perately. In 1845, after less than two years' "retirement" at Marlbourne, Ruffin admitted to Hammond that he had "departed somewhat from my *entire* separation from the public" and had agreed to write an agricultural column—at his own "discretion or caprice"—for the Richmond *Enquirer.* Then, at the suggestion of a neighbor, he wrote up the results of his marling experiments at Marlbourne and submitted them in article form to the *American Farmer,* which promptly accepted it. The essay was so popular that the magazine's subscription list substantially increased, especially in Virginia, and Ruffin recorded his secret pleasure at this "evidence of approval" from his native state.[2]

Ruffin continued writing for the *American Farmer* and the *Enquirer* and even began a fifth edition of his *Essay on Calcareous Manures,* but he very rarely left his plantation. By 1850, though, the situation had started to change. His new political activism made him less inclined to be reclusive. So, when the Agricultural Society of Eastern Maryland invited him that year to deliver the keynote speech at its annual meeting, Ruffin surprised everyone by accepting. He had declined many similar invitations from local Virginia societies but made an exception for Maryland, where he believed that, unlike in Virginia, he had many "friends and approvers."[3]

Once he had crossed the Chesapeake, though, Ruffin did nothing to ingratiate himself with his audience. He had come not to flatter his listeners but to be blunt and critical. He accused Southern agricultural societies, including their own, of "mis-placed deference to, and humble imitation of" Northern agricultural societies, which represented "an agriculture very different from and far inferior to our own." By operating mainly through cattle shows, livestock exhibitions, and "those things in which only our northern exemplars possess any agricultural wealth," Southern societies strengthened the false impression of Northern superiority and of their own inferiority. Meanwhile, Southerners "passed over" their own unique agricultural products and improvements with "scant notice," as though they had "no existence." Virginians, he added acidly, were particularly guilty of this "humbug policy." That was why their first attempt to organize a state agricultural society had been "still-born" and subsequent attempts all ended in "abortion."[4]

Despite their guest's sharp words, the Marylanders took Ruffin's censure in good spirit, treating Ruffin as an honored guest and public benefactor. He returned to Marlbourne satisfied that outside of Virginia, at least, there were people who valued his achievements and his advice. Then, shortly afterwards, he received a letter from *DeBow's Review,* a New Orleans periodical dedicated to Southern industry and agriculture, requesting his biography and portrait for their "Gallery of Industry and Enterprise" series. Ruffin felt flattered, because he knew that the purpose of the series was "to present the labour of *working* men, who had been of eminent service to themselves and their country." And, as he observed later, *DeBow's* had not yet "abused" the Gallery plan by "presenting galleries . . . of *nobodies,* & of any who would pay for a place, & were not ashamed to have their nothingness so prominently exhibited to public view & contempt." Ruffin knew that he was *somebody* and that his inclusion in the gallery was well deserved. So he accepted *DeBow's* invitation and furnished a friend, William Baulwane, with a picture of himself and enough of his published and private materials to write a short biographical sketch.[5]

In October, 1851, *DeBow's* "Gallery of Industry and Enterprise" introduced "Edmund Ruffin, of Virginia, Agriculturalist." The public's response was so favorable that Ruffin became something of a celebrity almost overnight. The United States Agricultural Society unanimously elected him an honorary member, the only such member, Ruffin suggested with pride, who had not "bought the honor" with a large financial donation. And although he considered his picture in *Debow's Review* a rather poor likeness, wherever he went even strangers recognized his "marked features & long gray hair" and rushed to greet him, shake his hand, and offer their congratulations and their thanks.[6]

Southern newspapers, particularly those in the Old Dominion, vied to outdo one another in praising the man they all recognized as Virginia's "Saviour," her "mighty public benefactor." Fascinated by the story of Ruffin's early attempts to restore his run-down Coggin's Point plantation and his unexpected success with marl, editors shared the tale with their readers, quoting long segments from the original article and enlarging upon and even exaggerating its main themes.

The *National Intelligencer,* for its part, claimed that Ruffin had rescued his native state from "an age of agricultural barbarism." The Old Dominion's once fertile fields had seemed "inevitably destined" to return to the desert or the forest, while "the *wolf,* driven from his native haunts two centuries before by the advance of civilization, returned to resume his ancient reign, and to howl over the desolation of Virginia." "We had reached the Nadir of agricultural depression," the Richmond *Whig* agreed, and "we were threatened with a general exodus of our most useful population."[7]

Then, just when the situation looked hopeless, Ruffin made his "great discovery" about marl, "stayed the mighty ruin," and arrested the tide of westward migration. "With an ingenuity, an energy and a logic, which belongs only to the order of great intellects," praised the *Whig,* "he demonstrated . . . the disease and the cure." He opened up "mines of wealth . . . in the bowels of our own lands" and taught Virginia's "struggling sons" that with the help of science, they could "enjoy abundant prosperity at home." Now the landscape "smiled," and gentlemen could once more afford to live like gentlemen. "Plenty presides over the board where meagre scraps of food were before served up," testified a grateful planter, and "hospitality once more invites the wayfarer to enter the doors where poverty so lately kept watch."[8]

The newspapers acknowledged that the farmers and planters of eastern Virginia owed Ruffin special thanks. The Virginia Census of 1850 showed that since 1837, land values in the eastern portion of the state had risen twenty-three million dollars, and the *Whig* reported that some planters were earning a 20 percent profit on lands they once considered useless for cultivation.[9]

In the Petersburg *Southside Democrat,* editor Roger Pryor paid eloquent tribute to the man who had made an "indelible impress" on his native state. With his agricultural contributions, wrote Pryor, Ruffin had built a monument to himself "more to be envied than 'storied urn or animated bust.' " "The poet may make classic ground of the most uninviting regions," Pryor admitted, "but greater still is the genius of him who converts the barren waste into the prolific field. The soldier may beat back the invading foe, but more valuable is the service of him who arrests the desolating sweep of poverty and depopulation. These are the deeds of Edmund Ruffin." Virginians should cherish and revere such a man; he was a patriot and a hero. "And yet we who literally reap the harvest of his toil," Pryor scolded, "regard him with less admiration and gratitude than we bestow on a windy 'legislator' or a bloodstained 'soldier.' " If Virginians neglected their "worthy son" and underestimated his value, he assured, other states did not. "In other States," Pryor observed, "the name of EDMUND RUFFIN is always mentioned with honor."[10]

2

At Marlbourne, Ruffin relished this unaccustomed—and in his mind long overdue—fame and publicity. Carefully he cut out all the flattering newspaper articles and editorials and pasted the clippings in his private journal. After he was done, he felt a sudden wave of shame. What if others thought him immodest, and accused him of false pride and conceit? Doubts that he had always tried to keep hidden began to surface. Was he indeed worthy of all this newfound praise? Did he truly merit his sudden popularity? Driven by his own insecurities, he concocted an elaborate argument for self-justification. Ordinarily, Ruffin admitted, he would have dismissed similar newspaper notices as worthless "puffs," because he assumed the articles were "begged or bought" to advance some individual's political ambitions. But his own case was unique, he reasoned, for "when such notices are of a person in private & almost recluse life—never seeking favors & having no reward to give for them—& when the praises proceed from strangers, &

from editors of all political sides, & none of my own peculiar political views"—then they must be "the prevalent opinions of the intelligent portion of the community."[11]

Perhaps the intelligent portion of the community had always appreciated his services, Ruffin mused. He remembered his previous feelings of neglect and ingratitude, his seclusion from the public. Wherever he had looked, he thought he saw "enemies." Even among his neighbors and personal acquaintances, it seemed that "there were many more who were . . . indifferent or . . . hostile to me, than truly friendly." But in light of his recent public favor, Ruffin wondered if he had not construed "many things wrongly." Perhaps he had been "morbidly sensitive" to criticism and had imagined slights and insults that had never existed. If the public had seemed hostile, much of that "was doubtless my own fault," he conceded generously. "I never possessed what are known as popular manners." If his neighbors had been unfriendly, they probably had "just causes of dislike." He was aware of "many errors of conduct" on his part, particularly "my habit of uttering my opinions . . . freely & strongly, & incautiously." But his neighbors, acquaintances, and the public in general had more than forgiven any past misconduct. Even former enemies, he reported happily, "are now among my warmest & devoted & . . . true friends."[12]

In return, Ruffin's hard feelings toward the public softened, and he was ready, once more, to love his fellow man. He even made up with the Virginia Agricultural Society, which he had once dismissed with the prediction that it "lived but to die." Early in 1852, when the Society tried to organize itself for the third time, Ruffin traveled to Richmond for the meeting, determined to cooperate at long last. There he met "a large & zealous assemblage" of old friends, former contributors to the *Farmers' Register,* and total strangers who, he marveled, "seemed like the others,—to be delighted to meet me."[13]

When the meeting started, the members chose Ruffin as their temporary presiding officer. Then they adopted every reform measure, no matter how controversial, that he proposed. "In organization, in principle, & prospective policy," Ruffin noted with satisfaction, "the meeting was made precisely as I advised." And, after the elections were over, Ruffin discovered that every ballot but his own had voted him president. This time he accepted the honor with thanks.[14]

As president, Ruffin worked diligently on the Society's behalf, preparing many of the principal addresses and, according to his own assessment, writing "*all* of the truly agricultural & important communications." He attended every Executive Committee meeting, even though winter sessions at Richmond worsened his health and gave him "wretched colds." And because of his tireless recruitment efforts, the Society's membership list more than doubled in its first year, but equally zealous attempts to obtain financial aid from the Virginia Assembly failed repeatedly. Ruffin denounced the legislature as "despicable" and blamed its "niggardly treatment" on a new state constitution which had expanded the popular vote.[15]

3

When he was not busy with his duties as the Society's president or with his work at Marlbourne, Ruffin honored the many speaking invitations he received from various Southern state and local agricultural groups. Several states even sent him complimentary railroad passes. So, during this first year in office, he traveled up and down the southeastern seaboard, addressing audiences in every state from Maryland to Georgia.

The main theme of his speeches, while not overtly political, still reflected Ruffin's growing hatred of the North and his commitment to Southern nationalism. Since he was well aware that talk of secession and Southern independence was unpopular with most Southern audiences, he never brought up the subject. Instead he spoke of the need for Southern agrarian reform, accused a "hostile and predatory" North of plundering Southern wealth and, above all, defended the economic and moral superiority of the South's slave-based plantation system of agriculture.

Ruffin knew that like Virginia, all the states of the Old South had suffered from problems of soil exhaustion and the consequent lure of fresher lands to the west. Some Southerners, jealous of the greater prosperity of Northern husbandmen, wondered if slavery and the plantation system were responsible for agricultural methods which depleted the soil. In his speeches, Ruffin denounced this theory as agrarian heresy. Slavery, he insisted, was not only indispensable to Southern profits but actually increased soil fertility more than "any purely agricultural labours and capital north of Mason and Dixon's line."[16]

He explained that wasteful, exploitative agricultural methods were common to the frontier regions in both the North and the South and had nothing to do with free or slave labor systems. The problem in the South was that long after the frontier had moved further west, planters and farmers had continued treating their worn-out land as though it were still in virginal condition. But the remedy was at hand. Older Southern communities, Ruffin said, must cease their former "land-killing" agricultural techniques and, with the help of their valuable slave force and calcareous manures, begin to refertilize the soil and restore the South to prosperity. He promised his listeners that if they followed his advice, they would soon behold "the dawn of a brighter day." And with uncharacteristic eloquence, he exclaimed, "The sun of agricultural improvement has already risen—

more glorious in every sense than the 'sun of Austerlitz'—already it is
rapidly ascending the heavens—and I trust that we shall soon see it at
meridian height."[17]

Then Ruffin asked his audiences to suppose, for a moment, that slavery
were less profitable than free labor. Even if this were true, he argued,
slavery's moral advantages would far outweigh any economic disadvan-
tages. For in the South, the presence of slavery confined the drudgery and
brutalizing effects of continuous toil to the inferior black race, thus affording the superior white race the leisure time to develop its "manners, morals,
and intellect" to their fullest. In the North, though, the absence of slavery
forced white yeomen and often their wives and children to do the work of
slaves, including "degrading menial tasks." Thus, with so little time for
self-improvement, these people became rude, ignorant, and brutish. They
might also be thrifty, industrious, economical, and wealthy, Ruffin admitted, but these were the characteristics of crass, materialistic Yankee society,
which believed that profit should be the goal of life. "No one appreciates
more highly than myself the advantages of producing and accumulating
wealth," he said. "Still, God forbid that we should deem the accumulation
of wealth . . . as compensation for the loss or deterioration of southern men,
and more especially of southern women."[18]

Because of slavery's refining influence, said Ruffin, Southern men of
culture, talent, and education engaged in agriculture and lived on farms or
plantations. But because of slavery's absence in the North, refined men
engaged in nonagrarian pursuits and lived in large cities. Yet farmers made
up the majority of the populace in both sections. The conclusion was
inescapable: the majority of Southerners were superior to the majority of
Northerners. He did not mention that the majority of Southern farmers
owned no slaves, for this would have meant that the majority of Southerners
were as ignorant and boorish as their Northern counterparts.[19]

Ruffin conceded that Southerners were inferior to Northerners in one
aspect only—their voting power. True, he deplored any expansion of the
electorate, even in the South, and had run unsuccessfully as an antisuffrage
candidate when Virginia held her last Constitutional Convention in 1850.
But at least "in the South," he pointed out, "the lowest, and necessarily the
most ignorant and degraded class . . . are not . . . citizens and voters, but
are negro slaves, who have no political rights," and the presence of slavery
discouraged the influx of equally ignorant European immigrants. Thus,
Southerners were able to "purify and exhalt" the popular vote by keeping
political power in the hands of a qualified elite, a situation, Ruffin reminded
planters, which was "most fortunate for the preservation of the political
freedom and safety of . . . the ruling class." But in the North, by contrast,
the majority of citizens and voters were stupid farmers and vicious foreign-

ers. Thus, political power remained in the hands of unprincipled leaders who pandered to and manipulated the masses. Yet because of the "tragic farce" of democracy and universal suffrage, inferior Northerners could control the federal government. In fact, though, because Southerners dominated the national Democratic party, they exercised political power far out of proportion to their actual numbers. Throughout the 1850s, Southerners controlled Congress, the Supreme Court, and the presidency. But Ruffin refused to acknowledge this. "Superior intellect has no influence," he kept insisting, "and we are governed by the brute force and cupidity of superior numbers."[20]

Ruffin saved his most political and anti-Northern remarks for sympathetic South Carolina audiences. Not long after a particularly vituperative speech in Charleston, where he "denounced the northern states & people, & the government of the U.S. for sustaining northern aggressions" in his "strongest language," he learned of a "strange & ludicrous" occurrence. Ruffin had doubted whether his "possibly . . . ungracious and distasteful" remarks were proper even in Charleston. He knew they would have been unpalatable anywhere in Virginia, and a Northern audience would have considered his words "highly offensive." Yet *DeBow's Review* had published the speech. Then, to Ruffin's vast amusement, the United States Agricultural Society reprinted the entire article, word for offensive word, in its Patent Reports for 1852 and distributed over one hundred thousand free copies throughout the country. The irony was delicious. "So," chuckled Ruffin, "my bitter denunciations of . . . the north, have thus been spread before all the people of the northern as well as southern states, by the action & at the expense of the U.S. government."[21]

4

Making speeches was never easy for Ruffin. The preparation of each address was a long and torturous procedure, and the delivery was no less difficult. Although he was never at a loss for what to say—ideas came to him as "rapidly as my pen moved"—he often lost track of his thoughts and unintentionally repeated the same point again and again. When he stopped to reread what he had written, this needless repetition embarrassed him, and he worried that he was no longer mentally competent. Nor had his long absence from public affairs given him more confidence in his speaking abilities. He invariably began each speech with an apology for the poor performance he was sure would follow. Did they expect a "fine speech?" Ruffin would ask his listeners. If so, he would disappoint them. "I have not the ability, nor the habit of attempting to frame or to utter the language of eloquent declamation," he said, "nor can I even offer . . . the ordinary smoothness and fluency ... of commonplace speakers." He explained that although others might find this hard to believe, he had grown old in Virginia without ever having been a lawyer, teacher, politician, or any other "seeker of popular favor." Thus, he was "unqualified" to be a public speaker. "I can scarcely hope to make you, intelligibly & without confusion, a plain statement ... in plain & rustic phrases," he added humbly.[22]

If Ruffin suffered at times like these from the "pride of having no pride," nobody seemed to mind. Perhaps his apparently genuine modesty and sincere self-deprecation charmed his audiences, for they overlooked his obvious flaws as an orator and responded to his "plain & rustic phrases" with warmth and enthusiasm. Occasionally, the usually nervous Ruffin even surprised himself at his own self-possession. An extemporaneous address to a Georgia society "succeeded well," he noted, because his audience seemed "well pleased," and "much evidences" of gratitude were offered in "marked cases by the ladies." And in South Carolina, a state Ruffin loved hardly less than Virginia, he received "the most cordial welcome & respectful attention" and enjoyed "a time of triumph ... without example."[23]

The time of triumph was not over. At the end of his year as president, Ruffin attended the Virginia Agricultural Society's first annual meeting and state fair at Richmond. The year's full round of activities had agreed with him, and he felt and looked better than ever. His previous symptoms of apoplexy had disappeared, and newspaper correspondents admired his "clear quick grey eyes, erect figure, firm confident step," and "fresh healthy, rosy cheeks."[24]

The meeting was held in the Virginia House of Delegates. As soon as Ruffin entered the great hall, the other members began to applaud. Then, one by one, they left their seats, surrounded him, clasped his hand and, according to one reporter, showed him "every mark of reverence and affection."[25]

John Tyler opened the proceedings with a valedictory address enumerating Ruffin's many agricultural achievements. "What can warrior or statesman do," Tyler asked, "to compare with the citizen who ... opened the way to resuscitation ... of his native land? Can too much praise be bestowed on that man?" The members of the Virginia Society thought not. Following Tyler's laudatory address, the Committee on Honorary Testimonials hailed Ruffin as "the field marshal of the army of farmers and planters of the Old Dominion" and pronounced him "Not Edmund Ruffin of Prince George—of Petersburg—of Hanover, but Edmund Ruffin of Virginia. He now belongs to us all."[26]

The following year, at the second annual state fair, Ruffin was surprised and delighted to discover that he was still a celebrity. Five of his children and several family friends circulated among the crowd at the fair and reported that, based on the conversations they had overheard, Ruffin was "the chief object of interest, & 'the observed of all observers.' " General Winfield Scott and former President Tyler were also at the fair, but Ruffin was the major attraction. "It was as obvious as [it was] remarkable," he noted with satisfaction, "that political & military fame here took a subordinate station to agricultural merit." All the attention made him feel "highly gratified," but he tried to hide his extreme pleasure, for fear someone would accuse him of ungentlemanly immodesty. "I endeavored . . . to bear my honors meekly, & never to appear conscious of them except when it was unavoidable," he insisted.[27]

But Ruffin was very conscious of his honors, and he ached to tell others of his new love affair with the public. So, in early December, 1853, just after the state fair closed, Ruffin went upstairs to his room at Marlbourne, sat down at his desk, and wrote Hammond a long letter. He recalled all the bittersweet experiences of the past—his retirement from public life, his gradual comeback, and his meteoric success of recent years. Then, unaware of his own conceit, he urged Hammond to follow a similar path back to public glory. A few agricultural articles and some personal speaking appearances outside his native state, Ruffin advised, would convince Hammond not to mistake "the hostility of the *many* to be the like feelings of *all.* " Even the gravest insults, if interpreted correctly, were compliments. "Envy loves a shining mark!" Ruffin reminded him. "Envy, hatred, and Calumny are the only tributes that many men can pay to worth—& for my own part, I have learned to esteem such tributes as compliments to superior merit."[28]

5

Hammond, though, was jealous of Ruffin's success and resented his advice. Secretly, he complained to others of his old friend's "vanity and egotism." As for himself, Hammond was ready neither to forgive nor to forget any past insults. He even refused the chance to have his portrait, like Ruffin's, displayed in *DeBow's* famous Gallery. But Ruffin had reentered public life with gusto and had no intention of turning back. In 1854, he became the Agricultural Commissioner of Virginia and two years later served as delegate to the Farmers' Assembly and again as president of the Virginia Agricultural Society. He continued his speaking tours and his prolific writing. In 1855, the publisher J. W. Randolph brought out a collection of fourteen of Ruffin's best articles in *Essays and Notes on Agriculture.* "Buy it," Randolph recommended in a newspaper advertisement, "and the earth will return the compliment with a smile."[29]

Again, as Ruffin's activities and fame as an agrarian reformer increased, his own interest in the practical day-to-day aspects of agriculture declined. No matter how many times he lauded Southern plantation life and hailed its elevating and refining influences, he proved repeatedly in his private papers and through his own actions that he was alienated from the typical boring, mind-dulling existence of the planter and was most eager to escape. He complained now that managing a plantation was "onerous & disagreeable"; he was too old and infirm for this sort of occupation, and he could give his work only "slight & general attention."[30]

Hoping to rid himself of this annoyance and thus be free to assume more satisfying public duties, Ruffin turned over Marlbourne's operations to his son Julian at the end of 1854. But the following year, family problems required that Julian leave Marlbourne and return to his own plantation, Ruthven, in Prince George County. That summer, within the space of a few weeks, three of Ruffin's daughters died. This heavy personal affliction left him less inclined than ever to resume his plantation work.[31]

But Ruffin realized that he either had to take charge of Marlbourne again or hire a white overseer to do the job for him, two choices which were equally disagreeable to him. For seven years, he and Jem Sykes had managed Marlbourne, and he feared that the introduction of an overseer now would stir resentment among Sykes and the other slaves and lead to "an entire revolution in the government & discipline of the farm." Insubordinate blacks were likely to provoke a new overseer, he would retaliate with harsh discipline and severe punishment, the slaves would complain to their old master, and Ruffin would "be annoyed & harassed beyond bearing by these difficulties."[32]

Because he wished to save himself from this unnecessary vexation and "do better for my slaves & defend them from maltreatment," Ruffin did not hire an overseer for Marlbourne. Instead, he decided to retire from planting completely and turn over the valuable Marlbourne estate, in equal but indivisible shares, to his children. Then he planned to set aside twenty-five thousand dollars for himself and divide the rest of his money and property among them.[33]

This was no small gift, for, according to Ruffin's estimates, he was worth at least one hundred fifty thousand dollars. But such generosity was not at all uncharacteristic, in that Ruffin was an extremely fond and indulgent parent who had frequently lavished his children with presents of money, land, or slaves. In return, he expected their love; their loyalty; and, most importantly, their obedience. When, as in most instances, his children gave these willingly, Ruffin enjoyed the closest and warmest kind of family relations. His letters and private papers often commended a son's or daughter's modesty, docility, "lack of levity," or "pure & strict moral conduct." But when they did not, when they were headstrong or disobedient, when they violated Ruffin's rigid standards of behavior, they bruised their father's fragile ego. Ungrateful children, an ungrateful public: they were one and the same to Ruffin, and he treated both in similar fashion. He tongue-lashed errant sons and daughters, hoping to shame them into good behavior. If that failed, he used punishment, taking away special favors, gifts, privileges. Finally, as a last resort, he withdrew his love, turning his back and rejecting his own flesh and blood. There were two such glaring examples: his eldest daughter Agnes and his youngest son Charles.[34]

Agnes had first incurred her father's great displeasure more than twenty years earlier in Petersburg when she flagrantly disregarded his wishes by courting and then wedding Stanley Beckwith, a poor country doctor of humble family background. Her romance was ill-timed, to say the least, for Ruffin's half-sister and ward, Juliana, had only just terminated a disastrous ten-year marriage to another penniless Petersburg physician. Her husband, Dr. William Coupland, turned out to be a shiftless, lazy, scoundrelly oaf. Ruffin had vehemently opposed that match from the start and, as Juliana's legal guardian, had even tried unsuccessfully to prevent the union from taking place. But Juliana had defied him, and when her marriage was finally in shambles—and she tearfully owned up to the error of her ways—Ruffin glowed with the satisfaction of a vindicated prophet.

What a bitter pill then for him to swallow when Agnes seemed only too willing to retrace her aunt's erring footsteps, ignoring his disapproval and taking up with a man who closely resembled the detestable Dr. Coupland. Nor was it likely that mere coincidence or the fickle dictates of her heart had determined Agnes's choice of suitors, since she picked a husband she must have known would infuriate her father. Her rebellion was deliberate and her motives unquestionably hostile.

Since their marriage, Beckwith, a ne'er-do-well and a spendthrift, had given his wife a dozen children, unpaid bills, and little else. All the Ruffins felt that Agnes had married "beneath [her] station." And because Beckwith was always in financial difficulties, no matter how many times his in-laws reluctantly bailed him out, Ruffin likened him to Charles Dickens's memorable character, the cheerful but inveterate debtor, Mr. Micawber. Relations between the two families had deteriorated so much over the years that Ruffin visited Agnes and his grandchildren only when he knew Beckwith would be away from home, and on more than one occasion, he expressed the hope that "if he [Beckwith] was gone so far that he never would be heard from, it would be the next best thing to his death." When Agnes tried to defend her husband and begged her father to stop treating him like a "criminal," Ruffin concluded that his "despicable" fortune hunter of a son-in-law had poisoned his daughter's mind. If he made Agnes a full and equal partner with her brothers and sisters at Marlbourne, he feared that somehow Beckwith would connive to get the property for himself. So, instead, Ruffin set up a trust fund for her and her children that Beckwith could not touch.[35]

He also considered making special financial arrangements for Charles, because his youngest son had long been a disappointment to him. Born when Ruffin was nearly forty years old, Charles never received the patient attention and loving confidence that his father had given to Edmund and Julian. His mother, Susan, ailing and tired after a dozen childbirths, died when he was fourteen. But even while she lived, the concerns of her large household occupied most of her time. So, much like Ruffin himself, Charles grew up feeling neglected, like an outsider, the family "outcast." Then, too, unlike his more serious and reserved older brothers, Charles was playful and high-spirited. He liked to sip mint juleps, wear expensive clothes, court neighborhood belles, attend lavish balls and barbeques, and generally enjoy the fancy trappings that went along with being the aristocratic son of a wealthy planter. He seemed to sense, like his sister Agnes, that inappropriate, even shameless behavior was an effective way to attract his father's attention. Ruffin, perhaps forgetful of his own youthful yearnings and indiscretions, disapproved of his son's frivolous behavior and accused him of being lazy and extravagant. Did Charles want to end up a common debtor like that wretched Dr. Beckwith? Ruffin would demand. And in letters signed "Your long-suffering father," Ruffin begged Charles to mend his ways, threatening to cut him off with "a bare competency" if he did not. Then in early 1856, after graduating from college, Charles took a job as a railroad engineer. Edmund had also been an engineer, and Ruffin hoped that this job would give his youngest son the "steadiness of purpose" to become a successful planter like his brothers one day. So, Charles, too, along with Edmund, Julian, Mildred, and Elizabeth, received an equal share of his father's estate.[36]

Still there remained the problem of who would actually live at Marlbourne and manage the plantation. Edmund and Julian had their own plantations to care for, and Charles was unwilling to give up his railroad job. Then William Sayre, Elizabeth's husband, made a startling announcement. He and Elizabeth would be moving soon to settle a new tract of land he had purchased in Westmoreland County. This presented the other Ruffins with a new problem. There was hardly a place the same distance from Richmond, they complained to one another, which was less accessible to public travel. They did not want Elizabeth, who was sickly, to move to such a remote spot, where she would have to cope with rough pioneer conditions and have little chance to see her neighbors, much less her family. "Such a home to Elizabeth," worried Ruffin, "would have been a dreary exile." As a solution to both these difficulties, the Ruffins decided to make William Sayre an equal partner in Marlbourne and offered him a salary of $1,000 a year, on the condition that he and Elizabeth live there and that he carry out the management duties as the plantation's resident superintendent. This way Mildred, who was still unmarried, could live at Marlbourne and act as her sister's nurse and companion, while Ruffin would also consider Marlbourne his home.[37]

Sayre accepted the offer, and Ruffin began making all the necessary legal arrangements. But before the transfer of property was complete, Edmund and Julian sat down with their father and urged him to reconsider his plans to retire. They were worried that without some kind of active employment, Ruffin would not be happy. That was very true, he agreed. "Occupation is necessary for me—& . . . if idle entirely, I should be miserable." But, he assured his anxious sons, he had no intention of becoming less active during his retirement. In fact, he expected to be busier than ever, but in a different, more pleasant way, one that was more "useful" to the public.[38]

He believed that the time had finally arrived when the public was ready to profit from his instruction not only on agricultural matters but on political topics as well. While he had no personal ambitions for political office, he envisioned himself as a sort of elder statesman, whose advice others would heed and whose wise counsel they would seek. Beaming with anticipation, Ruffin told his family that he planned to spend the rest of his life as an intellectual evangelist, traveling throughout the South; publishing his opinions on various subjects; and, most importantly, "acting as an itinerant missionary of disunion."[39]

But before starting this new phase of his career, Ruffin wanted to speak to his slaves. When the more than forty black men, women, and children had assembled in front of the main house, he explained that he was no longer the master at Marlbourne and that he had sold the plantation and all of them jointly to his five children and William Sayre. The slaves looked at one another, puzzled. They were aware that as their master's property, they could be sold, inherited, even given away at any time. But six masters and mistresses? Joint ownership? This was unusual and hard to understand. Nor were they happy to learn that Sayre would be the new plantation manager. Sayre, who had never owned many slaves, was uneasy around blacks, and they in turn distrusted him. But Ruffin either did not notice their displeasure or, if he did, he mistook it for loving sadness at the news of their old master's retirement. He did recognize their bewilderment, though, and immediately realized that if he stayed at Marlbourne, the slaves would continue to treat him as their master. He must leave Marlbourne, he decided, at least for a few months, to give the new owners and Sayre in particular a chance to establish their authority.[40]

Early that summer, in 1856, Ruffin packed a few belongings and headed for Prince George County to visit his other children, making Edmund's plantation, Beechwood, his temporary residence. But after several weeks, he became restless. Soaring temperatures made life almost unbearable in the Tidewater, and the malaria season was approaching. Soon thousands of prominent Southerners and their families would leave the unhealthy coastal regions to blacks and poor whites and escape to one of the refreshing mountain spring resorts in western Virginia. There, under a cool shade tree, beside clear sparkling waters, on a lovely veranda, or on a grand ballroom floor, Ruffin knew he could buttonhole any one of a number of important guests—politicians, planters, lawyers, merchants, editors—and chat for hours about disunion, his favorite subject. What better place, he thought, to combine pleasure and politics and begin to preach the gospel of secession.[41]

7

Missionary of Disunion

1

In MID-AUGUST, 1856, Ruffin joined his daughters Mildred and Elizabeth at one of the family's favorite spas, White Sulphur Springs. The cottages there resembled Greek temples, so the Ruffins and other Southerners who believed in a slave "aristocracy" felt quite comfortable and at home. But Ruffin found little time to admire the fine architecture or the exquisite natural scenery, for he was busy conversing with other gentlemen, using "every suitable occasion"—and there were many—to advocate immediate secession and the formation of a Southern confederacy "as the only means of warding off the continued & increasing assaults of the northern people to impair & finally destroy our institution of slavery." His purpose was not so much to argue with or convince his listeners as to conduct an informal canvass, testing the reactions to his ideas. He had not forgotten how, in the wake of the 1850 Compromise, disunion talk had been "odious" to most Southerners, and he was well aware that his strong words, if uttered then, would have branded him a traitor.[1]

But no one accused Ruffin of treason this summer. Political events, particularly those of the past two years, had all but shattered the fragile, uneasy sectional truce of 1850, dramatically altering Southern attitudes and making even "odious" disunion words more palatable.

The controversy again centered around the issue of slavery's expansion into federal territories. In 1854, after furious debate, a bitter and divided Congress passed the Kansas-Nebraska Act, and on May 30, President Franklin Pierce signed the fateful measure into law. The brainchild of Stephen A. Douglas, the act wiped out the old Missouri Compromise line, which would have organized Kansas and Nebraska as free territories. In its place was the old principle of popular sovereignty, leaving it up to the settlers in each territory to decide for themselves at some future date whether or not to allow slavery.

At once, a storm of protest broke out in the North. Outraged abolitionists, politicians, and newspaper editors denounced the new bill as part of a monstrous Southern conspiracy to undermine American democratic institutions. A sinister "Slave Power," they charged, was trying to extend slavery first into Kansas, then to the West, and finally to the North, until the vile institution had spread throughout the United States. Not only was the Kansas-Nebraska Act "a gross violation of a sacred pledge," charged Senator Salmon P. Chase of Ohio, but it was clearly "part and parcel of an atrocious plot to exclude from a vast unoccupied region immigrants from the Old World, and free laborers from our own states, and to convert it into a dreary region of despotism, inhabited by masters and slaves."[2]

Thousands of Northerners who were not abolitionists but nevertheless wished to ban slavery from the frontier also had considered the Missouri line sacrosanct. When they realized that for the first time, land once guaranteed as free soil might be lost to slavery, they too began believing in a "Slave Power" conspiracy. Determined that Kansas should be free, Northerners then organized Emigrant Aid and Save Kansas societies and began pouring men, money, and guns into the new territory. At the same time, Senator William H. Seward of New York flung down the free-state gauntlet, challenged the "gentlemen of the Slave States" to a contest over Kansas, and prayed that "God give the victory to the side that is stronger in numbers as it is in right."[3]

While the majority of Southerners supported the Kansas bill, a few, such as Ruffin, had ambivalent feelings about it. On the one hand, Ruffin had frequently protested that the Missouri Compromise unjustly kept slavery out of the Old Northwest. Yet, on the other hand, he believed that the Missouri line kept "freedom" out of the Southwest and that its existence had thus served as a protective barrier, however feeble, against Northern abolitionism. With this barrier gone, he feared that the South was even more exposed and vulnerable to abolitionist penetration and incendiary attack. Every Northern emigrant would "become a potential abolitionist." He was wary also of popular sovereignty. This democratic principle, which favored the side with superior numbers, seemed to him just another devious Northern trick calculated to ring the South with hostile free states and then launch a mightly and vicious antislavery assault. "If Abolitionism sets its fatal seal upon Kansas," he worried, "then the Union itself will be abolitionized."[4]

But frontier politics often had little respect for democratic theories or superior numbers, and the situation in Kansas was no exception. Although free-state Kansans greatly outnumbered their proslavery neighbors, they were unable to win control of the territorial government. In election after election, hordes of "border ruffians" from the slave state Missouri crossed into Kansas to vote illegally and terrorize free-state settlers, thus insuring proslavery victories. Hostilities flared and, before long, both sides had shed blood, each accusing the other of committing unspeakable "atrocities." By the spring of 1856, a full-scale civil war was raging, and newspapers nick-named the new territory "bleeding Kansas."

The violence that swept Kansas even spilled over into the halls of the United States Congress. In May, Senator Charles Sumner of Massachusetts delivered a brilliant but inflammatory anti-Southern speech blaming slave-holders for "The Crime Against Kansas." Two days later, in retaliation, South Carolina's congressman Preston Brooks marched into the Senate chamber, caught Sumner seated at his desk, and beat him savagely about the head and shoulders with a heavy gutta-percha cane.

Sumner was a member of the newly formed, all-northern Republican party. A coalition of several disparate groups—former Whigs and Demo-crats, freesoilers, nativists and immigrants, farmers and businessmen—the Republicans united mainly in opposition to the Kansas–Nebraska Act. Content to leave slavery alone where it already existed, they were deter-mined nonetheless to protect the territories for free laborers and free white men only. In mid-June, they gathered in convention at Philadelphia and nominated John Charles Fremont for President. Rallying their supporters with reminders of "bleeding Kansas" and "bleeding Sumner," Republicans campaigned under the slogan "free labor, free soil, Fremont."[5]

This intense Northern opposition to the Kansas-Nebraska measure genuinely baffled Southerners at first; then they became angry and suspi-cious. Didn't slaveholders have as much right as any citizens to take their property—their human chattels—into lands all states owned in common? Were Southerners second-class citizens? There was no "Slave Power," they assured their Northern brethren. But there was most assuredly a gigantic abolitionist plot to invade the United States territories, control the federal government, and emancipate the slaves.

When violence erupted in Kansas, many Southerners believed they were witnessing the first stage of this diabolical Northern conspiracy. The emergence and rapid growth of the strictly sectional Republican party seemed like the second step. In reality, though, Republicans advocated a hands-off policy on slavery in the South. In fact, like the majority of North-erners, most Republicans were racists who feared and hated blacks and who had no quarrel with slavery as long as it stayed off the frontier. But few Southerners saw any real difference between the nonextension and the abolition of slavery; to them the terms were interchangeable, and they referred to members of the new party as "Black Republicans." Fremont's nomination raised the horrible specter of an abolitionist sitting in the White House, where he could direct the third and final stage of the conspiracy—freedom for blacks, doomsday for Southern whites.

2

That summer at White Sulphur Springs, conversation naturally centered around the forthcoming presidential election. Even moderate states' rights partisans joined extremists like Ruffin in hot debate over whether or not, in the event of a Fremont victory, the South should secede immediately or wait for an overtly hostile Northern act. Ruffin naturally favored the former course, but he encouraged any kind of secessionist talk. He was surprised and very pleased at the number of guests who agreed with him in private, though they were more cautious than he in airing such extreme views publicly. One guest, Roger Pryor, now an editor for the Richmond *Enquirer,* even offered to print any article Ruffin cared to submit to him, no matter how controversial the content.[6]

In the autumn, Ruffin returned to Marlbourne, and on election day, he dutifully cast his ballot for the Democratic party candidate, pro-Southern James Buchanan of Pennsylvania. Secretly, though, he prayed for Buchanan's defeat, hoping that a Republican victory would precipitate the breakup of the Union. "If Fremont is elected," predicted Virginia's Governor Henry A. Wise, "there will be a revolution."[7]

But Fremont lost the election, and there was no revolution. Most Southerners welcomed Buchanan's victory over "Black" Republicanism, relieved that another possible sectional clash had been averted and that the South—and slavery—were still safe within the Union. Confidently, they reminded themselves that the South, despite its minority status, had always wielded tremendous political power and would continue to do so. Hadn't the recent election proved that point? Southern influence dominated all three branches of the federal government: another "doughface" Northerner was President; the Democratic party controlled both houses of Congress; and Roger Taney, a Southerner and former slaveholder, presided over a sympathetic Supreme Court. If Southerners and their peculiar institution needed further protection, they could depend on the sacred guarantees of the United States Constitution.

Ruffin's view of the recent election was less sanguine. He read in Buchanan's slim victory over Fremont an ominous portent for the future. He could not understand why his countrymen were unable to recognize the obvious danger signals. At night, he lay awake wondering how he could rouse the South "from its sleep of fancied security." Then he remembered

Pryor's offer from the summer before and, in early December, he began writing "On the Consequences of Abolition Agitation and of the Separation of the Union" for the Richmond *Enquirer.* [8]

First, he urged Southerners not to misinterpret Buchanan's election as a decisive victory over Republicans or Northern abolitionism. Foiled "for the present time," the Republicans were neither weakened nor discouraged; they had lost a battle but not the war. Buchanan had won the presidency, but only by the narrowest of margins. The Republican candidate had picked up over half the popular vote in the North and carried all but four Northern states. Had Republicans "more adroitly marshaled and directed" their present forces, warned Ruffin, Fremont, not Buchanan, would be taking the presidential oath of office.

Certainly, he conceded, Southerners had dominated the national government in the past. This was only natural, for slavery's elevating influence trained Southerners to be superior statesman. Men like George Washington, Thomas Jefferson, Patrick Henry, and John C. Calhoun were proof that slaveowners were best "qualified to teach and to lead in public affairs." But politics was no longer the preserve of a qualified elite; there would be no more Southern Presidents. Democracy had turned into a mere numbers game. And as political parties increasingly divided along geographic lines, it was a game in which the North held every trump card, and the South was bound to lose.

Ruffin pointed to the swelling population in the North and demanded how long Southerners could expect to compete for political power and their fair share of the western territories. Every day, overwhelming numbers of newly arrived, newly enfranchised Europeans crowded into northeastern cities or pushed onto the frontier and, he insisted wrongly, joined the ranks of the Republican party. And who were the leaders of this party? he asked. What were their designs? In Ruffin's view, they were "knaves and hypocrites," political abolitionists who cared nothing about the Negro but who whipped up hatred against the slaveholder and used abolition as an ingenious device to satisfy their lust for public office. So clever and devious were these men that they had managed to delude even "sincere abolitionists"—antislavery men of conscience and religion—and easily fooled the ignorant masses into believing that the emancipation of slaves and the South's financial and social ruin would somehow benefit them personally.

And this party of demagogues, of dangerous and unscrupulous abolitionist fanatics, had almost succeeded in placing one of its own in the most powerful office of the land! Ruffin exclaimed. Unless the South acted quickly to sever its relation with the Union, he predicted, Republicans would capture the presidency and the Congress in 1860. Then Southerners would learn, to their sorrow, what flimsy stuff the Constitution was made of.

Once in office, Ruffin explained, the Republican administration would pretend to adopt a conciliatory policy toward the South; it would commit no overt act against slavery. Then, having lulled Southerners into a false sense of security, Republicans would proceed to institute a series of measures—all of them strictly constitutional—designed to undermine the peculiar institution. "The forms or letter of the Constitution," Ruffin reminded Southerners, "may be so used as to destroy its spirit and substance."

First, the President would hand out lucrative patronage jobs only to known abolitionists, until Southern politicians capitulated to their own greed, desperation, or corruption and became antislavery converts. Thousands of these federal appointees would be deployed strategically throughout the slave states, where they could aid the many secret abolitionist agents already hidden there. Naturally, every military officer would also be an abolitionist, so federal forts and arsenals within the South would serve as refuge for runaway slaves and as bases for slave insurrections. Slavery would cease to exist in Washington, D.C., and the nation's capital, located dangerously within slave territory, would become the center for all abolitionist operations. Next, Congress would pass a law forbidding states with excessive numbers of slaves from selling them to states and territories where they were in demand. Since, in some older parts of the South, blacks outnumbered whites by as much as five to one, this law would create a socially dangerous concentration of slaves. Then, to further cement its political grip, the Republican Congress would divide each of the largest free states in half and would refuse to admit any more slave states into the Union. Finally, when Congress was sure it had the necessary approval of three-quarters of the states, it would pass a constitutional amendment abolishing slavery.

Emancipation. Southerners knew only too well what would follow, warned Ruffin. Amalgamation. Degradation. Racial catastrophe. These would be the inevitable results of an abolitionist victory in 1860. And "true abolitionists"—even nonviolent moral suasionists and Christian pacifists like Garrison or Henry Ward Beecher—would not flinch at this awful and bloody tableau but "would welcome all the evils and horrors" befalling their Southern brethren. "Fanaticism," Ruffin cried, "has no moderation, no reason, no mercy."

Even as he wrote, Ruffin heard reports that insidious Northern abolition agents, angry at their recent electoral defeat, had instigated several slave insurrections, which were scheduled to occur simultaneously throughout the South on Christmas day. Panic-stricken, Southerners tightened slave discipline, and in the Beechwood neighborhood, slave patrols went out every night to hunt likely insurrectionists. When Christmas came and went without incident, Ruffin noted, "As usual, all was unfounded & absurd rumor." Yet, "justly or unjustly," he added sadly, "many of the negroes have been put to death." But where he would once have condemned these needless executions as evidence of "community insanity," this time he put the blame entirely on Northern abolitionists. "Such are the only possible results of all such plots of insurrection," he said: "the speedy punishment" of guilty and innocent alike, "increased strictness of general discipline," and a withdrawal of the indulgences "the negroes had before enjoyed." Only increased suffering and misery followed all abolitionist attempts "to benefit & to free the slaves." So, for the sake of their poor slaves, if not for their own safety, begged Ruffin, Southerners must seize the present moment, as the colonists had once done to Great Britain, and declare themselves free and independent of the Federal Union.

If only the South had firmly resisted the first piece of abolitionist legislation, the Missouri Compromise, in 1820, "the spirit of political abolition would have been crushed in the bud," Ruffin said. But since then, and particularly after 1850, "abolition has been hastening toward its object with gigantic strides." Now it was too late to save the nation, so Ruffin openly proclaimed himself a disunionist. And just as he had done in 1850, he assured Southerners that they had everything to gain from secession and nothing to lose. Act now, he promised, and there would be no hostile Northern repercussions, no war between the states. The South would certainly not attack the North, and if Northerners were so foolhardy and reckless as to invade the South, they would suffer a quick and decisive military defeat. In any case, he exhorted his confederates, it was better to fight for freedom than to surrender without a struggle.[9]

3

In February, 1857, Ruffin carried his struggle for Southern "freedom" to Washington, D.C., to the seat of the government he wanted to subvert. He checked into Brown's Hotel on the thirteenth and scurried about the capital for the next ten days, hunting up old friends and former congressional acquaintances, acting as a one-man lobby for secession.

Almost every day he attended Congress, perched high in the Visitors' Gallery of the Senate or the House of Representatives, watching and listening intently to the proceedings below. Once he witnessed "an exciting scene," when the House "corruption committee" found four representatives guilty of accepting bribes. All four, Ruffin noted with satisfaction, were "northerners & abolitionists," and he concluded that, "as a body, the majority of the northern members of congress are as corrupt, & destitute of private integrity, as the majority of southern members are the reverse."[10]

When Congress adjourned after a full day's session, Ruffin usually lingered about, hoping to meet and talk to firm Southern rights supporters and perhaps win others to the cause. He refused an introduction to Sam Houston, the senator from Texas, though, because there were some men, no matter how "great & distinguished," whom a gentleman ought not to acknowledge. "The hero of San Jacinto," Ruffin explained mockingly, was nothing but "a bully & a western rowdy," who had betrayed the South with his "northern" stand on slavery. But he actively sought out Senator Robert Toombs of Georgia to compliment him on recent letters to the Savannah Commercial Convention proposing that the Southern states levy taxes on Northern manufacturing, in order to build up their own home industry. Ruffin urged Toombs to press the matter in Congress, for although he suspected that such discriminatory sectional "tariffs" were unconstitutional, he sensed they might provide one more controversial Union-splitting issue.[11]

On one of his rare days away from Congress, Ruffin paid a visit to the United States minister to Nicaragua, who happened to be in Washington at the time. He was interested, as were many Southerners, in the possibility of United States expansion into all or parts of Central America and the West Indies, countries where the climate and soil seemed well suited to slave-based plantation agriculture. He was somewhat hesitant, though, about colonizing lands which had a large mixed-blood native population; he had a horror of racial intermarriage and feared that some light-skinned mulattoes might escape detection and "contaminate the purity of blood of Caucasian settlers." The two men had a long discussion about the necessity of assuming the white man's burden in all "backward" "colored" countries, and Ruffin left satisfied that "the conquest of these mongrel & semi-barbarous communities, by any civilized power, would be a benefit to the conquered, & to the world." Still, he preferred to postpone annexation until after secession, when the South would be free of the Union and Northern abolitionist interference.[12]

In the evenings, Ruffin dined with Virginia's Senator Robert M. T. Hunter and his "mess" on F Street. Other members of the "mess" included Senator James Mason, Representatives William O. Goode and M. H. R. Garnett of Virginia, and Senator Andrew Butler of South Carolina—a powerful Southern political clique, which dominated weakling Northern Democratic Presidents like Pierce and Buchanan. Although none of these influential and ambitious politicians favored secession, preferring instead their present strong, if impermanent, control of the Democratic party, Ruffin was still flattered that they included him at their dinner table, allowing him to share in their conversation and their political gossip. He learned, for instance, that during the 1856 presidential race, Northern Democrats in New York and New England had spent enormous sums of money to bribe Pennsylvania into the Democratic column and thus insure Buchanan's election. "The victory over Fremont & abolitionism," he exclaimed in shocked surprise, "is worth even less than I had before estimated it." As for Buchanan, members of the F Street "mess" had little use for him and privately called him an "imbecile," even though their support had been crucial to his election. "Never has there been a president . . . who was so plainly denounced & spoken of so contemptuously . . . as Buchanan," marveled Ruffin afterwards. The new President's "reign," he predicted, would bring him little "pleasure or honor."[13]

On February 23, Ruffin packed his bags and prepared to leave Washington. Buchanan's inauguration was less than two weeks away, and already the city was filling with visitors, many of whom came for the sole purpose of begging political favors and collecting patronage spoils from the new administration. Ruffin hastened his departure, for fear someone might mistake him for one of these "base office seekers." But before he left the capital, he saw James D. B. DeBow, who promised to publish "On the Consequences of Abolition Agitation" in his magazine. Delighted, Ruffin returned to Virginia, looking forward to the "attention" as well as the "censure & abuse" his "bold propositions" would receive "in a work of such character as this Review."[14]

4

In May, Ruffin took his "bold propositions" to Charleston, South Carolina. There, through the columns of the Charleston *Mercury,* he laid out a plan for gradual secession. Let the states of the Deep South make use of "the period of truce presented by the late election," he proposed, to declare their independence. For a short time, the states of the Upper South would remain in the Union, serving as a protective buffer zone, in case Northerners got any foolish ideas about invading the infant confederacy. Then, gradually, Virginia and the remaining slave states "would be *forced* to join their southern brethren" and form an invincible new slave nation.[15]

Ruffin's plan impressed Robert Barnwell Rhett, who, recognizing a kindred spirit, made a point of calling on the old Virginian at his hotel. Rhett's impeccable credentials as a fire-eater dated back to the nullification crisis of 1832. Although, like his political archrival, Hammond, he was presently in rather ostentatious retirement from public life, Rhett's interest in secession had not waned in the least. Even Ruffin thought there was no one "more ardent for the measure than he was, & is," but Rhett despaired of "any early or efficient action by any of the southern states." The South, he moaned, lacked "proper leaders."[16]

How heartily Ruffin agreed, and how much he wished he could provide the needed leadership. But these were "degenerate times," in which "the purest integrity & correct morals" and "education of the highest order" were handicaps, obstacles "to an able & [scrupulous] seeker of public honors." For the present, at least, superior intellect and morals had to take a back seat to unprincipled demagoguery. His experience in Washington convinced him, he told Rhett, that some of the South's "strongest men" were aspirants for high federal office "& therefore are self-bribed to a course of inactivity, or submission," while "many others, formerly among the most earnest & zealous for resistance or secession, have abandoned the struggle in sullen despondency or despair."[17]

Among these, Ruffin immediately thought of Hammond, who was still "rusting in solitude" on his Savannah River plantation. Ruffin went to visit his old friend and came away with the impression that, despite Hammond's long absence from public affairs, "he has unquestionably the most powerful mind in the southern states." What a pity that such talent should go untapped.[18]

On July 4, Ruffin wrote to Hammond, begging him once again to come out of seclusion and actively lend a hand to the secession crusade. "A leader is wanting for the south," Ruffin pleaded. "There is no one left of the talent & influence necessary. You are the man for the occasion." Another Southern commercial convention would meet in Knoxville, Tennessee, in August, and Hammond must be there. "Come to the Southern Convention & show that you are not dead for all useful action," Ruffin coaxed. "I will meet you at Knoxville . . . & will be rejoiced to follow your leading in whatever you shall move rightly."[19]

Since the Panic of 1837, Southern commercial conventions had met more or less regularly every year in various cities, for the principal purpose of discussing ways in which the South could improve agriculture, diversify industry, and thus free itself of Northern economic domination. The early conventions were generally innocuous entrepreneurial affairs attended almost exclusively by businessmen and political leaders with commercial interests. But after 1854 and the rise of the Republican party and the "bleeding Kansas" controversy, these commercial bodies increasingly became pseudopolitical forums for promoting Southern unity and Southern rights, and the delegates were mostly politicians or men chiefly concerned with the South's political rather than economic interests. Twice before, Ruffin had attended these gatherings, but he suspected that most of the other delegates were "agents of northern merchants," who "would have lost their profits, if not their bread, by . . . the cessation of commercial dependence on the northern states." Ruffin wanted "a true *southern* convention, in which southern men . . . shall lead & direct the proceedings for the real benefit" of the South. "If you will only do what you are well able to do," he promised Hammond, "this would be but a beginning to a career of usefulness & of high & distinguished honor open to you." But "if you fail to render the service you can do at this juncture," he threatened, "you will forfeit every claim to patriotic feelings and motives."[20]

Promises and threats were of no avail. Hammond, who was at that very moment secretly eying a vacant Senate seat, refused, he said, to "drop my line again into the muddy waters of politics." It is up to "you & the *other* young men," he told the sixty-three-year-old Virginian, to "take care of the country."[21]

5

When the Knoxville Convention opened the next month, Ruffin was not among the delegates; a death in the family kept him at home. Mary Ruffin, Edmund's wife, had been like a daughter to Ruffin, and he mourned her passing as though he had lost one of his own dear children. Mary's death also triggered painful memories of previous family losses—his wife, his three daughters—and made him more aware of his own health and increasing old age. A period of deep depression followed.

He could not sleep at night and wished he could use his many "hours of involuntary watchfulness" to some advantage. As he lay awake tossing in bed, he tried mentally composing future essays on agriculture or secession. But when he tried to write, he discovered regretfully that his composition was as extemporaneous as his day-to-day speech. "I know no more, when beginning a sentence, how it is to be worded, or how it will end, than in the words of my ordinary conversation," he admitted, "& can scarcely think deliberately without having pen in hand." But when he picked up a pen, his quivering hand made legible script impossible. "If I drank intoxicating liquors at all," Ruffin anguished, "my trembling hands, & red face, would cause many strangers to think I was a drunkard."[22]

To Ruffin's further embarrassment, his hours of insomnia cleared up on Sundays during church services, when, despite "all my best efforts," he would doze off repeatedly for short snatches of sleep. Utterly humiliated by this uncontrollable habit, Ruffin debated seriously whether or not to skip future Sunday services, rather than insult the minister and "render myself ridiculous to observers."[23]

Ruffin was generally miserable that autumn, and he took it almost as a personal injury when he weighed himself in September and discovered that he had gained at least five pounds. Weight was a sign of health and happiness. "I am rather ashamed of becoming fatter," he confessed to his diary, "& that it should be generally observed, within the last years, when so many things have occurred to cause me grief & distress."[24]

Outward signs of health to the contrary, Ruffin insisted he was feeble and close to the grave. Hammond, who was somewhat of a hypochondriac himself, read about all his friend's complaints in a letter, then laughed and teasingly offered to insure his life to age eighty. Ruffin declined, preferring, he said, "the uncertainty of my actual life." Besides, who knew how many more children or grandchildren he would lose if he lived another seventeen years. And things even "more grievous" than the death of loved ones might occur. Even now his son Charles, who had resumed his flighty, extravagant ways, gave Ruffin "no pleasure or comfort," while Agnes and the Beckwith family offered him "nothing but subjects for grief, condemnation, & growing alienation." No thank you, he told Hammond, he would not even accept a *guarantee* of seventeen years, for there were so many times now that he "earnestly wished & prayed" for "immediate & unexpected death."[25]

On Tuesday morning, October 6, at Marlbourne, Ruffin's wish almost came true. A few hours before daybreak, he heard loud shouts of "fire." By the time he was outside the entire barnyard was ablaze. Flames consumed the barn, two stables, three corncribs, and all the seedwheat, and although the mansion and all its occupants luckily escaped any harm, financial losses amounted to more than six thousand dollars.[26]

Marlbourne's great fire was the talk of the neighborhood, and at church that Sunday, whites speculated nervously about the suspicious origins of the blaze and the identity of the arsonist or arsonists. Arson was a fairly common mode of slave resistance, and several people suggested that Marlbourne's own blacks might be the guilty culprits. Ruffin vehemently denied these accusations. He did not believe "a tittle of such deductions." *His* slaves were loyal; they would not try to burn their old master and his family in their beds! At the Marlbourne plantation, he argued, "there are no slaves more carefully & properly treated, having better allowances of food & clothing & proper indulgences, & . . . better contented." Yet to himself he admitted that the fire "may have been accidental—or it may have been the incendiary act of a secret enemy."[27]

In any case, the fire jolted Ruffin out of his moodiness and self-pity. Shortly thereafter, he made this seemingly noncommital entry in his diary: "Began to write an article on the institution of slavery—to furnish me with occupation."[28]

8

The Divine Institution

1

ЅOUTHERN ATTITUDES toward slavery had undergone a tremendous shift during the first half of the nineteenth century. In the wake of the egalitarian theories of the American and French revolutions, the tempestuous Missouri debates, and the British emancipation of the slaves in their colonies, most Southern whites felt ashamed, anxious, and apologetic about slavery. Guilt-ridden, they questioned but still clung to their peculiar institution. Then in the 1820s, under the mounting pressures of abolitionist agitation and real and alleged slave conspiracies, these attitudes began to change. A decade later, many Southern whites were boasting that slavery was a positive good, a blessing for both whites and blacks, masters and slaves. And by the 1850s, the new attitude was almost universal throughout the South. "Formerly," Ruffin recalled, "it would have been difficult to find, in Virginia, a man of education who did not deem slavery both a public and private evil. Now there are almost as few such men who do not deem the institution a positive and great benefit." "It would be difficult," exclaimed Hammond, "to find a Southern man who feels the system to be the slightest burthen on his conscience."[1]

Yet despite such ardent protestations of solidarity, Southerners still seemed to require periodic reassurances of the rightness of their position. In the 1850s, as Northern abolitionists stepped up their attacks and the question of slavery's status in the territories kindled sectional disputes, a new and even more militant army of slavery defenders sprang up, apparently in an effort to convince the already convinced. Edmund Ruffin, just

104

retired from management of his Marlbourne plantation and now a full-time secessionist, enlisted in their ranks.

First, he immersed himself in the existing proslavery literature. He subscribed to almost every major proslavery magazine—*DeBow's Review, The Southern Literary Messenger, The South,* and *Russell's Magazine*—and familiarized himself with the current works of authors such as George Fitzhugh, James Hammond, Thornton Stringfellow, Josiah Nott, George Gliddon, John Fletcher, Albert Bledsoe, Joseph Stiles, and George Armstrong. Then for additional inspiration, he turned back to the classic defenses of men like Thomas R. Dew, Edward Brown, John C. Calhoun, William Drayton, Thomas Cooper, Edwin Holland, and others. Dew and Fitzhugh were his favorites. He read Dew's *Review of the Debate in the Virginia Legislature of 1831 and 1832* three times and considered the arguments sublime. Fitzhugh, on the other hand, was "a careless writer—sometimes altogether wrong," but Ruffin judged him "a profound thinker," and each of his major works, *Sociology for the South, or the Failure of the Free Society* and *Cannibals All! or Slaves Without Masters,* merited reading twice.[2]

Having studied and absorbed all the stock arguments of his contemporaries and their predecessors, Ruffin felt that he too could make a contribution to proslavery literature. Like the others, he was also interested in self-justification, for his own identity and sense of worth were unalterably linked to the Southern way of life. His essay, "The Influence of Slavery, or of its Absence on Manners, Morals, and Intellect," originally part of a speech he had delivered in 1852, was in pamphlet form the following year. In 1857, he began writing his most important paper, "The Political Economy of Slavery." He followed this in 1858 with "African Colonization Unveiled" and in 1859 with "Slavery and Free Labor Described and Compared." In addition to these four major works, he sent numerous articles about slavery to *DeBow's* and other friendly Southern journals.

2

Few proslavery authors showed much originality in their arguments, and Ruffin was no exception. Like most of the others, he looked to history for slavery's origins and justification. Bondage in one form or another, he claimed, had existed everywhere in the civilized world. Egyptians, Greeks, and Romans practiced individual slavery; Puritan Massachusetts practiced religious slavery; revolutionary France under Robespierre knew political slavery; masses of Irish and British subjects suffered the slavery of poverty; and throughout the northeastern United States, class, wage, and industrial slavery were advancing rapidly.

Ruffin could think of only one type of individual slavery that was cruel: the slavery of "equals to equals"—that is, the enslavement of people of the same race as their masters. But even this form of slavery had brought riches, culture, and refinement to ancient Egypt, Greece, and Rome. And only Negro slavery had made settlement and civilization of the southern part of the United States possible, giving slaveowners the leisure time to cultivate their mental faculties and enabling the northern section of the country to concentrate on industrial advancement. Thus, for ages, slavery had contributed to the civilized world's mental, moral, and economic progress.[3]

Seventeenth- and eighteenth-century Europeans and Americans never questioned slavery's morality or expediency, and no slaveholder considered himself a sinner, because, claimed Ruffin, slavery was not the South's fault. The British government, greedy and anxious to reap the profits of the lucrative African slave trade, had forced the institution on innocent colonists. The first serious opposition to slavery, he said, arose during the American Revolution, when theoretical doctrines of man's equal natural rights led some Americans, like Thomas Jefferson, to condemn slavery and hope for its ultimate extinction. But Ruffin was sure that even Jefferson would never have advocated immediate abolition.

True, Ruffin conceded, the Fathers of the Revolution, among them Southern slaveowners, had admitted the legitimacy of that "indefensible passage" of the Declaration of Independence which proclaimed that all men are created equal. But at the time, they had understood this to mean the guarantee of equal rights for all free-born Englishmen, not for all mankind. Thus, he insisted, the slaveholding Southerners who wrote and signed the Declaration of Independence did so inadvertently, for they "no more thought of legislating for, or producing the freedom and equal political rights of their negro slaves, than they did of their horses and oxen." "Yet," he complained, "this mere sounding verbiage, these empty reverberations of a baseless and obscure theoretical doctrine . . . have since served as the citadel of defense for the new and zealous party of abolitionists of negro slavery, and the arsenal to supply their chosen weapons to assail that institution." This doctrine of inalienable rights was not only "false and dangerous," but also "foolish," for the next legitimate deduction might be that every *woman* had natural political rights equal to those of men. Ruffin understood that just such a heretical women's rights doctrine had infected parts of the North, but he was relieved that the ladies and gentlemen of the South seemed to be immune.[4]

Mankind, he said, was born neither free nor equal. He subscribed to the doctrine of the inequality of natural rights. To him, the moral authority for the institution of Negro slavery and the rights of slaveholders corresponded with the authority of government and the rights of private property. Likewise, the duties of the slave to obey his master corresponded with the "duties of the destitute & the powerless to respect & obey the possession by others of all the property & all the political power of the world."[5]

The master–slave relationship, he argued, was no more unjust than the inequalities of wealth, property, and political power found in almost every society. The majority of people always had less of these than did the very few. And no one but "rabid socialists" found fault with these inequalities. In England and in the North, where abolitionists wrote and spoke so eloquently in favor of equality and freedom for black slaves, there existed visible inequalities in all the aforementioned categories. Yet "no English philanthropist, or Northern antislavery writer, has denounced all hereditary magistrates and rulers as usurpers, and all property-holders as unjust and fraudulent possessors—and declared that both these classes of usurpers and robbers ought to be deprived of their acquisitions for the benefit of the multitude of destitute persons, whose equal rights had been thereby violated."[6]

By 1830, partly because of the fallacious natural rights philosophy, both England and the North had ended slavery or taken steps to abolish the institution, Ruffin explained. Their climates and economies did not depend on slave labor, and their population of blacks was small. But for the South, slavery was an economic necessity and, because of the presence of so many blacks, an indispensable means of racial control. Abolition meant economic destruction, social chaos. Most Northerners and British were willing to leave slavery alone in the South, but in Ruffin's view, the English and the Yankees, after ridding themselves of slavery and safeguarding their own property interests, had turned on the South with complacent and hypocritical self-righteousness. Alleging benevolent motives, they urged slavery's extinction at the expense of the South, and this would mean the ruin of the master class.[7]

3

As part of this anti-Southern plot, charged Ruffin, Northern abolitionists supported the efforts of the American Colonization Society. Formed in 1816, the Society's earliest patrons were slaveholders themselves, and the Society's object was to induce free blacks to voluntarily emigrate and colonize Liberia, a country in Africa. These free blacks, Ruffin explained, had become a nuisance, particularly in the Upper South, where their presence made slaves "discontented with their more constrained, though really much better condition."[8]

But the Society's members did not content themselves merely with trying to export the potentially troublesome free black population. They also promoted a program of gradual emancipation, offering to transplant slaves whose masters volunteered to set them free, a program which would eventually have emptied the South of its cheapest source of labor. Meanwhile, he said, Northern members who hoped to ruin the planter class hired abolitionist agents to pose as ministers and travel throughout the South, preying on the "morbidly tender consciences" of religious slaveowners. Individual acts of manumission, the agents would assure gullible masters, were signs of virtue and piety—practically an admission ticket to heaven —while removal of free blacks from the United States was a public benefit.[9]

Not all American Colonization Society members acted out of selfish or malicious intentions, Ruffin admitted. Many joined the organization out of "mistaken philanthropy," "sickly sentimentality," and a "false theory" which believed to an incredible and absurd extent in the potential of black intelligence. Some colonizationists even thought blacks and whites possessed equal mental powers and blamed Negro ignorance and vice on the black man's inferior social, economic, and political status in the United States and not, as Ruffin felt truth required, on inherent black physical and mental inferiority.

The American Colonization Society also believed that blacks were capable of self-government, and in 1820, they attempted to prove their theories by sending the first colony of eighty-nine American blacks to Liberia. Africa and the whole world would benefit, they hoped, from the example set by this civilized, industrious, and Christian black colony. Through this first handful of colonists, Ruffin believed, the Society expected to spread the Christian gospel to the sixty million "savage pagans and brutal idolators" inhabiting "the Dark Continent."[10]

For a variety of reasons, the Liberian experiment failed. Few free blacks, most of whom were born in the United States, wished to emigrate to Africa, and those who did were often unprepared for the harsh and unfamiliar conditions: an unhealthy climate, large snakes, and hostile natives. Moreover, despite many petitions for financial aid, the colonists received only meager support from Congress. As a result, the birth rate plummeted, the death rate soared, and after almost forty years, the colonists were not only unable to produce a single commodity export, but they could not even raise enough agricultural produce to support themselves. Famine was common, and many of the settlers sent pathetic letters to their former masters bemoaning their terrible fate.[11]

For Ruffin, Liberia's failure was an immense source of satisfaction. He contended that the problems in the colony only proved that blacks were inferior and that slavery was a humanitarian necessity. Liberia, he said, "affords the clearest evidence that the negro will not work, nor take care of his support, unless compelled by a master of the white race." To buttress his arguments, he read dozens of British and American journals and newspapers, clipping out all the "evidence" he could find on the failure of the colonization, emancipation, and black self-government not only in Liberia but in black-ruled Haiti and Jamaica as well. He even attended some American Colonization Society meetings and read the Society's official organ, *The African Repository,* but he always discounted all but the most pessimistic reports. Then he shared his findings with fellow Southerners in his article "African Colonization Unveiled."[12]

Negrophilists, he wrote, had blamed the degradation of blacks on slavery's "depressing" influence. But the Liberian colonists were free men and women who had had every opportunity to make their experiment a success. Some of them even had the added advantage of some white blood! And "experts" had testified to Liberia's soil fertility. So it was obvious, he concluded, that blacks, even under the best of circumstances, were incapable of self-direction without the help of an "enlightened master." "The true cause of the great and general neglect of agricultural pursuits, and the omission of labor," he argued, "is simply the natural aversion of the negro to regular and laborious toil—and his unwillingness to resort to continued labor so long as he can live, though ever so poorly, in idleness." Ruffin suggested that the colonists' only real chance for survival would be to enslave the native Africans and force them to work.

Colonization, Ruffin decided, was "a delusion and a snare." The colonists themselves knew this better than anyone else, and many of them, he insisted, would welcome the chance to return to the South and voluntary reenslavement. And if Virginia's own free black population had to choose between emigration to Liberia or perpetual servitude, he was willing to wager that three-fourths would opt for slavery. But members of the American Colonization Society and its supporters were "benevolent dupes," who stubbornly refused to recognize their mistake. "The longer the aid and support to the Colonization Society, and to Liberia," he predicted, "the more complete will be the experiment of the measure of the negro intellect, and the more conclusive will be the end result, in evidence of its inferiority, and its need for the direction and control of masters of a superior race."[13]

4

So convinced was Ruffin of the Negro's intellectual inferiority that he dismissed or explained away any contradictory evidence. Once, after reading a book extolling black mental capabilities, he learned to his amazement that the author was a black man and a graduate of Cambridge University. Cambridge, he sniffed, had no doubt awarded the man a diploma simply because he was black. But he conceded that "I would not deny the possibil-

ity of one negro in a hundred thousand cases being capable of receiving a
college education, & being competent to write a commonplace address."

Still, he was surprised whenever any black showed signs of intelligence.
When Jem Sykes, his black foreman, boasted that Marlbourne's present
abundant crops were the result of his old master's early marling efforts,
Ruffin was "especially gratified." But Sykes startled him too, for he "did
not expect a negro, even of superior intelligence as he is, to look back to
causes so remote, & of such gradual action." Nor could Ruffin accept the
musical genius of a slave known only as "Blind Tom," a self-taught pianist
and composer whose master had him performing in concerts throughout the
South. Ruffin remarked that Tom resembled an orangutan and then
dismissed his genius as mere "tricks."[14]

If anyone needed further proof that blacks were inherently ignorant
and lazy, Ruffin declared, he need only examine the lack of progress of free
blacks in the North. During all their long years of freedom, Ruffin declared,
few Northern blacks had acquired any considerable property or wealth, and
not a single individual displayed "remarkable, or even more than ordinary,
power of intellect—or any power of mind that would be deemed worth
notice in any individual of the white race." This observation was even more
astonishing, he exclaimed, because in the North, blacks and whites had
equal access to free schools, and many blacks were college graduates.[15]

This was, of course, far from a true picture of life in the North. There,
abolitionist and black demands for economic, political, social, and educational rights for blacks usually met with community resistance and often
violence. Nevertheless, Ruffin insisted that "nothing but the immutable
decree of God, fixing on [Negroes] mental inferiority, has prevented high
grades of intellect and of learning." "God," he said, "has created and
designed the negro race to be inferior in intellect to the white," superior only
in obedience, docility, and the ability to endure the heat and diseases of
tropical climates. In other words, God had Southern slavery in mind when
He created blacks. This was "an indisputable fact."[16]

The defenders of slavery had often invoked God's name to explain and
justify human bondage. Men like the Reverend Thornton Stringfellow
hunted through the Bible for evidence that the God of the Old and New
Testaments endorsed slavery. The institution began, they said, in Genesis
9:25 when Noah, acting as God's mouthpiece, cursed his son Ham, declaring, "A servant of servants shall he be unto his brethren." Blacks were the
descendants of Ham, and whites descended from "his brethren." By "servants," God had meant slaves. Turning to the New Testament and pointing
out that the Apostle Paul had sent the runaway servant Onesimus back to
his master, Southerners concluded that Jesus himself had underwritten the
fugitive slave laws.[17]

Ruffin, though, refused to accept such biblical justifications for slavery. He also read the Bible but could not find any logical proof in Genesis that Africans or blacks were Ham's descendants. Furthermore, he reasoned, Ham was guilty only of "an act of unfilial conduct, . . . not worse than almost every parent has had to bear from some child." A just, merciful God would not approve and carry out Noah's curse, which punished "not the truly guilty son, but his innocent posterity," dooming a third of the human race to live for all time "in degradation & misery."[18]

In the 1850s, Ruffin and other Southerners who rejected slavery's biblical defense turned to an increasingly popular scientific justification for the institution. Josiah C. Nott and George R. Gliddon, a doctor and an archaeologist respectively, zealously compared hundreds of Negro and white skulls. In 1854, they published *Types of Mankind,* which put forth the proposition that blacks and whites were not two different races of mankind but two entirely different and separately created species. Blacks were at the lowest end of human creation, their species falling somewhere between homo sapiens and the chimpanzee or orangutan. This doctrine contradicted the biblical account of man's creation and naturally raised storms of protest from clerics and biblical apologists who insisted on the unity of mankind. Ruffin confessed that he was deeply interested in this controversy and read every book he could find on the subject. But in the end, he refused to endorse either the scientists or the biblical scholars, finding more "amusement" than reliable information on either side. All the writers, he noted, had the same shortcoming. They made facts secondary to their own beliefs, a fault Ruffin did not recognize in his own proslavery arguments.[19]

For instance, although he privately rejected the story of Noah's curse and the biblical justification for slavery, Ruffin did believe that God favored slavery. In his lectures and speeches, moreover, he often referred to the institution's divine origins. And despite his own religious skepticism, he appreciated the value of having organized religion, if not God, on his side. He was pleased when those he called "ultra abolitionists" in the North denounced the Bible because it supported slavery. "This must array against them the power of the Christian Church," he gloated, "& that power is enough to put down an opposing doctrine." To audiences in South Carolina and Virginia, he swore, "If there is any institution of divine origin, slavery, and especially African slavery is such an institution." Hadn't the patriarchs of the Old Testament—"the most virtuous and the most favored of God's ancient worshippers"—been slaveholders? Judging from slavery's early existence and continued duration, its promotion of industry, culture, and all the good things in life, he concluded, "it seems to me an inevitable deduction, that the institution of slavery is as surely and manifestly established by the wise and benevolent design of God, as the institution of marriage and of parental rule—and it is next to these, and inferior to these only, in producing important benefits to mankind."[20]

One of slavery's most important benefits, according to Ruffin, was its Christianizing effects on heathen Africans. He argued that the institution of slavery was the world's most effective proselytizer of religion, successful in bringing black savages to a Christian God, where the best efforts of colonizationists and missionaries had failed. "There is no possible mode of either civilizing or changing the religion of a savage and numerous people," he stated, "other than by . . . subjecting them to slavery." He followed with great interest the missionary exploits of Robert Livingstone in South Africa. Livingstone had reported that the natives he met were "good & kind in disposition," but Ruffin thought it was more significant that after five years of extensive travel and missionary work, Livingstone had not made a single Christian convert. Livingstone, Ruffin admitted, was "a most pious & devoted Christian, & a brave man," but he would have done the Africans a greater favor had he purchased a large tract of land from a friendly chief and then enslaved the natives. Enslaving Africans under a civilized Christian white master, he asserted, would have made more converts out of heathens "than the mere preaching of 100 missionaries for as long a time."[21]

Southern slaveowners, therefore, were among the world's most successful missionaries. Ruffin pointed proudly to statistics which showed that in 1855, "heathen churches" all over the world held only 180,000 members, while the Southern Methodist Church alone claimed a membership of 175,000 slaves and twice that number belonged to other Southern churches. As for colonization, he said, there was no guarantee that former Christian slaves would act to spread the faith as freedmen. In fact, he had heard rumors that there was a great deal of religious backsliding among Liberians. There were numerous cases, he asserted, where once Christian freedmen refused to attend church and slipped back to their former heathen and savage ways.[22]

5

For these and other reasons, Ruffin opposed any emancipation plan, even if it included compensation to slaveholders and colonization of free blacks outside the United States. The cost of compensating every slaveholder would be far too great for any slave state government, he said, and money-grubbing Yankees certainly would not allow the federal government to foot the bill for Southern slaves. Moreover, despite its intentions, the American Colonization Society would never be able to remove all free blacks to Liberia. Most would remain inside the United States, primarily in the

South. The presence of millions of free blacks would mean that a race war was inevitable. "Let it never be forgotten," another proslavery voice, Edwin C. Holland, had warned years earlier, that "our NEGROES are truly the *Jacobins* of the country; that they are the *anarchists* and the *domestic enemy,* the *common enemy of civilized society,* and the barbarians who would, IF THEY COULD, become the DESTROYERS *of our race.*" Ruffin recalled how the Jacobin leader Robespierre, having urged France to free its slaves in Santo Domingo despite warnings of calamity, had shouted, "Perish the colonies, rather than sacrifice one iota of our principles!" Northern abolitionists subscribed to this same "atrocious declaration," said Ruffin, when they knew full well that the result of black emancipation would be "discontent, insubordination, & bloody insurrection."[23]

Ruffin accused Southern colonizationists of being the unwitting dupes of bloodthirsty Northern abolitionists. First, their efforts to convince masters to manumit their slaves discredited the South's peculiar institution in the eyes of the rest of the world by casting doubts on slavery's benevolent aspects. After all, some people might wonder why, if slavery was such a blessing to blacks, slaveowners would "reward" their slaves with freedom. Worse still, the Society's campaign to convince freed slaves to emigrate to Africa drained the South of needed laborers and promoted servile rebellion, for the same words used to induce reluctant blacks to colonize Liberia filtered into the slave community and made formerly happy slaves feel wronged and discontented.[24]

6

Ruffin favored one type of colonization scheme, though, and he worked it into a unique plan which he presented in 1858 in his article, "The Free Negro Nuisance and How to Abate It." Since slavery was so good for blacks, he proposed a method to enslave Southern free blacks or "colonize" them to the North. He stated that the number of free blacks living in the South was a nuisance. As a class, they were "lazy, improvident, degraded in every respect, vicious, incorrigible and shameless." To get rid of this nuisance, Virginia and the other slave state legislatures should pass a series of laws converting present prison sentences for black criminals into terms of slavery. The length of enslavement would vary from five years to life, according to the seriousness of the crime. In addition, the state should require all free blacks either to show evidence of honest employment or be classified as idle, destitute, and vicious. This latter class, wrote Ruffin, although guilty of no crime except "bad habits," should be sold to the highest bidder for two years. At the end of the two years, these slaves would be free again, but if they resumed their bad habits, the punishment would be perpetual servitude.

Before these Black Laws went into operation, Ruffin suggested, the state should allow free Negroes to emigrate and "colonize" the Northern states. Honest, hard-working free blacks would stay in the South, he believed, while the loss of potential criminals to the free states was really the South's gain.

These ideas on how to deal with free Negroes were not entirely original. In 1854, Fitzhugh had asked "What Shall Be Done with the Free Negroes?" and suggested that the answer was to return them all—criminal and law-abiding—to slavery. And several Northern states, fearful of black "colonization" within their borders, had already adopted Black Laws to restrict or exclude Negroes. Still, former President John Tyler thought Ruffin's penal reforms added a new twist to an old theme. He congratulated his old friend on finding "the *juste milieu,*" the perfect solution to Virginia's free Negro problem, enabling the state to rid itself of lazy, good-for-nothing blacks and to keep honest and industrious blacks. "Expel the first by all means," Tyler urged, "and give to our *Northern brethren* the full benefit of their darling race."[25]

Ruffin felt that he had also found the perfect solution to a problem which bothered free blacks themselves. He was sure that there were countless unhappy, impoverished free Negroes who would jump at the chance to become slaves. A small population of sober, honest, hard-working blacks would remain free, but soon even they would die out. Sobriety, honesty, and industry were uncommon traits in the Negro, he maintained, and rarely extended to a second or third generation. Confidently, he predicted that within a few generations after his plan went into effect, "there would probably remain in Virginia no negroes except such as were in their proper and only suitable condition—that of being slaves to white masters."[26]

7

In Ruffin's view, Southern blacks were not only in their most proper and suitable condition as slaves, but they were actually much better off than most free white laborers. For proof, he pored over federal census returns, Parliamentary reports on the operation of the Poor Laws, and reviews from British and Northern periodicals, searching hungrily for the flaws and failures of free society. Like other proslavery apologists, he accepted the descriptions of horrible factory and industrial conditions at face value. He made no allowances for reformers' occasional exaggerations.

After a determined investigation, all of it secondhand, he concluded that the term "free labor" was a misnomer. "Free labor," in so-called "free society" was really wage and pauper slavery, "the slavery of labor to want." The "miserable millions" of Northern and British free laborers were "as truly and fully slaves to want, cold, hunger, and every threatened greater misery of destitution," he contended, "as even *lash-driven* negro servants of Virginia are slaves to their masters."[27]

Ruffin rarely spoke of lash-driven slaves. In fact, he hotly denied abolitionists' accusations that slaveowners were brutal men who mistreated their slaves, and he alleged that the free labor system was a much crueler institution. Whenever some men had power over others, he admitted, there was bound to be some cruelty and injustice in the exercise of that power. This was a "deplorable truth." Slavery had its evils, its injustices, but so did all social institutions, including marriage and the family. Why weren't "sickly philanthropists" calling for their abolition? Indeed, argued Ruffin, cases of cruelty to slaves were as exceptional as cases of wife beating or child abuse.[28]

Like the majority of husbands and parents, he continued, slaveowners were kind, just, and benevolent masters, who realized that it was in their own best interest to preserve the life and health of their dependents. Slaves, after all, were valuable property, and cruel or capricious treatment might damage that property or make it surly and disobedient. Thus, the owner would not receive the maximum return on his investment if he did not treat his slaves properly. Besides, genuine ties of affection and devotion, which went beyond mere self-interest and the profit motive, bound many masters and slaves. These lifelong personal attachments between master and slave should be contrasted with the purely economic feelings of Northern employers toward their frequently changing "free" employees. These heartless Northern capitalists had only one rule, Ruffin said, and that was to obtain the most labor for the least wages.

And in times of financial depression, what was the fate of free labor? he demanded. Without jobs, free labor was free only to starve in the North or enter the poorhouse in England. But in good times or ill, Southern slaves had employment, roofs over their heads, and the comforts of family, health, and old age care. The death of a Northern wage slave was no concern to his employer, and the loss of an English pauper was a gain for his parish. But in the South, slaveowners cherished and valued the lives of their bondsmen, and the death of a slave was a tragedy. Who could doubt that the life of a Southern slave was "immeasurably superior & preferable" to the life of a free laborer? Compared to the latter, the slave's life was "one of comfort, ease and happiness."[29]

"Even among the most fanatical denouncers of negro slavery," Ruffin was certain, "there are few who, if acquainted with both conditions, would not admit that the far greater amount of suffering is to be found in the class

which they falsely term 'free laborers.' " If the Northern and British abolitionists were not such hypocrites, they would cease their harassment of
innocent slaveowners and work to abolish the evils of industrial wage
slavery in their own midst. "Yet," he declared, "all these statesmen, theoretical reformers, and socialists of every sect, who have all the horrors of class
slavery standing and growing under their eyes, neglect its miseries and
victims to unite in one universal howl of denunciation of negro slavery."[30]

8

Ruffin believed that socialists were "the most malignant enemies of slaveholders," but he was perplexed that this should be the case. He felt that
logically, they should be slaveholders' best friends. Both socialists and
slaveholders combated the evils of industrial capitalism through a form of
"associated labor." But slaveholders had improved on the socialists' doctrine by supplying "the first and great motive power, which is to be found
only in one directing mind, and one controlling will." Add this "single
ruling power"—the master—and "the association is thereby converted to
the condition of *domestic slavery.*" For Ruffin, then, domestic slavery was
the best form of socialism, "the realization of all that is sound and valuable
in the socialists' theories and doctrines." As Fitzhugh had said, the Southern plantation was "the beau ideal of Communism."[31]

As in Fitzhugh's case, the more Ruffin thought about the South's
peculiar institution, the more convinced he became that domestic slavery
would be the best form of associated labor not just for blacks but for most
whites too. He said that in every society, whether free or slave, savage or
civilized, there existed a lower class of individuals—a "mud-sill," Hammond called them—who were naturally lazy and who, if left alone, would
avoid all work, preferring lives of abject poverty. "In all such cases," Ruffin
believed, the best solution to this problem "would be the enslaving of these
reckless, wretched drones and cumberers of the earth, and thereby compel-
ling them to habits of labor." In return, the master would provide for all
his slaves' material needs, while "raising them and their progeny in the scale
of humanity, not only physically, but morally and intellectually." The
majority of free white laborers in the North would be much better off as
domestic slaves, he argued, than as wage slaves to heartless industrial
capitalists.[32]

9

But when it came to the subject of profits, Ruffin was every inch a capitalist.
Fitzhugh's feudal inclinations had made him critical of the profit motive,

but Ruffin thought Fitzhugh was "foolish." "What inducement would there be to accumulate, if it could yield no profit?" he demanded. And what could be more profitable than slave labor?[33]

In both "Slavery and Free Labor Described and Compared" and "The Political Economy of Slavery," Ruffin argued that the common expression, "free labor is cheaper than slave labor," was both hackneyed and untrue. He denied what he called the popular misconception that a free worker, laboring for his own profit, worked harder and more efficiently than a slave laboring under fear and coercion.

On the surface, he conceded, free labor seemed cheaper and more profitable than slave labor. The free man had more incentive to work hard, while the slave, he said, "has every inducement to spare himself as much as possible, and to do as little work as he possibly can, without drawing on himself punishment, which is the only incentive to slave labor." Ruffin may not have realized that this admission cast grave doubts on his previous assurances about the infrequency of slave mistreatment. But he did point out that slave labor was continual service, while free labor was not. Moreover, few truly "free" laborers were industrious. The majority, he contended, were indolent men and women who worked only two or three days per week, enough to acquire life's necessities. The rest of the week, they loafed. So, while it was true that slaves were rarely as efficient as industrious free workers, they were far superior to the great numbers of lazy and improvident free workers. And, he added, free workers were much less docile, contented, and tractable than slaves. Therefore, slavery was the cheaper and more profitable labor system.[34]

Even if free labor were cheaper than slave labor, Ruffin said, the institution of slavery had many human and social benefits which outweighed any of free society's materialistic advantages. The slave South was clearly a superior civilization. If anyone needed proof, he could consult Thornton Stringfellow's 1856 study, *Scriptural and Statistical Views of Slavery.* Stringfellow had used the United States census of 1850 to compare five of the oldest Southern states—Maryland, Virginia, North Carolina, South Carolina, and Georgia—with the six New England states. On the basis of this comparison, which left out most of the states in the North and South, Ruffin drew definitive conclusions about the differences between slave and free society.

First, the census revealed that the Southern states had higher birth rates and lower death rates than the Northern states. Second, the South had more churches than the North, which proved to Ruffin the religious superiority of slave society. The Northern states, on the other hand, were "superior" only in their far greater number of blind persons, deaf-mutes, paupers, idiots, lunatics, and criminals.[35]

But an even more shocking difference, Ruffin noted, was a "condition of moral debasement and depravity" which was "extremely common in the North, and so rare in the south, that cases of parracide and incest are not more infrequent occurrences." "This," he asserted, "is the marriage, or cohabitation, of white women with negro men." Pointedly, he omitted any mention of sexual relations between white men and black women, because on this issue Southerners themselves were extremely vulnerable. One unusually frank Southern woman, Mary Boykin Chesnut, the wife of a senator from South Carolina, complained to her diary: "Like the patriarchs of old, our men live all in one house with their wives and their concubines; and the mulattoes one sees in every family partly resemble the white children." According to the 1860 census, over half a million mulattoes lived in the South. How could southerners explain this embarrassingly large mixed population? But unlike the forthright Mrs. Chesnut, most Southerners either ignored the problem or tried to hide it. "Any lady is ready to tell you who is the father of all the mulatto children in everybody's household but her own," Chesnut exclaimed. "Those, she seems to think, drop from the clouds."[36]

Privately, Ruffin deplored these "revolting cases of vice among slave-owners," because they gave "color" "to the general libel of such writers as Mrs. Stowe" and provided ammunition to other Northern abolitionists who accused slaveowners of lechery and called the South a giant brothel. Publicly though, Ruffin, like Mrs. Chesnut's lady friends, hid his own reservations, ignored the evidence of racial mixing, and pretended that it simply did not exist in the South. As usual, whatever shamed Ruffin he denied and attributed to others. So, like many other anxious Southerners, he responded to abolitionist accusations with unintentional irony, attacking Northern free society for its inferior morality while claiming superior virtue for the South and slavery.[37]

10

Even with all this "evidence" of Southern superiority, Ruffin admitted that statistics showed that the North, with its more diversified economy, was wealthier than the South. But these figures were deceptive, he maintained. While it was true that land was more valuable in the North, the difference in prices was a result of two entirely different systems of agriculture and not of the inferiority of slave labor. Furthermore, if Northern society was wealthier than Southern society, it was because Northern profits came out of Southern pockets. In Ruffin's opinion, discriminatory federal legislation had fostered and protected Northern commerce and manufacturing at the South's expense. Northern prosperity, then, was really founded on Southern

Negro slavery and not, as critics alleged, on the superiority of the free labor system.[38]

Besides, Ruffin could see a time fast approaching when there would be no more free laborers left in the North, only class and wage slaves. Free labor, he explained, depended on the law of supply and demand. When the demand for labor was greater than the supply, the laborer was free to choose his employer and demand higher wages and shorter hours. But when supply outstripped demand, capitalists gained the upper hand, and free laborers became wage slaves, forced to toil almost continuously for mere subsistence pay. At present, Ruffin admitted, most Northern workers were free, but this was because of a peculiar and changing set of circumstances. The availability of abundant, fertile, and cheap western lands drained off the excess labor supply from the industrial northeast, keeping the population sparse in comparison to the territory and enhancing labor's bargaining position vis-à-vis capital. But, he warned, "whenever the valuable vacant lands shall have been all settled upon" and the frontier was gone, "the supply of labor shall ... greatly exceed the demand." "Then in New England, as has already been effected in Old England," he predicted, "*slavery to want* will be established rigidly, and in the form most oppressive and destructive to the laborers, but the most profitable of all slavery to the employers, the capitalists."[39]

Wage slavery, he conceded, was even cheaper and more profitable than black domestic slavery. But the long-term social and economic costs were disastrous. Wage slavery brought with it class slavery and widespread ignorance, poverty, and crime among the masses. Capitalists enslaved the bodies of their employees, and unscrupulous political demagogues would soon enslave their minds. When that happened, Ruffin argued, revolution would follow. The "spirit of agrarianism, communism, and anti-rentism ... will govern!" And "then may be looked for such regard to property, liberty and life, as was seen in the like calamitous time of the Reign of Terror and of Robespierre."[40]

There was only one way for Northerners to prevent this "threatening consummation." Propertied men of the North and South must unite in defense of African slavery. Like Calhoun, Ruffin thought slavery was "the balance wheel of the government" and that its conservative influence protected the lives and property of all Americans. Abolish slavery in the South, he thundered, and the North will fall into the "abysses of class slavery" and revolution.

In the South, where labor and capital were identical and the institution of slavery united whites of all classes by promoting the idea of white supremacy, there was no labor–capital conflict, no sign of class warfare. Slaves loved their masters; poor whites mingled with gentlemen on terms of easy familiarity. How Ruffin pitied the uneasy sleep of wealthy Northerners, whose lives and property were menaced by their workers and poorer neighbors. Southern slaveowners, he insisted, slept soundly, secure in the knowledge that even if they left their doors and windows wide open and put deadly weapons within reach of every slave, they were far safer than their brothers and sisters in the North.[41]

11

In March, 1858, Ruffin was at the Beechwood plantation finishing "The Political Economy of Slavery" when word came that there had been another fire at Marlbourne. No one was hurt, but the new stable and granary had burned to the ground, causing considerable financial loss. Even more disturbing was the fact that this was Marlbourne's second fire in less than six months, and the circumstances surrounding the second blaze were almost identical to the first. Even Ruffin had to conclude that the fires were not accidental.

But who, he asked himself, could be the "malignant & unscrupulous" incendiary, the "secret enemy, against whom it is impossible to guard?" Perhaps it was some jealous poor white of "bad habits" who lived nearby. But Ruffin's neighbors had different suspicions. Again they hinted that Marlbourne's blacks might be the secret enemy, and again Ruffin vehemently denied their accusations and defended his slaves' fidelity. To have done otherwise would not only have jeopardized his version of Southern slavery, but it would also have undermined the core of his social and political philosophy. The plantation system Ruffin described in his proslavery literature represented his idealized vision, his dream of what Southern society should be: a place harmoniously ordered on the principles of man's natural inequalities, governed benevolently by enlightened masters like himself, stewards whose legitimate authority and power to control others derived from their special talents as thinkers and their demonstrated moral superiority.

"But still," Ruffin later confided to his diary, "it was entirely within the power of any slave on the farm, safe from discovery or suspicion to have caused the great fires. And the very idea that some one whether on or off the farm, has twice so acted, & can again so act, is enough to cause bad & uneasy feelings in us all."[42]

9

Cassandra's Warnings

1

MARLBOURNE'S FIRE was the only excitement Ruffin had that winter. By mid-March, 1858, he was bored. He tried to tell himself that he didn't regret having given up Marlbourne to his children. He was glad that business matters no longer bothered him, that retirement from the plantation had freed him for other occupations. Yet there were still so many empty hours to fill. "My time is hanging heavy on my hands," he complained to his diary. "I must find something to do."[1]

So, in April, he went searching for "amusement" in Washington, D.C. He wanted to see some friends, and perhaps he could find a publisher for "The Political Economy of Slavery." On the fifteenth, he checked into Brown's Hotel but discovered that he would have to pay as much as $2.50 to $3.00 per day for "wretched accomodations" and worse meals. After one uncomfortable night "on the hard lumps of an old mattress," a disgusted Ruffin paid his bill, checked out of this "first-class hotel," and moved to a private boarding house. Then he called on James Hammond, who had recently emerged from political retirement to accept a seat in the Senate.[2]

Hammond told him that all of Washington was in an uproar over Kansas and the Lecompton bill. Ruffin was not surprised. He knew that the Buchanan administration had pressured Congress all winter to admit Kansas into the Union as the sixteenth slave state under the notoriously fraudulent Lecompton constitution. This proslavery constitution was a product of the rigged elections and stuffed ballot boxes which had become the norm in Kansas politics. Free-state Kansans had shown their contempt for the bogus constitutional convention and the equally bogus document it produced by staying away from the polls and refusing to participate in any way.

In the North, Republicans and many Democrats denounced Lecompton as a flagrant violation of popular sovereignty. Abolitionists saw Lecompton as one more step in a growing Slave Power conspiracy. Southerners, who were equally conspiracy-minded, defended Lecompton as the people's choice and pushed for Kansas's admission as a slave state.[3]

Ruffin had mixed feelings about the Kansas situation. Initially, he had hoped that Congress would defeat the Lecompton measure. "By adhering to & sustaining the slave-constitution of Kansas, which is universally admitted not to express the will of the people," he said, "the south will appear to support what is wrong for selfish ends." Worse, Southerners would play into the hands of conniving Northern abolitionists.

Following his own special logic, Ruffin explained that free-soil Kansans had deliberately stayed home from the polls in order to give abolitionists an issue to use in the next presidential campaign. In other words, abolitionists wanted a proslavery victory in Kansas, and the Lecompton constitution was really a diabolical antislavery tool. So if Kansas came into the Union as a slave state, he argued, "it will be an apparent gain & victory to the south, but in a bad cause." Besides, the free-soil majority in Kansas would soon overturn Lecompton and substitute a new constitution prohibiting slavery. So "even if the south conquers in Congress, it will be defeated soon after."[4]

But when Democrats Stephen A. Douglas, senator from Illinois and architect of the Kansas–Nebraska Act, and Henry A. Wise, governor of Virginia, expressed similar anti-Lecompton sentiments, Ruffin abruptly changed his mind. He did not want to identify himself with "these two distinguished demagogues," these presidential hopefuls with their "immeasurable & unscrupulous ambition." Southerners *should* vote to admit Kansas under Lecompton, he now argued. The constitution had arrived in Washington according to all the forms of legality, and it was not up to Congress to investigate the matter any further. The fight for Kansas had never been fair anyway. Northern abolitionists had secretly conspired with Buchanan's administration (an administration, Ruffin forgot to mention, which was dominated by Southerners) to flood the territory with antislavery emigrants. Illegal proslavery electoral maneuvers, he said, were a necessary, if regrettable, effort to even the odds and win the contest.[5]

When Congress took up the Kansas question early in February, Ruffin quickly recognized that Lecompton could be a marvelous secessionist tool. The administration-controlled Senate acted swiftly to pass the bill, but the House of Representatives balked. The debates had barely begun when a fistfight broke out on the House floor between South Carolina Congressman Laurence M. Keitt and Pennsylvania Congressman Galusha Grow. Another dozen or so Representatives joined them, turning the fistfight into a free-for-all. Ruffin read about the fracas in the Richmond papers. He was both shocked and delighted. "All such brawls are disgraceful," he clucked. "But it seems to be as probable a manner of the beginning of a separation of the states as any other."[6]

Just that April, a few days before Ruffin arrived in Washington, Hammond had defended Lecompton in a Senate speech that was so stridently proslavery and anti-Northern that Yankee congressmen and newspapers were still furious. Ruffin congratulated his friend on his fine speech and urged him to keep up his agitation for Southern rights. Meanwhile, Ruffin would do his part, too. He had convinced publisher William O. Goode to print 5,000 copies of "The Political Economy of Slavery"—purely as a public service, Ruffin insisted—and before he left Washington, Ruffin placed a free copy on the desk of every Southern senator and representative.[7]

2

When he returned to Marlbourne in late April, Ruffin learned that the voters of Hanover County had chosen him to represent them at the May 10 Southern Commercial Convention in Montgomery, Alabama. "These conventions have been of no *direct* use," he mused, but they might be "of indirect benefit." After all, these congresslike meetings provided a forum for states' rights men and disunionists like himself to exchange views and plan for future Southern independence. He would go "for the possible chance of forwarding the union . . . of the southern states, & in my private capacity instigating secession from the northern states."[8]

On Monday, May 3, he began the five-day journey that would take him to Montgomery. During the train ride, he sounded out fellow passengers on his favorite subject. He was disappointed when a Virginian from his own county turned out to be "one of those who will submit to every possible wrong from the north, before resisting to the extent of secession or separation." He hoped he wouldn't find many of these "submissionists" at the convention.[9]

But when his train pulled into the Montgomery station and he checked into the Exchange Hotel, he was relieved to meet men whose opinions were much more to his liking. The Exchange was buzzing with secessionist activity. South Carolina's Robert Barnwell Rhett was there, and Alabama's leading fire-eater, William Lowndes Yancey, was like a permanent fixture in the hotel lobby. Part of Virginia's delegation was also there, and Ruffin decided to room with two of the strongest Southern rights men, Lewis E. Harvie and Roger A. Pryor.

Ruffin was still changing out of his traveling clothes when callers arrived. Yancey was one of the first to knock. Then came Judge Seaborn Jones of Georgia and Noah Cloud, editor of the *American Cotton Planter.* Others also were eager to meet the distinguished delegate from the Old Dominion. Ruffin was amazed at how many men outside of Virginia had heard of him "& were rejoiced to know me personally." Perfect strangers "offered me attentions," he boasted in his diary. Former Virginians who had moved to Alabama begged him to honor their plantations with a visit. He was "almost oppressed with invitations," he complained good-naturedly. In truth, his dizzying popularity and unexpected "attentions" pleased and flattered him. The Virginia delegation made him even happier when it chose him as its chairman. No matter what the convention's eventual outcome, Ruffin knew that he had scored a personal triumph.[10]

The convention began on Monday, May 10. Ruffin and the rest of the delegates gathered in a large empty cotton warehouse which had no roof or floor. The obvious acoustical problems may have bothered some of the delegates, but not the opening speaker, William L. Yancey. Yancey's almost magical voice could expand or contract with the size of any audience, and he welcomed the other delegates with an address to "my countrymen of the South." He told them that the convention had a noble purpose: to stimulate and improve Southern commerce and industry in order to free the South from Northern economic domination. But more importantly, this convention was a rehearsal for another assembly of men that must soon gather, "if injustice and wrong shall continue to rule the hour and councils of the dominant section of this country."[11]

The next day, the convention took up an extremely controversial topic —a resolution to repeal the constitutional prohibition against the African slave trade. Yancey, speaking for most of the Lower South, gave an electrifying speech in favor of the proposal. He argued that an increase in the supply of Africans would bring down the present high slave prices, enabling nonslaveholding whites and small slaveowners to purchase more blacks, thus tying Southern whites even more firmly to the institution of slavery. Without importation from abroad, he warned, there would be no future slave states. James DeBow, the convention's presiding officer, agreed with Yancey, announcing, *"we must have Africans."*[12]

Ruffin also favored reopening the slave trade. He had not always done so. He remembered how, for a long time, even after he had learned to accept slavery as a positive good, he still abhorred the foreign slave trade. "At a former time," he said, "I would have as soon expected that I would become the approver of piracy & murder, as of the slave trade in any possible form."

He still opposed the present illegal African slave trade. "Nothing, he admitted, "can exceed its horrors." But his opposition was because of the traffic's very illegality. Slave traders, fearful of capture and capital punishment, packed their human cargo, spoon-fashion, into tiny, cramped, swift-sailing vessels, he explained. Disease and despair carried away most of their shipment. But legalize the now prohibited slave trade, he argued, and humane conditions would prevail on the slave ships. Traders would want to bring their goods to the American market in the best possible condition. Economic self-interest would prompt them "to take the best possible care of the health, and lives, and consequently of the comfort, of the slaves when on their passage across the ocean." Ruffin, though, ignored the fact that the slave trade had been legal for almost 200 years. In all that time, self-interest had not in the least mitigated the evils of the business. The effect was quite the opposite. Even so, Ruffin stubbornly insisted that "there is no reason why the African slaves, even on the 'Middle Passage' should not be even more comfortable . . . than their lives were before under their barbarous & inhuman African masters and rulers."[13]

Ruffin never doubted that these black "savages" were better off as slaves in a civilized white society. He was certain that even the captured Africans, rattling in their irons, realized what a favor the slave traders were doing them. A Georgia planter swore to Ruffin that he had personally witnessed the unloading of an illegal cargo of thirty Africans near Columbus, Georgia. Not only were these blacks gentle and in the best of humor after the nightmare of the Middle Passage, but "when a return to Africa was intimated to them, all showed marked repugnance to it."[14]

Besides, there were very practical reasons for reopening the trade. Southerners needed more cheap labor. Meanwhile, shiploads of European immigrants arrived each day to replenish the North. And were the conditions on board the crowded, filthy immigrant ships much better than on the slavers? Ruffin demanded. Why hadn't the government in Washington forbidden the importation of this form of cheap labor, for humanitarian reasons?[15]

Ruffin soon learned, however, that he was one of the few men from the Upper South and the only member of the Virginia delegation to favor the slave trade resolution. Pryor was on his feet at once to speak against the proposal. On behalf of the Old Dominion, he stated that the foreign traffic in human flesh was outrageous and morally repellent. Virginians, Yancey retorted, were selfish hypocrites whose only real concern was their own pocketbooks. He insisted that Virginia was a slave-breeding state and that planters there wanted to keep slave prices expensive and guard their monopoly over the domestic slave trade.

So far, Ruffin had remained seated in the audience, silently listening to the heated debates. But Yancey had besmirched the honor and integrity of his native state, and Ruffin could sit still no longer. He got up, strode to the speaker's platform, and refuted Yancey's accusation point for point. Virginians were *not* slave breeders, he said. "No man is so inhuman as to breed and raise slaves . . . as a western drover does with his herds of cattle." Ninety-nine out of a hundred Virginia planters wanted to keep their slaves and even purchase more. But exorbitant prices for blacks reduced and sometimes eliminated agricultural profits, thus forcing owners reluctantly to sell their surplus slaves outside the state. Far from adding to Virginia's wealth, Ruffin informed Yancey, these high prices only drained away a needed labor force, endangered agriculture, and would soon make the Old Dominion "a desert and a ruin."[16]

If this were so, Virginians should have favored renewal of the African slave trade, but evidently Ruffin's arguments didn't convince his own delegation, which still refused to budge from its original position. Ruffin had known all along that even if the convention passed the slave trade resolutions, Congress would never agree to lift the ban. But he and other extremists had hoped that by involving the South in an impossible demand, they could use the issue to destroy the Union. Apparently, though, the touchy subject only served to undermine whatever unity there was among Southerners, and Ruffin confessed his relief when a unanimous convention finally tabled the proposal. "Fortunately," he sighed, "we have thus avoided exhibiting to our northern neighbors the division of the South." To all outward appearances, the South had maintained a united front.[17]

3

After the convention was over, Ruffin decided to stay in Alabama an extra week or two. An admirer had offered him free use of the railroads, so he accepted several long-standing invitations to inspect the famous prairie lands and test for calcareous manures. He regretted that the convention had taken no substantive steps toward secession, but he thought he sensed a disunionist spirit in most of the individual delegates. In fact, after conducting his own private poll, he reported in his diary that only two persons outside the Virginia delegation were out-and-out unionists.[18]

Before leaving on his inspection tour, Ruffin contacted his newest disunion friend, Yancey. Despite their slight tiff during the slave trade debates, Ruffin recognized the fiery Alabamian as a kindred secessionist spirit. During the convention's proceedings, he had observed Yancey closely. Physically, the man was unimpressive: dour, pudgy, and pastey-faced. But when he began to talk, people forgot how he looked. His style —influenced in no small part by his stepfather, a Northern abolitionist minister—was emotional, thumping, and revivalistic. His voice, soft as a whisper, kept suspenseful listeners glued to their seats, or loud as a thunderbolt, pulled entire audiences, screaming and shouting, to their feet. Even Ruffin, who distrusted fine oratory, usually classifying the talent for it as demagoguery, described Yancey as "a very eloquent & powerful speaker."

Of course, no one knew this better than Yancey himself, who loved nothing so much as the sound of his own voice. Ruffin noted disapprovingly that Yancey once made a speech for two hours, stopped for dinner, got drunk, and then continued speaking for two more hours. "He is so fluent," Ruffin complained, "that he does not know when to stop." But drunk or sober, the man was a spellbinder, and Ruffin immediately spotted a valuable ally. Yancey could sway the Southern masses, win their hearts and minds over to the disunion cause. He could become the Pied Piper of secession. Yancey's critics might accuse him of demagoguery, but in Ruffin's judgment, there were different kinds of demagogues. A demagogue on the side of secession and Southern independence was no villain. Besides, Ruffin had devised a bold new scheme that he was eager to share with Yancey. He would meet him back in Montgomery on the twenty-seventh of May.[19]

4

Ruffin spent almost two weeks examining the Alabama prairies. Then on May 26, he boarded a crowded steamboat for his return to Montgomery. Navigation was difficult, and the steamer ran aground several times that night. Worse, Ruffin had to rest his sixty-four-year-old bones "on a dirty & very bumpy mattress laid on a table." The next morning, tired and rumpled, he landed at Montgomery and made straight for the Exchange Hotel, where he and Yancey had arranged to meet. In his carpetbag, he carried plans which he hoped would lead to the breakup of the Union.

What the Southern nationalist cause needed, he explained to Yancey, was an organization of dedicated "patriots" who could protect the South's welfare while preparing its citizens for secession. The Southern Commercial Conventions were too cumbersome, too divided on important issues, to be effective. But a small group of revolutionaries, an advance cadre in each state, could accomplish this end with much greater ease. Taking out his plans, he proposed that he, Yancey, and other sincere and committed separationists set up what he called a League of United Southerners. The League would establish clubs throughout the South. Acting like Committees of Correspondence, each League club would educate the Southern mind by publishing and distributing Southern rights propaganda. And in a strictly nonpartisan manner, members would support only those political candidates who were true to Southern nationalist principles and work hard to defeat those who were not. Each local club would send a representative to a League Council, which would direct and coordinate the activities of the member organizations.[20]

Ostensibly, the purpose of the League of United Southerners was to purge national political parties in the South—which meant the Democratic party—of any man who was weak on Southern rights. But the organization's real purpose, Ruffin admitted, was to "endanger the national Democracy, to undermine the South's loyalty to the party." If the League could undermine the party, it would destroy the South's loyalty to the nation.

Yancey, bitter at his own frustrated political efforts within the Democratic party, thought this was a marvelous idea. He promised to launch the movement with a secessionist speech on July 4. He would appeal to the "spirit of 1776" and use all his persuasive talents to make this the Southern Independence Day. *"We shall fire the Southern heart,"* he wrote confidentially to a friend, "instruct the Southern mind—give courage to each other, and at the proper moment, by one organized concerted action, we can precipitate the Cotton states into a revolution."[21]

Ruffin had drawn up an official League "Declaration," which he now showed to Yancey and two other trusted conspirators, Alabama's Judge George W. Stone and Mobile attorney F. B. Shepherd. All expressed admiration for the plan and willingly signed the "patriotic" document. Yancey promised to promote the League in Alabama and, true to his word, set up a club that very day. Wasting no time, Ruffin boarded the late-afternoon train and set out to do the same in North Carolina and Virginia.[22]

5

Ruffin stopped for a few days in North Carolina to visit his favorite cousin, Judge Thomas Ruffin. As Ruffin's carriage pulled up at the Alamance plantation, he was still recalling all the flattering attentions he had received in Alabama, and he felt particularly buoyant over prospects for his League. He felt so good, in fact, that when the judge's two attractive, unmarried daughters welcomed him at the door with their customary hugs and kisses, he began "returning their caresses as if they were more than daughters to me." Delighted and then horrified by his own behavior, he feared he might actually be in love. And love between an old man and a young woman, in his opinion, was "foolish & reprehensible." Love would lead to marriage, and he was sure that "such marriages . . . could produce nothing but unhappiness to both parties." Besides, other people—"enemies"—would laugh at him behind his back, and how he hated to be mocked. Fortunately, he was used to a lifetime of repressing appetites and desires that did not square with his strict code of behavior, but if he allowed desire and selfish inclinations to rule, Ruffin confessed, "I might be as great a fool as most other old men, & seek to marry a blooming young girl." He was relieved that there were *two* blooming young girls at Alamance, for he could not make up his mind which one he loved best. Indecision, he hoped, would save him from an old man's folly and indiscretion.[23]

The following day, Ruffin pushed aside all thoughts of May and December romances and turned his attention to serious business. He was eager to enlist his Cousin Thomas's support for the League of United Southerners. Judge Ruffin was an eminent jurist, whose career on the North Carolina Supreme Court had spanned twenty-four years. A noted agriculturalist, too, he was president of the State Agricultural Society. Ruffin admired and respected him enormously, even when they disagreed. But the Judge wanted nothing to do with Ruffin's League. Although he believed in Southern rights, he was a strict constitutionalist. Secession, he told Ruffin, was not only illegal, it would mean violent revolution. The judge was "too cautious —perhaps too wise," Ruffin reflected afterwards, "to go with me."[24]

Ruffin soon discovered that his cousin was not the only Southerner suffering from an excess of caution. Throughout the summer, he labored with Yancey and Rhett to make the League of United Southerners a success. In June, Yancey published plans for the League in the *Montgomery Advertiser,* and Rhett followed suit in the Charleston *Mercury.* On July 4, both men began simultaneous speaking campaigns to promote secession. The very same day, Ruffin was at Old Point Comfort, trying to drum up League members from among the hotel's sixteen hundred guests. But this was a bad time for agitators, and the League never caught on. Yancey and Rhett received cool receptions, and Ruffin found that vacationers preferred fishing, billiards, tenpins, cards, smoking, drinking, and especially a new form of gambling called faro bank—in fact almost anything at all—to a serious discussion about Southern rights and secession.[25]

Besides, most men thought these topics poor politics. Presidential fever had already broken out in the South, and every Southern political hopeful and his lieutenants knew they needed Northern as well as Southern votes to win the national election. No one wanted to join an organization that would weaken, much less one that would destroy, the national party. In Virginia, Robert M. T. Hunter's wing of the Democratic party—once extreme in its states-rights stance—suddenly turned accommodationist and tried to soft-pedal the slavery issue. Hunter's lieutenant, Roger Pryor, published two articles that summer in *The South* which attacked the League of United Southerners. Southerners had no need for this traitorous and conspiratorial association, he argued. Slavery and Southern rights were perfectly safe, as long as the South controlled the Democratic party.[26]

Ruffin was disgusted with what he considered Pryor's treachery. But

Pryor was not the only Southern turncoat. There were "scarcely a dozen men in Va.," Ruffin informed his diary, "who will even now speak openly, much less act, in defence of the south to the extent that was avowed very generally a year or two ago." Representatives James L. Orr and Laurence Keitt—two South Carolina firebrands—had recently made pro-Union speeches, while Jefferson Davis of Mississippi, a strong opponent of compromise in 1850, was also "fishing for northern votes." Even Hammond had disappointed him. Almost a year in public office had mellowed Hammond's attitudes about the dangers from Northern abolitionists. In a recent letter, he had accused Ruffin of raising "false issues." "We can whip them in the Union," he had promised. "We have them dead."[27]

What had changed these Southern leaders into "such good union men"? Ruffin demanded angrily. It must be their vain delusions of political grandeur, he told his friend Willoughby Newton that August. Ruffin had gone to visit Newton at his plantation in Westmoreland, Virginia, and to discuss "the great Southern question" and the future of the League of United Southerners. Newton urged him to abandon operations, at least for the present.

He told Ruffin how his own strenuous efforts to promote the League and set up local clubs in his part of Virginia had met with much resistance and had made him the target of severe public criticism. A bit shamefaced, Ruffin confessed that he had deliberately avoided linking his own name with the plan and had thus escaped much public censure. In fact, few persons outside of Montgomery knew he was the League's original architect and founder; most gave all the credit—or blame—to Yancey. This secrecy was necessary, Ruffin explained, because he still had many "enemies" in Virginia, and he didn't want to jeopardize the League's success with his own unpopularity.

The two men agreed that as the 1860 presidential contest approached, Southern politicians would fall all over themselves protesting their loyalty to the Union and their devotion to its permanence and integrity. In this unfriendly atmosphere, secessionist sentiments were "addressed to deaf ears." Not even one out of a hundred disunionists would publicly admit his true feelings by joining the League, and the few who did would make the disunion cause look weak. Besides, Ruffin decided, it might be unwise to identify "our true & boldest men" until the South was ready to strike for independence. "Under these circumstances," he concluded, "there is no use in attempting . . . to make any arrangement for action."[28]

But how he hoped and prayed that every "cowardly" Southern politician would suffer defeat in 1860. This would be just "punishment" for not heeding the advice of their prophet, a lesson they would not soon forget. Total victory for the "Black Republican" party, the election of an abolitionist President, and "the speedy overthrow of the national democratic party"

—the very idea was exhilarating! Deprived of their coveted political offices, he predicted, "the dishonest & timid southern men" would be "as strongly *bribed* by their selfish views to stand up for the South, as now to stoop & truckle to the North." Secession would follow. The South would be saved. "If not," he prophesied, "then submission to northern oppression will be the fixed course of the South, & its fate sealed."[29]

6

Still downcast over the failure of his League, Ruffin said good-by to Newton and returned to Marlbourne. When he arrived, there was a letter waiting for him from Rhett's editor son, Robert Barnwell, Jr., inviting him to submit all the articles he liked to the Charleston *Mercury.* Ruffin accepted gladly. He knew he could no longer write for *The South,* because the paper's editor, Roger Pryor, was now an "enemy." Nor did he trust any of the other Richmond papers. The *Enquirer* was Governor Wise's "mouthpiece," the *Examiner* a "mere tool" of the Buchanan administration. If critics responded that the *Mercury* served merely as the mouthpiece and tool of Robert Barnwell Rhett, Ruffin could not have cared less. *The Mercury* was pure on Southern rights and secession. This outweighed any other consideration.

But only a few weeks after accepting Rhett's offer, Ruffin had cause to regret his decision. The *Mercury's* politics were still correct, but while thumbing through a back issue of the paper, he noticed one of his own articles, "Suggestions for the Southern States. No. 5." Startled, he realized that he had forgotten ever having written the essay and had just submitted another called "Treachery to the South—active or passive," in which he repeated the same arguments in almost same words. He was terribly embarrassed. Would the paper's readers notice the mistake? Then, to make matters worse, he discovered that he had been dating his diary a day ahead for some time. "I cannot remember the day of the month from one day to the next," he complained. His memory was fading. Maybe he was becoming feebleminded. All the old fears came flooding back, fears of senility and mental decay. Again he wished for death—sudden, unexpected, and painless. But his physical health had improved so much, he lamented, that he would probably live another five to ten years. In the meantime, perhaps he should spare himself and his family further humiliation and give up written work altogether.[30]

Ruffin, though, could no more give up writing than he could give up breathing, and in his better moods, he knew it. He loved to write. It was therapeutic for him. If he were interested in a subject, he could sit down at his desk any time of the day or night and write for twelve hours, even longer, until cramped fingers made him rest. But he never rested long, for he found that if he allowed too much time to pass, his writing skills deteriorated. So, to keep them finely honed, he had begun an irregular diary shortly after he retired in 1856. He had promised not to burden it with trivia or everyday happenings, nor would he ever intentionally use his diary as a vehicle for critical self-examination. Instead he vowed to make frequent entries and allow his pen "to run ever so wildly" on any number of fascinating topics. "Nothing suits me so well . . . as writing," he stated unreservedly. "There is no employment so pleasant & engrossing to me."[31]

Nothing, perhaps, except for reading. He once remarked that reading was "the greatest pleasure I ever enjoyed." If anything, his youthful appetite for books had increased with age. On the average, he read a book each week. If he ran out of new material, he went back to old favorites. Reading was a reliable way to chase away boredom and depression.

On mail days, Ruffin received such a deluge of newspapers and periodicals that it took him six to ten hours to look through them. He subscribed to all the leading Richmond papers and the Charleston *Mercury*. In addition, he sent for three New York papers: the *Tribune*, the *Daily Herald*, and the *Journal of Commerce*. He thought the *Herald* was "the most unprincipled & infamous . . . paper of Yankeedom," and the *Tribune* was "a vile abolitionist paper." But he examined them "for the purpose of seeing the worst words & movements of [the South's] enemies." From London came reviews like *Blackwood's Magazine* and the *Westminster Review*. He took many major American magazines also—*DeBow's Review, Russell's Magazine,* the *Southern Planter, Littel's Living Age,* the *Southern Literary Messenger,* and *Harper's. Harper's* was "trashy," but he read it anyway.[32]

The library at Marlbourne and later at Beechwood housed over a thousand volumes—histories, travelogues, scientific works, religious tracts, biographies—all testifying to Ruffin's wide range of interests. For light reading, there were Hans Christian Andersen's fairy tales or the *Diary of Samuel Pepys.* For more serious stuff, he could pick up something by one of the classical liberal economists—preferably John Stuart Mill or Adam Smith, his favorites. Smith's *Wealth of Nations,* Ruffin decided, was "one of the most useful works ever written." Ruffin liked books on political philosophy, especially Calhoun's *Disquisition on Government.* He also owned a copy of Montaigne's famous *Essays* but thought them "tiresome" and "indecent to a disgusting degree."[33]

Naturally, there were several crowded shelves of well-thumbed pro-slavery books. But Ruffin gave some room to the opposition too. Though he disapproved of them, he glowered through *Uncle Tom's Cabin* and Hinton Rowan Helper's *The Impending Crisis.* Occasionally this antislavery collection received an unsolicited addition from Benjamin Coates, a Philadelphia abolitionist, whom Ruffin had never met. Coates evidently hoped that abolitionist books and tracts would convince slaveowners of the errors of their ways and somehow managed to slip this forbidden literature past Virginia postal censors. Ruffin, of course, returned the favor and sent his correspondent all the latest proslavery literature.[34]

But of all the books he owned, Ruffin returned most often to his novels. He never outgrew his boyhood infatuation with fiction. Sir Walter Scott was still his favorite British author, although Charles Dickens, William Thackeray, and Lord Byron also ranked high with him. He tried very hard to patronize Southern writers, although this was not easy. Edgar Allan Poe was undoubtedly the South's preeminent author, but Ruffin hated him. "Whatever of genius, or other talent, his strange writings may exhibit," he sneered, "they are as abominable as his morals." As for less well-known Southern writers, their books were almost too boring to read. Even though Ruffin had once claimed that he "would rather read the lightest & more trashy tales on the score of profit or intellectual improvement" than take part in any other form of entertainment, he complained that he could not wade through even one of the four new Virginia novels he had tried to read. All these novels had received rave reviews in the South, and a few had been published in Europe. "If so," Ruffin commented dryly, "it shows that there is more bad taste there than here."[35]

Ironically, he much preferred the novels of Northern writers like Herman Melville and Nathaniel Hawthorne. But when Charles Mackay, a Scottish journalist, wrote a book called *Life and Liberty in America,* stating that Southern literature was inferior to Northern literature because slavery was incompatible with high literary achievement, Ruffin leaped to the South's defense. Were literary achievements wanting in ancient slave civilizations like Greece and Rome? he demanded. True, the North had produced far greater quantities of superior—and inferior—fiction and poetry than the South. But this was the result of Yankee greed and thirst for profits, not of a superior society. Northern writers pushed themselves to work harder than Southern gentlemen, because they had to produce or starve. "Writing for gain is a business not yet begun in the southern states," he explained. "But even without that incentive or reward, our productions on the far higher subjects of government, philosophical argument, & politics, are as far above any of the north, as are southern statemen superior to those of the north."[36]

7

Statesmen Northern or Southern, American or European, were all fair game for Ruffin's pen. From his reading and his personal experiences, he formed definite and critical opinions about famous men, living and dead, and he liked to record these evaluations in his diary. Because he was a man whose likes and dislikes were always intense, his character descriptions often fell into simple villain or hero categories.

The list of heroes was short, and most of the men on it were dead. Virginians Patrick Henry, Richard Bland, and Richard Henry Lee were "among the sages, patriots & heroes" of the American Revolution, while contemporary Italian freedom fighter, Guiseppe Garibaldi, was "the noblest of modern patriots & heroes." John C. Calhoun was another particular favorite; Ruffin had mourned his death as though he were a member of his family.

The list of villains and enemies was much longer and more geographically mixed. High on the list were the biblical figures King David and Judas Iscariot. Nor far behind were most of Europe's rulers. Ruffin disliked France's Emperors Napoleon I and Napoleon III, abhorred revolutionists Jean Paul Marat and Maximilien Robespierre, and detested most of England's kings. Charles II, he wrote, was "one of the most depraved & despicable of all the English monarchs." James I was "far more contemptible." James II was a "stupid bigot." Henry VIII was "a monster of selfishness, injustice, & cruelty." And George IV was "the most infamous scoundrel . . . that has worn the crown of England since James I."[37]

Ruffin didn't rate American Presidents much higher. George Washington was a sincere patriot but only a mediocre military commander, whose second-rate mind had never generated an original or important political thought. Thomas Jefferson was a man of "giant intellect" but a covert and cunning abolitionist all his life. James Madison, a professed Republican, was really a political apostate, who had promoted Federalist policies and principles. Andrew Jackson was an "illiterate & ignorant soldier" and a "vulgar despot," who had surrounded himself with "sycophants & base tools" to feed his vanity, while they feasted like vultures on the spoils of high office. Buchanan, too, was "a great political scoundrel." And included among the lower-ranking scoundrels, rascals, villains, enemies, and traitors scattered throughout Ruffin's diary were former Supreme Court Chief Justice John Marshall; Democratic senators Sam Houston and Stephen A. Douglas; Republican John C. Fremont; Governor Henry A. Wise; editor Roger A. Pryor; and all Northern politicians, just on general principle.[38]

One President whom Ruffin did admire was John Tyler. Tyler was now retired from political office and living on a nearby plantation, and Ruffin visited him occasionally. The man was not an adroit politician, and he had been one of the least popular Presidents, but to Ruffin, these were endearing qualities. Ruffin was always drawn to men like himself who had felt the sting of public neglect, who wore their rejection like a badge of honor. Also he liked Tyler's "plain & unassuming manner," his lack of conceit. Ruffin thought Tyler was a model country gentleman.

He also enjoyed Tyler's companionship. Sometimes after an early breakfast at Marlbourne, he would row across the Pamunkey River, catch a steamer to Kennon's wharf, and then walk the three and a half miles to Sherwood Forest, Tyler's plantation. Ruffin loved a good conversation, and the two men would talk for seven, eight, or even nine consecutive hours, usually weighing the relative merits and demerits of past and present political leaders. Ruffin especially relished gossipy tidbits about the well-known Washington insiders Tyler had met as President.

Tyler also admired Ruffin. Over his sitting room fireplace he had hung two neatly embroidered, identically framed portraits: one of Daniel Webster and the other of Edmund Ruffin. "The one," Tyler explained, is "the first among American statesmen, & the other the first of American Agriculturalists." Ruffin stared at the two pictures for a long time, thinking that Webster's morals were much too low to deserve such an honor and wishing very hard that Tyler could have reversed his tribute.[39]

8

Politics would always be Ruffin's first love. Ruffin no longer harbored any personal ambitions, but he preferred to be near the centers of power and was a frequent visitor to both the Virginia legislature and the United States Congress. State legislators and Southern congressmen were no longer surprised when they returned from a recess or a break and found on their desks presents of Ruffin's latest articles on slavery or secession.

Shortly after New Year's, 1859, Ruffin traveled to Washington, bringing with him copies of "African Colonization Unveiled." Early on January 4 he went to the Senate and placed a gift copy on each senator's desk. Then he climbed up to the Visitors' Gallery and nervously waited to see what kind of reaction there would be. But when the senators arrived and took their seats, they paid no attention to Ruffin's article. Indifference was something Ruffin dreaded. It was a sign, he believed, that what he said and did—his very existence—was of no importance. "I had a rebuff to my vanity," Ruffin reported sorrowfully in his diary that evening. "No one, whether acquaintance or stranger, was taking any notice of the pamphlet, or seemed conscious that it was before their eyes." He'd been ignored again. But then, he was used to public ingratitude.[40]

John Tyler was also in Washington that January, and at first Ruffin was delighted to see him again. But when Ruffin brought up the question of how best to split the Union, the ex-President launched into a three-hour pro-unionist "harangue" that left Ruffin speechless with anger. Privately, he fumed at Tyler's "grand airs & artificial mock tragic acting," his "glaring exhibition of vanity and self-conceit." Why hadn't he noticed this before? Ruffin decided that Tyler never had been very bright. His "intellectual powers" had "always been more showy than solid, or deep."[41]

Anyway, Ruffin much preferred the company of Hammond, who discussed the possibility of annexing Cuba, or of the slavery advocate Elwood Fisher, who regaled him with stories about the illicit African slave trade. Only a few months earlier, Fisher confided, the slave ship *Wanderer* had successfully evaded British and United States authorities and landed a fresh cargo of blacks in Georgia. What a capital move! Ruffin exclaimed. The Southern states would nullify the federal law against the foreign slave trade the same way the Northern states had nullified the federal Fugitive Slave Act with their personal liberty laws. If only the government in Washington would try to recover these illegal Africans. Naturally, Southerners would resist, and this might lead to bloodshed, secession, and an independent South. What a thrilling prospect![42]

9

There was nothing thrilling, though, about the rest of Ruffin's winter or most of the spring. He tried to amuse himself in various ways: tracing the legitimate and illegitimate members of his family tree, sorting out and cataloguing old letters, and even acting as a secret matchmaker between his son Edmund—a widower—and Jane or Patty Ruffin. Since his own rather straightlaced sense of propriety wouldn't allow him to make either of these girls his bride, he thought having one close by as a daughter-in-law would be the perfect substitute.[43]

Occasionally he traveled to Richmond to hear a concert or an opera or to attend the theater. But his tastes, he admitted, were "singular, odd, & paradoxical," and he was a hard critic to please. He listened to the world-famous Austrian pianist and composer, Sigismund Thalberg, and the equally renowned Belgian violinist, Henri Vieuxtemps, and complained that he had heard no "music." The execution was wonderful, he admitted, but there were too many frills and flourishes. Likewise, opera star Caroline Richings had filled her performance of *The Enchantress* with too many unnecessary "trills & cadences." He thought Thalberg, Vieuxtemps, and Richings were show-offs, and he distrusted fancy music as much as fancy oratory. Their performances stirred his envy, reminding him of his personal shortcomings. He compensated by making a fetish out of plainness and simplicity—qualities he apologized for in his own speeches—and insisted that he much preferred "simple airs correctly & plainly played or a band, or harmonized songs, by a few good voices."

The rest of the audience on both these occasions had clapped long and hard during and after the performances. But Ruffin was never a slave to popular tastes. The public, he reasoned contemptuously, never appreciated the merits of true genius like his own. So, public favor—unless aimed in his particular direction—was a reverse barometer for measuring genuine talent. The concert audience, he sniffed, had only pretended to understand the difficult pieces of music when actually half of them would rather have listened to "an ordinary fiddler playing common reels, & Yankee Doodle." The opera audience, which had clapped loudest during Richings's "trills & cadences," would have applauded her imitation of a mewing cat or a braying ass, "provided they had been assured that these imitations had been applauded by all preceding audiences and persons of musical taste."[44]

Convinced that the citizens of Richmond had no artistic sense, Ruffin spent most of his time in Prince George County, either with Edmund at Beechwood or with Julian and his wife at Ruthven. He enjoyed being around his children and especially his many grandchildren. With adults he was always serious, but children made him almost playful. Once, he taught a grandson how to make a proper fishnet. On another occasion, he personally supervised three grandchildren who were trying to learn the intricacies of hoop-rolling. At night, before their bedtime, the children would often beg their grandfather for a special treat. Then, gathering the youngsters around him, Ruffin would settle himself into a comfortable chair, pick up a favorite storybook, and read in an imitation Irish brogue that delighted his audience.[45]

But happy as Ruffin was with his children and grandchildren, family pleasures were not satisfying enough to occupy all his time. He longed for something else to do, something more exciting to fill his hours. Even his diary was boring him. "I am weary of keeping this diary," he said late that spring, because it "has become a series of entries of the most commonplace & uninteresting incidents of my daily life."[46]

10

Prospects for excitement didn't show any signs of improving that summer. Secessionist talk was still unpopular. When the Southern Commercial Convention met at Vicksburg, Mississippi, only eight states bothered to attend; Virginia, Ruffin observed sadly, had not sent a single delegate. Unionist sentiment was particularly strong in the Old Dominion, where, with few exceptions, both Democrats and former Whigs downplayed any issues that might divide the country. The widely circulated Richmond *Dispatch,* a nonpartisan paper, estimated that 99 percent of the men in eastern Virginia were staunch unionists, while westerners had never been more loyal. Fire-eaters were unwelcome.[47]

Despite this discouraging news, Ruffin was not about to abandon his Union-splitting dreams. He had to do something to shake Southerners to their senses and awaken them to the increasing dangers of the Northern abolitionist conspiracy. In July, he began an article for the *Mercury* entitled "Cassandra's Warnings," named after the Trojan prophetess whose countrymen had ignored all her counsel and advice until it was too late to save themselves from disaster.

"Cassandra's Warnings" catalogued every Northern insult and oppression from the Missouri Compromise to the present. The South must sever its ties with the Union now or suffer the consequences: an abolitionist President in 1860, the almost simultaneous admission of enough free states to pass a constitutional amendment abolishing slavery, and then general emancipation. And every Southern white knew what that meant: once docile slaves reverting back to crazed savagery, engaging in an orgy of lust, blood, and carnage. The nightmare was all too familiar. Northern abolitionists had already dispersed their secret agents throughout the slave states, Ruffin declared. Preachers, teachers, businessmen, workers, magazine peddlers, even pretended invalids—all used any excuse to infiltrate the South and encourage slave rebellion. The South was crawling with abolitionists. Incendiaries were everywhere.[48]

In August, Ruffin preached "Cassandra's Warnings" at White Sulphur Springs, where he met Cassandra's fate: no one believed a word he said. The vacationers had come to the Springs to relax and enjoy themselves, not to hear some ancient prophet of doom and destruction. Then Ruffin's daughter Mildred landed a personal blow. She was getting married. William Sayre's brother Burwell had asked for her hand, and they were planning an October wedding. Mildred was her father's favorite; he did not want to let her go. But she was determined, and he reluctantly gave his consent.[49]

His cup of bitterness had overflowed. Suddenly he was exhausted. He felt like a very old man. Once more, death looked inviting to him.

But unknown to Ruffin, another old man, who also fancied himself somewhat of a prophet, was preparing at that very moment to fulfill "Cassandra's Warnings" and arouse Ruffin as he'd never been aroused before. Holed up in a dilapidated Maryland farmhouse not far from the Virginia border, old John Brown and a small band of followers plotted a raid on Harper's Ferry, Virginia. When the time was right, Brown said, they would attack the town, capture the federal arsenal there, arm and liberate the slaves, and begin a wholesale insurrection that would sweep the South. Even if their bold attempt failed, he prophesied, it could well ignite a sectional conflagration, a civil war that would wash away the sins of slavery with blood.

In October, just before John Brown struck at Harper's Ferry, Ruffin was probably the unhappiest man in the Old Dominion. Mildred was married, and his career as "an itinerant missionary of disunion" seemed finished. Ruffin was almost suicidal. Then came the news of John Brown's raid, and Ruffin decided that life was worth living.

10

The Approaching Storm

JOHN BROWN'S RAID was the answer to Ruffin's prayers, "Cassandra's Warnings" vindicated. Northern abolitionists had actually invaded the South, had shed Southern blood on Southern soil, for the avowed purpose of instigating a slave rebellion. The news was almost too good to be true. This "practical exercise of abolition principles," thought Ruffin, was exactly what the South needed to stir its "sluggish blood." He figured that the Harper's Ferry fiasco would win more converts to the disunion cause than the speeches and essays of a thousand secession crusaders.[1]

Ruffin was correct. Brown had tapped into a primal Southern white fear—that of servile insurrection—a fear that cut across class and political lines, uniting slaveowner with nonslaveowner, conservative with extremist. "Even the most bigoted Unionist," shrieked the Charleston *Mercury,* must now realize "that there is no peace for the South in the Union." "More than any other event that has happened since the formation of the Government," the Richmond *Enquirer* commented, "the Harper's Ferry invasion has advanced the cause of Disunion."[2]

Northern "fanatics" had warred upon the South, and, unlike Ruffin, most Southerners found nothing to cheer about. For months after the initial and rather pitiful attack on Harper's Ferry, newspapers kept the entire Southern populace on edge with false reports of fresh abolitionist incursions. Beardless youths and gray-haired old men alike shouldered their muskets and began forming volunteer militia units. Troops of soldiers marched to and fro across the Southland in response to constant new insurrectionary scares. Local vigilance committees and companies of "Minutemen" often took matters into their own hands, beating, whipping, tarring and feathering, even hanging any man—black or white—who looked the slightest bit conspiratorial. States from Virginia to Mississippi girded themselves as if for Armageddon. Not since Nat Turner's uprising in 1831 had Southerners known such panic, such hysteria. A Great Fear enveloped Dixie.[3]

But no state, naturally, was more frightened than Virginia. From October through late December, terrifying rumors flew from city to city, from plantation to plantation, as jittery Virginians spotted imaginary John Browns behind every tree and bush. On December 10, riders galloped through the Marlbourne neighborhood. Pick up your guns, they shouted to the men. Run and hide, they told the women and children. An army of blacks, led by Northern abolitionists, was advancing through the countryside. At once, hysterical women and weeping children barricaded themselves inside central homes for protection, while their menfolk grabbed every weapon in sight, ran for their horses, and rode out bravely to do battle with the black army that never appeared. Still the horrible stories persisted: abolitionist troops were headed in this direction; stampeding slaves were headed in that. Nowhere was safe.[4]

Threatened, it seemed, with external invasion and internal rebellion, Virginians shed their former moderate unionist stance and assumed a more bellicose and anti-Northern posture. Virginia-born students who were studying in the North dropped out in mid-semester and transferred to Southern colleges. Southern Rights Associations—which had lain almost dormant since the sectional hostilities of 1850—began a crusade to boycott Northern manufacturers. Public meetings passed resolutions pledging all those present "to use, eat, drink, wear or buy nothing under the sun from north of the Mason and Dixon line." Citizens in nearly every city or town formed "Homespun Clubs," and Southern belles proudly wore homespun gowns made from cheap Virginia fabrics to their balls and barbecues.[5]

At the same time, calls for military preparedness rang out in the General Assembly. "All Virginia should stand forth as one man," General James L. Kemper exhorted the legislators, "and say to fanaticism, in her own language, we will welcome you with bloody hands and hospitable graves." In response, local militia from the Tidewater to west of the Blue Ridge drilled and drilled, preparing "to let the 'nigger worshippers' know that Virginia intends to maintain her institutions, peacefully, if possible, but with force if necessary." "Virginia is arming to the teeth," exclaimed John Tyler to a friend. "An indiscreet move in any direction may produce results deeply to be deplored." "Never before, in the history of this commonwealth," reported the usually conservative Richmond *Whig,* "were the people so aroused, and so bent on maintaining their rights and honor *at any cost!*"[6]

2

At Marlbourne, Ruffin consumed every unfolding detail about the Harper's Ferry raid with obvious relish. He was happy to learn that John Brown had been the notorious leader of a gang of "brigands, murderers & robbers" who had stalked the Kansas territory, terrorizing and slaughtering proslavery settlers during the Kansas Civil War. This proved that Brown was a Northern abolitionist agent, a hired gun for the New England Emigrant Aid Society, and that abolitionists lied when they professed nonviolent and peaceful aims. Moreover, a satchel full of letters discovered at Brown's hiding place incriminated many prominent Northern antislavery men and women, while secret maps indicated that Brown had not intended to confine his bloody expedition to Virginia alone. While other Southerners staggered under the impact of these new revelations, Ruffin and other tireless agitators stood their ground and smugly asserted that Brown was just a typical Northerner and that Harper's Ferry was only a logical step in the developing and ever present abolitionist conspiracy they had warned about for years.[7]

The majority of Northerners, though, denied this kind of logic and rushed to repudiate John Brown and his "insane and villainous scheme." Brown, they assured, was in no way a representative Northerner. He was a madman, a lunatic, and his attempt to stir up a slave revolt in the South was atrocious and unspeakable. But traumatized and suspicious Southerners refused to believe the conservative protestations of their Northern neighbors. Instead they concentrated on the well-publicized words of New England transcendentalists like Ralph Waldo Emerson and Henry David Thoreau, who glorified Brown and made him a martyr, and mistakenly identified these individual sentiments with the main body of Northern opinion.[8]

All the "thorough abolition papers & speakers," Ruffin decided, had justified and applauded the raid at Harper's Ferry "for every thing except its rashness and imprudence—and would have rejoiced," he was positive, "at its success, even if ever so destructive to the whites." What was he to think when he picked up the Charleston *Mercury* in early November and read that, according to a recent lecture given by abolitionist Wendell Phillips, the typical Northern reaction to news of Brown's attempt to incite slave rebellion was "what a pity he did not succeed"; or that, according to a sermon delivered by Massachusetts minister Reverend Wheelock, if John Brown were a free man, he could easily command enough Northern votes to become the next President of the United States? Because Southern papers favored the atypical words of Northern abolitionists, Ruffin could draw but one conclusion: John Brown, "the attempter of the thousand-fold horrors in Virginia, is, for these reasons, the present popular idol of the north."[9]

While Brown was far from becoming a popular idol, he was the object of increasing expressions of Northern sympathy during the weeks before his execution. His sincere and eloquent antislavery ideals, his integrity during his hurried and almost mock trial at Charlestown, Virginia, and his courage while awaiting death in the land of his enemies impressed many Northerners who still despised the old man's warlike tactics. Even Ruffin felt impelled to give Brown a grudging compliment: "He is as thorough a fanatic as ever suffered martyrdom." Given the opportunity, Ruffin would gladly have sacrificed himself on the opposite altar of secession and slavery, so he could understand Brown's singular drive. Of course, Ruffin detested old Brown's abolitionist goals as well as his methods. But, he confessed, "it is impossible for me not to respect his thorough devotion to his bad cause, & the undaunted courage with which he has sustained it, through all losses & hazards."[10]

But neither Ruffin nor most other Southerners were capable of distinguishing between Northern admiration and respect for John Brown, the man, and admiration and respect for his deeds. The wound Brown had inflicted at Harper's Ferry was still festering deep within the Southern psyche, and for Southerners, sympathy for the man meant sympathy for his deeds.

When a number of Northern Democrats as well as Republicans began to plead with Virginia to spare old Brown and commute his sentence to life imprisonment, Ruffin, like many Southern whites, saw this as evidence of complete Northern betrayal. "The mass of the people of the north," he decided, "even embracing many who have been deemed most our friends, are more or less enemies of the south." Even he was astonished at what he interpreted as "so *general* an excitement & avowed sympathy" among Northerners for Brown and his fellow villains. He admitted privately, though, that every speech, sermon, or article that he could possibly construe as pro-Brown or pro-Harper's Ferry "gratified" him. "This must open the eyes of the people of the south who have heretofore trusted to the justice & forbearance of the northern people," he declared, "& it will be evident to many who have most feared & abhorred disunion, that that will be the only safeguard from the insane hostility of the north to southern institutions & interests."[11]

3

Despite the minor jolt it had received at Brown's rough hands, the South's main institution and interest—Negro slavery—was undamaged. After the raid, most Southerners were still frightened, yet some whites assumed tones of supreme confidence and tried to reassure themselves that they had nothing to fear from their slaves. Why, even at Brown's peak strength during the Harper's Ferry attack, boasted the Richmond papers with bravado, not a single member of the slave community had voluntarily responded to his call for insurrection. Let this be a lesson to the North, agreed Ruffin, that Southern slaves were happy, contented, and fiercely devoted to their white masters and mistresses. Hadn't Brown's "malignant, atrocious, and devilish" conspiracy proved "to the world the actual condition of entire obedience and general loyalty of . . . negro slaves"?

Ruffin was so certain of black fidelity that he deliberately took Jem Sykes aside one day at Marlbourne, outlined the history and rationale of slavery in the South, discussed John Brown's raid, explained the reasons why all such attempts at slave liberation must fail, and sent Sykes back to the slave quarters to pass on the "correct information" to the other Ruffin slaves. Few masters were so trusting. Most rarely even mentioned Brown's name, much less spoke of his awful deeds in front of their slaves, for fear of spreading incendiary ideas. Ruffin, too, may have thought better of his own loose tongue when, shortly after Brown's trial and death sentence, another family plantation went up in flames. At almost the same time, unknown arsonists torched the barns and "other property" of Brown's jurors. Newspapers blamed these fires on slaves and their abolitionist allies. For once, Ruffin agreed.[12]

Still, he insisted that Southern slaves were inherently faithful and loving toward their owners; problems arose only when evil-minded abolitionists preyed on ignorant and malleable Negro minds. So, after some thought, Ruffin came up with a plan that would decrease if not eliminate all contacts and communications between slaves and any Northern abolitionist agitators operating within the South. According to this plan, Southern businessmen would form local commercial organizations and pledge to boycott Northern products. This way "vagrants or temporary sojourners" in Dixie, who were really hired abolitionist agents, would not have any pretext to talk with slaves. State governments would also join in on the official boycott, negotiate direct trade treaties with Europe, and begin to "devise suitable and efficient measures for the defense of the Southern people . . . from the increasing hostility and unscrupulous assaults of Northern enemies, fanatics and conspirators." Putting all these suggestions into petition form, Ruffin first circulated his "Harper's Ferry Memorial" around the Marlbourne neighborhood and then carried it to the November 25 meeting of the Richmond Southern Rights Association.[13]

The Richmond meeting welcomed Ruffin, applauded the "Harper's Ferry Memorial" and voted unanimously to adopt his petition. Ruffin remembered that at one time in the not too distant past, these same resolutions would have met harsh criticism and defeat because of their violence and extremism. Now his own views were not so peculiar. He marveled at the changed attitudes of his fellow Virginians. "Many persons," he noticed, who were once "the most conservative, or submissive to the Union under all circumstances, are now saying that *something* must be done by the south —& separation is admitted by others as the coming result."[14]

Ruffin believed that something would happen soon—probably at Charlestown, where the imprisoned Brown was awaiting his turn on the gallows. And if secession were to result from some blow struck at Charlestown, Ruffin wanted to be there to witness the fulfillment of his heart's desire. So he did not tarry long in Richmond. He delivered his "Memorial," spent one night in a hotel, rose the next morning at dawn, and hurried to the railroad station. By 6:30 A.M., he was on his way, heading as fast as possible toward "the seat of war."[15]

4

First Ruffin stopped off at Harper's Ferry, because he was interested in seeing the scene of the recent crime and hoped to talk to some of the eyewitnesses. After inspecting the bullet-ridden engine house where Brown and what was left of his gang had been captured, he spoke to Alfred W. Barbour, superintendent of the federal arsenal. Barbour showed his wide-eyed visitor the 1,500 long metal pikes that Brown had brought with him to change "slaves into men." Ruffin stared at the weapons in horrified fascination, an idea slowly forming in his brain. These pikes were fearsome, terrible. But might they not still serve some useful—albeit unintended— purpose? Were they not by themselves eloquent spokesmen for disunion? Please, Ruffin begged the startled superintendent, could he have a spear for himself?[16]

Barbour, who probably thought he was just indulging an old man's curious whim, delivered the souvenir spear to Ruffin several days later in Charlestown. Then Ruffin, not trusting the weapon to speak entirely for itself, pasted a label on the handle: "Sample of the favors designed for us by our Northern Brethren." Later, he would add this encouraging message: "The most precious benefit derived from the Northern States by the Southern, if, rightly using it, out of this nettle *danger,* we pluck the flower *safety.*"

Next, taking spear in hand, he lugged his trophy through the streets of Charlestown. Naturally he attracted a lot of attention. Crowds of curious spectators gathered round him wherever he went, and he used "every suitable occasion to express [his] disunion sentiments."[17]

He did not always encounter friendly audiences. In fact, he noticed right away that the people of Charlestown were "much more unionists than in lower Virginia." While some citizens cheered his secessionist appeals, he could sense that most listeners "generally disapproved." Once, after what the New York *Herald* called a particularly "treasonable harangue," the commander of the Harper's Ferry militia scolded Ruffin and warned him that if it were not for the gray hairs on his head, which protected him, "he would be taken down to 'the run' and well ducked, and then driven out of town." When Ruffin read the article, he immediately dashed off angry letters to several newspapers, denying that the alleged incident had taken place or that anyone had treated him with such disrespect.[18]

Instead, he had received many pleasing signs of courtesy and special attention. Companies of soldiers from all parts of the Old Dominion had saluted him as they clattered by on Charlestown streets. And on several occasions, the officer of the day had invited the grateful old agitator to accompany him at night on military "grand rounds." For Ruffin, this was "a stirring time."[19]

This was also a very volatile time. The normally sleepy little village of Charlestown was abnormally astir that week before Brown's hanging. Despite the presence of some four thousand soldiers, rumors persisted that Northern abolitionists were plotting to spring their hero from his jail cell or somehow save him from the gallows. A guard told Ruffin that two thousand desperadoes had pledged their lives to obey, defend, and avenge John Brown. Even now they were mobilizing across the border in Maryland, Pennsylvania, and Ohio, waiting for the signal to attack. One night, several sentries reported seeing rockets thrown from neighboring mountaintops. Was this the attack signal? Soldiers and citizens tensed for the expected abolitionist onslaught until someone discovered that the "rockets" were simply chimney sparks. Another false alarm.[20]

But Virginians were still edgy after Brown's original invasion, and they were not about to risk his possible escape. Authorities took every precaution against abolitionist infiltration. They searched incoming railroad cars and sent back suspicious-looking people, including four congressmen from Ohio. Strangers had to produce vouchers of good character or else face deportation to the other side of the Potomac. Sentries posted day and night around Charlestown had orders to arrest any unidentified person who tried to enter or leave town. Ironically, Ruffin was one of the first men they pulled in. On his way to dinner at a friend's home just outside Charlestown one evening, he was arrested, marched through the main street, and questioned in the guardhouse. Of course, once the soldiers learned his true identity, they released him with profound apologies. Ruffin took the whole episode with good humor, commending the men who had arrested him for executing their orders so well.[21]

Secretly, Ruffin harbored hopes that Northern abolitionists *would* penetrate Charlestown's defenses and try to liberate Brown. Whether their mission was successful or not made no difference to him. Their success, especially if accompanied by bloodshed, would be "a certain cause of separation of the southern from the northern states," while their defeat, he smiled, would mean that all the rescuers would be "put to death like wolves."[22]

5

John Brown was to hang on December 2. As the day of his execution drew nearer and no rescuers had yet appeared, Ruffin wondered whether Northern abolitionists would try to snatch their hero from the ropes of death on the very day of his hanging. How Ruffin wished that he could be there to witness the event and perhaps spill some blood for Southern independence.

But Virginia authorities, fearful of just such a rescue attempt, had restricted viewing of the hanging to the military guard. Ruffin fretted about his predicament until one day shortly before the execution, when he caught sight of his old friend Hugh Nelson, age sixty-seven, marching jauntily in step with the Petersburg volunteer militia. Filled with envy at first, Ruffin suddenly realized that his friend had shown him the way he too could be present at the hanging.

On December 1, he cornered Colonel Smith, commander of the Virginia Military Institute Cadets, and begged permission to join his troops on the morrow for that one special day. Smith smiled at Ruffin, who at sixty-five would be the "youngest" recruit in his "company of boyish soldiers" and indulgently granted the old man's wish. Ruffin, who was aware that he would be in a "somewhat ludicrous position" among the fresh-faced cadets, suppressed any feelings of embarrassment. Instead, he felt a surge of almost youthful military vigor flow through his aging body, and he eagerly hurried over to the armory to pick up his private's uniform and arms.[23]

That night, he went on the "grand rounds" for the last time. He returned to his room at 4 A.M. but was too excited to go to bed. Instead, he lay down on a sofa and remained half dozing until drumbeats awakened him at daybreak. Pulling on his uniform with its long gray overcoat, he picked up his gun, hurried over to the parade grounds, and looked for his comrades. He spotted them easily. The other cadets, smartly outfitted in specially purchased uniforms—scarlet shirts, gray pantaloons, and criss-crossing white bandoliers—could barely suppress their giggles when Private Ruffin fell in behind them. "It required all the constraint of their good manners," he observed, "to hide their merriment." But despite his advanced years and rather comical position, Ruffin marched and wheeled with the best of his young companions that day, and afterwards the "Society of Cadets" elected him an honorary member.[24]

The troops paraded for an hour and a half. Then around 9 A.M., each company marched silently to the execution grounds, where they stood waiting for the next two hours. Ruffin noted that the day was clear and beautiful, and he was thankful. If the weather had been gloomy, he was sure that "northern fanatics would have seen in it an indication of God's anger with the execution, for which the Heaven was draped in mourning."

Shortly after 11 o'clock, John Brown appeared, arms bound together at the elbow and seated on his own black walnut coffin, riding in a light and open wagon. Standing at attention some fifty yards from the gallows, Ruffin watched Brown intently as he stepped down from his coffin and "ascended the steps of the scaffold . . . with readiness & seeming alacrity." Then, without betraying a trace of terror, the condemned man "went through what was required of him apparently with as little agitation as if he had been the willing assistant, instead of the victim."

Ruffin's mouth was agape. For him, Brown was a villain, an "atrocious criminal" and "eulogized miscreant," who deserved to die. Yet he had to admire the man's "animal courage," his "complete fearlessness of & insensibility to danger & death." "In this quality," Ruffin said by way of epitaph, "he seems to me to have had no equals." [25]

6

John Brown was dead, but his ghost still hovered over the nation. Nowhere was this more apparent than in Washington, D.C., where on Monday, December 5, just three days after Brown's execution, Congress assembled in a highly charged atmosphere filled with intense sectional hostility and mutual mistrust. At Charlestown, Ruffin heard rumors that senators and representatives were brandishing knives and pistols as they filed into their respective legislative chambers. Not wanting to miss any potential disunion action, he stuffed his belongings into a suitcase, grabbed his pike, and boarded the night train to the capital. He wanted "to witness something of the present turmoil" and "see, if possible, to what early end it is tending."[26]

Tuesday morning, December 8, Ruffin checked into Brown's Hotel, because that was where most of the other Southern visitors were staying. Someone told him that the Senate was about to organize an investigating committee to ferret out any Republican "subversives" who were involved in the John Brown conspiracy. But the real fireworks, he heard, were taking place in the House of Representatives, which had just begun what would turn into a bitter and acrimonious two-month debate over the election of a Speaker. Naturally, Ruffin was in the House's Visitors' Gallery almost every day.

So many curious spectators crammed the Gallery that Ruffin usually had to squeeze into the ladies' section. From that vantage point, he noticed how the members of the two political parties had separated themselves physically—Republicans to the left of the middle aisle, Democrats to the right—a division he hoped would foreshadow future national developments. He also commented on a distinct lack of courtesy between Democrats and Republicans. This lack of courtesy occasionally erupted into physical violence. Only a few days before Ruffin arrived in Washington, the representative from Mississippi had unsheathed a bowie knife and lunged at Pennsylvania Republican Thaddeus Stevens, who managed to escape unhurt. Ruffin himself witnessed another scrape, when two Illinois men— one a Democrat and the other a Republican—tried to settle an argument with their fists and had to be pulled apart by friends.[27]

This "contant irritation" in the seat of government pleased veteran disunionists like Ruffin, who hoped it might provoke bloodshed and "serve to foment & increase the general exasperations" that John Brown's raid had first set in motion. Ruffin perceptively understood that Harper's Ferry "afforded the best practical ground for dissolution that the South ever had." In private conversations with Southern rights congressmen from North Carolina, South Carolina, and Alabama, he frantically pleaded with them not to "pass over" such a wonderful opportunity to promote secession. Continue to dramatize John Brown, he urged. Keep his terrifying image constantly before Southern eyes and "agitate & exasperate the already excited indignation of the south."[28]

7

Meanwhile Ruffin was perfecting his own scheme for agitation. Wherever he went in Washington, he carried his John Brown pike with him, and he could see that the spear "attracted much notice." The weapon conjured up nightmare visions of slave insurrection and was in itself a silent but dramatic advertisement for secession. He decided to send one to the governor of each of the fifteen slave states with the request that it occupy some "conspicuous" position, preferably in the state legislature, where it could not escape public attention. "Each one," he contended, "will then serve as a most eloquent and impressive preacher," rousing Southern patriots to defend themselves

and their country "against all assaults from [the] unscrupulous and mea-
sureless enmity of Northern Abolitionists."[29]

While he was still in the capital, Ruffin chanced into Colonel Barbour
of the Harper's Ferry arsenal and pleaded with that unfortunate man to
send him the requisite additional pikes. Barbour agreed but evidently had
second thoughts and stalled his delivery for six months. In the meantine,
not anticipating any delay, Ruffin sat in his hotel room and wrote out neat
labels for each weapon.

To Virginia he offered the honor of formally distributing his gifts.
When the Virginia legislature ignored the offer, Ruffin decided to carry out
his plan alone. Along with every pike, he sent a letter to each Southern
governor explaining that this horrid present was originally designed "to be
imbrued in the blood of the whites of the South." "Northern Conspirators,"
"Northern Factories," and "Northern funds," he claimed, had devised,
manufactured, and paid for this weapon. Exhibit John Brown's pike, he
implored, "as abiding ... evidence of the fanatical hatred borne by the
dominant northern party to the institutions & the people of the Southern
States, and of the unscrupulous & atrocious means resorted to for the
attainment of the objects sought by that party."[30]

8

After he had completed all his labels and letters, Ruffin had another brain-
storm. "Under a sudden thought & impulse," he dashed off an article for
the Richmond *Examiner* and another for the Virginia *Index* exhorting the
Old Dominion, as "the now especially aggrieved & endangered state," to
secede immediately and lead the rest of the slave states out of the Union.
According to Ruffin, Virginians had only two alternatives: the "Subversion
of Negro Slavery, or the Dissolution of the Present Union."[31]

Ruffin thought he saw some real evidence that Virginia—once so full
of devoted unionists—might choose the latter alternative. Every time he
picked up a Richmond newspaper, he seemed to find reports that one
county meeting after another had passed anti-Northern and Southern rights
resolutions. At the same time, the state legislature had taken up similar
proposals such as taxing or excluding Northern imports, enslaving or ban-
ishing free Negroes, forbidding postobituary manumission, and tightening
slave discipline in general. Even Governor-elect John Letcher, who was far
from an extremist, had confided to Ruffin that he thought the Union's days
were numbered. "The spirit of disunion seems to be growing fast in Virginia," Ruffin concluded excitedly. "I hope that it is not all gas."[32]

More than anything, he feared that Virginia secessionists would fail to
exploit their opportunities and that "the warm & angry spirit now pervad-

ing the people of Va. will subside, & cool, before it is put to use for asserting
our independence." Several otherwise sympathetic disunionists argued with
him that Virginia—indeed every Southern state except maybe South
Carolina—was totally unprepared to defend its independence, should
Northerners try to force it back into the Union. Wait a while, they cautioned. Postpone secession until Virginia has had enough time to arm. But
Ruffin had waited too long already; he would not hear of any further delay.
The time was "ripe for striking the first blow for secession," he insisted. "I
would prefer that Va. should secede unprepared as we are, but with this
noble spirit of resistance prevailing, to having a year of preparation, &
losing that spirit."[33]

Ruffin's own spirits continued to rise and fall with the prospects for
Southern secession, as he perceived them. Still in Washington on New
Year's Eve, he reflected on the past year's events and contemplated the
future. "This year closes with appearances of awful portent to the Southern
States & to the whole union," he recorded in his diary. "Never has there
been such an opportunity for secession. But I fear it will be allowed to pass
unused—& that after the present fever of excitement & indignation, & spirit
of resistance, there will succeed a general chill & collapse."[34]

9

In January, Ruffin returned to Virginia, where, just as he had feared, the
"warm & angry spirit" of December had cooled considerably. Even Governor Wise, whose fiery and impassioned orders had set thousands of men
marching and drilling throughout the state, was now counseling Virginians
to fight for their rights within the Union. And when South Carolina
proposed that the Old Dominion issue a call for an all-Southern conference
to discuss plans for secession and common defense, the legislature flatly
refused.[35]

Ruffin's friends in South Carolina were simply astonished at Virginia's
response. Reverend John Bachman wrote from Charleston demanding to
know why Virginia had hesitated to break the bonds of Union. Didn't
Virginians realize that the fate of the entire South was at stake? "Frenzy
and madness rule the hour," Bachman declared in exasperation. Soon
Northern abolitionists would have "their feet on our necks and their dag-
gers in our throats." Virginia had already "had a fair specimen of Northern
sentiments in the tender mercies of old Brown." Was it "waiting for something more of the same sort"? "If so," threatened the angry preacher, "you
will have it before long."[36]

Virginia's stubborn moderation continued to frustrate Ruffin. But he
took heart, since extremists and fire-eaters were gaining the upper hand in

other parts of Dixie. Although they represented a numerical minority within each state, men like Rhett and Yancey sensed that the tide of public fear was with them after Harper's Ferry, and they pressed their advantage.

Slavery, they knew, was the basic issue, and over and over secessionists drummed their dire warnings for Southern ears: the South's peculiar institution was not safe within the Union; John Brown and his fiendish raiders had made that fact emphatically clear. In response, Southern rights politicians began to insist on new and extraordinary guarantees for slavery's security, guarantees often deliberately calculated to split first the national Democratic party and then the nation.

The Democrats had scheduled their national convention for late April. But already in January, the Alabama delegation was making plans to disrupt the affair by introducing a plank which would repudiate the party's allegiance to popular sovereignty and substitute a congressional slave code for the federal territories. If the convention refused to endorse this plank or its equivalent in the national platform, Alabama had commanded its delegates to bolt the proceedings. Such a platform, though, would mean political suicide for Northern Democrats and their frontrunning candidate Stephen Douglas, a man whose name was practically synonymous with popular sovereignty. Both sides would meet in Charleston—not the best place for cool and dispassionate politics. Some sort of clash seemed inevitable.[37]

Ruffin, meanwhile, cheerfully anticipated the party's breakup in the spring and spent the preceding months working tirelessly as usual, trying to ready his reluctant state for disunion. At Beechwood and Ruthven that winter, he endeavored to keep up a "general ferment" and even organized a "Ladies Shooting Club" to teach local matrons and belles how to defend themselves against "danger or insult" should secession provoke a conflict that would leave their honor temporarily deprived of male protection. And when the state Democratic party met in Richmond that February to choose delegates to the national convention, Ruffin was there too, dressed nattily in a cheap suit of Virginia homespun and toting his trusty spear. Looking like some queer apparition of the Ancient Mariner, he would corner startled delegates and earnestly exhort them to demonstrate their "patriotism" at Charleston by following Alabama out of the party and from there out of the Union.[38]

10

While he awaited the outcome of "the final struggle" at Charleston, Ruffin embarked on a new project for secession: he began writing a political novel called "Anticipations of the Future." Although he had never attempted fiction before, he got his inspiration from a sketch entitled "Wild Scenes of the South," whose plot revolved around the likely results of disunion. Ruffin thought this sketch was "very foolish," but the central theme intrigued him. After all, was he not a veteran political prophet himself? For years he had written serious articles like "Consequences of Abolition Agitation" and "Cassandra's Warnings," which forecast the South's future in and out of the Union. Perhaps, he decided, he could put his talents to better use and attract a wider audience if he rewrote these same articles as fiction.[39]

Assuming the voice of a blatantly biased, pro-Southern English correspondent for the *London Times*, Ruffin wrote his book in the familiar and comfortable style of letters to the editor. The first letter, dated November, 1864, announced the reelection—by a strictly sectional vote—of Republican William Seward to the presidency. In the story, Seward's first victory in 1860 had prompted "southern patriots" to call for secession, but Southern unionists—"submissionists" the reporter labeled them—had counseled delay. Wait, they had cautioned, for an "overt act" of Northern aggression, a direct violation of the Constitution.

But Seward was much too cagey to commit any clearly illegal or hostile acts. During his first administration, he pretended to adopt a conciliatory attitude towards the South. At the same time he used his patronage powers to undermine slavery, replacing every incumbent Democratic official with a Republican or an abolitionist. In the South, where he could find neither Republicans nor abolitionists, he appointed Southern submissionists, who, he reasoned, were practically the same thing.[40]

Growing even bolder during his second term of office, President Seward gave every major and minor political post to "abolitionists only." Salmon P. Chase replaced Roger Taney as Chief Justice of the Supreme Court. Each of the sixty-eight Republican Congressmen who endorsed Hinton R. Helper's notorious antislavery book, *The Impending Crisis*, and all the conspirators involved in the John Brown affair who had escaped death received "lucrative and important offices." John C. Fremont became Commander-in-Chief of the Army. Nathaniel Banks, Charles Sumner, and Francis P. Blair received European ambassadorships, while Joshua Giddings became United States Minister to Haiti and black abolitionist Frederick Douglass went along as his Secretary of Legation.[41]

Douglass's appointment was only the beginning of a general Republican movement to raise Negroes to positions of political and social equality with whites. The highlight of the Washington social season was a visit from the Haitian Minister, the "Count of Marmalade." The Count was crude, clumsy, and ugly, with "intensely African features," but he was also very rich and a bachelor. "No doubt," commented the *Times* reporter, "his attentions will be acceptable to sundry fair daughters of distinguished abolitionists."[42]

Meanwhile, the Supreme Court reversed the *Dred Scott* decision, making it possible for blacks to become United States citizens and for Congress to keep slavery out of the federal territories. The "Black Republican" Congress, which had been having a heyday passing high protective tariffs and other crippling anti-Southern economic legislation, took its cue from the Court and refused to allow any more new slave states to enter the Union. Instead, Congress admitted free state after free state until there were enough votes to pass and ratify a constitutional amendment abolishing slavery.

For desperate Southerners, this was the final humiliation. The Deep South seceded in December, 1867, and set up an independent confederacy. The states of the Upper South lingered in the Union for a few more weeks, serving as a "protective barrier" against Northern invasion. But in January, when Seward tried to send troops across their borders to coerce the Rebel states to return, they dissolved their Union ties and joined the new Southern nation.[43]

During the brief but costly civil war that followed, Northern abolitionists tried twice to make allies of the Southern slaves and foment servile rebellion, but to no avail. According to the story, loyal and contented blacks rebuffed abolitionist bribes of free land and emancipation and steadfastly defended the gentle white folk they loved and respected.

In Maryland, slaves themselves foiled the plans of their would-be liberators by giving their masters advance warning of the plot. Thus alerted, whites easily beat back the antislavery invaders. Not a single insurrectionist escaped death. As soon as Southerners could erect a gallows, they strung up all captured prisoners. Many abolitionist preachers and lecturers, both black and white, mounted the scaffold; but the prize catch and the first one hanged was that arch-abolitionist and "apostle of insurrection," William Lloyd Garrison, who had come "to witness the expected certain success and triumph of his long and zealous labors in the cause of negrophilism."[44]

While the Maryland incendiaries were being shot or hanged, another abolitionist army was marching toward a similar fate in Kentucky. Led by Owen Brown, son of the notorious John Brown, the army consisted of 3,500 soldiers—800 whites and 2,700 blacks. But, unknown to Brown or the other whites in his company, the majority of black troops had come south not to liberate their brothers and sisters but to join them in bondage. Most of these soldiers were fugitive slaves who were miserable as free men and only wanted a chance to beg their old masters—or any willing white person—to reenslave them. Once inside Kentucky's borders, they deserted en masse.

Kentuckians then easily disposed of Brown and what was left of his tiny army.[45]

The civil war lasted until October, 1868, when the South, joined at the last moment by a secessionist West, emerged battered but victorious. Ruffin's story ended with the North—now threatened by internal insurrections of its own from lower-class whites and "undigested foreigners"—financially ruined and totally prostrate. The South, on the other hand, having established favorable treaties and direct trade relations with Europe, looked forward to a great and prosperous future.

Ruffin secured a publisher for "Anticipations of the Future." But the story would not come out in book form until September, 1860, and Ruffin anxiously awaited the reviews. At times he feared that the last section of his 416-page book "dragged" badly and showed evidence of a "failing mind," but secretly he hoped that his work would create a furor in the South like *Uncle Tom's Cabin* had in the North. He liked to imagine himself toasted by his Southern friends as a hero and denounced by Northern "enemies" as a traitor. Attention was what he craved. To be overlooked would be the cruelest fate of all. But when more than half a year elapsed before he received even a single review, Ruffin had to admit the "mortifying truth": friends and enemies alike had ignored his masterpiece. Far from creating a sensation, his book might just as well have "fallen dead from the press."[46]

11

Ruffin was just putting the finishing touches on "Anticipations of the Future" when word reached him in early May that the Charleston Convention had broken up in a shambles. Northern Democrats had rejected the Alabama platform, and the Alabama delegation, led by a smiling Yancey, had marched out of the hall. Delegates from six Deep South states followed them.

Ruffin was jubilant. Not only did the sectional voting at Charleston demonstrate that Northern Democrats had really been "moderate abolitionists" all along, but surely, he believed, the Convention's results made it painfully clear that no Southerner could ever gain enough Northern votes to become President. Ruffin also rejoiced that the "archdemagogue" and "consummate intriguer," Douglas, had probably ruined his own political chances for November. And if this forwarded "the election of Seward, or any other abolitionist," he decided, "so much the better."[47]

Naturally Ruffin desired Seward's nomination as the Republican standard-bearer in 1860, not only because he had prophesied the choice in his book, but also because Seward was the strongest candidate and stood the best chances of winning the election. Seward's name was anathema to most Southerners because of a speech he made in 1858, which described an "irrepressible conflict" between slavery and free labor. For this very reason, he was just the man Ruffin wanted in the White House: his election would provide an excellent provocation for secession.

Imagine Ruffin's surprise and subsequent disappointment when he learned that the Republican "abolition convention" at Chicago had passed over its best man as well as the other leading contenders and instead had chosen the relatively unknown Abraham Lincoln of Illinois, a man Ruffin considered "inferior in ability & reputation to all." His friend Bachman had warned him in a letter that the Republicans might try "to lull us to sleep a little while longer" by putting "an ass into the presidential chair," where Seward could "lead or drive him." In any case, there would be a "Black Republican" in the White House come November. "Will old Virginia nestle under the wing of that black buzzard?" Bachman taunted. Will it "swallow black republicanism—nigger, tariff & all"?[48]

Appalled at the very idea, Ruffin was astute enough to realize that the cause of Southern secession probably hinged on the fate of the Democratic party. After Charleston, the main body of the Democratic convention had adjourned until June 18, when it would reassemble at Baltimore; the bolters meanwhile planned to hold their own convention one week earlier at Richmond. To Richmond, then, Ruffin would go and urge the Deep South to turn its meeting into a secession convention and form a slave-based republic. Next he would go to Baltimore to implore the rest of the slave states to join the new confederacy.

But first he paid a visit to Columbia, South Carolina, where the state party was in the process of choosing delegates for Richmond. On May 30, he conferred with Rhett, the leader of the new delegation, and assured him that although Virginia would not "now or ever" begin the secession movement, she would follow the lead of South Carolina or any one of the bolder states of the Deep South.[49]

The next day, Ruffin attended the state convention, where, by a unanimous vote, the members formally asked him to take a seat. Since he had already *"assumed"* a chair, Ruffin found the offer disconcerting and not a little embarrassing. Then the convention officers invited him to sit with them on the elevated dais, but he shyly declined "so conspicuous a position."

Ruffin appreciated the honor and attention he received at Columbia, especially compared to Virginia's "neglect" of him, but he was distressed to see how little unanimity there was for disunion even in South Carolina. "There are not many more avowed advocates for secession" in the Palmetto state, he glumly informed his diary, "than there are in Virginia." Perhaps he ought to consider moving deeper south—to Texas or Florida—where his family and slave property would be safer from both Northern aggressors and southern submissionists.[50]

Pushing these dark thoughts aside, Ruffin hurried from Columbia to Richmond. There the rump convention met for only two days before adjourning to await the outcome at Baltimore. Ruffin proceeded on to Maryland but first stopped in Washington in order to survey the national political scene and discuss disunion prospects with friends like Laurence Keitt and James Mason. Keitt thought Lincoln's election was certain, while Mason foresaw "the end of government" approaching rapidly.[51]

Cheered by the good news, Ruffin arrived in Baltimore on June 19, the day after the convention opened. Through persistent wheedling, he managed to obtain a complimentary ticket to the Front Street Theatre, where the delegates were gathered. Regretfully, he noticed that all but two of the state delegations which had walked out in Charleston had returned —looking somewhat abashed—and were asking to resume their seats. More submissionism. But then, to Ruffin's delight, newly elected delegations, friendly to Douglas, were on their feet challenging the credentials of the old delegates and demanding that they be seated instead.

While the party's Credentials Committee retired to wrestle over the conflicting claims to legitimacy, Ruffin returned to the capital. Here he suffered several days and nights of trepidation, fearing that wily Northern Democrats might reconcile with their Southern colleagues and heal the party breach. But he worried for nothing. On June 22, shortly after 9 P.M., he opened a telegram from Baltimore: the Democratic convention had voted to oust the "legitimate" Southern delegation and seat the "bogus" Douglas contestants. In response, all slave state delegates—including those from Virginia—had risen up and left the convention floor. No one expected them to return.

The Democratic party had split, finally and irretrievably. The Northern half went on to select Douglas as its presidential nominee, while the Southern half returned to Richmond and nominated John C. Breckinridge of Kentucky. But there was no longer a national political party to bind the country together. It seemed inevitable that a "Black Republican" would become the next President. Ruffin shivered with anticipation and delight. The day of Southern independence could not be far away. He gave thanks to God: "Laus Deo."[52]

12

More gladdening news—this time of a personal nature—arrived in July. Burwell Sayre, who was now a schoolteacher in Frankfort, Kentucky, wrote to announce that his wife, Mildred, had given birth to their first child, a baby girl. Would Ruffin like to visit them and meet his newest granddaughter?

Ruffin thought the offer over carefully. He had never liked either of the Sayre brothers—they had robbed him of his precious daughters and made him "a miserable & desolate old man." There was also the unfortunate incident just before Mildred's wedding when the Sayres had tried to pressure the Ruffin brothers into selling their shares of Marlbourne. Otherwise, they had threatened to sell their own shares to strangers and move so far west that the Ruffins would never see Mildred or Elizabeth again. Although the Sayres had eventually backed down, bitter feelings remained on both sides. Still, Ruffin had not seen Mildred for almost a year. What was more, he had never seen Kentucky, and he was curious to test the disunion waters in another border state. So he accepted the invitation.[53]

But before he started on his journey, Ruffin spent a few weeks in August at White Sulphur Springs. When he arrived, he found all the gentlemen discussing the presidential contest and the difficult problem of what the South should do if Lincoln were the winner. Ruffin, predictably, pleaded for immediate secession. Why wait for the election? he demanded impatiently. But to his dismay, he found that out of 1,600 guests, he was the only "avowed disunionist *per se.*"[54]

Undaunted, Ruffin pushed on with his crusade. He had come to the Springs armed with his his "usual travelling supply of pamphlets" on slavery and secession. He proceeded to hand them out "to all proper persons." Such a person was Judge John C. Perkins, a wealthy Louisiana cotton planter, who drew Ruffin aside one day and asked if he would be interested in joining a "Publication Society," whose object would be to broadcast firebrand pamphlets and articles like Ruffin's own throughout the South. A full-fledged propaganda effort which played on all the old Southern fears, explained Perkins, might create an irresistable momentum toward disunion. Ruffin needed no more incentive. Without a moment's hesitation, he pledged one hundred dollars annually for the next three years.[55]

13

A crisis atmosphere was building in the South over the probable election of a "Black Republican," and the fire-eaters' hyperbolic warnings and incendiary speeches and writings were beginning to have their desired effect. Abraham Lincoln loved "niggers," they said. His mother was a slut who had had sexual intercourse with black men. His running mate was a mulatto. He was, at the very least, another John Brown, whose election would unleash hordes of blacks on innocent and trusting white Southerners.[56]

Southerners had never fully recovered from John Brown's raid. Now, faced with what many perceived as a new abolitionist threat, they began again to discover slave conspiracies everywhere. Rumors of servile revolts, poisonings, arson, and other acts of sabotage swept the South from late August until election day.[57]

Ruffin was on a train to Frankfort in early September when Johnson A. Hooper, a fellow passenger and the editor of an Alabama newspaper, began talking about all these suspected slave plots. Hooper assured Ruffin that conspiracies were indeed widespread. In fact, he whispered secretly, Alabama papers had concealed hundreds of other incidents involving slave sabotage. In one case, he told Ruffin, whites discovered over one hundred bottles of strychnine hidden in slave quarters. The poison had come from Lincoln's henchmen—"white inciters to murder, arson & insurrection." Shocked, Ruffin loudly denounced these "deplorable" atrocities, but after some thought, he decided that if more such incidents were to occur, he wished they would happen in "dull & lethargic" states like Georgia—extreme but perhaps necessary incentives for secession.[58]

The same thought might have crossed his mind when he reached Kentucky. Although he had had no illusions that Kentuckians were anything better than "contingent or conditional" secessionists, he had never expected to find so many "thorough unionists & submissionists." His son-in-law informed him that there were even wealthy planters who would rather give up their slaves than risk disunion. Sayre also loved the Union, but, unlike his neighbors, he loved slavery more and favored secession if the federal government ever moved to abolish the institution. For this reason, Sayre was "almost a submissionist" in his father-in-law's eyes, while his neighbors regarded him as a political extremist, almost a fire-eater.[59]

Ruffin, however, was the genuine article—a fire-eating secessionist, whose "notorious reputation" had preceded him to the Bluegrass State. He bragged to his diary that among such die-hard Union devotees, "I must be deemed a sort of speculative Benedict Arnold—a traitor & enemy of the country in wishes & design, though not yet in action." Still, despite Ruffin's reputation and "odious" opinions, Frankfort's exclusive, well-bred society treated him so cordially that the old agitator decided to make a special effort to behave himself and control his troublesome tongue.

This was not easy. At a party given by Senator John J. Crittenden, Ruffin first tried valiantly to avoid all political conversations. Finding this "a difficult part to play," he switched tactics and attempted not to offend anyone "directly." He pulled off this coup rather cleverly, he thought, by passing off his most extreme remarks "in jocular fashion" and with "exaggerated expressions."[60]

Before he left Kentucky in late September, Ruffin finally met one man with whom he could relax and to whom he could frankly express his true disunion opinions. Governor Beriah Magoffin was decidely "the most southern man" in Kentucky. Magoffin confidently told Ruffin that if any slave state seceded after Lincoln's election and the new President raised troops to coerce that state back into the Union, then "if that army attempted to march through Kentucky while he was still governor, every night's encampment should be made a graveyard." But despite his bellicose words, Magoffin was no immediate secessionist. He would not use Lincoln's election as an excuse to take Kentucky out of the Union.[61]

14

Sentiments in Virginia were not much different. Ruffin was at Marlbourne in October when he picked up the Richmond *Whig* and learned that "Virginia will *not* unite . . . in 'resistance' to the mere Constitutional election of Abraham Lincoln." "It would be the height of folly and madness for the people of any State to take their stand before the country and before the world on a ground so untenable and so absurd," the *Whig* added. "The intelligent and patriotic people of Virginia entertain no such idea themselves, and will administer a withering rebuke to those who do."[62]

No one in Virginia considered himself more intelligent and more "patriotic" than Edmund Ruffin, but he put down the newspaper with mingled feelings of disgust and panic. It now appeared that most Virginians really were willing "to swallow black republicanism—nigger, tariff & all." But then he had long ago despaired of placing Virginia in the vanguard of the secession movement. What really disturbed him and robbed his nights of sleep was the gnawing fear that this unionist "poison" would infect the rest of the South and not a single slave state would secede after Lincoln's election.

As usual, Ruffin turned to South Carolina which was still the stronghold of secessionist sentiment. Through the columns of the Charleston *Mercury,* he encouraged the Palmetto State to ignore the "conservatism" of its less stalwart fellow states and press forward toward disunion. Southerners needed a single shining example of secessionist courage. "One state will be enough to begin the movement," he proclaimed. "South Carolina will not fail."[63]

South Carolina would not fail, Rhett promised him. On October 20, Rhett wrote his fellow agitator in Virginia that the South Carolina legislature was packed with disunionists. "I believe we are going to break up the Union," he exulted, "if Lincoln is elected."

But Ruffin still needed convincing. He had just come from the State Agricultural Fair in Raleigh, North Carolina, where he had been privy to political news which elated him and then left him crestfallen. On the one hand, Governor Ellis of North Carolina had told him about a secret letter from Governor William Gist of South Carolina, in which Gist revealed his plan to ask the legislature to call a secession convention in the event of Lincoln's election. South Carolina, he stated, would leave the Union—alone if she had to. On the other hand, North Carolina's two United States senators—Thomas L. Clingman and Thomas Bragg —had shrugged off Gist's threats as just so much hot air. If Lincoln were elected, they assured Ruffin, South Carolina would submit. So would every Southern state.[64]

On Sunday, October 28, with the election less than two weeks away, Ruffin lay awake all night, frantic that his countrymen were about to lose another golden opportunity for secession. What more could he do, could anyone do, to insure that Lincoln's election would break up the Union? Finally an idea came to him. The next morning he posted a long letter to William Yancey.

"Within a few days after this letter can reach you," Ruffin began, "the popular vote will have been given in the presidential election, and the results will be known to you. According to all present indications the result . . . will give the election to the avowed abolition candidate." Ruffin did not have to remind Yancey, the "Prince of Fire-Eaters," what that meant: Northern domination "& the beginning of a sure & speedy progress to the extermination of negro slavery, & the consequent utter ruin . . . of the south."

How could patriots like Yancey save their countrymen from "this impending and awful danger and calamity"? Ruffin was ready with an answer. Become another Patrick Henry, he beseeched Yancey, another "great defender of freedom." "You are gifted," he told Yancey, "with the power of eloquence, & through it, the power to sway the public will." Use your silver-tongued voice to rouse your fellow Southerners and convince them to throw off the yoke and manacles of Northern tyranny. As soon as you learn of Lincoln's election, Ruffin directed, swing through the South, stop at every state legislature and secession convention, and preach a mighty sermon for disunion.

How Ruffin wished that he could trade places with Yancey. What a thrill to stir popular passions with magnificent oratory. But he was all too aware of his own oratorical limitations. If Yancey's tongue was silvery, his own was leaden. "I do not urge on you what I would not attempt myself, if endowed with your peculiar power as a public speaker—or even with a far less share," Ruffin stated truthfully, "instead of being, as I am, entirely destitute of such talent." Ruffin would use his own "meager talents" for the rest of his life to assist Yancey in his noble efforts. "But all that I can do is nothing to what you can do," he coaxed, "& with the sure prospect of earning imperishable fame."[65]

15

Although he had no hopes of "imperishable fame" for himself, Ruffin kept his promise to Yancey, and during the week before the presidential contest, he handed out secession propaganda to all his neighbors. But "Virginia," he lamented, "is as yet a bad soil on which to sow such seeds." The soil was so bad that Ruffin had made plans to leave it very soon. He would stay until November 6, he told Yancey, just long enough to cast his ballot for Breckinridge. Then he would head for more hospitable political grounds in South Carolina to await the outcome of Lincoln's election.[66]

Then a terrible thought struck him: what if Lincoln lost the election? What if the Republican candidate moderated his policy toward slavery in the federal territories and alienated his most fanatical supporters? What if Northern Democratic newspapers and politicians convinced voters that Southern threats of secession were genuine? And what if those same voters —moderates and extremists—switched their ballots from Lincoln to one of the other candidates? All these doubts made Ruffin miserable. A Republican defeat would set back the cause of secession for at least another four years, perhaps longer. For this reason, there wasn't a single Republican partisan who prayed with more fervor for Abraham Lincoln's victory than Southern fire-eater Edmund Ruffin.[67]

Ruffin's sons Edmund and Julian felt differently. On Friday night, November 3, the three men sat down after dinner at Beechwood to argue politics. Edmund and Julian were secessionists, of course, but unlike their father, they did not think a single slave state would secede if Lincoln won the election. As a consequence, they both hoped for Lincoln's defeat.

"I most earnestly & anxiously desire Lincoln to be elected," Ruffin answered. He had faith, he told his skeptical sons, that at least one state— probably South Carolina—would secede and that the rest would follow. But "even if otherwise," he added "I wish the question tested & settled now." If there was "general submission" to the election of a "Black Republican," Ruffin foresaw "the end of negro slavery." "I can think of little else," he finished, "than this momentous crisis of our institutions & our fate."[68]

On election eve, Ruffin packed his bags for South Carolina. Too excited to sleep, he sat down at his desk and opened his diary. "No news," he reported, "but the roaring of the approaching storm is heard from every part of the southern states."[69]

11

Striking the First Blow

1

ON THE MORNING of November 6, Ruffin woke up early, his heart pounding with anticipation. "This is the day for the election of electors," he wrote in his diary, "the momentous election" whose results would seal the fate of Southern civilization. Would the Southern states resist Lincoln's victory, preserve the institution of Negro slavery—an institution "on which," he said, "the social & political existence of the south rests"—and thus "remain free"? Or would they submit to Republican rule, accept black emancipation, and thus "be politically enslaved"?[1]

Slavery or freedom. The irony and paradox contained in this ordinarily clearcut choice escaped the fiery old Virginian. But in the context of the world the slaveholders made, with its inverted hierarchy of values, Ruffin longed to become a freedom-fighter. The election of Abraham Lincoln would give him his chance.

That afternoon he drove to the local courthouse and deposited his vote for the Southern candidate, Breckinridge, but he did not stay around to learn the election's outcome. Virginia, as he told Yancey the week before, was still "sterile soil" for disunion, and he was eager to shake its dust from his shoes. In South Carolina, though, the state legislature was about to call for a secession convention. So, before nightfall, Ruffin caught a train bound for Columbia.

The trip southward took almost twenty-four hours, but he found plenty of secession work to occupy him. At every stop along the way, he threw out generous handfuls of disunion broadsides—supplied courtesy of

the "Association of 1860," Charleston's own propaganda agency—and between stations, he walked up and down the train aisles distributing appropriate reading material to his fellow passengers. Recipients in Virginia and
North Carolina tended to regard him rather sourly—citizens from these
states, he noted, were visibly "conservative" and pro-Union. But as soon as
the locomotive puffed into the Palmetto state, a "universal secession feeling
appeared." Young bloods sporting the blue cockade—the revolutionary
badge of the Minute Men—on their hats, climbed aboard at nearly every
station; friendly hands reached for copies of "secesh" leaflets; and Ruffin,
son of the Old Dominion, began to feel less and less like a stranger "in a
strange land."[2]

He felt even more at home when he stepped off the train the next day
in Columbia. A holiday atmosphere permeated the entire city. Business was
nearly at a standstill; men pressed close to bulletin boards and hurrahed
each new confirmation of Lincoln's election; bands played the "Marseil-
laise"; soldiers and para-military troops paraded through the busy streets;
on nearly every corner, soapbox secessionists attracted admiring, cheering
audiences. Anticipating a Republican victory and South Carolina's withdrawal from the Union, Columbians had begun a fiesta of freedom that
would last until after Christmas.

Ruffin beamed at the disunion orgy around him. He picked up his
carpetbag and threaded his way to the Congaree House, the city's main
hotel. Inside the packed lobby, he spotted some of South Carolina's leading
citizens: there was Rhett, tall and bespectacled, with his two strapping sons;
the fiery Keitt; Senator Chesnut, who would resign his office in a few day's
time; editor Richard Yeadon of the Charleston *Courier;* General Bonham;
Congressman William W. Boyce; and many of Ruffin's other old friends and
past acquaintances. Immediately they recognized the snowy-haired visitor
from Virginia and rushed over to shake his hand, clap him on the back, and
draw him into their conversation.[3]

Secession, naturally, was the "all-absorbing topic" of discussion, and
before long, Ruffin was the center of attention. He had begun what turned
into a heated argument with Patrick N. Lynch, the Catholic Bishop of
Charleston, over whether South Carolina should secede alone or wait to act
in concert with other slave states. Lynch favored concerted action, and he
was an eloquent man, "greatly my superior in argument," Ruffin realized.
To make matters worse, a group of curious spectators had encircled the two
debaters and were waiting expectantly for Ruffin's response. He felt terribly
self-conscious, and his palms began to perspire. Bravely, and with more
earnest passion than reason, he turned to answer. The election of a "Black
Republican" President was too gross an insult for South Carolina to ignore,
he said. Even certain defeat was preferable to outright submission.

A "storm of applause" burst from the crowd, and Ruffin, somewhat dazed at his own success, seized the opportunity to bow out gracefully and retire to his room. Very soon afterwards, serenaders gathered outside the hotel beneath the veranda and called for speeches from their favorite orators. The first man they summoned was Edmund Ruffin of Virginia.

Sensing that the sympathy of the crowd was with him, Ruffin faced his audience with unaccustomed self-possession. Southern independence, he declared, "has literally been the one great idea of my life. The defense of the South, I verily believe, can only be secured through the lead of South Carolina. As old as I am, I have come here to join you in that lead."

Amidst cheers and whistles, he urged Carolinians to sever their Union ties *"the sooner... the better."* He scoffed at the danger of a civil war. There would be no harmful repercussions from the North, he promised. Cowardly, money-grubbing Yankees would not tolerate an expensive conflict just to satisfy the blood lust of fanatical abolitionists. And European nations like England and France, whose economies depended so mightily on Southern cotton, would smash any Northern "paper blockade." Should the North be so foolhardy as to initiate hostilities, he said with a confident smile, so much the better. "The first drop of blood spilled on the soil of South Carolina will bring Virginia and every Southern state with you." There was no way South Carolina could lose, but she must act soon and decisively. Honor demanded bold, even desperate, measures. "Precipitate action," he shouted in conclusion, "is better than none."[4]

2

Action was exactly what South Carolina wanted. Her citizens were itching for a fight. Having clamored for secession so often in the past, they could not bear another retreat, another humiliation. Pride and honor were at stake. Fire-eaters warned that if South Carolina backed down again, she would be the laughingstock of the nation. Already Yankees were snickering. "The North claims that the South cannot be kicked into disunion," taunted Rhett.[5]

Indeed, some Northern newspapers unwittingly played into secessionist hands with their derisive comments about Southern "windy bombast" and "empty bluster." Ruffin cut out a particularly insulting article from the *Chicago Democrat* entitled "The Southern Braggarts" and pasted it in his diary. The *Democrat* observed that on election day, eighteen million "free" men had spoken so loudly that "even the most stupid secessionist" could not fail to understand their message: "We will endure your insolence, suffer your tyranny, bear your assumptions no longer!"

Northerners had elected a President who would not "bow the knee" to the "slave oligarchy" and who would place the "accursed institution of slavery" on the road to ultimate extinction. "You have sworn that if we dared elect such a man you would dissolve the Union," the article goaded. "We have elected him, and now we want you to try your little game of secession. Do it if you dare!"

What would the Yanceys, the Rhetts, the Keitts, the Jeff Davises and "all that noble army of traitors" do now? queried the *Democrat.* "Will they eat dirt?" Yes, "the chivalry will eat dirt," the editors predicted. "They will back down. They never had any spunk anyhow. The best they could do was to bully, and brag and bluster." The Union had nothing to fear from these fire-eating "knights of the Sunny South," for they were "just such heroes as Sancho Panza was—wonderful hands at bragging and telling fantastical lies, but when it comes to action count them out."[6]

What "blindness," thought Ruffin, after reading "The Southern Brag-garts." What "astonishing delusion." But he, for one, prayed that North-erners would continue to ignore and ridicule secessionist threats until the South was safely out of the Union. That way there would be much less chance of any federal interference.

Still, the charge of Southern cowardice rankled. To prove that at least one member of the "chivalry" was ready for action and would never "eat dirt," Ruffin set out the next morning to find General Jones, head of the South Carolina Minute Men, and offer his services. Before noon, he was an official enlistee, and the Reverend Bachman's sister, Catherine, was sewing the blue cockade on his wide-brimmed hat. "With such a cause, & such defenders," she told him admiringly, "the daughters of Carolina need not tremble."[7]

The sons of Carolina felt the same. On November 8, a deputation of seniors from the College of South Carolina called on Ruffin at the Congaree and invited him to address their student body. Governor Gist received him at the State House and thanked him profusely for the John Brown pike that now graced his office. And in the House and Senate chambers, legislators extended a warm invitation to their honored guest from Virginia to take a seat among them.

Two days later, Ruffin witnessed the unanimous passage of a resolution calling for a state convention, whose purpose would be to consider "the value of the Union." "Thus this great & important measure, which I have so long anxiously desired, is adopted," he recorded in his diary, "& on this hereafter glorious day, the 10th of November, is inaugurated the revolution which will tear the slave-holding states from their connection with the northern section, & establish their separate independence."[8]

The serenading began early that evening, but Ruffin's tired old bones required rest from all the unusual excitement; so, after listening to the first five speakers, he retired to his room. Later he learned that Rhett had spoken, and he sorely regretted missing the speech. Rhett had become quite a hero over the past few days, and Ruffin took a great deal of personal satisfaction from his friend's newfound popularity. For, like himself, Rhett had been a prophet without honor in his own country. Even in hotheaded South Carolina, Rhett had championed the disunion cause with such fire and persistence that many of his colleagues had dismissed him as a nuisance and a crank. But Rhett—again like Ruffin—had borne the criticism of his countrymen with the air of a persecuted martyr, convinced that he was right and everyone else was wrong. Now South Carolina hailed him as "the father of secession." Local communities organized Rhett Guards in his honor, and a restaurant even decorated its window with a life-sized portrait of him that glowed after dark.[9]

3

The time for prophets had finally arrived—at least in the Palmetto state— and Ruffin, too, was in his glory. Four days after he arrived in Columbia, he wrote a letter to his son Edmund, claiming that "the time since I have been here has been the happiest of my life." South Carolina's citizens had always treated him with kindness and respect but never before with such an outpouring of genuine love and popular admiration. "My coming was hailed as if a subject of public interest and rejoicing," he said. "What a contrast to my position in my native state!" "No prophet," Edmund duti- fully consoled his father, "is without honor except in his own country."[10]

If South Carolina knew how to honor her prophets, she also exacted what for Ruffin was a stiff price: public speeches. Suddenly the shy little Virginian found himself in great demand as a speaker, and although this flattered his "self-love," he could never feel completely at ease in front of an audience. Yet on November 14, he agreed to visit the county seat at Sumterville and speak on the necessity of electing immediatists to the state convention in December.

No visiting dignitary could have received a more enthusiastic welcome. One hundred fifty Minute Men met his train and escorted him to his lodgings, while someone fired off a cannon as a personal salute. At night there was the inevitable serenade, and the next morning, amid equal fanfare, Ruffin made his way to the crowded courthouse and mounted the podium.

Speaking without notes, he rambled on for three-quarters of an hour, then ended abruptly, having forgotten to mention most of his main points. Fortunately for him, the audience cared less about what he said than what he symbolized, and they gave him a rousing round of applause. Several spectators assured him afterwards that his very presence in South Carolina had immeasurably forwarded the cause of disunion. Others even congratulated him on his "plain," unadorned style of oratory.[11]

The next day he took the train to Charleston, where more triumphs awaited him. At the Citadel—South Carolina's military college—the parading cadets glimpsed him sitting in their grandstand and whooped for joy. Ruffin responded with a graceful bow. That evening, a group of the city's most prominent citizens, headed by Mr. Carlisle, editor of the *Courier,* knocked at his hotel room door. The townspeople would like to serenade their distinguished guest, Carlisle explained. Would Ruffin be so good as to oblige with a few words?

The request touched the old man's heart. Stepping out onto the balcony, his eyes ablaze with emotion and his head jerking so defiantly that the locks of long white hair danced upon his shoulders, he pledged his loyalty to the Palmetto state and announced his intentions to become a Virginia expatriate. He would punish the Old Dominion for her insults to Southern pride and honor. She would lose the prophet she had so callously ignored. "If Virginia remains in the Union, under the domination of this infamous, low, vulgar tyranny of Black Republicanism, and there is one other state in the Union that has bravely thrown off the yoke," he swore, "I will seek my domicile in that State and abandon Virginia forever. If Virginia will not act as South Carolina, I have no longer a home, and I am a banished man."[12]

4

But before he condemned himself to exile, Ruffin wanted to give his native state every chance to come to its senses and join the growing disunion movement. Already there were rumors that the cotton states would follow South Carolina if she seceded. He noticed that even "lukewarm" states like North Carolina and Maryland were starting to show signs of "ferment." The Old Dominion's "universal calm" in the present crisis puzzled Ruffin. Perhaps, he thought hopefully, "the quiet of Va. is but the lull which precedes a storm."[13]

For the moment, though, disunion clouds looked like they might burst over Georgia, where even staunch unionists like Alexander Stephens and Benjamin Hill were advocating "resistance" to Lincoln's election and where the legislature had recently imitated South Carolina by calling for its own state convention to meet in January.

On November 21, Ruffin accompanied Rhett on a short visit to Millegeville to confer with dedicated secessionists like Governor Joseph E. Brown. At night the two unofficial ambassadors for disunion and their colleagues celebrated the legislature's action by breaking out several bottles of vintage champagne. Even the usually abstinent Ruffin "committed the unusual excess of drinking half a glass to the most speedy secession of Georgia." "Oh!" he sighed afterwards. "If I may see such a time in Va.!"[14]

Suddenly homesick, Ruffin packed his trunk—a "miserable Yankee cheat" that promptly fell to pieces and had to be replaced—and departed for Virginia. On the way back, he relived in his mind all the "glorious" events of the past two weeks, dwelling especially on the visions of his personal successes. But what good were the honors and praises of strangers when "accompanied by the powerful & mortifying reflection" that his native state still rejected and abused him, when his "own country," where he had "long lived & labored, & had so much served & benefitted," continued to deny him the "rewards" and public affection he so desperately wanted? When at home he felt he could count on "far more enemies to depreciate & censure me, & many to calumniate" than on "friends & approvers to applaud"?

"A prophet is not without honor except in his own country," Ruffin repeated over and over in his diary. And nowhere was this homily more apparent than when he reached Richmond. There no honor guard waited to greet his arriving train, no cannon saluted his return, no cheering throng offered a serenade or begged for a few words of secessionist wisdom. Instead, the governor greeted him with a cold shoulder, the townsfolk saluted him with hostile glares, and a group of angry citizens offered to ride him out of town on a rail.[15]

Still, despite his lack of popularity and the "disgusting" Union spirit he encountered in Richmond, Ruffin thought he could detect a slight shift in Virginia's political winds. While "conservative" newspapers like the Richmond *Whig* were still standing with the federal government and getting ready to bid good riddance to South Carolina, more extreme Democratic organs—like the *Enquirer* and the *Examiner*—were beginning to take on a belligerent, prosecession tone, even going so far as to suggest that Lincoln's election was equivalent to a Northern *"declaration of war."* Some of Ruffin's Prince George neighbors—formerly loyal Union men—were saying fatalistically that since the Union was bound to split anyway, Virginia "ought to go with the southern fragment." And in several parts of the state, a friend wrote to inform him, "secession is now the universal sentiment." Even many "life long unionists" were clamoring for "immediate dissolution."[16]

But others in the Old Dominion, particularly slaveholders living in the Northern section of the state—and therefore most vulnerable, should there be an enemy invasion—were not so sure about forsaking the federal government. They felt themselves pulled in two directions: fire-eaters told them that if they did not secede from the Union they would lose their slaves;

unionists countered that secession would sound "the death knell of slavery," would provoke civil war and servile rebellion and thus destroy the
very institution it sought to save. Who would protect the master class
against black insurrectionists and "Black Republican" armies? the Union
men wanted to know. Certainly not that "unreliable" class of overseers and
poor whites who declared without hesitation that "they would not lift a
finger in the defense of the rights of slaveholders." Since committees in the
Senate and House of Representatives were already seeking new guarantees
for slavery's protection within the Union, moderates pleaded with extremists to postpone any secession action and give the forces of compromise a
chance to succeed.

All these fears were groundless and ridiculous, Ruffin responded impatiently. There would be no Northern attempts at coercion, no war, no slave
revolts, no chance for class conflict—as long as the slave states acted immediately to leave the Union. There must be no further postponement of
Southern independence. Any hopes of working out a just compromise with
Yankee "fanatics" were vain indeed. The time for foot-dragging was over.
"Delay," he warned all those who would listen, *"is Submission."*[17]

5

Virginians hedged so much over disunion that it nearly drove poor Ruffin
to distraction. But South Carolinians, at least, had made up their minds.
When Ruffin returned to Charleston in late December for the state convention, he discovered a wonderful unanimity among the delegates. No one
wanted to waste time debating the proper course of action; immediate
secession was a foregone conclusion. The presiding officer, David F. Jamison, epitomized the prevailing mood when he banged his gavel—which had
the word "secession" carved into it—and urged his fellow conventioneers
not to think but to do or, in the words of the revolutionary Danton, "To
dare! and again to dare! and without end to dare!"[18]

At one o'clock on December 20, with Ruffin cheering them on, 169
daring souls resolved, without dissent, "that the union now subsisting between South Carolina and the other States, under the name of 'The United
States of America,' is hereby dissolved." That evening, they reassembled at
Institute Hall—now renamed Secession Hall—to sign and ratify the secession ordinance. Ruffin was there too, seated among the delegates as special
guest of former Governor John Manning. Other less privileged spectators
jammed the galleries and spilled over into the rear and sides of the audi-
torium. The ceremony, which began at 7:00 P.M., lasted almost two hours,
yet, Ruffin observed, "No one was weary & no one left." Finally, when the
last member had affixed his name, Jamison held up the piece of parchment

and solemnly announced: "The Ordinance of Secession has been signed and ratified, and I proclaim the State of South Carolina an independent Commonwealth."[19]

With these words, joyful pandemonium broke loose. The men in the audience jumped up and down, whistled, cheered, shouted, stamped their feet, and tossed their hats into the air; the ladies fluttered their handkerchiefs and cried. Outside, the people of Charleston were dancing in the streets. Church bells rang, cannon boomed, and fusillades of firecrackers lit up the sky. Men marched by carrying bold disunion placards; others waved specially designed flags like the one depicting "Abe" Lincoln vainly attempting to split a palmetto log.

Gazing out his hotel room window late that night, Ruffin watched the merrymakers below and fondly touched the "secession pen" he had pocketed from the convention as a valued memento. Although his old bones were too tired to join the young folks in their nightlong celebration, there was no happier individual in all of South Carolina. As he drifted off to sleep, he could still hear the distant sounds of military bands and the crack of exploding fireworks—a fitting disunion lullaby.[20]

6

The secession bandwagon got rolling in South Carolina, and Ruffin—always a tireless disunion worker—was willing and eager to push it across the entire South, personally if he had to. Six days after South Carolina officially broke with the federal government, he was headed for Florida to urge the state convention in Tallahassee to climb on board. From there, he expected to bring his one-man campaign to conventions in Alabama, Mississippi, and Georgia.

He must have been an appealing figure, an inexhaustible emissary for secession. A reporter for *Frank Leslie's Illustrated,* a New York weekly news journal, thought he was good enough copy to introduce him to Northern readers in an article which included a photograph. Ruffin kept the clipping for his diary.

As the reporter described him, Edmund Ruffin was a quaint and picturesque character: a Virginia patriarch and born secessionist, who must have "imbibed with his mother's milk the desire to break up the compact that binds this great Confederacy together." Although he was "laden with years" and his shoulder-length hair was "perfectly white," Ruffin had "not yet by any means reached the doddering state." His form was "not bent" nor his gait "slow or uncertain." "To meet him in the street," the reporter assured readers, "he would seem like one who had just stepped out from the Past into the new world of the Present." But his clothes—of "patriotic homespun"—were cut in the modern fashion, and on the left side of his hat he wore the "ever-present cockade." "And so," the article concluded, "with this symbol of resistance hoisted at the peak, the old man goes from Convention to Convention, a political Peter the Hermit, preaching Secession wherever he goes."[21]

And his preaching was not ineffective. On January 7, two days after his sixty-seventh birthday, Ruffin delivered a brief but impassioned disunion sermon to the convention delegates at Tallahassee; three days and several "tedious" Union speeches later, Florida seceded. The next day, Ruffin was on his way to Montgomery when a telegraphic dispatch interrupted his journey by informing him that Alabama and Mississippi no longer required his presence: they were both newly declared independent countries. The Georgia Convention was scheduled to meet next on January 19, and Ruffin would have gone there to lend a helping hand, had events in Charleston which suddenly recalled him to South Carolina not cut short his convention-hopping.

7

When Ruffin first departed from Charleston in late December, the only vestiges of federal authority still remaining there were three Union forts in the harbor. All three—Castle Pinckney, Moultrie, and Sumter—were in partial stages of completion, and only one—Moultrie—was garrisoned. Still, South Carolinians considered the presence of a "foreign" power on their soil an affront to their new nationhood and immediately sent commissioners to Washington to negotiate the transfer of the forts. In the meantime, there was a kind of gentlemen's agreement between President Buchanan and the South Carolina authorities to the effect that the military status quo in Charleston bay would remain unchanged.[22]

But on December 26, the very day Ruffin set off for Florida, Major Anderson, the Union commander at Moultrie, secretly transferred his troops from Moultrie to the more defensible Sumter. Outraged by the President's "egregious deception," as Ruffin put it, South Carolina militia seized the other forts and ringed the harbor with guns. A few days afterwards, Ruffin heard stories that a Northern vessel, the *Star of the West,* was sailing toward Charleston with reinforcements for Sumter. Rumors flew that South Carolina's shore batteries would never allow the ship to land; fighting was expected to break out at any moment. Ruffin could have kicked himself for leaving.

He almost turned back; to witness a little bloodshed would be good, he thought, "both for my health & pleasure." But he decided to push on, figuring that news of armed conflict between Yankees and Southerners would give a tremendous boost to immediatists, deflate submissionists, and "stir doubly fast the sluggish blood of the more backward southerners" like those in Virginia and the other unionist border states.[23]

Once Florida was safely out of the Union and Mississippi and Alabama had seceded without his help, Ruffin rushed back to Charleston "to commit a little treason to the northern government" by shoveling some dirt for the strengthening of Fort Moultrie. He observed with pleasure that defense work in and around the city was proceeding at top speed, although few persons, including himself, actually anticipated war. In fact, fire-eaters were generally fond of boasting that they would drink all the blood spilled in any conflict or wipe it up with a handkerchief.[24]

Privately, though, Ruffin half expected a show of federal military force, particularly if only one or a few slave states seceded. But Buchanan failed to take any action beyond sending the *Star of the West*. When Charleston batteries opened fire on the ship and it turned and sailed away, Ruffin knew that he could "trust in the President's general imbecility" and his "desire to do nothing" but serve out his term of office peacefully and leave the problems of a divided nation to his successor.

The key to avoiding war with the Lincoln government, contended Ruffin, was his native Virginia, for she was the anchor holding the eight states of the Upper South in the Union. By February, the Lower South was already out. If Virginia seceded before Lincoln took the oath of office on March 4, most of the other border states would follow. Faced with a fait accompli—a united Southern confederacy of thirteen to fifteen states—the new President would be helpless. Ruffin could not conceive what sort of "folly or infatuation" would then prompt Lincoln to initiate hostilities. But he predicted that if Virginia did not secede in time, emboldened Republican abolitionist "fanatics" would likely provoke a civil war.

Meanwhile, unaware of the awesome responsibility that Ruffin envisioned for them, Virginians had taken tentative steps both to preserve and destroy the Union. After issuing a call for a national Peace Congress to meet in Washington on February 4 to discuss possible ways of enticing the seceded states back into the Union, the legislature announced that on the very same day, the people of Virginia would elect delegates to a state secession convention. In Charleston, Ruffin cursed the first move but applauded the second. Then he hurried home to agitate for the election of immediate secessionists.[25]

8

On February 4, Ruffin suffered what he considered a bitter personal insult as well as a severe political setback. He had badgered his reluctant son

Edmund into running as an avowed secession delegate to the upcoming convention, but voters in Prince George and Surry counties not only rejected his son's candidacy but handed an overwhelming victory to Ruffin's longtime political "enemy," unionist Timothy Rives. "Demogoguism & submission" had triumphed once again, Ruffin concluded ruefully. He blamed himself, too, for Edmund's defeat: "enemies" were striking at the father through the son.

But the younger Ruffin's political beating was the result of more than just his father's lack of popularity. All over Virginia, the electorate rejected secession candidates and sent moderates and Union men to represent them at the Richmond convention. To Ruffin's further chagrin, he learned that Pennsylvania had fired a thirty-four-gun salute to celebrate the news and that several towns in New York had done the same. "This marked applause offered by the abolitionists & the north," he declared disgustedly, "ought to cover" Union savers in the Old Dominion "with shame."[26]

Still, Ruffin did not give up hope. As was his habit concerning matters of secession, he could always find a ray of victory gleaming through the darkest clouds of defeat. The Union triumph in Virginia, he prophesied, would cause "Black Republicans" to grow overconfident, to "harden their hearts" against compromise, to "yield nothing," and thus would sabotage the "useless & ridiculous" efforts of the Washington Peace Congress.[27]

Throughout the month of February, Ruffin carefully followed the glacial progress of the peace conference and the Virginia Convention, hoping that the failure of the former would provoke immediate secession by the latter. He was terribly eager to get his state and himself out of the Union before inauguration day. But both parties moved with such exasperating slowness. The Virginia Convention, Ruffin complained impatiently, took "as much time to elect door-keepers . . . as the Convention of S. C. used to dissolve the Union." What a contrast also to the seven seceded states, which boycotted the Washington conference and sent their representatives instead to Montgomery, Alabama, where they swiftly dispensed with "time-consuming" and "inefficient" democratic procedures and adopted a Constitution, elected a President and Vice-President, and organized a new Southern republic—the Confederate States of America.

By the end of the month, Ruffin saw plainly that the Old Dominion would not join the Confederacy, at least not until the incoming Congress had had a chance to act on the proposals put forth by the peace delegates. Fed up with Virginia's dawdling, he began to pack his suitcases. He would keep the promise he had made last November in Charleston; he would abandon his old "country" and seek a new home in South Carolina. "I will be out of Va. before Lincoln's inauguration," he vowed, "& so wiil avoid being, as a Virginian, under his government even for an hour. I, at least, will become a citizen of the seceded Confederate States, & will not again reside in my native state . . . until Va. shall also secede, & become a member of the Southern Confederacy."[28]

9

On March 4, Ruffin was in Charleston, standing outside the telegraph office and jockeying for position with the excited crowds in front of the bulletin boards. Lincoln's inaugural address was just coming over the wires, and Ruffin was interested in learning the new President's intentions toward the Confederacy.

Lincoln's message was mild and conciliatory, but Ruffin read in it only more evidence of "northern blindness" and unyielding "anti-slavery fanaticism." Lincoln pleaded with his countrymen for mutual forbearance and brotherhood. He denied the legality of secession and maintained that the Union was still whole, but he also promised not to invade the South or to coerce the seceded states back into the federal fold. "The government will not assail *you*," he assured Confederates. "You can have no conflict, without being yourselves the aggressors."

But as President, Lincoln had sworn a sacred oath to uphold and faithfully execute the laws of the United States. He would not violate that oath by relinquishing federal property—including forts and military installations—that were on Confederate soil but still in Union hands. To Ruffin, these were fighting words. This "settles the question," he exclaimed as he pushed his way through the crowd. "There must be war."[29]

Ruffin was far from being upset at the prospect of a civil war, which even his daughter Mildred had warned him would be "the more violent for being between brothers." On the contrary, he was impatient for the conflict to begin at once. He had just heard "alarming" news from former Governor John Peter Richardson of South Carolina, a recently returned representative to the Confederate Convention at Montgomery, who confided that the other delegates believed that the majority of Southerners in every state but South Carolina were against secession and that if the question were ever put to a popular vote, the Confederacy would dissolve in a twinkling. "Unless you sprinkle blood in the face of the Southern people," one delegate had advised Confederate President Jefferson Davis, "they will be back in the old Union in less than ten days." A sprinkle of blood, agreed Ruffin, was also just what fence-straddlers like Virginia needed to drive them out of the Union.[30]

10

The situation at Fort Sumter—where Major Anderson and his crew were still grimly hanging on—was ideal for provoking bloodshed, and the people of South Carolina were in a bellicose mood. Anderson desperately required supplies and fresh troops, but the Confederate commissioners in Washington made it clear that their government would interpret any attempt to provision Sumter as an act of war. Throughout the month of March, contradictory reports from the North kept Charleston on edge: now Lincoln was about to evacuate Sumter, now he was about to send reinforcements. In the meantime, volunteer troops poured into the city by the thousands, recruitment being a simple matter, since female "patriots" threatened to secede from any man who shirked his duty. By early April, the soldiers were bored with their constant inactivity, and the natives were growing restless.

On April 5, Ruffin observed that "the troops & citizens of Charleston are becoming feverishly impatient for the reduction of Sumter." On April 6, he wished "with all [his] heart" that Lincoln would "send a strong squadron to force the passage & attack the defences of Charleston." On Saturday, April 7, Charleston authorities cut off Sumter's food and communications, and on Sunday morning, Ruffin—whose own patience had run out—borrowed a musket and ammunition and cajoled his way on board the first supply boat making its daily rounds to the Confederate fortifications.

Ruffin was well aware that without Northern reinforcements, Anderson now had only three alternatives: surrender, starve, or fight. Hoping that the major would choose the latter option, Ruffin saw his little boat as a lightening rod which might draw Sumter's fire and thus provide the opening incident for civil war. He dismissed the possible danger to his own person and to the other passengers as "very trifling," but his courage and motives were not entirely unselfish. He was a man who yearned for recognition, and the feeling that he had nothing to lose but his anonymity made Ruffin brave to the point of recklessness. "I greatly coveted the distinction & *éclat* which I might have acquired if the steamer had been fired upon, & we had refused to yield," he admitted frankly afterwards. A few lost lives, a few wounded bodies—these were a small price to pay for the glue that would bind the Confederacy together.

As the boat passed within a few hundred yards of Sumter, one of the passengers spied federal soldiers loading a cannon. For a few minutes, Ruffin felt his heart beat faster, and he clutched his gun tightly to his side. But Sumter held its fire.

Deprived of his distinction and éclat, the dejected old warrior returned to the docks that afternoon. He found the people of Charleston in a frenzy of excitement, and soon his own spirits brightened. For while he was out trying to tease Sumter into an attack, a courier from Washington had arrived announcing Lincoln's officially stated intentions to provision the fort with food. The mission would be peaceful, the President had insisted, but Ruffin and the Charleston citizenry knew that this was their signal to "strike a blow!"[31]

11

Determined that South Carolina should not strike without him, Ruffin arose early the next morning, dressed quickly, and paid his hotel bill. Then with his gun in one hand and his carpetbag in the other, he scurried toward the wharves, where the ten o'clock steamer would take him and other recruits out to Morris Island. He chose Morris Island purposely, because its batteries commanded the main ship channel into the harbor—the channel through which an enemy fleet would have to pass to reach Fort Sumter—and thus afforded him an excellent position to observe any hostile action and perhaps even help drive the invading Yankees into the sea.

While he waited dockside, attired (just as *Leslie's Illustrated* had pictured him) as an ancient secession hero in a suit of Southern homespun, he was an inspiration to the other volunteers, most of whom were young enough to be his grandsons. They gathered round him, lavishing him with compliments and making such a fuss over his bravery and Southern patriotism that Ruffin was quite overcome. He modestly protested that he feared they were exaggerating his "very small effort or sacrifice."

Despite his protestations, the praises continued throughout the voyage to Morris Island. As the ship approached land, Ruffin could see a large crowd of soliders who had gathered on the beach to greet the new arrivals. One man, Captain George B. Cuthbert of the Palmetto Guards, immediately recognized the familiar figure with the flowing white hair standing on the ship's deck. "Three cheers for Mr. Ruffin!" he sang out. And the men obliged with stirring cries.

Blushing with embarrassment and pride, Ruffin stepped ashore, took off his hat, and acknowledged the cheers with a deep sweeping bow. Right away, several officers rushed up and invited him to join their respective units. Finally, after a great deal of consideration, he chose to stay with Cuthbert's Palmetto Guards because of their select membership—"no one being admitted who is not perfectly respectable," he assured his diary—and because the Guards were attached to the Iron Battery under Major P. F. Stevens, who was the toast of Charleston for having fired on the *Star of the West*. [32]

12

Stationed with this illustrious group at Cummings Point on the northernmost tip of the island, Ruffin looked for the arrival of the Yankee supply ships and awaited orders to seize Fort Sumter. In the meantime, he dined in the officers' mess and chatted amiably with his superiors, but otherwise, he insisted on sharing all the hardships and fatigues of an ordinary private, even rejecting the camp commander's offer of a soft warm bed, sleeping instead on a hard straw pallet in an open tent exposed to the cold night air.

When after almost three full days of expectant waiting, neither the ships nor the attack had materialized, Ruffin and his youthful companions grew impatient at the delay. "Excitement increases hourly," he reported on Friday, April 11. "To myself & others not in authority . . . every hour passed before attacking Fort Sumter seems a loss of precious time & opportunity."

But Confederate authorities—namely President Davis and his lieutenant in Charleston, General Pierre T. Beauregard—still hoped to avoid the onus of initiating open warfare and possibly drawing the first blood. Accordingly, they sent their aides on several missions to Sumter to demand Anderson's peaceful surrender. Each time Anderson refused. But he admitted that if the Northern relief expedition did not arrive before April 15, he and his men would be forced to evacuate. The Confederate high command found these conditions unacceptable, and Davis reluctantly issued the order to take Sumter.[33]

Word reached the restless troops on April 11 that a bombardment would begin that evening. At six o'clock, Ruffin and his comrades paraded around the sand dunes and then marched to their batteries, loaded the cannon, and trained their sights on Sumter. But the orders were premature —Beauregard would make one more fruitless effort to get Anderson to give up without a fight. At eight o'clock, Ruffin and the others, feeling downcast and terribly disappointed, marched back to their quarters.

Later that night, though, Ruffin was cheered considerably when Captain Cuthbert visited his tent and informed him that the attack would definitely commence at daybreak. What was more, Beauregard had ordered the Palmetto Guards to fire the first shot at Sumter, and the other men had unanimously agreed that that honor ought to go to their eldest recruit. "Highly gratified by the compliment," Ruffin accepted the offer without hesitation, assuring the captain repeatedly that he was only too "delighted to perform the service." Surely, he reasoned privately, Cincinnatus would have done no less for his country.[34]

13

Shortly before four o'clock the next morning, drums summoned the soldiers to their battle stations, and Ruffin, who had slept in his clothes, hurried immediately to his position. At 4:30, as scheduled, a mortar battery at Fort Johnson, located across the harbor, threw up a signal shell. With a roar that "woke the echoes from every nook and corner of the harbor," said a Confederate officer, the shot swung out in a high red arc, hung over Fort

Sumter for a split second, and then exploded—according to the claims of several spectators—in the perfect pattern of a palmetto leaf.[35]

Ruffin, standing proud and erect next to his loaded cannon, a heavy-duty sixty-four-pound Columbiad, recognized the attack signal. Without a qualm, he jerked the lanyard, stepped back, and watched as his shell speeded toward its target, plunging deep into Sumter's northeast parapet. The shot may have landed in uncomfortable proximity to the ear of the dozing Abner Doubleday, a Union captain stationed at the fort. At least Doubleday liked to think so. In later years, he would always describe the shell that had jarred his sleep as "the one that probably came with Mr. Ruffin's compliments."[36]

In any case, further Union slumber was impossible as one by one, each of the fourteen Confederate batteries took its turn firing into the gray mist at the enemy fortress. But for two hours, Sumter failed to answer, and Ruffin became "fearful that Major Anderson . . . did not intend to fire at all." Victory over a foe who refused to fight back lacked the essential romance and glory he craved and "would have cheapened our conquest of the fort," Ruffin complained. So, when the first Federal shell came ricocheting over the water a little while later, he and the other Confederates were relieved and grateful.

The volleying continued back and forth all day with neither side managing to inflict much damage on the other. Over at Fort Moultrie, carefree Confederate soldiers chased after spent Union cannon balls—an activity, Ruffin noted with amusement, that lasted throughout the siege. Deferring his own search for wartime memorabilia until later, Ruffin spent most of his day perched high atop a parapet in the Iron Battery, from which he shouted helpful advice to the Confederate gunners below him. Now and then, he climbed down to fire off a shot himself.

After dark, the cannonade stopped, but Confederate mortars kept up their rhythmic blasts all night. Ruffin retired early to his bed, determined to get some much-needed rest. But he was too excited to sleep. Stepping outside his tent, he stood for hours watching the luminous course of the shells as they skimmed across the sky and burst in a final brilliant explosion over the beleaguered enemy fort. This was a grant moment, a historic occasion, he realized quite suddenly—the Confederacy's Fourth of July.[37]

14

The next morning, bleary-eyed but happy, Ruffin resumed his post at Stevens' Battery. But his lack of rest was about to play him a cruel trick. Shortly after breakfast, having nothing else to do at the time, he innocently leaned back against the wall of a mortar battery. Before he knew it, he was fast asleep. Suddenly a ten-inch mortar directly over his head fired its shot. Even Abner Doubleday could not have suffered a ruder awakening. Ears ringing from the shock, Ruffin staggered to his feet. His hearing, already poor, had received severe and permanent damage; though there would be some gradual improvement over the next few days, for the moment he could make out nothing softer than a shout.

Luckily, he needed only his eyes that day to tell that Sumter was doomed. Confederate cannoneers, whose aim had steadily improved with practice, had torn the fort's brick walls to pieces, and at eight o'clock that morning, a red hot shot from Moultrie ignited the officers' barracks. From his position at Stevens' Battery, Ruffin watched the fiercely raging flames race from building to building, until a dense cloud of white smoke enveloped the entire fort. The spectacle filled him with joy and exultation. Yet he also pitied the brave Federals, who kept up their fire through it all and steadfastly refused to surrender. At noon, though, Ruffin rejoiced when the flag of the United States, the Stars and Stripes, toppled to the ground as a result of the bombardment. And he cheered mightily a short time later when a waving white flag announced that Anderson and his men had finally had enough. Surrender was unconditional. For Ruffin, it was a glorious triumph.[38]

The next day, April 14, 1861, was victory Sunday. It was a gala holiday, and Charleston Harbor swarmed with ferries, launches, skiffs, dories, rowboats—anything that would float—all carrying curious residents out to gawk at the first prize of war.

At ten o'clock that sunny morning, the Palmetto Guards fell out for parade with Ruffin in the lead, proudly bearing the company flag. Then they all boarded a steamship and made their way across the shimmering waters to Fort Sumter, where they waited politely for several hours for the federal occupants to vacate and depart.

Around four o'clock, Ruffin heard the Union band strike up "Yankee Doodle" and watched as Anderson and his soldiers solemnly filed through Sumter's battered gates for the last time. A few minutes later, the Confederate Stars and Bars and the Palmetto ensign of South Carolina floated side by side over the rubble of Sumter. Ruffin cheered, but his voice was lost in the general triumphant din that encompassed the whole harbor.

The Palmetto Guards had the honor of being one of the first detachments to take possession of the fort. Once inside, Captain Cuthbert dismissed his men, and Ruffin went off by himself on a sight-seeing and souvenir-hunting expedition. Poking the charred ruins, he discovered pieces of shell fragments and eagerly stuffed them into his knapsack as keepsakes. Once choice bit of shrapnel he set aside to give Jefferson Davis as a personal gift. A few hours later, Ruffin bid a fond farewell to his comrades in arms and took the next boat back to Charleston, where, unknown to him, a hero's welcome awaited.[39]

15

Charlestonians had always liked Edmund Ruffin, but now they adored him. All the local papers had followed his military exploits during the recent battle. He was the nearest thing the Confederacy had to a genuine folk hero. Wherever he went for the next few days, men, women, and children followed him just to catch a glimpse, shake his hand, or hear the story of the first shot directly from the old soldier himself.

Newspapers heralded his bravery. An Alabama reporter compared him to Cincinnatus—a comparison Ruffin liked—and raved about the "sublime spectacle" of this silver-haired planter–aristocrat, "who, when the warcloud lowered over the gallant city of Charleston volunteered as a private, and with his knapsack on his back, tended his services to South Carolina." "All honor to the chivalric Virginia[n]," proclaimed the Charleston *Courier.* "May he live many years to wear the ladeless wreath of honor placed upon his brow on our glorious Friday!"[40]

Tributes poured in from all over the South. In Mississippi, a volunteer regiment christened itself "The Ruffin Rangers." In Georgia, a legislator cast a ballot for Edmund Ruffin as President of the South. In Virginia, Julian and Lottie Ruffin named their newborn son, Edmund Sumter. A sourer note came from the North, where the New York *Post* suggested that "a piece of the first hemp that is stretched in South Carolina, should be kept for the neck of this venerable and bloodthirsty *Ruffian.*" But the old man laughed the threat off and counted this enemy article among his sweetest tributes.[41]

Official recognition followed quickly. In his army report, General Beauregard commended the "noble & gallant Edmund Ruffin, of Virginia," who "fired many guns" and had done as much to capture Fort Sumter as "the youngest of the Palmettos." President Davis sent his "best wishes and grateful acknowledgement of your heroic devotion to the South, of truth and Constitutional Government" and then added his thanks for the shell fragment.[42]

The ladies of Dixie were no less grateful. Dozens of scented letters, addressed to Ruffin on behalf of all Southern womanhood, expressed "high admiration" for his noble deeds. One woman wrote to say that she and her young daughter had read an article that said of Ruffin, "He is always on the right side—a true-hearted southerner!" Is Mr. Ruffin a Christian? the child inquired. "I do not know," replied her mother, "but I hope so. I should be sorry to think he was only on the right side in this life."[43]

But Christian or not, Ruffin was for the time being an extremely glamorous and inspirational figure to many Southerners. He posed in full uniform for the photographer Quinby, and his portrait was then sold throughout Dixie—a sort of Confederate pin-up poster and an appealing advertisement for secession. Fire-eating orators loudly praised Ruffin's heroism, hoping to shame the border slave states, particularly Virginia, into the Confederacy. The selfless example of Edmund Ruffin and the single ball he fired at Fort Sumter, predicted the New York *Tribune's* Charleston correspondent, "will do more for the cause of secession in the Old Dominion than volumes of stump speeches."[44]

16

Is it really true that "you fired the first gun upon Sumter?" Edmund wrote his father. "I hope it is so for Virginians are already proud of it—and congratulate themselves that as backward as she has been she yet fired the first gun."[45]

The firing on Sumter now gave Virginia what it had been waiting for: an overtly hostile Republican act. On April 15, Lincoln called upon the states to furnish 75,000 soldiers to put down the rebellion. The same day, Ruffin and Roger Pryor—who was now hot for secession and war and therefore no longer an "enemy"—received an important telegram from a delegate at the Virginia Convention: "An ordinance of secession will pass in sixty hours."

Ruffin could scacely believe that "so vile a submission body" would change its stripes so quickly, but three days later, a messenger knocked at his hotel room door with wonderful news: on April 17, Virginia had voted to cut her Union ties. Unable to contain his joy, Ruffin hurried as fast as he could to the *Courier* office and fired off the "secessionist cannon" eight times—one shot for each Confederate state. That night he celebrated as he had never celebrated before and in a burst of intemperance downed a glass of ale and another of wine.

The next day, he made arrangements to leave his adopted home and return to Virginia. He was ready to reembrace his native state. "The formal act of secession & withdrawal of Lincoln's government," he explained, "terminates my voluntary exile." The Old Dominion would get back her prophet. Perhaps this time she would know how to honor him properly.[46]

12

Once More into the Fray

1

FORT SUMTER MADE Edmund Ruffin famous. On April 21 he left South
Carolina and returned to Virginia. Three times along the way, cheering
crowds gathered at train stations to chant his name and call for a speech.
When he arrived in Richmond two days later, he marveled at the "complete
& wonderful change here since I left."

All traces of the "revolting unionism," which had driven him from his
native state the previous February, had vanished. Now everyone was a
secessionist, and even former "submissionists" vied with fire-eaters in their
loud protestations of deep hatred for Yankee "oppressors" and in their
rock-like loyalty to the Confederate cause. To Ruffin's surprise, his political
"enemy" William Rives, a man he had always despised as "a complete
union-worshipper," stopped him on the street one day and expressed his joy
that they were both finally fighting on the same side. Even Captain Harrison
Cocke, once "the most thorough, slavish & base submissionist," Ruffin
claimed, now "goes beyond me in extreme measures for disunion."

Along with this "complete & wonderful change" in public attitudes
toward secession came an equally remarkable change in opinion toward
secessionists. Ruffin, whose extreme Southern rights and disunion politics
had made him an outcast everywhere but in renegade South Carolina, was
now the toast of Virginia. The people of Richmond, many of whom had long
regarded him as a traitor, greeted his homecoming "with marked appearances of welcome & cordial regard." Friends and "enemies" alike went out
of their way to be pleasant, showering the indefatigable old fire-eater with

thanks and congratulations for his recent services at Sumter. They were all grateful, Ruffin boasted to his diary, "that I . . . alone, upheld the honor of Va. abroad." Why, no less a personage than the Confederate Vice-President, Alexander Stephens, had sought him out, thumped him on the shoulders, and insisted on shaking his hand.[1]

Even Yankees had begun to take the measure of Virginia's aged but feisty prophet-soldier of secession. "Mr. Ruffin is the mainstay of secession in Virginia," claimed a Northern newspaper article that Ruffin treasured. "He is a brave, determined ultraist—a match for John Brown in his devotion to his principles—a crazed Secessionist."

But crazed or not, Ruffin ranked number one "of all the traitors in the South." "He is our enemy, and a terrible one," the paper warned Northern readers. "He will not [only] spill his 'last drop' of blood for the Southern Confederacy, but he will not hesitate to bleed first if necessary." And though it made the Yankee writer's "blood boil" to have to admit this, he believed that with a few more men like Edmund Ruffin, the South would be unbeatable. "If the new republic is not ungrateful and unwise," suggested the newspaper, "it will insist upon making him . . . their President. He has more brains than a hundred Hunters and a den of Davises."[2]

2

Beloved throughout the South and especially in his native Virginia, feared and respected in the North, Ruffin had never been happier. He was finally a prophet with honor in his own country. For the first time, he was the champion of a popular political cause; he was an insider. But the role did not suit his character, and he had barely been back in the Old Dominion two weeks before he began attacking the way politicians were running the government at Richmond.

In anonymous newspaper articles like the one he signed "X," Ruffin accused the state legislature of woeful negligence in its military preparations. After calling Virginia's Governor John Letcher "a great clog," Ruffin demanded his impeachment. He was outraged, too, when President Davis began handing out political and military appointments to men Ruffin considered "inferior" and even "incompetent." While Ruffin always vehemently denied any personal political ambitions or desire for office, it still rankled when the Confederacy consistently passed over a man like himself, whom even Northerners recognized as "worth a hundred Hunters and a den of Davises," and over men like Rhett and Yancey, "the earliest & staunchest movers of secession," to offer its highest honors and the most important offices to "eleventh hour secessionists" and men "who were submissionists to the last moment of free choice."[3]

Shrewdly, Ruffin realized that he could not continue to snipe away at public officials and still expect to bask in the limelight of public approval. Rather than jeopardize his hard-won new status, he would prefer to die. "I feel, in sincerity & earnestness, that I have lived long enough," he thought, "& for my own future place in the opinion & regard of my countrymen, it will be best for me to die very soon."[4]

Alas, the prospects of an imminent death were not promising. Despite increased deafness, a trembling left hand, and frequent burping spells, Ruffin's health was as good as it had been in years. This left no choice for him, he decided, but to leave Richmond immediately. "If I live again . . . in society, I shall lose all my present popularity," he concluded regretfully, for "I could not (& never can) bridle my tongue." Like his model, Cincinnatus, he would lay down his arms and retire to the countryside, where he could express all his pent-up unpopular opinions in the safety of his family circle.[5]

3

Ruffin had retired to Beechwood for only a few days when in early May he learned that the Confederate Congress had issued a formal declaration of war against the United States government. War fever quickly spread throughout the South, as troops hurried to Richmond to protect the recently named capital of the Confederacy. Even Ruffin came out of his self-imposed exile briefly to welcome the Palmetto Guards and present them with their own genuine John Brown pike.[6]

The feeling in Richmond and among Southerners generally was that the coming conflict would be short, lasting at best only a few weeks or a couple of months. One Confederate soldier, they bragged to one another, could outfight a dozen Yankees, and a quick Southern victory was certain. Fearful only that the war might end too soon and thus deprive them of the chance to cover themselves with a sufficient amount of glory, thousands of eager, fresh-faced young boys and mature able-bodied men flocked to join the armed forces.

One of the first to enlist was Edmund Ruffin, Jr., forty-seven years old and a recently remarried widower with six children. Gathering together a group of his neighbors, he organized a volunteer troop, which thoughtfully elected him its captain. Then, with his eighteen-year-old son Thomas at his side, he led his men off to find General Robert E. Lee's army.

Surprisingly enough, Ruffin was not pleased with his son's decision and tried to dissuade him from leaving. The older man still doubted that there would be any major military clash between Confederate and Federal armies. He believed that Lincoln and his Secretary of State, Seward, were too cowardly to launch a real invasion of Virginia. At most, the Yankee troops would occupy the pro-Union northwestern area of the state, where, he hoped, they would "be left undisturbed to weary & wear out the hospitality of the residents." These calls into active military service, he complained, were "harassing," "ridiculous," and "absurd." They took planters and overseers away from their plantations and unnecessarily interrupted the texture of Southern life.[7]

Ruffin voiced no objections, though, when his son Charles announced that he also intended to take up arms and fight for the Confederacy. Charles had always been something of a wastrel. His profligate habits so distressed his father that the previous summer, Ruffin had confessed to one of his daughters that his love for his youngest son had "much abated." Shortly after this, Charles made one of his frequent promises to reform and mend his ways. He begged his father "to welcome the returning prodigal." Then in late May, about one month after Ruffin distinguished himself at Fort Sumter, Charles seized the opportunity to reinstate himself in his father's good graces: he enlisted as a private in the Palmetto Guards.

Ruffin softened toward Charles. "So far he has lived for no good purpose," Ruffin commented after learning of his son's plans. "God grant that this step may be a new direction & turning point in his progress. May he now deserve & achieve success, & acquire justly an honorable reputation, if not distinction & glory." Otherwise, Ruffin hoped Charles would have the good sense to die in battle. "An early . . . death in fighting for his country's rights & defence," he reasoned rather coldly, "is preferable to a useless & inglorious life extended to old age."[8]

4

With both Edmund and Charles in the army, Ruffin was the only adult white male left at Beechwood and was thus responsible for the care of the plantation and the protection of its occupants. He enrolled right away in a home guard composed of men and boys who were too young, too old, or too infirm for regular military duty. Armed only with fowling pieces, the home guard expected to act as a guerilla force in the event of a Union army invasion. In the meantime, they spent their nights patrolling the neighborhood for runaway slaves and ferreting out suspected servile rebellions. As an extra precaution at Beechwood, Ruffin taught the ladies how to shoot a gun and took them out for daily target practice so they could sharpen their aim and better defend their lives and honor against "insurrectionary" blacks and "depraved" Yankee soldiers.[9]

Still, Ruffin insisted that the danger from the enemy within—the four million Negro slaves—was minimal. After all, he had invested much of his time and energy over the past ten years trying to calm Southern white racial fears. In the event that secession led to civil war, he had assured, blacks would remain loyal to their masters. Slaves would neither run away in large numbers or, worse, rise up in bloody insurrection.

Ruffin's article entitled "The Fidelity of Slaves to Their Masters," published in January, 1861, at the height of the secession crisis, contained all his major arguments. Blacks, he contended, had certain inherent traits which made them unlikely runaways. Laziness was one. While it was true, he admitted, that a naturally lazy Negro might want to run away in order to avoid work, that same inertia was a powerful force keeping him or her on the plantation. "The negro," he asserted, "is naturally timid, unenter-prising, fearful of, and adverse to change, to any new and untried condition" —and this included freedom. As proof, he cited the experiences of two previous wars, the American Revolution and the War of 1812, in which few slaves had rebelled or tried to escape, even though the British army prom-ised to emancipate them if they did. Slaves then and now, Ruffin concluded, feared far worse treatment from their so-called liberators than from the Southerners who kept them in bondage. Besides, he assured his readers, before the "happy" and "docile" blacks grabbed guns and knives and began butchering whites, they would have to forget the great love they bore for their masters and mistresses.[10]

Over and over again, like a man whistling in the dark, Ruffin pro-claimed his perfect trust in the loyalty of Southern slaves in general and of his own blacks in particular. Even the five suspicious fires at the family plantations could not shake his confidence. Only a few months before the war broke out, he boasted that he and his sons and grandsons all slept with their doors and windows unlocked. Most slaveowners, he insisted, slept in the same unguarded manner. "It may be truly said that every house & family is every night perfectly exposed to any attempt of our slaves to commit robbery or murder," he wrote in his diary. "Yet we all feel so secure, & are so free from all suspicion of such danger, that no care is taken for self-protection."

Ruffin knew that this state of Southern domestic affairs would seem "incredible" to Northerners, "who suppose that every slave in the South wants nothing but the safe opportunity to kill his master." "We all know," he admitted, "that if our slaves so choose, they could kill every white person on any farm or even through a neighborhood, in any night." But the danger of such a horrible event was so remote that "no fear is entertained by the most timid of whites." "Consequently," Ruffin complained, "there is a blameable & general neglect of all proper police regulations, & of means for defence against such possible violence."[11]

No Southerner, not even Ruffin, could forget the terrifying example of the Nat Turner insurrection. But Ruffin repressed that awful memory and tried to ignore the harsh and repressive internal security measures Southerners had instituted in its wake, measures that made the possibility of another servile revolt extremely unlikely. He also tried to ignore the continuing and all-pervasive Southern fear of slave uprisings, which manifested itself in periodic insurrectionary panics and in the kind of mass hysteria that swept the slave states following John Brown's raid.

Nor did Ruffin feel "so secure & . . . free from all suspicion" as he pretended. On May 26, only a few weeks after the official Confederate war message, he heard that blacks at nearby City Point had been meeting secretly at night in prayer groups, supposedly for religious services, while in reality they plotted the best way to kill their masters and escape to the Union army. Luckily for the whites, two of the conspirators were loyal slaves who informed on the others, and Southerners had quelled the alleged uprising before it began, punishing those involved with up to thirty-nine lashes apiece. Ruffin tried to take the news calmly. "A conspiracy discovered & repressed," he told himself, "is better assurance of safety than if no conspiracy had been heard of or suspected." But when he retired that night, he slept with a loaded gun beside his pillow.[12]

5

Southerners must be ever vigilant against attacks from internal enemies, Ruffin finally was willing to concede, but what troubled him more was the threat posed by the external foe, the invading Union army. Almost daily, he read reports in Southern newspapers describing Yankee soldiers in less than human terms: as lascivious devils foaming at the mouth at the prospect of raping helpless Southern belles or as fiendish monsters drooling in anticipation of the murderous carnage they would inflict on the Confederacy.

Some Northerners even helped contribute to this distorted image of themselves. In an effort to frighten Southerners and bolster Union morale, many Northern papers printed articles that boasted about the vicious nature of Yankee troops and the terrible fate in store for the South. The Davis government recognized that these inflammatory words made excellent wartime propaganda and saw that they received widespread circulation in all the major Southern newspapers.[13]

For his part, Ruffin clipped out and saved two pieces he found particularly insulting. One was from the *Westchester Democrat* of Pennsylvania, which threatened to sully the purity of Southern womanhood. The *Democrat* lewdly reminded several troops of Pennsylvania volunteers who were marching through Maryland that Baltimore "has always been celebrated for the beauty of its women" and suggested that "the fair were ever the reward of the brave." "*Beauty & Booty,*" cried the paper, "[is] the watchword in New Orleans."[14]

Equally threatening, the New York *Herald* promised to unleash "at least three hundred thousand of the most reckless, desperate men on the face of the earth." "The Goths and Vandals who descended on Rome and ensanguined the Tiber with patrician blood," bragged the paper, "were angels compared to these fellows." Foreign-born, living in the cities of the North, and known only by the generic name of "roughs," these fellows were interested in the spoils of war and would "fight like demons for present enjoyment." Their leaders having excited them "to the boiling point" with promises of extravagant plunder, they would not stop until they had "a farm and a nigger each."

Horrified, Ruffin read on. The "roughs" would strike first in Maryland and Virginia, said the article, and "will sweep these states with fire and sword." There was no protection against their wrath: "where one is killed twenty more will spring up in his place." Southern traitors would regret having picked a fight with the North, warned the *Herald,* because, without exaggeration, "the character of the coming campaign will be vindictive, fierce, bloody and merciless beyond parallel in ancient or modern history."[15]

6

Late in May, Union General Irvin McDowell led the Army of the Potomac into northern Virginia and took over Alexandria and Arlington Heights. Ruffin was astonished. He had to admit that it looked like the Yankees really intended to carry out their war threats, even though, in Ruffin's estimation, the Union did not have a shred of a chance for victory. "Even if we should be beaten in one or two important battles," he declared confidently, "it would be but temporary loss to the South. One or two important victories gained over the North would be to them tenfold more disastrous."[16]

A few days later, Charles Ruffin said good-by to his relatives and left to join the Palmetto Guards on the Confederate front lines at Manassas Gap Junction. Manassas was located about thirty miles from Washington behind a sluggishly winding brown stream known as Bull Run. There the principal Southern army, commanded by General Beauregard of Fort Sumter fame, awaited McDowell's advancing troops. Ruffin sensed that very soon the first serious battle of the Civil War would be fought at Manassas. He began to wish with all his heart that he could be there in the thick of the action.[17]

But he was stuck at Beechwood, responsible for the smooth running of plantation operations and the safety of its women and children. He had promised to retire from public life, and he regretted the decision. His hero, Cincinnatus, may have genuinely preferred the simple, solitary pleasures of rural life, but Ruffin had gotten used to more excitement. After a few monotonous weeks at Beechwood, he was bored, restless, and miserable. He longed for the chance to drop his plough, pick up a gun, and go to the defense of his country. Throughout June he sulked about the plantation, praying for "a leave of absence" and threatening "to decamp."[18]

Leave of some kind evidently arrived at the end of the month: on July 1 Ruffin was in Richmond picking up food, blankets, and camping supplies. The next morning he donned his familiar homespun uniform, pulled on a new pair of boots, packed two coarse blankets and a half barrel of crackers into his knapsack, strapped a small head of cheese to his side, and proceeded to Manassas Junction. The Palmetto Guards, he learned, were stationed just a few miles forward of the line at Fairfax Courthouse. It was late that afternoon before a hot, tired, and dust-covered Ruffin trudged into camp. His feet were blistered and his corns ached from the new footgear, but he was grateful nonetheless to be with his old army buddies again.[19]

For the next two weeks, the men prepared for the coming battle. Ruffin was too weak physically to perform drill, guard, or fatigue duties, but he pitched in gladly whenever he could be of help, even grabbing a gravel shovel—the same tool he had once used to scoop up marl—to assist the younger men who were building trenches and earthworks. Most of the time, though, he had nothing to do. To chase away boredom, he read newspapers and tried to engage the officers and their men in intelligent conversation.[20]

Newspapers and camp talk were filled with stories of "atrocities" committed by the "undisciplined" and "unruly" Northern soldiers: they ransacked buildings, plundered houses and even burned them to the ground, and encouraged slaves to run away. Ruffin talked to Colonel Ferry, the leader of a band of Confederate raiders, about the best way to counter these Yankee "outrages." Ferry favored guerrilla tactics against the enemy, and Ruffin agreed with him. Normally Ruffin would have disapproved of such an "uncivilized" manner of conducting war. But he decided that the South was not fighting a civilized enemy: it was fighting Goths and Vandals, who deserved no gentlemanly consideration. The Yankee barbarians were no better than murderers and insurrectionaries. Take no prisoners, Ruffin recommended. Shoot them dead without mercy.[21]

7

Ruffin was just beginning to complain about the boredom of camp life when on Wednesday, July 17, in the dead of night, General Beauregard sent word to the troops at Fairfax Courthouse to prepare for a sudden march. Confederate scouts had spotted Yankee soldiers advancing from nearby Falls Church. Beauregard had his army of approximately twenty thousand men spread out along the eight miles of Bull Run, and there he intended to make his defensive stand. He ordered the Palmetto Guards to fall back to Manassas Junction in "double-quick time."

Double-quick time meant marching at a full trot, and Ruffin's ancient legs could keep up this demanding pace for only two miles. Dropping back, he became separated from his unit and started to panic. Forms passed him in the darkness and he could not make them out. He realized for the first time in his life that he suffered from a malady called "night blindness" and that he just might stumble into the enemy's camp.[22]

Fortunately, the first soldiers he bumped into were Virginia militiamen under the command of Captain Delaware Kemper. Anxious not to be left behind again, Ruffin begged Kemper for permission to ride on one of the caissons in the light artillery. Kemper offered no objection, so Ruffin gratefully climbed aboard a cannon and let younger men carry him into battle.

But the ride itself was an ordeal. The surface of the highly polished weapon was so slippery that Ruffin could barely maintain his balance, while the roads were so rocky and rutted that his old bones winced with each painful jolt. Swaying back and forth and from side to side, his back aching terribly from the lack of support, he spent the entire night astride this precarious and uncomfortable mount.

At dawn, the light artillery set Ruffin down at Bull Run near Mitchell's Ford, where he rejoined the Palmetto Guards. He was in camp only a few hours, though, before Beauregard again ordered the Palmettos to move out, this time to support and defend the artillery, which had made brief contact with a division of Union soldiers. Stiff, weary, and sore to the bone, Ruffin was unable to follow and spent the day in a trench with a lame soldier.[23]

Still, he was "determined to have a hand in the affair." He dug out a kneeling hole in his entrenchment, shouldered his musket, and positioned himself so that he could take aim and get a fair shot at any Yankee who was so unlucky as to come within range. The battle, though, never came close enough for Ruffin to pull the trigger. But, said a Charleston newspaper correspondent, South Carolina's adopted son had once again willingly risked his life for the Confederacy. Enemy bullets whizzed over his gray head, and according to an officer who was there at the time, a Union ball struck the dirt in front of Ruffin's face and "came very near snuffing out the veteran Virginian's life." Unafraid, the old soldier listened rapturously to the sounds of faraway fighting. He envied a man in a neighboring foxhole who had picked up a piece of burst Union shell and who graciously allowed him to fondle the fragment, which was still warm from being fired. Secretly, Ruffin wished he could keep this new trophy as another wartime souvenir, but his shyness restrained him from asking a favor of a stranger.[24]

When the fighting ended that evening and the Palmettos returned to camp, Ruffin found out that although the Confederates had successfully repulsed the Union regiment, the former had sustained fifty-four casualties. Tragically enough, about half of those wounded or killed were the victims of "friendly fire," of Confederates shooting at their own troops. Someone told him that this kind of mistake was common in both armies, because Southerners and Northerners alike dressed in blue and gray uniforms as well as in all sorts of fancy costumes. Indeed, some Confederates wore no particular uniform at all. Under these circumstances, distinguishing friend from foe was extremely difficult. The mark of Rebel recognition that day, Ruffin noted, had been the military salute, and the number of unnecessary casualties demonstrated its worthlessness. Beauregard tried to remedy the situation by having his men pin similarly colored badges—scarves or rosettes—to their shoulders, but there were never enough of these to outfit the entire army, and deadly errors continued.[25]

8

Ruffin had managed to escape any battle injuries, but the rigors of army life were taking their toll on his frail and aged body. He was tired, hungry, and sore all over. And he was wet. All day long, a steady rain had pelted his face and uniform, till by nightfall he was soaked to the skin. Numb and shivering with the cold, he lay down to sleep in his wet clothes, no tent above him but the open sky, no mattress but a borrowed overcoat between him and the damp, furrowed ground.

He awoke the next day looking haggard and feeling like he had not slept at all. A stabbing hunger pang made him remember that he and the Palmetto Guards had not eaten a decent meal since they retreated so rapidly from Fairfax Courthouse two days before. Only a handful of gingerbread nuts, which he had stuffed into his pockets and munched on from time to time, had stood between him and starvation.

But when food finally arrived from the kitchen at the main camp that morning, Ruffin discovered that he could not eat it. He tried the fresh beef, but it was too tough and leathery for his few weak old teeth. The stew looked tasty but was so highly salted that Ruffin choked on his second mouthful. He gnawed on a few hard crackers, but again, his poor teeth made this slow, painful work. Then he tried to wash down the crackers with some liquid refreshment, but the sugarless coffee was "unpalatable," and water was scarce and dirty. Finally, driven by great thirst, he accepted some muddy water and even drank a little undiluted whiskey, something he had not done since he stood guard duty during the War of 1812 almost fifty years earlier. The raw liquor "burnt . . . like pepper," but he had to confess that its effects were "pleasant" and "refreshing."

While the crackers and whiskey eased Ruffin's hunger, they could not hide the visible effects that lack of sleep and exposure to the elements had had on his appearance. He was pale and thin and so sickly looking that he shocked his son Charles, who implored him to go home and recover. Other men in his outfit chimed in with the same appeal, urging him at least to fall back to the rear for some rest and recuperation. Ruffin stubbornly ignored their entreaties. He had "no notion of leaving until after the great battle."[26]

9

After one more sleepless night, though, Ruffin decided that the "great battle" was still weeks away. So, on Saturday morning, July 20, he reluctantly gave in to the advice of his companions and headed behind the lines. He recuperated at the main camp for less than twenty-four hours, because at Sunday breakfast he heard the booming of distant cannons. Immediately his appetite for adventure overcame all thoughts of food and rest. Without a word, he left the table, lifted his rifle to his shoulder, and hiked two miles back to join the Palmetto Guards.[27]

Unwilling to be stuck all day in a trench again, where he could not see any action, Ruffin secured permission to station himself on McLean's Hill, which offered a commanding view of the countryside. He realized that he was too feeble to seek out the enemy, but he was eager to engage in mortal combat, if only the enemy would come to him.

Maddeningly, though, the fighting never came in his direction. After more than an hour of watchful waiting, Ruffin decided that if the battle would not come to him, he would have to go to it. Setting off in the direction of the gunfire, he had not gone very far when he ran into at least a hundred Confederate soldiers headed the opposite way. Confused, he asked where they were going and learned that these men were "skulkers"—also called "stragglers"—men who had deserted the battlefield because they were exhausted, afraid, or fed up and disillusioned with a less-than-glorious war. They informed Ruffin that the fight was lost, that Southern troops were firing on one another in confusion, and that the entire Confederate army was in retreat. Heartsick at the news, the old warrior nonetheless attempted to rally the skulkers around him and lead them back into the fray. But no one seemed to hear his fierce battle cry. All stared at him in silence.[28]

10

But the skulkers were wrong. The tide of battle, which had been going badly for a while, had shifted decisively in favor of the Confederate forces. As Ruffin pressed forward alone, vainly searching for his regiment, he caught sight of the Secession Guards of Mississippi hotly pursuing a retreating

Union division. Then from a ridge off to his left, Kemper's field artillery suddenly swung down to give chase, stopping only long enough to scoop up a befuddled Ruffin and deposit him again on one of their caissons.

Up and down the narrow paths they ran, over rocks that bounced Ruffin about and jolted his body severely, through clouds of dust that left his lungs choking for air, and at a pace so swift that his teeth rattled. Yet even during brief halts, he kept his seat, fearful that if he came down even for a minute to stretch his legs he might be forgotten, left to follow on foot, and then captured as a prize of war by Yankee "roughs." Besides, climbing onto and off of a cannon was no simple task for a soldier of sixty-seven.

Straddling the cannon's long barrel, clutching his gun with one hand and clinging desperately to his slippery mount with the other, Ruffin must have presented a remarkable if somewhat ludicrous sight, that of a sort of Confederate army mascot. The boys of Colonel Hampton's Legion yelled their approval with three rousing cheers as they marched by. The Palmetto Guards did the same.

From his elevated perch, the indomitable fire-eater shouted down to them. Which side was winning? he wanted to know. The enemy was on the run, the soldiers yelled back, but Ruffin was too deaf to hear their answer. So, for some time, he labored under the false impression left by the skulkers that Manassas was a Union triumph and that he was taking part in a humiliating Confederate retreat.

Soon, however, the evidence of Union defeat became increasingly obvious. Dozens of Yankee muskets—shiny new Springfield rifles—lay scattered along the paths and roadsides, where fleeing Federals had tossed them in their rush to get away. Ruffin eyed the gleaming weapons with admiration and immediately wanted one for his collection of secession souvenirs and wartime mementoes. A soldier was kind enough to pick one up and hand it to him. Thus, seated on a cannon, a Yankee rifle grasped in one hand and a Confederate musket in the other, Ruffin rode after the enemy.[29]

11

Eventually Kemper's battery halted near a small stream called Cub Run, over which arched a suspension bridge that connected with the Warrenton Turnpike, the main highway leading back to Washington. Unlimbering their big guns, the Confederates prepared to hammer away at the ragged column of retreating blue uniforms. As soon as the first cannon was in position, the men invited the "Chief of Rebels," Edmund Ruffin, to fire the initial shot.

As he readied himself to yank the lanyard, Ruffin could see that the main body of the Northern army plus a great many Washington civilians, who had come down to the field of battle expecting a Sunday's entertainment, were all trying to crowd over the narrow bridge at once, thus clogging the escape route and creating a terrific traffic jam. The old fire-eater's carefully aimed shell landed in the center of all this havoc and confusion, overturning a wagon on the bridge and barricading the road.

This created pandemonium and turned a disorderly retreat into a tumultuous rout. Horses reared, mules kicked, ladies shrieked, and men swore. Carriages careened and buggies collided. Soldiers on horseback plunged into the icy waters of the Run, swam across, scrambled up the muddy embankment, and never looked back until they reached Washington. Foot soldiers, who only moments before had thought they were too tired to walk another step, suddenly began to run. Into the creek they pitched their guns, canteens, haversacks, and other gear—anything that would lighten their load as they hotfooted it for home. When someone yelled that the Black Horse cavalry—the Confederacy's version of Yankee "roughs"—was coming up to kill off what was left of the Northern army, the panic was complete. Ambulance drivers abandoned the wounded. Teamsters left wagons full of valuable military supplies and equipment by the roadside. Thousands simply ran for their lives.[30]

Safe behind a Confederate battery, his eyes glittering with joy, Ruffin watched the chaos in the enemy ranks. The South had won a glorious victory. In his view, McDowell's disintegrating army proved the superiority of Confederate soldiers and of Southern civilization as well. That night he slept soundly, confident that Confederate independence would soon be a reality.

12

The next morning, Ruffin borrowed a horse and rode out to the battlefield, expressly "to see the dead bodies," but even he was not prepared for such "a horrible sight." Grotesquely postured corpses and injured men, whose faces "indicated the suffering of agonizing pain," carpeted the landscape, covering over thirty acres of open ground and stretching a distance of almost three miles. "Clotted blood, in what had been pools, [was] under or by every corpse," Ruffin recalled. "From bullet holes in the heads of some, the brains had partly oozed out. The white froth covering the mouths of others was scarcely less shocking."

He spotted half a dozen or so Northerners who were still alive and was about to pass one of them when he noticed the man reaching for a tin cup of water that lay just outside his grasp. Dismounting, Ruffin offered the thirsty soldier a drink from his own canteen, then did the same for the other wounded men. He spoke consolingly in tones of gentle compassion, assuring them they would receive good care at Confederate hospitals.

Several hundred other curious Confederate soldiers were also picking their way about the field, gawking at the dead and dying. Some even stood over the bleeding Yankees and indignantly demanded to know the reason why they had left their homes in the North to come kill innocent Southerners. Ruffin realized that these thoughtless questions only added to the suffering of the wounded, so he reprimanded his younger comrades sharply and shamed them into silence. He despised Yankees too. But when they lay before him hurt and bleeding, the enemy no longer seemed like monsters or barbarian "roughs" and instead took on all too human forms that stirred his pity. "No one more bitterly hates the northerners as a class than I do, or would be more rejoiced to have every invading soldier killed," he explained in his diary, "but all my hatred was silenced for the wounded."[31]

But his pity and compassion were short-lived. At twelve o'clock he rode over to Cub Run, where he had personally had a hand in the enemy's defeat. Lying on the road near the bridge were only three dead Union soldiers, and Ruffin feared that these might have been carried over from the battlefield. Crestfallen, he thought his shot had not killed a single Yankee. "This was a great disappointment to me," he complained bitterly. "I should have liked not only to have killed the greatest possible number but also to know, if possible, which I had killed, & to see & count the bodies." Nor was he willing to let the matter drop. The same need that made him a compulsive souvenir hunter operated here. He wanted tangible evidence that his presence at Bull Run had not been superfluous, positive affirmation that his actions had made a genuine contribution. This was why he developed what seemed like an almost ghoulish interest in his personal body count, and in the following months he persistently tracked down other eyewitnesses, who swore that at least six and maybe even eight Yankees lay dead on the road after Ruffin's first cannonade. The official army report— which he copied carefully into his diary—noted an additional twelve to fifteen enemy wounded. Much mollified, Ruffin convinced himself that his shot had felled every one of them.[32]

13

Two days later, Ruffin was back in Richmond. Confederates there were boasting about their spectacular success at Bull Run, and naturally the eyewitness accounts of Virginia's eldest soldier were much in demand. The city was so crowded with excited visitors that Ruffin had to sleep on the floor of the Common Room at the Columbian Hotel.

He did not mind the inconvenience, however. He met several of his old fire-eating friends, and they rejoiced together over the recent Confederate victory. He and Judge Perkins sat down one evening and reminisced about old times and their former fruitless campaign to promote secession. They remembered how at first they had had to fight *"union"* men, North and South; then they had fought *"compromise"* schemes; next they had fought *"reconstruction"* of the seceded states. Now, they told each other, they had to fight against *"reconciliation"*—the danger of a premature peace treaty, before the South had had a chance to separate itself completely from the North in feelings, habits, and business relations. Both men were supremely confident that the South held all the cards. This was the Confederacy's finest hour. The battle of Bull Run, Ruffin promised anyone who seemed doubtful, "will be virtually the close of the war."[33]

13

Fight or Flee

1

BULL RUN DID NOT end the Civil War. Contrary to Ruffin's bright expectations, this bloody battle marked only the beginning of a long, drawn-out conflict that would last almost four more years. But for the time being, there were no more military confrontations in Virginia. The defeated Army of the Potomac had slunk back to Washington, and the North would not risk another major assault in the eastern theater until the following spring.

Despite the lull in fighting that summer, 1861, Ruffin and the other Beechwood residents practically lived and breathed war. "We think & talk of nothing else," he wrote earnestly. Each member of the family did his or her best to aid the Confederate cause. Edmund and his son Thomas were in the army, and the ladies of the house had joined a sewing circle and were busy knitting socks and stitching shirts for Southern soldiers. Ruffin, too, fresh from his stint at Manassas, paid frequent sick calls at the Richmond hospitals, cheering the wounded and inquiring solicitously after the health of injured Palmettos. He also visited several Confederate forts in the Old Dominion, making unannounced spot inspections to assure himself that these vital defense centers measured up to his standards of military preparedness.[1]

Most of the summer, though, he was stuck at Beechwood, where he quickly ran out of things to do and reverted to his usual pattern of boredom, then bitterness, and finally depression. Time, he complained over and over in his diary, lies "heavy on my hands."

Reading had always been one of his main pleasures, but the war had cut off his source of books from Northern cities. Until an alternate supply arrived from Europe, there was nothing new to read except the stories of Fanny Fern—a writer whose sentimental material catered especially to women—and other "trashy stuff."

Writing had also been a major occupation as well as an amusement in the past, but Ruffin still harbored his lifelong grudge against a public that had never shown the proper appreciation for his literary contributions. What an "impressive & mortifying fact," Ruffin complained bitterly, that even his own children—"sons as well as daughters"—usually ignored their father's writings. He practically had to force them to give their opinions of his published works; they never volunteered their reactions. And not a single one of his offspring had ever asked to see any of his many unpublished essays, a circumstance which wounded his pride. "Their usual silence in this respect," he noted sadly, "has served me as the strongest indication of the want of interest or worth of my writings . . . & more strong than any direct or indirect indication of disapproval from any other quarter." He was a prophet without honor even among his own kin. An extremely sensitive man, Ruffin resolved again that he would no longer write for an ungrateful audience, explaining that he kept up his diary only "to avoid the misery of idleness."[2]

As usual when he was miserable and idle, Ruffin began to dwell on his own mortality. He was sure his health was failing rapidly. He had, after all, returned from Bull Run feeling much weaker than ever before. Walking up a single flight of stairs caused his aged thigh muscles to "fail," he remarked, and even climbing the gentle hills of Richmond left him "winded."

As for his hearing, that too was much worse. At church, he strained to hear the sermons. Even though he sat in a front pew, he found it impossible "to take in the preacher's sentences in connection." All he could make out were meaningless reverberations of sound which hurt his ears and annoyed him even more than his deafness. Giving up church attendance was undoubtedly a sacrifice that Ruffin made gladly, but his poor hearing also deprived him of another great pleasure: conversation. Unable to hear more than one person at a time—even when the speaker was shouting—he avoided the company of almost everyone outside his family. Yet, in the intimacy of his family circle, Ruffin often felt shut out, even a little jealous. "The more cheerful & talkative they are," he once confessed, "the more lonesome & unamused I am." So, for most of the day and evening, he would sit in his chair brooding silently, without anyone or anything to make him happy.[3]

Deprived of the enjoyments of conversation and writing, with fewer and fewer books to read, and fearing "the marked approach of general debility," Ruffin offered his customary prayer for "a sudden, unexpected, & painless death." "My remaining life will be a burden to me," he explained. If only he could have died a hero's death on the battlefield. "A cannon-ball, at Bull Run, or Manassas, . . . would have been the most desireable termination of my life."[4]

Moody and despondent, Ruffin somehow got the impression that he was no longer welcome at Beechwood. For three years he had more or less made his home with his eldest son Edmund and Edmund's six children, and he was happy with them. Although Marlbourne was still his official residence, he had rarely visited the plantation since his daughter Mildred married and moved away and his daughter Elizabeth died. In fact, it was shortly after Elizabeth's unexpected death in December, 1860, that Edmund's daughter Nanny—Ruffin's favorite grandchild—sent over to Marlbourne for her grandfather's furniture, books, and other belongings and set up a comfortable private apartment for him in the east end of the old house fronting the Beechwood mansion. Ever since, Ruffin had considered himself a permanent member of the Beechwood household.[5]

Yet, for some unstated reason, that summer he began to feel like an unwanted guest, even an intruder. Perhaps this had something to do with Edmund's recent marriage to his cousin Jane. Although Ruffin had helped to kindle this romance and had applauded the match, he had also once loved Jane and had toyed with the notion of marrying her himself. Now with Jane mistress of the house and Edmund away in the army, the old repressed longings may have reasserted themselves, a situation the very straightlaced Ruffin must have found unbearable. Edmund, too, for all his filial devotion, might not have been entirely comfortable with this domestic arrangement, and Jane may have expressed some uneasiness. More likely, Ruffin just imagined their discomfort. He was so touchy, so quick to perceive hostility, that he came to expect and find rejection everywhere he looked. In any case, he concluded that it was time for him to leave. "I feel neither energy nor inclination to seek for change," he protested, yet "uneasiness drives me to go abroad."

So, in October, Ruffin moved from Beechwood into a boarding house on Clay Street in Richmond. There he rented a tiny room and furnished it as cheaply as possible, sleeping on a narrow wooden cot with an uncomfortable hair mattress, a single sheet, and three coarse blankets. His son Julian took one look at his father's lodgings and pronounced them cramped, desolate, and cheerless. Still, Ruffin was determined to stay in Richmond on a "trial" basis for at least three months to see if being away from his family made life "more tolerable."[6]

2

Ruffin had some positive reasons, too, for establishing his new headquarters in Richmond. In the capital of the Confederacy, he could be close to all the war news and the latest political gossip. Despite his hearing problem, he found lots of old acquaintances to talk with, and strangers often recognized him and stopped to chat. Eminent Confederate statesmen like Secretary of the Treasury Christopher Memminger and Secretary of State Robert M. T. Hunter warmly invited the crusty old fire-eater to call on them, and though Ruffin still retained his fear of being tainted as a "base office-seeker," he accepted these invitations with obvious relish.[7]

He was talking with Congressman James A. Seddon in November when the topic of discussion turned, as it usually did, to the war and specifically to the recent *Trent* affair. On November 8, an over-eager United States naval officer had illegally stopped and boarded an unarmed British merchant steamer, the *Trent,* and had plucked off two Confederate Commissioners—James M. Mason of Virginia and John Sliddell of Louisiana—who were on a diplomatic mission to England and France. Northerners heartily approved of the capture and imprisonment of these two distinguished Rebels, but an enraged Great Britain considered the federal action an affront to its national honor and began making serious war threats.

Like most Southerners, Ruffin and Seddon hoped the *Trent* incident would redound to the South's benefit. "Something good is obliged to come from such a stupid blunder," wrote Mary Boykin Chesnut. Surely now, both Ruffin and Seddon agreed, England would smash the Union coastal blockade, formally recognize the Confederate government, and perhaps even launch military reprisals against the North. Seddon believed that President Lincoln had deliberately engineered the entire affair in hopes of provoking Great Britain into a declaration of war. According to Seddon, Lincoln was looking for just such an excuse to withdraw from the present civil conflict, because he realized that the North could never conquer the South. A war with England would extricate his administration from a sticky no-win situation without political embarrassment to the Republican party. The Civil War, Seddon and Ruffin concluded happily, would soon be over. The day of final Confederate victory was at hand.[8]

But in early January, 1862, Ruffin learned that Lincoln had released Mason and Sliddell and had offered apologies sufficient to smooth ruffled British feathers. Naturally, Ruffin was disappointed, and he had only words of contempt for the Northern government. "Such an act of abject humiliation has not been paralleled by any civilized nation in the last century," he sneered. The Union had tried playing the "boastful & threatening bully" but had revealed itself as a "timid poltroon."[9]

England had also let Ruffin down. Before the war began, many Southerners had feared that Britain's antislavery sympathies might ally that great nation with the North, but Ruffin had always maintained that England would never allow its abolitionist "fanaticism" to interfere with its "greatest interest," Southern cotton. So he had fully endorsed King Cotton diplomacy and the Confederacy's early decision to prohibit the export of cotton and thus force economically dependent European countries like Britain to intervene in behalf of the Rebel cause.

In May, 1861, England had granted the Confederate government the status of a "belligerent power" but withheld full recognition. By February, 1862, King Cotton still had not worked its expected magic, and Ruffin glumly concluded that England despised both the Union and the Confederacy. The North was a hated commercial rival; the South was "odious" because of its peculiar institution of slavery. So England was quite content for the present to stand aside and let the Yankees and Rebels tear each other to pieces. But, Ruffin predicted with doubtful optimism, the British would never allow the North actually to win the war and reconstruct the former Union. At the moment of federal victory, England would immediately step in, break the Northern blockade, and recognize Southern independence, if only for its own selfish interests.[10]

3

By the winter of 1861–1862, Ruffin no longer expected a quick and easy Confederate victory, no "short & slight struggle." "Most of our people have been lowered in their sanguine hopes of signal success over our enemy, & a speedy & triumphant end of the war," he wrote at Christmastime. Yet Southerners remained rosily optimistic. "There are no indications of discouragement," Ruffin insisted, "or doubts of our final success."

The Yankees had to be "demented" if they truly expected to conquer the South, Ruffin bragged. Still, even he was amazed at the amount of materiel and the number of troops the Federals commanded. He had predicted that the North could never bear the financial burden of a civil war, but when the Yankee economy perversely refused to collapse, he changed his mind and argued that Seward and other "corrupt" Republican leaders were making so much money from war profiteering that they would never willingly stop the fighting. Mostly, though, he credited Northern warmaking abilities to Lincoln's "dictatorial" administration and the President's wholesale violation of civil liberties.[11]

Ruffin charged that Lincoln, "a president, who is neither wise, nor brave, nor even very popular, but a low & vulgar blackguard & buffoon," had trampled on the United States Constitution and set up an "unlimited despotism." Acting without congressional approval, the President had declared war, raised an army, erected a naval blockade, suspended the writ of *habeus corpus,* and restricted the rights of free speech and free press. To hold the key border states of Maryland, Kentucky, and Missouri in the

Union, Lincoln had acted boldly and sometimes ruthlessly to root out disloyalty. Shortly after the Confederate declaration of war, he had ordered Federal troops to occupy Baltimore and put Maryland virtually under martial law. "Md. is trodden under foot by Lincoln's government," Ruffin raged, "& is made to 'drink the cup of humiliation to the dregs.' "

Yankee submission to this kind of tyranny, exclaimed Ruffin, "is a stinking evidence of the ignorance of the northern people of constitutional obligations & rights." Blinded by an "inferior" belief in majority rule, Northerners "never can conceive that a constitution of government is adopted for the very purpose of controlling majorities, & preventing them from oppressing minorities." He was inordinately proud that Southerners, with their superior understanding of constitutional safeguards, had conducted their war effort in a strictly legal fashion.[12]

But not all Southerners, it seemed, were equally appreciative of these fine constitutional principles. For instance, when the Confederacy formally went to war against the North in May, 1861, "a convention of traitors" from northwestern Virginia had quickly assembled at Wheeling and resolved to cut their ties with the Old Dominion and adhere to the Union. "I should not be sorry if this most disaffected section should be occupied by 20,000 of Lincoln's troops," Ruffin cursed, "& would not have their occupancy disturbed for some time."[13]

But he was greatly upset as well as astonished to learn that Union sympathizers were to be found even in the Tidewater region, particularly among lower-class whites who were declaring themselves ready to surrender to the Yankees the first chance they got. The war had placed a heavy burden on these poor whites. Many lived near the rivers most exposed to enemy attack, while those who had supported themselves and their families peddling supplies to the Northern boats that navigated these waterways saw their only source of income ruined. To make matters worse, in order to prevent slaves from escaping to Federal ships or garrisons, Confederates sunk the small sailing vessels along the Tidewater shores, vessels which generally belonged to lower-class whites and which often represented their only property and means of subsistence. Meanwhile, wartime inflation sent prices soaring and naturally hit the poorest classes the hardest.

Ruffin knew that economic deprivations were partly responsible for this kind of Confederate disloyalty, but he blamed mostly the political "demagogues" who, he claimed, had taught "white trash" to hate the rich planters and envy their possessions. According to Ruffin, this envy was the reason these impoverished classes failed to appreciate the value of slavery to even the poorest white man. Whatever the reasons, anti-Confederate sentiments appeared rampant in Virginia's Northern Neck, where Willoughby Newton overheard poor whites saying that "the object of the secession & the war is to protect the negroes of the rich men, who own all the negroes & all the good land—& that they own neither, & have no interest in fighting, or opposing the North."[14]

4

Most of the war news that winter was disheartening to a sincere Southern patriot like Ruffin. In February, he gritted his teeth as successive Union victories at Fort Henry, Fort Donelson, and Roanoke Island made the North "wild & crazed with rejoicing." These losses infuriated him, and he suggested to his diary that defeated military commanders ought to be shot.[15]

Ruffin also began to lose faith in the abilities of Confederate political leaders, particularly Jefferson Davis. As word of Rebel defeats filtered back to Richmond, he bemoaned Davis's policy of appointing "incompetents" to generalships, merely because the men had been his cronies at West Point. He was equally critical of Confederate military strategy, which kept the army always on the defensive. "I believe that we owe most of this war especially to three things," he exclaimed one day in exasperation, "West Point, 'red tape,' & strategy. I heartily wish that our civil & military affairs were in the hands of leaders who knew nothing of either." He talked to men in the Confederate Congress who opposed Davis, men like Rhett, Seddon, and Robert Barnwell. Rhett denounced the President for his "dilatory" and "improper" handling of military affairs, and the others, including Ruffin, nodded their heads in vigorous assent. Ruffin was aware that Rhett, the "father of secession," had coveted the presidency for himself and that political disappointment had prompted part of his sharp attack. But Ruffin, too, worried that "Mr. Davis is far from being the right sort of leader for our country in our present difficulties."[16]

In March, though, Ruffin concentrated on good military news, as the sensational ironclad *Merrimac*—renamed the *Virginia*—battled her way out of Norfolk Harbor and, but for the last-minute arrival of the Northern ironclad, *Monitor,* almost broke through the Union blockade. That same month, General-in-Chief of the Union Armies, George B. McClellan, began his cautious campaign up the Virginia Peninsula. His object: to capture the capital city of the Confederacy. McClellan would probably come up the Pamunkey River, despaired William Sayre. He feared that the Yankees would sack and destroy Marlbourne because of its connection with his notorious secessionist father-in-law. If so, Ruffin replied coolly, he would consider the Federal action a personal "compliment."[17]

Despite his brave words, when Ruffin heard rumors that Lee's army was falling back toward Richmond, he packed his suitcases and returned to Beechwood. An apologetic letter from his son Edmund, chiding him for

being overly sensitive and urging him to come home, had reassured him of
his family's love and thus sweetened the move. At home, Ruffin recovered
his courage. Although he realized that if Richmond were to fall, Yankees
might soon overrun all of Virginia, he refused to give up hope of the
Confederacy's "ultimate success." Northerners might have more men, mus-
cle, and supplies. "But our superiority to our enemy," he sniffed with
aristocratic pride, "is in the much higher moral & intellectual grade of the
Southern people, & of the superior principles by which they are actuated,
& the holy cause which supports their patriotism & courage." Even military
disasters, he claimed, made ultimate victory the more certain, for defeat
only served to stoke the fires of Southern nationalism, strengthening Confederate resolve and the willingness to make even greater sacrifices.[18]

5

Perhaps the greatest sacrifices were made by the men in the Confederate
army—and not always with the willingness Ruffin liked to boast about.
Julian Ruffin had enlisted that spring—over his father's strenuous en-
treatries that he hire a substitute—and that meant all three of Ruffin's sons
were fighting for the "holy cause." Their letters home reflected the changing
attitudes of Confederate soldiers.[19]

At first, the letters were high-spirited, filled with anecdotes and good-
natured complaints about army life. Ruffin's grandson Thomas was stationed with Julian's company at the head of the Warwick River. Enemy
troops were stationed on the opposite riverbank. There was a great deal of
fighting, Thomas wrote his sister Nanny, with both sides firing away at each
other. He told her not to worry, though; scarcely anyone was ever hit. When
they were not engaged in battle, the Rebel and Yankee soldiers were often
so close that they carried on long conversations and even ribbed one another, with Federals making fun of Confederate "a dollar and a quarter
guns." Army life, Thomas added teasingly, "is taking the polish off of us;
we don't wash but twice a week, and have not commenced combing our hair
yet." His father complained that he had to sleep in his clothes every night,
and he feared "I shall forget to feel like a gentleman."[20]

Soon the messages became more serious, even somber in tone. Thomas
was ill. His company had no tents and no protection from the weather
besides the clothing they wore. Ruffin worried when he read this letter and
not just about his grandson's welfare. He knew that these hardships would
lead to sickness and that "sickness . . . serves to kill or disable ten times as
many soldiers, as blood-shed in battle." Julian, who had been so eager to
join the army, was in uniform less than a month before he confessed that
the widespread disease and the rigors of military life were not what he had

anticipated when he volunteered. He had expected romance and glory. He found none. When his ninety-day enlistment was up, he informed his father in April, he intended to come home.[21]

Charles Ruffin wanted out also. In October, 1861, after almost half a year with the Palmetto Guards, Charles was physically and spiritually sick of war. Home on furlough the next month, he announced to his startled family that he had no intention of ever going back.[22]

Ruffin was appalled. He had been so proud when Charles literally followed in his footsteps by enlisting in the Palmetto Guards. After Bull Run he had even written to several of his friends in the Confederate Congress and to Jefferson Davis—whom he had criticized roundly for appointing friends to military offices—and requested that Charles receive a captain's commission in the Confederate army. For Ruffin, this was an extremely unusual act. He prided himself on never asking political favors for himself or for his family, but he had made an exception for his youngest son, though he felt "reluctant & even ashamed to do so." Ruffin's request was either ignored or denied, for Charles remained a private, but his father still insisted that he belonged in the army. At least then, Charles pleaded, let him transfer to another unit, his brother Edmund's company perhaps. But Ruffin would not hear of it. Charles must return to the Palmetto Guards, and that was that. Brothers Edmund and Julian sided with their father. So, when his furlough was over, Charles very reluctantly rejoined Ruffin's old unit.[23]

Almost immediately, though, Charles became "sick," obtained another leave of absence, and checked into a Richmond hospital. For the next six months, he dropped almost completely out of sight. His letters to his father and brothers grew more and more infrequent, then stopped completely. By early May, 1862, Ruffin had begun to suspect the worst: his youngest boy was a deserter. A chance meeting with Charles's commanding officer, Captain Cuthbert, confirmed Ruffin's suspicions. Cuthbert had no idea of Charles's whereabouts and told the humiliated father that sick or well, Charles should have returned to his company long ago.

Disgraced, angry almost beyond words, Ruffin begged Cuthbert to punish Charles as he would any ordinary deserter. Do not spare my son, he implored, out of any "tenderness" or consideration for me. Ruffin himself had written several articles advocating that the army execute all deserters. He would make no exception, even for his own flesh and blood.

Ruffin was willing to give Charles one last chance to redeem himself and the family honor. He wrote Charles a letter and in it delivered an ultimatum: go back at once to the Palmettos or I never want to see you or speak to you again. If only Charles could die on the field of battle, he might vindicate his past misconduct. "His honorable death would be to me a blessing," wrote Ruffin, "compared to his continuing to live & act as he has done." A few weeks later, at the end of May, Cuthbert wrote Ruffin a letter assuring him that Charles had indeed returned to his duty. Not long afterwards, though, Charles deserted again, this time for good.[24]

6

Personally and politically, Ruffin found little to be happy about that spring. In April, a string of Union victories in the West, starting with General Ulysses S. Grant's triumph at Shiloh and climaxing with Admiral David Farragut's capture of New Orleans deflated even Ruffin's persistently buoyant spirits. The loss of New Orleans, the largest city and port in the Confederacy and the key to controlling the great Mississippi River, was an especially "heavy blow." For the first time, Ruffin had to admit "the supposition of the *possibility* of the subjugation of the southern states."[25]

He trembled as he tried to imagine a conquered South prostrated by Northern "roughs," whose cruelty, he was certain, rivaled the "barbarian hordes that . . . laid waste to the Roman empire." "If we are to be held as subject provinces," he decided, "I would prefer that our despotic ruler & master should be any power of Europe, even Russia or Spain, rather than the Northern States." But the very possibility of a brutal enemy triumph stiffened the old fire-eater's resistance, his readiness to sacrifice literally everybody and everything for the sacred cause. "Rather than to submit to Yankee domination, it would be better for all to be killed in battle."[26]

If there was a bright spot in any potential disaster, Ruffin could always find it, though. Should the Yankees succeed in winning the war, then, he predicted, they would lose the peace. Even if the victorious Northerners put every secessionist to death, they would still be left with almost eight million destitute whites and five million "lazy" blacks, who would refuse to lift a finger to work after they had been handed their freedom. To control this rabble of starving paupers and desperate plunderers, claimed Ruffin, the Yankees would have to garrison the South with more troops than it had taken to win the war. Eventually, Ruffin prophesied, gnawing hunger plus the thirst for revenge against their oppressors would drive the defeated Confederates into servile insurrection. In a burst of frenzied energy, "enslaved" Southerners throughout Dixie would rise up and massacre their Northern "masters."[27]

Even as Ruffin contemplated the likelihood of Northern victory and made plans for future revenge, more immediate concerns demanded his attention. Confederates had abandoned the Norfolk Naval Yard, leaving the James River plantations exposed to attack. In the Beechwood area, Ruffin's neighbors began to pack up their valuables, debating whether to stay where they were or flee before the enemy's arrival. In early May, the occupants of Beechwood spotted Yankee gunboats chugging up the James, and the fear of capture suddenly clutched at Ruffin.[28]

How simple it would be, he imagined, for a small party of Yankee soldiers, guided by some treacherous runaway slave, to row ashore one night and, under cover of darkness, "capture & carry off any especially obnoxious & noted residents." The ladies of Beechwood thought Ruffin fit this description perfectly and urged his "speedy departure." Friends assured him that he would be "an especial object for Yankee hatred & outrage," and Willoughby Newton added that Northerners would probably put both of them to death for their infamous antebellum secession activities. After all, wasn't the New York *Tribune* saving a piece of rope for the neck of the "traitor" who had fired the first shot at Fort Sumter?

Less afraid of death than the possibility of a long prison term, Ruffin was in a dilemma. Despite what the female members of his family were pleading, he had to take into consideration the fact that he was the only adult white male protector at Beechwood. He could not leave. But at night, recurring visions of himself rotting away, lonely and despised, in some stinking Northern jail cell haunted his dreams. He tried to lock out the Yankees, bolting his bedroom door and fastening the frail window shutters, but he could not lock out his nightmares. "I must try to avoid being captured," he admitted.[29]

7

A couple of weeks later, in mid-May, Edmund resigned his army commission and came home, thus allowing his much-relieved father to leave Beechwood. But instead of escaping, Ruffin headed toward the enemy. Word had arrived that the Confederate army on the Peninsula was retreating toward Richmond, and Ruffin wanted "to personally witness what is there going on" and "give my feeble aid to the defence of our capital." He knew that Richmond's capture by Union troops would probably mean the loss of all Virginia and a devastating blow to the Confederacy. "But before . . . surrendering, or retreating, without fighting," he said fervently, "I hope that our army may fight bravely until destroyed, & that Richmond may be bombarded & laid in ashes." If he could not have a stunning victory over his foes, he would settle for an equally impressive defeat. Honor was at stake.[30]

No sooner had Ruffin reached Richmond on May 17 than he learned that hundreds of McClellan's cavalry were near Marlbourne, occupying neighborhood plantations and encouraging slaves to join them. Ruffin, who had been contemplating a visit to his old home, shuddered to think of his narrow escape. A week later, though, as Yankee troops pressed close to

Richmond, Willoughby Newton advised his old friend to hurry away. But events were swirling out of control, and even Ruffin's bowels—usually constipated—betrayed him now. A sudden and severe attack of diarrhea left him temporarily disabled. "I am not fit now to fight or flee," Ruffin moaned piteously. Still, weak as he was, when the mayor of Richmond called for volunteers to form a Home Guard, Ruffin submitted his name without a moment's hesitation.[31]

Feeling a little better on the morning of May 31, Ruffin learned that a fight between Union and Confederate forces was about to begin somewhere on the Chickahominy River, not far from Richmond. Dressing quickly, he hurried over to the Capitol, climbed the steep staircase—his thighs did not fail him now—and stepped out onto the roof to join the dozens of other spectators, who were also hoping to catch "a whiff of battle." But the day was overcast and the sky leaden. It was hard even to distinguish the gray puffs of gunsmoke that appeared now and then on the horizon just over the trees. And although others assured Ruffin that the cannonfire was very rapid and noisy, he could hear only the most terrific explosions.[32]

Determined to have a closer look, Ruffin borrowed a horse the next day and rode off toward the battlefield. Once there, he could see that the number of casualties on both sides was awesome. Bleeding corpses and wounded men were sprawled out even more thickly than at Manassas. But after a quick body count, Ruffin felt relieved, for he was certain that he saw more blue uniforms than gray.

Despite the horrid presence of dead and dying soldiers, Ruffin was only one of hundreds of distinguished Southern citizens out for a day's sightseeing. Richard Yeadon of the Charleston *Courier* was another. He spotted South Carolina's favorite adopted son almost immediately and, perhaps recognizing a good news story, rode over to greet him. Later Yeadon would report to his readers how at the battle of Seven Pines, he had bumped into none other than the elderly but fearless Edmund Ruffin, the veteran of Fort Sumter and Bull Run, who, armed with his musket, was "always ready . . . to face danger wherever there is likelihood of striking at Yankeedom, or for southern independence."

And Seven Pines was a dangerous place to be, even for civilian spectators. The ground itself was so muddy and "rotten" from a previous night's downpour that Ruffin's horse lost its footing several times and almost fell. Worse, enemy shells were coming uncomfortably close. One Federal fragment missed Ruffin's gray head by only a few feet, landing fifteen yards behind him. Excited more than scared, Ruffin climbed down from his horse, picked up the shell as still another memento, and tried to guess just how close he had come to a hero's burial.

With Yeadon at his side, Ruffin rode on until he reached a captured Union campground. Some of the Confederate soldiers there recognized him and began "an irregular cheering." Puzzled, Ruffin asked his companion what all the noise was about. "It is a compliment to you," answered Yeadon. Then he yelled, "Three cheers for Edmund Ruffin of Virginia, the brave veteran, who fired the first gun at the bombardment of Fort Sumter." The men in gray responded with "loud & joyous huzzas." The object of all the fanfare simply lifted his hat and gave his customary bow.[33]

After seven rather uncomfortable hours in the saddle, Ruffin returned to Richmond. Before he reached his room, someone brought him sad news: his grandson Julian Beckwith had fallen in battle. Ruffin was stunned. Estranged from his daughter Agnes and her husband, Dr. Beckwith, for almost six years, he barely knew his own grandson. Still, Julian was the first member of Ruffin's family to lose his life because of the war, and the old man was unable to sleep that night. Yet he could not bring himself to write a letter of condolence to the bereaved parents. He could neither forgive nor forget their past "insults." "My temper is neither quick nor violent," he tried to rationalize. But "when my slow anger has been raised to the point of hostility & vindictiveness, my resentment is implacable." He cheered himself with the comforting circumstances of Julian's death: his grandson had died honorably, facing and firing upon Yankees.[34]

8

Confederate armies managed to check the Union advance at Seven Pines, but they did not clear Virginia of Northern troops. Yankee warships still patrolled the James River, and McClellan was able to establish secure headquarters on the Pamunkey. Thus, both Marlbourne and Beechwood were in constant danger of enemy attack.

Still in Richmond on June 10, Ruffin picked up a Northern newspaper and happened to see an article announcing that Yankees had captured Mrs. Robert E. Lee. Mrs. Lee had been hiding at a Hanover County plantation, and from the newspaper description, Ruffin knew that the plantation was Marlbourne. The article also said that when captured, the high-spirited and indignant Mrs. Lee had given such a lecture to the enemy officers on the duties of male chivalry toward women that they agreed to release her. She arrived in Richmond on June 11, and Edmund Ruffin was one of her first callers.

Mrs. Lee told the old gentleman terrible tales of Yankee plunder at Marlbourne. The horses, the mules, and most of the other livestock were gone. Soldiers had broken down the doors to the barn and the main house and then carried off the corn and wheat and two cabinets full of Ruffin's valuable fossil shell collection. And as if these catastrophes weren't bad enough, Mrs. Lee told her distraught visitor how most of the "loyal" slaves at Marlbourne had run away. The rest were in "quiet rebellion," staying on at the plantation but refusing to do any work.[35]

This unexpected and open show of resistance among the Marlbourne slaves—no matter how "quiet"—alarmed Ruffin. His son-in-law William Sayre, who was also in Richmond hiding from the enemy, told him what he could about this sudden "unchecked rebellion." Sayre swore that up until the night of Saturday, May 17, when Northern troops first arrived in the Marlbourne vicinity, none of his blacks had ever given him the slightest indication of unhappiness. (Evidently he never connected the plantation's two suspicious fires with slave discontent.) Yet that very Saturday night, Sayre continued, twelve of his males had escaped to join the Union army. Ironically, these were the very first slaves in the neighborhood to do so. Two days later, the remaining sixty blacks at Marlbourne—including the faithful Jem Sykes—went on strike.

Sayre had tried to reason with the rebellious blacks, he assured Ruffin, to show them gently the error of their ways. They had listened to him politely enough, without a trace of insolence or hostility. Yet no one budged either, and the work strike continued. "It was evident," commented Ruffin, "that all were convinced that they had in their reach the negro's heaven, of being relieved from labor, & were not at all troubled by any misgivings or fears of how they were to be fed & supported in idleness."[36]

Beechwood, too, was experiencing similar difficulties with its slaves. Twelve adult blacks whom Edmund had sent to help General J. E. B. Stuart had not been seen or heard from since the Confederate retreat at Williamsburg in early May. By June, twenty-eight more Negro men, women, and children had also deserted the plantation. Among these were two cripples and a dwarf, who, according to Ruffin, were never even required to do enough work to support themselves. Unaware that this evidence contradicted his theory about why slaves escaped to the Union army or refused to work, he could only shake his head in bewilderment. Why, he asked himself, should Marlbourne and Beechwood suffer from this "epidemic" of runaways, "for no where were they better cared for, or better managed & treated, according to their condition of slavery"?[37]

When Ruffin returned to Beechwood on June 12, he found his family in sad shape. He noticed right away that meals were skimpier than before and the dishes less varied. Conversation was also gloomy, with everyone packed and wondering out loud how soon it would be necessary for the entire household to escape out of enemy reach. The answer came less than two weeks later, when the Federal army moved so close to Beechwood that Ruffin; Edmund; five of Edmund's children and his wife Jane; William

Sayre; and the widow, Mrs. Lorraine, fled the plantation and crowded in with Julian, Lottie, and their four children at Ruthven.

At the same time, Edmund arranged to send the slaves who remained at Beechwood and his other plantation, Evelynton, to Petersburg for safe-keeping until most of them could be sold further south. This meant the "painful necessity" of splitting up slave families, Ruffin admitted, but he soothed his conscience by recalling how several black runaways had gone off "in utter disregard to family ties & affection." His son, Ruffin decided, was treating his slaves no worse than they treated one another.[38]

Thoughts of his own family and happier times brought Ruffin back to Beechwood a week later. The deserted mansion looked desolate. Wandering through the house, he looked into his bedroom and the rooms where several of his children had died, gathering sweet and painful memories along the way. Outside, he strolled around the lovely grounds, down the walking paths he had carved out with his own hands, past the thinned and open woods, "the Wilderness," and the marl knolls covered with bright red wildflowers. His heart ached to think he might never see these things again, as long as the war made him an exile from his beloved home.

Next he visited his old Coggin's Point plantation. Distinguished now only by a few huge shade trees, most of which Ruffin had planted himself, the place blended into the surrounding wheatfield. Last of all, Ruffin came to the family graveyard. Falling to his knees, he prayed aloud for the welfare of his family and country, for the restoration of their former prosperity and happiness, and for the "extinction" of all Yankee "vile public enemies."[39]

9

On July 1, Edmund and Julian Ruffin and William Sayre rode over to Marlbourne. They were able to return, because General "Stonewall" Jackson had launched a surprise attack on the neighborhood only a few days earlier and had successfully driven off the enemy troops. The Marlbourne slaves were simply astonished at the sudden flight of their newfound "Yankee friends & protectors."

All the black women and children were still on the plantation. But only two adult males—Jem Sykes and one other man—remained with them. The others had escaped behind Union lines and had even led the enemy on marauding expeditions to Marlbourne and neighboring plantations and farms. The slaves who stayed showed no special loyalty to their owners. Some of the bolder and more enterprising blacks had taken wheat out of the barn and sold it for seventy-five cents a bushel; others slaughtered approximately forty hogs and then cooked and sold the delicious meat to Yankee soldiers who were camped nearby.

When their Northern customers hastily retreated and Marlbourne's owners unexpectedly reappeared, these slaves were disappointed, and it showed. No one welcomed the masters' return. "But there was general & complete, if not willing acquiescence," and Edmund generously offered them "amnesty" for all past acts of disobedience and insubordination. If their future conduct was good, he promised, former misdeeds would be "overlooked & forgiven." But any further transgressions, he threatened, would result in the offender's immediate sale to the Deep South, where masters were not so "liberal" with their Negroes. This amnesty offer applied to all Marlbourne's slaves, Edmund concluded, even those who had run away. He urged the other blacks to communicate his message to the fugitives who were still hiding in the neighborhood and persuade them to return home.[40]

Ruffin was delighted that his son had put down this servile "rebellion" so quickly and without the use of force or violence. He was positive that now that the enemy was gone, the rest of Marlbourne's blacks would soon come back and voluntarily take up the yoke of bondage again. And indeed, by the end of the week, most of the missing men had returned. But after debating among themselves, they decided not to trust Edmund's generosity. Amnesty, they figured, was their master's trick to lure them back so they could be punished and then sold south. So they escaped again. A few trickled back to Marlbourne over the next five months: two fugitives returned because they were too sick to follow the Northern army; two were captured and sold immediately. Only one healthy male ever took advantage of "amnesty."[41]

10

The same day Ruffin's sons were surveying their losses at Marlbourne, Ruffin was engrossed in a different activity. That morning he awoke before sunrise, mounted a horse, and headed for Coggin's Point. He knew that McClellan's army, badly beaten during the Seven Days' Battles at the end of June, had abandoned headquarters on the Pamunkey and were retreating toward the James. Rumor had it that another fight would begin soon at the Berkeley plantation just below Coggin's Point, and Ruffin certainly did not want to miss such a spectacle. Climbing to the top of a hill called, appropriately enough, "Ruffin's Bluff," which offered a panoramic view of the broad inclined fields at Berkeley, the old man waited expectantly for the action to commence.[42]

What he saw, though, confused him. On the river he spotted a large enemy steamer, four transports, and several gunboats. A great number of Union wagons already lined the public roads, and clouds of dust signaled that more would be arriving shortly. But where were the Yankee troops? Ruffin wondered. Why weren't they accompanying the Union supply wagons? A fellow spectator informed him that Lee's army had managed to cut McClellan off from his line of supply. The news made Ruffin certain that Lee would now be able to crush the Army of the Potomac. Joyfully anticipating a Union disaster, he did not want the other members of his family to miss such a splendid sight. So, he immediately sent a messenger back to Ruthven summoning all the ladies and children to join him on the bluff. The family came willingly, the ladies swinging picnic baskets. Though no battle took place that day, Ruffin was glad to see that "they were delighted with the novel & unexpected scene offered to their view."[43]

Every morning for the next few days, Ruffin resumed his position on Ruffin's Bluff, carefully noting the number and disposition of enemy vessels and wagons and then sending reports to the Confederate Secretary of War in Richmond. He was standing at his customary spot on July 4, Independence Day, when he heard the Yankee gunboats fire off a salute in honor of the occasion. "What striking inconsistency—what a farce," he grumbled. How could Northerners be such hypocrites? How could they pretend to glorify the Declaration of Independence, a document that guaranteed the right of every oppressed people to assert their separate nationality, while at the same time conducting "this murderous war" against the South?[44]

11

The proximity of the enemy still made it impossible for the Ruffins to return to Beechwood. But Marlbourne was safe, so Edmund began making plans to move his family, including his father, to the Hanover County plantation. But on July 8, he received a startling telegram that made him change his mind. William Sayre wired from Richmond saying that he had reliable information that Lee was about to fall back again. Yankee soldiers, warned Sayre, would be at Marlbourne very shortly.

Heartily disappointed at this news, Edmund purchased a house in Petersburg, and on July 21, he and his family left Ruthven. Ruffin, though, would not budge. He had hated Petersburg since his unhappy days there as editor of the ill-fated *Farmers' Register,* and he nursed a lasting grudge. He would follow Edmund and his family anyplace, he declared, but Petersburg. So, until they moved to a more congenial spot, he would prefer to remain with Julian at Ruthven.[45]

After the departure of his eldest son, Ruffin's routine still consisted mainly of daily trips out to Ruffin's Bluff. On July 22, he met a General Raines there. Raines confided tentative plans to mount an artillery attack from the bluff, thus clearing the James River of enemy ships and cutting off a main source of Union army supplies. Ruffin could not have been more enthusiastic, and he eagerly showed the general all the available routes for the artillery to approach and retreat, including the best shortcuts.

A week later, though, Ruffin was distressed to hear that the Confederates wanted to mount several cannons in front of Beechwood and from there launch the Southern attack on the Yankee fleet. In a way, Ruffin had to admit that Beechwood was a perfect choice, for it offered a commanding view of the river, while the surrounding belt of trees screened the plantation and its occupants from prying river eyes. But he also knew that even a successful surprise attack from Beechwood would eventually draw enemy fire and all but guarantee the plantation's destruction. So, on July 29, he galloped over to Beechwood, pleaded convincingly with a half dozen officers to change their strategy, and then gladly guided them to a more promising position atop Ruffin's Bluff.[46]

Two days later, Confederate guns began pounding the enemy, but Ruffin's plans backfired. Instead of ridding the area of Northern vessels, the attack provoked severe Yankee reprisals. Even Ruffin voiced no protest this time when in early August, Ruthven emptied out and his entire family took to the road toward Petersburg. On their way, they met scores of neighbors as well as retreating Rebel soldiers.

Meanwhile, Union soldiers swarmed up the banks of the James River. An elderly slave woman told them how old Master Ruffin had helped to guide the recent Confederate artillery attack on Northern gunboats, and angry Yankees immediately headed for the Ruffin plantation. They were most eager to lay their hands on this notorious Rebel.[47]

14

Warfare of Extermination

1

YANKEE SOLDIERS wasted no time getting to Beechwood. When they found that neither Ruffin nor his son nor any of his kinfolk were on the plantation, five Northern regiments from the Pennsylvania Cavalry and the Sixteenth Michigan decided to make themselves at home.[1]

"We lived while we were over there," one soldier wrote to his sister. Few of the men, officers included, had ever seen such beauty or known such luxury. "It is the only place I have yet seen," swore the same trooper, "that gave much evidence that the owner is anything more than in name and pretension an F.F.V." What an "excellent farm" the Ruffins had. Why there were acres upon acres of corn—"the largest corn I ever saw," the soldier marvelled—growing sixteen feet high. And, since "guarding secesh property is played out," he added merrily, "we had full liberty to 'acquire' anything we could find to eat."

The Yankee soldier tried to describe everything he saw at Beechwood but explained apologetically that words could not capture or convey the exquisite loveliness of the plantation. Picture if you will, he told his sister, the greenest, thickest carpet of a lawn, magnificent shade trees of oak and tulip "that look as though they have seen a century's growth at least," winding walkways and twisting avenues, shady bowers, and rose-covered summer cottages "drooping with graceful festoons of flowers." Even the slave quarters were attractive. At other plantations the writer had seen, the slaves lived in miserable log huts; at Beechwood, they enjoyed "clean painted frame buildings tastefully arranged in the shade of those old trees."

In front of the main house, continued the letter, there was a smaller dwelling—Ruffin's quarters—where the Yankee writer imagined that the master of Beechwood spent most of his time. Inside, there were an office, a study, and "the largest library I ever saw." Thousands of books—subsequently "acquired" by other Union soldiers—attested to the fact that the owner must have been "a scholar and a writer of no mean ability."

Last and most impressive of all in the eyes of this Northerner was the Beechwood mansion, which sat high upon a hill almost one hundred feet above the James River, encircled and shielded by a grove of tall trees. "There is an air of aristocracy and luxury about these old southern mansions that time alone can give," he concluded. Beechwood was "a palace almost," an "abode of wealth and taste," the stuff dreams are made of, "the realization of the imaginary residences of the heroines we read of in romances."[2]

2

It was not until the middle of August, 1862, that Federal troops evacuated the James River area. On August 17, reports reached Ruffin in Petersburg that McClellan had taken his defeated army back to Washington. Beechwood was safe again. So, saddling up a horse that same afternoon, Ruffin raced over there to survey the damages. A nagging fear made him suspect that enemy "vandals" had wreaked special vengeance on the homes of infamous Rebels like himself, and he was right.

Beechwood was a shambles. The storybook palace looked more like a dump. As Ruffin alighted from his horse, his joints stiff and sore from the long, hurried ride, he stepped into knee-deep rubbish. Scattered across the once clean-swept yard were bits and pieces of dishes, plates, and crockery, broken chairs, and mangled furniture. Feathers torn from pillows and bedding floated freely through the air. Unstuffed mattresses lay ripped and shredded on the ground.

Almost in shock, Ruffin went up to the main house where, if anything, the wreckage was worse: windows smashed, mirrors shattered or stolen, doors wrenched off their hinges. Kicking aside the debris that covered the mansion floors "even more thickly than the yard," Ruffin made his way to his private living quarters. Most of the rooms were bare, totally stripped of their belongings. What remained was useless, the Yankees having destroyed "everything that could not be conveniently stolen & carried off." A terrestrial globe lay in pieces on the floor. The beloved harmonicon no longer held its pretty glass panes. Gone too were thousands of library books, some rare shells and crystals, and personal correspondence spanning more than twenty years. Union soldiers had even unscrewed the knobs from doors and dresser drawers, looted all the bells, and pocketed the closet hooks—souvenirs, perhaps for their own collections of wartime memorabilia.[3]

Heaping insult upon injury, the pillaging Yankees had spat streams of tobacco juice over the exterior and interior mansion walls. Then, using their own spittle plus chunks of charcoal, they boldly signed their names and scrawled messages "of the most rascally character." Among them: "This house belonged to a Ruffinly son of a bitch." "Old Ruffin don't you wish you had left the Southern Confederacy to go to Hell (where it will go,) & had stayed at home?" "You did fire the first gun on Sumter, you traitor son of a bitch."

Union scribblings were everywhere. An "*elegant* epistle" on the mantelpiece mockingly thanked the owners of Beechwood for the "sumptuous accomodations," called Ruffin a "brick" for keeping such a good "hotel," and boasted of what fine care Northern troops had taken of Confederate property. The flyleaf of an old book bore this inscription: "Owned by Old Ruffin, the basest traitor rebel in the United States. You old cuss, it is a pity you go unhanged." The language contained in most of the other messages was too "vulgar & disgusting" for Ruffin to copy, but he refused to let the enemy's personal insults bother him anyway. "I take the scurrilous abuse thrown upon myself very complacently," he explained, "as the only compliment or eulogism that a low bred Yankee can bestow on me."[4]

He was less complacent about the "wanton mischief" done to Beechwood's lovely grounds. In a place the Ruffins called "the Grove," Union troops had hacked down almost ten acres of innocent trees, including many fine old oaks. One particularly magnificent shade tree, standing apart from all the others, had been cut around its middle, Ruffin noted angrily, killed by "wilful & malignant design." In addition, Yankee "bandits" stole the livestock, took almost every farm tool, broke the reaper and the thrashing machine, damaged and plundered the slave quarters, and abducted eighty-six blacks. Total losses came to some one hundred fifty thousand dollars.[5]

3

The destruction at Beechwood did not dampen Ruffin's enthusiasm for war. Instead it whetted his appetite for revenge. Drawing up his own scheme for a "war of retaliation," he submitted the plan to his old friend Judge Perkins and to several Richmond newspapers.[6]

First of all, his plan deplored the Confederacy's present defensive military strategy, which enabled even a defeated enemy to ravage Southern land and loot Southern property. Abandon this accursed policy, pleaded Ruffin. Seize the initiative. "Put the cost & sacrifice of war on the enemy's territory, & . . . make them feel the horrors of war."[7]

How easy it would be, he thought, for some daring and clever Confederate cavalry officer—the dashing Jeb Stuart, for one, or the wily John Hunt Morgan, or the equally slippery Stonewall Jackson—to lead a small guerrilla force of ten to twenty-five thousand men into a Northern border state like Pennsylvania, Ohio, or Illinois, where they could "lay waste" to the major cities "with fire & sword." A smile lit his wrinkled face as he imagined Philadelphia burning, Cincinnati buried in its own ashes, Chicago reduced to rubble.

But destroying the cities was not nearly punishment enough for Northern war crimes, Ruffin insisted. As the Southern raiders charged toward their targeted urban centers, they must live off the countryside, ransacking Northern farms, stripping the fields of their crops, bringing the war home to the civilian population, just as Union soldiers had done when they invaded the South. And just as Union troops had encouraged black slaves to run away and turn against their masters, trying to stir up servile insurrection, Confederate guerrillas must encourage Northern "wage slaves" to rise up and rebel against their capitalist employers, fomenting class revolution. "If the enemy were thus made to bear the cost & the worst evils of war, as they have inflicted them on us," Ruffin prophesied, "they would weary of the then unprofitable contest."

After the raiding parties had spread a sufficient amount of terror and destruction throughout the North, and once the Yankees had learned a lesson they would never forget and were begging for mercy, Ruffin would have the Confederate government call a halt to these scorched-earth tactics and declare that past Yankee "atrocities" had now been officially avenged. If the enemy would promise to conduct itself in a manner befitting honorable gentlemen, the South would agree to return to its former strict observance of the laws of civilized war. Otherwise, Ruffin would willingly carry forward a "warfare of extermination."[8]

4

That autumn, 1862, as if in response to Ruffin's ardent wishes, there was a sudden and unexpected turn of the military tables. For the first time, the Confederate government was mounting a concerted—though ultimately unsuccessful—military counteroffensive. In the West, General Braxton Bragg outmaneuvered the Yankee high command, slipped through western Tennessee, and set out to "liberate" Kentucky. In the East, Lee thwarted McClellan's Peninsular Campaign, rolled over General John Pope's troops at the second battle of Bull Run, then took the Army of Northern Virginia into Maryland and seemed hell-bent on an invasion of Pennsylvania.

Naturally, Ruffin could not have been more pleased, and he followed newspaper accounts of Lee's progress that September with great interest. On the seventeenth, Lee engaged McClellan at a little town named Sharpsburg on Antietam Creek. Neither side decisively defeated the other, and tactically the battle was a draw. But when the fighting was over, Lee decided to halt his advance northward and to withdraw his men back into Virginia. This made Antietam a crucial strategic victory for the North.[9]

Back at Beechwood, though, Ruffin had no way of knowing what had actually taken place in Maryland. He read contradictory Confederate and Union newspaper dispatches—each side claiming victory—and put his trust in Southern reports that the invincible Lee had triumphed once more over the enemy. After all, Ruffin reasoned, Yankees were "monstrous liars," who always tried to win in the press what they had lost on the field of battle. Later, he would severely berate Confederate authorities for concealing military disasters, calling it "a pity & a shame" that Rebel war reporters "seem to emulate Yankee commanders in their monstrous falsehoods." But for the present, he felt confident that Southerners had won at Antietam. "I cannot help believing that the last of our great and bloody battles has been fought," he wrote optimistically in his diary, "& that negotiations for peace will be on foot before winter is over."[10]

5

Less than two weeks after Antietam, Ruffin received what he believed was even more encouraging news. On Sunday, September 28, a neighbor galloped over to Beechwood, waving a newspaper and shouting hysterically. Abraham Lincoln had issued a preliminary emancipation proclamation, he cried. Unless the seceded states ceased hostilities and returned to the Union before January 1, 1863, the President had promised to free all Rebel slaves and to abolish the South's peculiar institution "thenceforward and forever."[11]

Ruffin greeted the announcement with a smile and a sneer. Like most Southerners, he interpreted the presidential proclamation as an open invitation to servile insurrection. But unlike Jefferson Davis, who damned the document as "the most execrable measure recorded in the history of guilty man," Ruffin, oddly enough, "rejoiced" at Lincoln's actions.[12]

Ever since the war commenced, Ruffin had been waiting—even hoping —for such a Northern declaration. After all, he pointed out, hadn't the Republican Congress already authorized the seizure of Rebel slaves as legitimate "contraband of war"; provided for compensated emancipation in Washington, D.C.; and enacted laws prohibiting slavery from the Federal territories? And hadn't Ruffin predicted years ago that this was exactly what "Black Republicans" would do, once they were in control of the national government? This latest Federal offense, declared the vindicated prophet, should come as no surprise, for it did no more than "strip off the disguise" from an old and long-established abolition policy.[13]

This emancipation proclamation was a sure sign of Northern weakness, Ruffin contended. Having given up all hopes of ever defeating the South militarily, the Lincoln government, he said, was trying to sweet-talk it back into the Union with "false promises of pardon and amnesty," while at the same time coupling its sugary words with threats of slave rebellion. Ruffin cautioned Southerners to distrust the promises and ignore the intimidation. For more than twenty years, abolitionists had failed consistently in their attempts to incite a slave revolt, he argued. Why should they be any more successful now?[14]

Ruffin was sure that Lincoln's latest ploy to win the war would backfire. In fact, he predicted, the emancipation proclamation "will do our cause good" both at home and abroad. Designed as it was to foment "another St. Domingo in the Southern States," the measure could not fail to "shock & repel" European countries, sending "a shudder of horror throughout England & France." Thousands of equally horrified unionists in the border slave states would become instant secessionists. And in the South itself, said Ruffin, the now undeniable certainty that slavery's very existence was at stake would redouble Confederate determination to win the war at all costs.[15]

The emancipation proclamation would not gain Lincoln many friends in the North either, Ruffin stated confidently. Indeed, it would only make him more unpopular than ever with everyone but "rabid abolitionists." Ruffin was overjoyed to read that Democratic politicians were bitterly protesting Lincoln's "criminal" proclamation, that even members of the President's own party deplored the act and called him an "imbecile." The ever-popular General McClellan had threatened to resign his army commission rather than fight "a nigger war." Thousands of Northern soldiers echoed his sentiments, adding that while they would willingly lay down their lives to save the Union, they would not lift a finger to liberate slaves. Ruffin had even found evidence of this widespread Northern negrophobia in his own backyard. A letter left behind at Beechwood by a Massachusetts trooper stated unequivocally, "I would not turn my hand over to free all the niggers of the South, for they are better off where they are than they could be if they were free."[16]

And just where exactly would the newly emancipated slaves live once they were free? Ruffin wanted to know. Would their Yankee liberators welcome them to the North? He doubted that very much, for he had come to realize that the majority of Northern people were not so much antislavery as antiblack and that working-class whites who lived in the cities and in the rural parts of the Midwest were particularly ferocious racists. The Northern laboring classes, Ruffin explained perceptively, "dread & detest the free negroes as rivals for employment." Already, stories of bloody Northern race riots made Ruffin confident that whites would never stand for black emancipation. Any freedmen who ventured North, he predicted, would soon be "murdered by their Yankee protectors."[17]

But the Lincoln administration, sensitive to the widespread racism of its constituents, tried to convince jittery citizens that emancipation would not flood the North with swarms of black immigrants. Ruffin read an editorial in the New York *Evening Post* that suggested putting the free blacks on Indian-type reservations located in desolate regions of the West, where, like the native Americans, their numbers would dwindle and they would soon die out. "It is the destiny of the free white working men of this country to possess it," the Republican editors claimed. Slaveholders had robbed free labor of half the land—"the richest & fairest half—*& devoted it to the blacks.*" Slaveholders, charged the *Post,* had "*preserved the negro race* from decline among us," and slaveholders had "increased the blacks from 700,000 in 1790 to four million in 1860." Remove Negro slavery from the United States, the paper seemed to promise whites, and you will remove the Negro.[18]

Few Northerners swallowed this kind of argument, and Lincoln himself, Ruffin noticed, favored a different sort of forced migration scheme: colonization of the liberated slaves outside the United States in black-ruled Haiti, Liberia, or some country in Central America. Ruffin, as always, was skeptical of any colonization plan. He was sure that no matter what anyone said, the only country Republicans intended to colonize was the South. He shuddered to think what that might mean: a reconstructed South that was economically, politically, and socially in the hands of its former slaves. Black governors ruling black legislatures. Black judges presiding over black courts. Black officers commanding black militia. "Africanization" replacing "civilization." Such an awful tableau might bring smiles of pleasure to the faces of "fanatical fools" like Horace Greeley and Wendell Phillips, but Ruffin believed that the majority of Northern whites would find the prospect "objectionable and disgusting."[19]

6

That fall Ruffin listened carefully for grumblings of discontent from the North. He guessed correctly that many Northerners were unhappy over the emancipation proclamation, angry at their President, and sick to death of war. In fact, if it were not for Lincoln's "reign of terror," his suppression of free speech, and his habit of throwing critics in jail, Ruffin thought, it would be well known that the vast majority of Northerners favored peace.[20]

Ruffin's contempt for Lincoln knew no bounds. Why, the man was "utterly incompetent," even as a tyrant. An Oliver Cromwell or a Napoleon Bonaparte would have made himself king of the North by now. But Lincoln did not possess "one-tenth part" of their "intellect & talent for command." To Ruffin, Lincoln was demagoguery incarnate, the kind of political usurper who had robbed him—a man of superior mental qualities—of the rewards of high office. Lincoln was just a "low-minded & narrow-minded" individual, "deficient in courage as well as in intellect & education." Yet Congress had given him enormous powers: the power to draft men between age twenty and forty-five into the army, the power to command government credit and revenue, the power to arrest and imprison citizens for seditious speech, the power to suspend the writ of *habeas corpus* and order military imprisonment without due process of law. "Will the people of the north . . . submit to this unconstitutional despotism?" Ruffin asked himself. "That is the question."[21]

No, he decided. "Base & abject" as Yankees were as a people, they would not quietly bow to these "deadly blow[s] to their rights & liberty." There must be some sort of revolution in the North. A single state—New York, perhaps—would refuse to obey the conscription law and thus fatally undermine the Union war effort. A whole section of the country would break off from the Union and perhaps even side with the Confederacy.[22]

The latter possibility intrigued Ruffin. Opposition to Lincoln and his policies had been increasing steadily, especially in the Northwest. Shouldn't the Confederacy take advantage of this situation? In a letter addressed to Jefferson Davis and in a separate article to the Richmond *Enquirer,* Ruffin advised that the South dispatch peace commissioners on a secret diplomatic mission to the northwestern states, where they should try to negotiate a separate treaty. The terms of said treaty should guarantee the Northwest free access to the Mississippi River and free trade with an independent South. In return, the Northwest must agree to cease fighting the Confederacy, detach itself from the Northeast, and "revolt from Yankeedom."[23]

In November, as off-year congressional and state elections approached in the North, Ruffin anticipated a different kind of revolt in "Yankeedom": a peaceful political revolution. By voting Republicans out of every available office, Northern citizens might force Lincoln to end the war. Ruffin rejoiced when the Democrats won five key Northern states—states that had gone for Lincoln in 1860—and only narrowly missed gaining a majority in Congress. He believed that the Democratic party was really a peace party in disguise. When Democrats controlled the Federal government, Ruffin predicted, they would take off their war masks and make peace with the South. Ruffin prayed that until that time, Copperhead peace politicians and other antiwar Northerners would counter every one of Lincoln's war moves with "obstinate & bloody resistance."[24]

7

But many Southerners were also weary of war and its harsh deprivations, and they were not kindly disposed toward fire-eaters like Ruffin, whom they blamed for most of their present hardships. Ruffin learned from one of his neighbors that the "white trash" living near Ruthven had "the settled & unquestioned opinion . . . that *I* was the whole & sole cause of the war." Naturally the accusation tickled him, and he only wished that it were true. "I would desire no more glory & fame than to be truly believed to have been the chief cause of effecting the separation of the Southern from the Northern states," he declared boldly, "even at all the general expense of blood & property . . . which it will cost."[25]

No genuine Confederate complained about the sacrifices he or she was asked to make during the war, Ruffin insisted, except for the ones who were lazy, low-born, and vicious. "Such people cannot have any exhalted sentiments of patriotism, & must regard the war almost exclusively in reference to the sufferings it has caused them," he added haughtily. More disturbing, though, was this same lack of "exhalted sentiments" among some of the South's more substantial citizens. Men like John Minor Botts of Virginia and William Woods Holden, editor of the *North Carolina Standard,* made no secret of their unionism. Ruffin, the defender of civil liberties and the right to dissent in the North, never uttered a word of protest when Botts was arrested and thrown into "a dirty, filthy negro jail" and kept there until he agreed to keep his unpopular opinions to himself. As for Holden and the *Standard,* Ruffin urged the "patriots" of North Carolina to use any means —legal or illegal—to shut down this traitorous paper and punish its outspoken editor. Later, when an angry Raleigh mob acted on these suggestions, sacked the *Standard's* offices, and forced Holden to run for his life, Ruffin was all smiles, having forgotten about constitutional niceties like freedom of the press.[26]

8

In December, Lee gave the Army of the Potomac another trouncing, this time at Fredericksburg, and Ruffin turned his attention back to the military arena. On New Year's Day, 1863, he delivered a state of the war message in his diary. "This year which is just closed has been almost everywhere glorious to our arms," he wrote. True, Northern troops enjoyed an advantage in the West, where they presently occupied Kentucky, Missouri, Louisiana, and West Virginia plus large sections of Tennessee, Arkansas, and Mississippi. True, four enormous Union armies were pressing down on all sides of the Confederacy. Yet Ruffin remained "sanguine," because he believed that the South needed just one more "signal victory" to end the war. "The Northern power apparently is already doomed," he concluded brightly. "Nothing can bring a reprieve but a series of great victories."[27]

The hope for a Yankee doomsday soon turned into Ruffin's one reason for living. "Except for the deep interest I feel in the present war, & all its incidents, & my wish to witness its termination, with success, glory, & the sure prospect of prosperity to my country," he confessed, "I have no inducement to desire the extension of my life. With this one exception, I should not care how soon the last summons may come to me."[28]

Why was Ruffin so ready to accept "the last summons"? On January 5, he had reached his sixty-ninth birthday, and as usual, he took the occasion to describe his health in great detail. He told his diary that all his old ailments had worsened considerably. His hearing was almost gone. His hands shook uncontrollably. His hair was falling out and even "my pendant locks are shorter," he wailed. His memory was fading too. He forgot the details of newspaper articles; he could not recall the faces of old friends. "My infirmities have deprived me of nearly all the pleasures I formerly enjoyed, mental as well as physical," he complained. "Especially do I suffer for the want of society, which I have lost the capacity to enjoy, & am unfit to mix with."[29]

The next day, January 6, Ruffin received news that only deepened his depression: his favorite daughter, Mildred Sayre, was dead. Frozen with grief, the old man was unable to cry, and this "calmness & apparent insensibility" upset him almost as much as his daughter's death. "Have age and decrepitude so impaired my faculties, paralyzed my affections, & dried up the sources of parental love & of all deep feeling," he asked himself, "that I scarcely grieve for the death of . . . my best beloved remaining child?"[30]

Age and decrepitude had not affected Ruffin's capacity to hate or to hold a grudge though. A few days after he learned about Mildred, Ruffin received another letter, this one from his daughter Agnes Beckwith, whom he had refused to communicate with or see for many years. Agnes expressed sorrow over her sister's death and then begged Ruffin to forgive and forget all their past misunderstandings. But Ruffin spurned her offer of reconciliation. He would "forgive" Agnes but never "forget" the misery she had caused him by her marriage. Although Ruffin liked to think of himself as a mild-tempered man who was always reluctant to take offense—an extraordinary, though unconscious, self-deception—still he admitted that "a real deliberate malicious aspersion, or act of hostility without just cause, I have rarely forgiven. Subsequent lapse of time, absence of or separation from the offender, or even his death, & the passage of many years thereafter, have not operated to alter my opinion of my enemy, or sensibly to abate my feelings of hatred & vindictiveness." So he sent Agnes's imploring letter back to her with just one terse comment: "I have *no daughter* left alive."[31]

9

Still despondent over his daughter's death and his own declining health, Ruffin suffered an acute attack of self-pity that winter. He dredged up all his old memories and past feelings of public "neglect." Ingratitude, he decided sorrowfully, had been the story of his life. He recalled all the commendable and disinterested contributions he had made on the public's behalf—as a politician, agricultural reformer, publisher, author, and most of all as a secessionist and soldier. And what had the public given him in return? he demanded angrily. "No thanks." Nothing but "neglect, ingratitude, villification, & persecution, from those I sought to benefit."[32]

The only reward he had ever wanted, protested Ruffin bitterly, was public approval and affection, but this he never received, at least not in his "country," not in Virginia. He thought that once the South had seceded, surely his personal star would rise. But after only a brief flurry of popularity, Ruffin felt forgotten. People who hated him before secession because of his disunion views continued to hate him afterwards. Although strangers outside his native state hailed him on the street, soldiers saluted and cheered him, and legislatures treated him like a special guest, in Virginia he was still "a prophet . . . without honor."

Nor had the Confederacy—this new and purified Southern republic which Ruffin had labored so hard to bring into existence—ever given him the kind of recognition and respect he felt he deserved. Ironically, the unusual and fleeting glory of his military adventures only heightened his sense of alienation, of being a social misfit, when he returned to everyday civilian life. What little fame he now had, Ruffin realized, he owed to his brief but dramatic moment at Fort Sumter. "It seems to me, that, but for the accident of Fort Sumter, my patriotic labors & efforts would have been unknown—& my name almost forgotten," he lamented. "I appeal to future generations for the due appreciation of my efforts, & their effects."[33]

10

Adding to Ruffin's general unhappiness and perhaps partially responsible for it was the fact that there was almost nothing for him to do that winter. The war made mail deliveries slow and irregular, and he had very little to read. Combined with "wretched weather," which kept him indoors all day, this situation made for "a wretchedly dull time."[34]

In March, just to "kill time," Ruffin started to take an interest in plantation work. He, Edmund, and Edmund's family were living at Marlbourne now, since this estate was in better shape than Beechwood and safer from the Yankees. William Sayre, Marlbourne's former resident superintendent, was no longer there. Edmund had bought his share of the plantation in January, and Ruffin now agreed to replace him as *"consulting agriculturalist."* Aside from giving his son advice and suggesting agricultural improvements, Ruffin took on the duties of overseeing the ploughing and directing the digging of drainage ditches.[35]

To his own surprise, Ruffin began to enjoy himself. But he had trouble at first dealing with the slaves. He found that despite the promise of complete amnesty, he could not treat these blacks with his former affection. He was unable to forgive their recent unfaithful behavior when Northern troops invaded the Marlbourne neighborhood. He could not forget that they had betrayed his trust. Their actions mocked him, belying his utopian vision of Southern society. And yet it was not very long before his fertile brain came up with an explanation for his slaves' disloyalty that made him feel better, because it squared with his previous beliefs about innate Negro character.[36]

In a way, Ruffin felt personally responsible for the trouble Marlbourne had experienced with its slaves. After all, it was he who had given the plantation to his children in six indivisible shares. This made for six masters when, according to Ruffin, "the negro needs to look up to, for protection & control, one individual master or mistress." Slaves just could not understand belonging to a copartnership. Their "strong disposition for loyalty," he concluded ruefully, "had no place for growth." It was "natural" for a slave to be faithful to one owner, but "it is contrary to negro nature to be loyal to a copartnership of [six] individuals."

It was particularly hard for the slaves at Marlbourne to be loyal to William Sayre, "a stranger whom they first disliked & subsequently hated heartily." Neither Ruffin nor his sons were aware of these hostile feelings until they actually came to live at Marlbourne in the autumn of 1862. Nor were they aware that Sayre was guilty of "gross negligence" in all his plantation duties. Ruffin cursed the day he had ever allowed his son-in-law a share of Marlbourne, calling the decision "the worst blunder of my life." It was Sayre he blamed for all the past incidents of slave infidelity: the two suspicious fires, the numerous runaways, the work slowdowns.[37]

Yes, Sayre and the copartnership arrangement provided convenient scapegoats for Marlbourne's past slave difficulties—but only up to a point. One problem still baffled Ruffin. At Beechwood, the slaves had proved no more faithful than at Marlbourne. In fact, Beechwood had had a worse "epidemic" of runaways. Yet at Beechwood there was only one master, a master who was "humane & judicious," Ruffin insisted. What had happened to those slaves' "natural disposition for loyalty"? As always, the answer eluded him.[38]

11

Ruffin spent very little time that spring puzzling over such contradictions. He was having too much fun getting reacquainted with plantation work. Like Cincinnatus, Ruffin felt that his return to the soil revived him and restored some of his old vitality. He no longer complained that farm duties were "tedious." He began to sleep soundly at night, untroubled by the habitual bouts of insomnia that had plagued him in the past. By mid-April, he swore that he felt better mentally and physically "than in any part of my previous life."[39]

On Monday morning, May 4, Ruffin got up, ate breakfast, and walked outside as usual to supervise work on his drainage ditches. He watched absentmindedly as the ladies of the house climbed into their carriage and departed on a trip to Richmond. Fifteen minutes later, though, he was surprised to see the carriage coming rapidly back in his direction. The ladies, Ruffin later learned, had gotten only as far as their neighbor Lewis Johnson's gate when someone there informed them that a large body of Yankee cavalry had plundered Spring Garden—a plantation just upriver from Marlbourne—that very morning and were probably still close by. Turning their carriage around, the Ruffin women immediately came back to Marlbourne to warn the others.

Meanwhile, Ruffin had no idea of the impending danger until a slave boy rushed up, breathless and excited, with the message that Yankees were in the neighborhood. Sending the child on to warn Edmund, who was out attending to the field labor, Ruffin proceeded back to the house. But before he even reached the yard, his young grandsons John and Meade intercepted him with urgent news: two enemy soldiers had spotted the Ruffin carriage, seen it make its sudden turn, and then chased it back to Marlbourne. Already Yankees were at the mansion door. Ruffin must hide quickly.

Concealing himself in some nearby shrubs, Ruffin waited anxiously for the intruders to leave. "Where are the damned Ruffin men?" he heard them ask the slaves. Gone, the slaves lied. Old Master and young Master were gone, and no one knew when they were coming back. Cursing, the enemy soldiers mounted their horses and left, but they would return, Ruffin heard them promise, for they "were bound to have our heads."[40]

12

The appearance of Yankees at Marlbourne had come so suddenly and without warning that it unnerved Ruffin. That evening, the family held a hurried conference, and everyone agreed that Ruffin must escape to Ruthven as soon as possible. The following morning, he was packed and ready to go. But before his carriage pulled away, a neighbor rode up bringing excellent news: Lee had just won a brilliant victory over General Joseph Hooker at Chancellorsville. The Army of the Potomac, disgracefully beaten again after still another vain drive toward Richmond, was retreating back to winter quarters north of the Rappahannock River. Southerners everywhere were predicting that the war was over. Elated, Ruffin climbed down from his carriage and began to unpack.[41]

A few days later, though, Federal troops were advancing through the Marlbourne neighborhood again. This time, the entire Ruffin household fled to Ruthven. Yet even this constant running away from Yankees did not dampen Ruffin's high spirits after Chancellorsville. Surely, he figured, this battle was the one "signal victory" that would successfully conclude the war. The Union government would have no choice now but to sue for peace.

In fact, he was so confident that one night after dinner, he sat down with his diary and dictated the terms of peace that a victorious South must impose on a vanquished North. The most important demands concerned heavy war reparations. Northerners must pay for all the valuable slaves they had "stolen" and for other "outrages contrary to the laws of war." Partial compensation should include a share of the United States Navy and a sizable chunk of the Federal territories. Finally, until the Union made good on all Rebel claims, the Confederate government should ban all commercial and business dealings with the North. And, he stipulated, no Yankee should ever be allowed to travel through the slave states without first posting a special bond that guaranteed that said traveler was no abolitionist.[42]

13

For the rest of May, Ruffin waited impatiently for the North to surrender. He was incredulous that the Northwest, at least, did not grab the opportunity to sign a separate treaty with the South. What ailed the people of these states? he wondered in amazement. Didn't they realize yet that an alliance with the Confederacy was their only guarantee of cheap and safe passage down the Mississippi River? Hadn't this "obvious fact" had time to impress itself on their "dull minds"? And why hadn't antiwar Northerners revolted against their President's continuing assaults on their civil liberties? When would they display some "spirit of manhood" and topple the Lincoln government?[43]

When the anticipated Union surrender failed to materialize by the end of May, Ruffin realized that his expectations of peace were premature. True, the battle of Chancellorsville had been another high-water mark for the Confederacy. Lee had won a smashing victory, yet he had made a grave mistake, a mistake common to generals on both sides during this war so far. He had allowed the defeated enemy to get away. Ruffin repeatedly criticized this lack of military follow-up after key battles. What good was winning, he would demand, unless Confederates reaped "the fruits of victory" by going after and then destroying the enemy's army and thus its ability to come back and fight another day?[44]

Lee, too, evidently had some second thoughts about strategy after Chancellorsville and decided to take the offensive for a change and invade a Northern state. Harking back to Ruffin's earlier suggestions, Lee hoped to seize some major Yankee city like Philadelphia and hold it captive until Lincoln agreed to a negotiated peace. In June, he began moving his troops toward Pennsylvania, where, in a month's time, they would clash again with the Army of the Potomac, this time outside a little town called Gettysburg.[45]

Naturally, Ruffin followed the military reports of Lee's progress in the East very closely, but it was the situation in the western theater that concerned him most. Since early spring, Grant's army had been floundering around in the low country near Vicksburg, trying without success first to reach and then to capture this last Confederate stronghold of the Mississippi Valley. If Vicksburg fell, Yankees would control the length of the great river, and the Confederacy would be cut in two. Ruffin also knew that such an important Union victory would be a tremendous boost to Northern war morale and would probably spell the end of any effective peace movement. If Grant succeeded in taking Vicksburg, he prophesied, Northern opposition to the war would melt away; dissident voices would hush. Not a soul would utter even a whisper of protest against Lincoln's foulest misdeeds. But if Grant's campaign failed—and Ruffin fully expected that it would— if the Union armies suffered yet another disastrous defeat, Northern citizens *"must revolt"* and force their government to capitulate. Vicksburg, it seemed, would be the key to war or peace.[46]

14

On July 6, Ruffin learned about the "incredible" twin Confederate defeats at Gettysburg and Vicksburg. The news stunned him. Initial battle reports from Gettysburg had sounded so promising: Rebels were whipping Yankees as expected, claimed the Southern newspapers, and Lee was supposed to have captured as many as forty thousand Union soldiers. But the truth was that on July 3, a defeated Lee had retreated from the battlefield, lucky to get himself and his demoralized army safely back across the Potomac. The forty thousand Yankee prisoners, naturally, had "vanished into thin air." The very next day, July 4, Vicksburg surrendered.

These back-to-back Union victories depressed even Ruffin's stubbornly "sanguine" war spirits. "Our prospect is extremely gloomy," he had to admit that summer. "I have never before felt so despondent as to our struggle."[47]

In the weeks that followed, though, his gloom changed to anger at the "infernal enemy." The Confederate government, hoping to boost civilian as well as military morale, was cramming the newspapers with dozens of sensational, lurid, and sometimes fabricated tales of Yankee "atrocities." Ruffin's fury mounted as he carefully recorded each new "unspeakable outrage": Southern citizens tortured beyond human endurance until they agreed to sign "traitorous" loyalty oaths to the Union; fugitive slaves ordered "to rob & maltreat . . . their late owners"; innocent noncombatants rounded up and "murdered in cold blood by their negro captors"; white men dragged from their homes, stripped naked, tied to trees, and then "scourged" by their former slaves; white women raped and "ravished by *parties* of these devils"; sadistic Northern soldiers watching the savagery, grinning broadly, egging the blacks on to new acts of barbarism.[48]

But the worst Yankee "outrage" of all—the one Southerners could never forgive—had to be the use of Negro soldiers. Nothing so thoroughly frightened and infuriated Southern whites as the sight of a black man armed and wearing a uniform. Jefferson Davis was so angry that he threatened to execute every black prisoner of war along with the white officers who always led Negro troops.[49]

But when Lincoln promised to retaliate in kind—to execute a Confederate prisoner for every Yankee prisoner killed in violation of the codes of war—Davis backed down. Ruffin was clearly outraged. He berated Davis in no uncertain terms for his "morbid tenderness of conscience," his "weak & childish policy of forbearance & mercy," and his general "imbecility." Ruffin wanted *every* Union prisoner of war, black or white, instantly put to death. This would make Yankees think twice before they invaded the South, he contended, and the extra casualties would stimulate the Northern peace movement. So what if this also meant sacrificing the lives of all Rebel prisoners? The price was not too much to pay. The honor of the South— the honor of Edmund Ruffin—made all-or-nothing tactics essential. Besides, this kind of ruthless policy would give Confederate soldiers an added incentive to fight with even greater valor and determination. And, he added, since there were more Yankees in Confederate prisons than Rebels in Union prisons, the net effect would harm the North more than the South.

Ruffin's cold calculations, of course, ignored the North's vast overall superiority in numbers, but Ruffin was interested less in logic than in revenge. He called for more "bloody executions," and when they were not forthcoming, he concluded bitterly that President Davis was as "soft-hearted & hard-headed" as President Lincoln was "hard-hearted & soft-headed."[50]

15

The Union's use of black troops did not worry Ruffin, he declared. He predicted that like the emancipation proclamation, this newest Republican tactic to win the war would backfire, because Negroes were too lazy, too docile, and too cowardly to make good soldiers. How he had laughed earlier that spring when he heard that Northern General Nathaniel P. Banks was trying to organize a "Corps D'Afrique" among free blacks and ex-slaves in Louisiana. At the first sign of battle, he scoffed, these raw recruits would run for their lives and hide themselves in the Louisiana bayous.[51]

But contrary to Ruffin's expectations—as well as the expectations of most Southerners and Northerners—the Negro regiments that fought in Louisiana and elsewhere did not turn and run. Even in the face of over-whelming odds and withering enemy fire, they kept on coming. Advancing over open ground at Port Hudson in May, beating back a Confederate assault at Milliken's Bend in June, leading a desperate charge against Fort Wagner in July, the black enlistees proved again and again that spring and summer of 1863 that they would fight with as much courage and heroism as any white man. In fact, after the battle at Milliken's Bend on the Lower Mississippi, Ruffin read a Northern article claiming that "*the negroes fought better than their white officers. many of whom it is said, skulked.*"[52]

At first Ruffin ridiculed these stories of black valor, dismissing them as a pack of Yankee lies. But after reading repeated accounts of how Negro soldiers had distinguished themselves on the battlefield, he had to find some explanation for what he considered extraordinary black behavior. He found his answer in a Confederate newspaper article that insisted Negro soldiers were "well dosed with whiskey" before each battle. According to the same paper, the white officers prevented blacks from retreating by telling them that the white regiments behind them had orders to kill any man who tried to fall back. Drunk and caught between two deadly forces—one Confederate and the other Union—these Negro troops "fought, or stood, with the desperate courage of martyrs for a time," Ruffin concluded.[53]

16

And how long would it be before millions of racist Northerners revolted against fighting what up to now had been strictly "a white man's war"? Ruffin soon had his answer. That summer, one of the bloodiest race riots in United States history rocked the city of New York. Mobs made up mainly of lower-class whites who were protesting the unfairness of the draft laws and screaming "Down with the rich" went on a three-day rampage through the city, destroying millions of dollars worth of property and maiming or killing up to a thousand victims. The favorite targets for their rage were blacks, abolitionists, police, and military officers. Ruffin read how a Negro orphanage burned to the ground. A man mistaken for abolitionist Horace Greeley almost lost his life. A Union officer was captured, "beaten to a jelly, & hung upon a lamp-post."

This orgy of violence in the North gladdened Ruffin's heart. It was, he reasoned, only just retribution for all the Union outrages against the Confederacy, and he prayed that this New York riot was the long-hoped-for precursor of a general class revolution that would soon spread to "every Yankee city."[54]

"And if such measure of calamity did not then soften the Pharoah-like heart of the Yankee race, & dispose the people to cease this atrocious war on the South," he declared, "*I* would rejoice to have effected if possible, the further destruction of every mansion & farmhouse, & . . . all other property in Yankeedom, & the putting to death of every individual who had urged on this war." The irony of Ruffin's curse was staggering, coming as it did from one of the South's foremost secessionists and the man who, symbolically at least, had started the Civil War with his shot at Fort Sumter. But the possibility that he could be pronouncing his own death sentence never occurred to him.[55]

15

Superfluous Lags the Veteran on the Stage

1

WHILE NEWS OF BLOODY Northern riots gave Ruffin some consolation in the summer of 1863, he was also painfully aware that the Confederacy was suffering from its own grave internal problems. "If our struggle was only in fighting our enemy, even with all their superiority in arms & munitions of war," he declared, "I should not entertain a shadow of doubt of our triumphant success." "But sanguine & confident as I am," he worried, "some fears for the result darken my views of the future in reference to our great disadvantage in commercial & economic matters."[1]

Indeed, by autumn, the Confederate economy had almost collapsed. The Northern naval blockade plus the lack of Southern home manufactures caused severe shortages of imported consumer products. Add to this a scarcity of specie combined with a superabundance of paper money, and the results were skyrocketing costs, an almost worthless currency, and a dizzying inflationary spiral that saw prices quickly outdistance incomes.

Periodically, Ruffin would take time to record examples of the fantastically high prices for commodities in his diary. For instance, during the winter of 1863, he noted that a pound of brown sugar cost a dollar. A year later, sugar would fetch twelve times that amount. During that same time span, Ruffin saw bacon's price go from $1.10 to $10 a pound, corn rose from $4.50 to $40 a bushel, and the cost of fresh beef quadrupled. Thirsty Southerners paid $90 for a gallon of French brandy, while less discriminating imbibers still had to shell out $30 for a gallon of "the meanest whiskey." Even "the most inferior kind" of coffee, Ruffin noted, cost more than sixty cents a pound. Flour sold for $325 a barrel, eggs for $6 a dozen, butter for $8 a pound. A single head of cabbage brought $1.50, and a turkey set its buyer back by as much as $30. As Southern pundits wisecracked, a shopper went to market carrying his money in a basket and returned with his groceries in his wallet.[2]

But runaway inflation was no joking matter to most Southerners, especially the urban poor. In the spring of 1863, "bread riots" had broken out in a number of major Southern cities. Edmund was in Richmond on April 2 buying household provisions when the high price of corn set off one of these food riots. "A mob of low men & women" broke into local stores and helped themselves to what they needed. Edmund, who fled with his own supplies down the backstreets and alleyways to avoid the rioters, considered himself lucky to have escaped the city with his hogshead of bacon intact.[3]

To Ruffin, this kind of civilian behavior was even more demoralizing than the loss of a military battle. It was "this state of things" that caused him "the first & only feelings" of "despondence for our final military success & triumph over our enemy." The newspapers told him that rioting and other economy-related crimes were on the upswing everywhere. In "orderly" Richmond, there were daily reports of assault, robbery, and murder. Southern "bandits" menaced the highways. Thieves roamed the countryside. "Soon," Ruffin feared, "portable property of every kind will be at the mercy of the necessitous & vile," and the South would suffer the kind of class revolution he had been predicting for the North.[4]

If food prices kept rising, there was no telling what desperate actions hunger-driven Southerners might take. His countrymen could withstand the severest hardship, the heaviest burden, Ruffin insisted, except this economic one, "which, & which only, *may* compel us to yield to our enemies." "We may not fail in resolution, constancy or courage—nor in soldiers, arms, or money," Ruffin wrote unhappily. "But I begin to lose hope of our Confederacy being able to carry on the war much longer, with such high prices & increasing scarcity of the necessities of life."[5]

2

The army, too, was suffering from drastic shortages in provisions and manpower. The Confederate government, despite its unpopular "impressment" policy, was unable adequately to feed, clothe, or supply its fighting men. "It is a dreadful sight to see so many of our soldiers barefooted walking over frozen ground, and muddy roads, their feet torn and lacerated by the stones, and unable to keep up, obliged to fall in the rear, and come under the head of stragglers," wrote young Thomas Ruffin, who was with Lee's cavalry. The cavalry itself was almost "worthless," Thomas informed his family, for not only the men but even the horses were "quite lame" or "completely broken down."[6]

Given these dreadful conditions and the fact that the war most men expected would last only a few weeks had dragged on for over two years and showed no sign of ending soon, it was not surprising that so many ragged, hungry soldiers deserted. In August, 1863, President Davis implored the thousands of missing soldiers to come back, promising total amnesty if they would only return to their units. But a year later, he would have to confess that at least two-thirds of the Confederate army was absent without leave. Many of those who remained in their ranks "showed themselves as unscrupulous as the Yankees," Ruffin was shocked to find out. Many times Confederate soldiers looted farms and plantations—stealing fruit and corn from Beechwood, hogs and chickens from Ruthven—and in general behaved "worse than . . . Yankees."[7]

Ruffin laid the blame for all the Confederacy's woes—economic and military—at the door of its "imbecile" President, Jefferson Davis, and his "despicable Congress." The Congress, Ruffin argued rightly, should have imposed heavy taxes at the beginning of the war to fight inflation. And Davis was personally responsible, he claimed, for the mass desertions and the "bad discipline & demoralization of our troops." Davis should have ordered all deserters shot without exception as a bloody but effective deterrent to the thousands of soldiers now missing without leave. Instead, Ruffin noticed with disgust, "during our great reverses in arms," the President had engaged in some pious soul-searching and decided to become a church member. "To the morbid tenderness of conscience of a 'seeker of religion,' and a new convert," snorted Ruffin, "I ascribe much of the imbecility of President Davis, in failing to punish military & political criminals." Davis was too lenient to suit a martinet like Ruffin. Confederate deserters and Yankee prisoners deserved the firing squad or the gallows, he argued. Anything less was "diseased sensibility."[8]

3

"Diseased sensibilities" or not, the Davis government chose to deal with its manpower problem not by shooting deserters but by drafting more men into the army. Late that summer, 1863, the Confederate Congress passed a new conscription law, including all men between the ages of eighteen and forty-five. This forced Julian Ruffin, age forty-two, back into service again. So, at the end of August, he reluctantly but dutifully rode off to Petersburg to join his regiment.[9]

With Julian in the army and Edmund managing the Marlbourne plantation, sixty-nine-year-old Ruffin was the only one left to take charge of

Ruthven. The responsibility made him miserable. The pleasure he had previously felt as a "consulting agriculturalist" disappeared when all the headaches of running a plantation were his alone. The slaves, he discovered, would not work half so hard for him as they had for Julian. He felt lucky if he got two hours of work per day out of them. Nor were the blacks as docile and obedient. He noticed that a disrespectful, impudent, even surly tone had come into their voices. He also knew they abused the farm animals when they thought he wasn't watching, and he suspected that they deliberately broke agricultural tools and machinery. "A farm thus left to the negroes to do as they please, must soon come to nothing," Ruffin lamented helplessly after only a few weeks. His nerves, he confessed, were "painfully agitated & disordered."[10]

Ruthven was doomed. Ruffin was sure of it and longed for the chance to leave, so that he would not be the one to preside over the plantation's ultimate ruin. Besides, newspaper dispatches reported that the Yankees were trying to hammer their way into his beloved Charleston, and he felt he ought to be there in the cradle of the Confederacy to lend his hand against the enemy and also to witness the "very interesting incidents of the bombardment & siege."

As luck would have it, in mid-September Julian's company set up camp at Beechwood. Since Julian was now living only four miles from Ruthven, he could easily perform his military duties and direct his plantation as well, thus leaving his much-relieved father free to go off in search of adventure in South Carolina.[11]

Ruffin arrived in Charleston on September 23, and within twenty-four hours, he was the newest volunteer in the city troop made up of the usual assortment of men and boys who were not otherwise eligible for regular military duty. Their leader, Captain Andrew G. Magrath, was a former federal district judge and one of the first Southerners impulsively to resign his office after the election of Abraham Lincoln in 1860. Ruffin held Magrath in high esteem and made the captain promise solemnly to wake him up day or night in case of enemy attack, so that he would not sleep through a moment's opportunity for field service.[12]

In the meantime, while he awaited Magrath's summons, Ruffin busied himself visiting and inspecting various companies around the harbor, saying hello to the Palmetto Guards, making detailed sketches of the forts, and reading all the Northern and Southern newspapers he could find at the *Courier* office. But after four weeks without a Yankee attack, Ruffin was bored, and on October 24, he concluded petulantly that he had come to Charleston "at the worst possible time." "I have remained here more than a month," he whined, "without the enemy's doing anything to relieve the dull monotony of the time & scenes." He had left his home in Virginia only because he supposed "that the crisis of the fate of Charleston was close at hand, & the last desperate defence would soon be made." He realized somewhat sheepishly that he, like the majority of Charlestonians, should be grateful for the delayed Union assault. "But personally," he confessed in all candor, "I cannot help being wearied with the inaction." Secretly he prayed that soon the enemy would renew hostilities "with the utmost vigor."[13]

Three more weeks passed before the Yankees responded to Ruffin's pleas, but at noontime on Tuesday, November 17, Ruffin was sitting in the company room of his Broad Street rooming house when he heard the unmistakable crack of cannonfire. Hurrying out to the street, where a crowd of curious citizens had already begun to gather, he was just in time to see several enemy shells explode near City Hall, only a few hundred yards from where he stood. Fearlessly and without regard for his own safety, Ruffin rushed over to the spot where one shell had hit the hard sidewalk and began digging frantically—but unsuccessfully—for a fragment to add to his already considerable collection.[14]

Fortunately, from Ruffin's point of view, the Northern bombardment kept up for several days, giving him plenty of opportunity, as he scurried about Charleston examining shell-damaged buildings and visiting sundry city batteries, to pick up battle souvenirs. He was proud of how Fort Sumter was able to withstand the Yankee attack. "Huzza! More glory for Fort Sumter," he boasted three days after the siege began. "Another assault was made last night, & repulsed." But when the enemy ceased fire around mid-December, Ruffin complained about the "general languor of the siege," packed his bags, and returned to Virginia.[15]

4

Ruffin wasn't back at Ruthven more than a week before he began complaining again that his life was "monotonous." Every morning he would get up shortly after sunrise, dress, and then read until it was time for breakfast. After breakfast, he continued reading until summoned for the midday meal. Dinner finished, he spent the afternoon reading until early evening, when it was too dark to see without a candle. There was no one to talk to, since the only other adult members of the household, Lottie and Mrs. Meade, were busy with their church work. Ruffin was too deaf to enjoy the chatter of his young grandchildren and too feeble to enter into their games. So from twilight until suppertime, he sat silently in his chair, lonesome and unamused, "with my own wearisome thoughts as companions." After supper, Lottie lit a candle, and Ruffin resumed his reading until the ladies retired for the night. No matter how early this might be, he put down whatever book he was holding, extinguished the candle, and went to bed too, even though he lay awake for hours and considered his sleeplessness a "great punishment."[16]

As the winter dragged on, Ruffin grew more and more depressed about his humdrum routine. "Every day of my life is a continuation of the same unvarying affliction of *ennui,*" he whimpered, "wearisomeness of everything, including life itself." He no longer even looked forward to mail days. The irregular deliveries of newspapers, he complained, "only vary the general sameness of the dull passage of my time."[17]

There was only one sure cure for Ruffin's low spirits: he needed some useful work to do. For a while, he tried to keep busy doing a variety of things: making envelopes out of old insurance policies, writing an article on how to make ink cheaply, devising an improved spelling primer for children and sending it to an educational convention in Petersburg. But very soon he had more envelopes than he or his family needed, and he was sure that the public would not pay "the slightest attention" to his article on ink or to his spelling ideas. "However, I will let it go," he wrote resignedly after mailing off his spelling reforms, "as one of many efforts to benefit my countrymen, which are not heeded, or remembered."[18]

Reading, then, became Ruffin's primary and usually only form of entertainment, and he devoted ten to twelve hours a day to this pursuit. But the Yankee raids had depleted his book collection to such an extent that sometimes he was "reduced . . . to the reading of my diary for killing time." He reread all his old books again and again until one Sunday, desperate for something new to read, he started thumbing through *Webster's Dictionary* and, to his great surprise, became engrossed in the Introduction. He had never cared to examine the dictionary before, because its author was a Northerner. "Ignorantly," he admitted, "I supposed it to be the embodiment of Yankee language, & the authority for Yankee deviations from standard English." Now he found himself heartily agreeing with Webster's spelling reforms, dropping the "u" from words ending in "our" like "labour" and "honour," substituting "s" for "c" in words like "defence." But he disagreed just as heartily with Webster's section on pronunciation. Ruffin loathed the sound of a Yankee accent. And yet, he asserted, "I shall be glad if the high authority of Webster shall induce all his countrymen to adopt all his wrong pronunciations." This way, even though Northerners and Southerners shared a common English language, "the dialects of the two peoples may become as much unlike as possible & . . . a Yankee may be known as such . . . as soon as he speaks a sentence."[19]

Along the same line of reasoning, Ruffin relished extracts from Yankee newspapers that claimed to have evidence of increasing numbers of black–white sexual liaisons in the North. The majority, if not all, of these articles were fabrications, part of a Copperhead propaganda campaign to defeat

Lincoln's bid for reelection in 1864 by linking him with an alleged Republican party program advocating racial amalgamation. Ruffin, though, was no more aware that these accusations were lies than were most Northern readers, and he accepted each story—no matter how fantastic—as the gospel truth.

In March, 1864, Ruffin read one of these clippings, taken from the New Hampshire *Patriot.* The *Patriot* carried the tale of a fictitious Reverend Liberty Billings, an officer supposedly in command of a black regiment stationed in Port Royal, South Carolina. Billings told the newspaper how nine months earlier, sixty-four Yankee spinsters had arrived in Port Royal as teachers for the newly emancipated blacks. Each of these unmarried white schoolmarms had become pregnant and was now a mother. Billings never mentioned the color of these "piously produced infants," Ruffin noticed, but he added meanly that "if they are not all of mulatto features, I am sure that the exceptions are due to accident—& not to any scruples or nicety of taste of these zealous ladies, who, in this respect at least, are truly what they claim to be, *philanthropists,* i.e. loving, or ready to bestow their love on, all of mankind, whether black or white."

When a follow-up article appeared in the *New York Times* that April and quoted the gossipy Billings as saying that all sixty-four babies born out of wedlock at Port Royal were mulattoes, Ruffin beamed with satisfaction. "I had certainly supposed that *some* of these 64 infants had been white," he exclaimed in gleeful mock astonishment. "Probably, these occurrences will give a new impulse to the benevolence of Yankee spinsters, & induce them to come on southward in increased numbers, & with increased ardor, to teach practically to their adult male pupils how to forward the new scheme of 'miscegenation,' for the improvement of the negro population."[20]

"Miscegenation" was a new word in 1864, coined by an anonymous Northern author in a twenty-five cent pamphlet entitled, "Miscegenation: The Theory of the Blending of the Races, Applied to the American White Man and Negro." "No race can long endure without a commingling of its blood with that of other races," claimed the writer, who was supposedly a shy abolitionist. "The condition of all human progress is miscegenation." The pamphlet, allegedly endorsed by such notable abolitionists and political writers as Wendell Phillips and Theodore Tilton, was really a hoax, another clever effort to discredit Lincoln and the Republican party with negrophobic Yankee voters. Ruffin read excerpts from "Miscegenation" in the Richmond *Examiner,* and he hoped Northerners would soon put its theories into practice. That way the entire Yankee "race" would be "negroized," and it would be even easier to distinguish "vile" mongrel Northerners from "pure" Southern whites.[21]

5

When Ruffin tired of the newspapers and the dictionary no longer held any charms for him, he often liked to go back and reread his own past publications. He was particularly fond of the four major proslavery tracts that he had "tried, in vain, to force upon the public" by selling them at cost or even giving them away free. Now, as he read them again early in the spring of 1864, he could not help but admire his own talent as a writer and a thinker, and he was genuinely perplexed "that the merit & ability of these writings [have] never been observed, or commented upon, by any person but their author."[22]

His modesty returned, though, after rereading his only novel, *Anticipations of the Future.* In his diary, Ruffin defended himself against an imaginary contemporary critic who mocked and taunted him about all the glib predictions he had made about secession, war, and slave loyalty. Characteristically, Ruffin found a way to blame others for his mistaken prophesies. Secession, he declared with some heat, should not have led to civil war. The fault lay with "submissionists" in the Upper South—especially in his native Virginia—who delayed secession until after the Fort Sumter incident. By tarrying so long in the Union, these states had given the North the "pernicious idea" that an "intimidated majority" of Southerners were really Union loyalists. According to Ruffin, this served as an open invitation for Lincoln's armies to invade the Confederacy.[23]

Slave behavior was more difficult to explain. Even Ruffin was frankly amazed at the "signal ingratitude & treachery" of what he considered "the best fed & clothed, the most easy-conditioned, comfortable & happy, of all the laboring & lowest classes on the face of the globe." The fault this time, said Ruffin, rested with Northern abolitionists who had "seduced [the slaves] into disloyalty." During previous wars like the American Revolution and the War of 1812, he argued, few slaves had tried to escape to the enemy, because they knew from bitter experience that by running away, they would only be exchanging their old owners for a crueler set of new masters. But for the past thirty years, since the time of Nat Turner's rebellion, abolitionist agents had been operating secretly in the South. Cloaked in a variety of seemingly innocent disguises—Ruffin believed that John Brown had come as an itinerant preacher and his chief aide, John E. Cooke, as a salesman —these undercover subversives traveled freely throughout the slave states, promising blacks that freedom meant no work and high wages and assuring them that the Yankees would treat them kindly and provide for all their wants and pleasures. So, when the Civil War began, Ruffin reasoned, many slaves ignored the psychological scare tactics of their owners, who warned them that the Yankee devils would skin them alive, boil them in oil, or drill holes in their shoulders and hitch them to carts. Instead, he noted bitterly, thousands of "duped" slaves willingly took their chances with the Yankees and ran behind Union lines at the first opportunity.[24]

These faithless fugitives would live to regret their infidelity, Ruffin predicted, when they got a taste of how cruel Yankee freedom could be. Already, he said, Northerners were heartlessly splitting up slave families. He almost laughed when he recalled how "hypocritical" abolitionists had leveled the same criticism at slaveholders during antebellum times.[25]

Personally, Ruffin had always maintained that family separation was a natural part of almost everyone's life. In New England, he used to say, it was the fate of many sons and daughters to migrate westward in order to earn a living and never see their parents and relatives again. Ruffin saw no difference between this voluntary separation of New Englanders and the forced family breakups imposed on slaves. Besides, he maintained, blacks suffered from a peculiar "obtuseness of affection." "The strongest of these affections, which is the love of a negro mother for her infant," he claimed, "is not more if so ardent as the maternal love of a brute animal, nor much longer-lived. The grief felt by a cow when her suckling calf is separated from her, either for weaning or for slaughter, is fully as acute, & nearly as long felt, as that of the negro mother deprived of her children by death or final separation." As proof, he cited the example of several Marlbourne, Beechwood, and Ruthven slaves who had abandoned their closest relatives when they ran off to the Yankees. Still, even he had to admit that escape as a family unit would have been almost impossible to accomplish, since, in most of these cases, husbands, wives, and children were living on separate plantations.[26]

But even if slave families managed the difficult task of running away together—and, in fact, the typical slave arrived behind Union lines in a family group—the Yankees quickly saw to it that they did not stay together, Ruffin noted. Ruthlessly separating the "stolen" Southern slaves into two groups, Yankees pressed the able-bodied males into military service. Women, children, the old, and the sick, they herded into freedmen's "receptacles"—pestholes teeming with filth, vermin, and disease. And they did this callously, Ruffin pointed out, "with no more compunction than if ordering the sending off of horses & cattle." He insisted that Southern slaveholders had always tried their best to keep black families together, despite the slaves' own "feeble" affections. But Yankee wartime policies, he contended, had separated more black fathers, mothers, and siblings than two hundred years of slavery.[27]

The Northern free labor system would further undermine and eventually destroy the black family, Ruffin believed. When black men, accustomed as they were to the care of some benevolent white master, learned that as free men they were responsible for supporting themselves and their families, predicted Ruffin, they would cast off wives, children, and dependent parents, leaving these unfortunates to fend for themselves or die of starvation. He boasted that under the beneficent influence of slavery, the black population had flourished and grown. Under freedom's baneful guidance, it would sicken and shrink. "In less than two years," he gloated, "the Yankee philanthropists . . . have caused more suffering to the 'emancipated' negroes than would have been produced in a century of slavery."[28]

6

But it was his own suffering and family misery that concerned Ruffin more that spring. In March, Edmund wrote that the Yankees had raided Marlbourne again and had ransacked the plantation "from top to bottom." He and his family were now living in a recently acquired home, "Redmoor," located in Amelia County, and he begged his father to join them there. Ruffin was feeling too sick to travel, but, spurred on by the fear of what the Yankees might do if they caught him, he fled to Redmoor at the end of April.[29]

Ruffin was at Redmoor less than two weeks before he felt absolutely certain he was going to die. In addition to all his old complaints, he suffered from severe chest pains; cold shivers in his back; and a giddy, light-headed feeling that twice made him lose his balance and fall down, resulting in a bumped forehead and a painfully wrenched right shoulder. The very thought of food "repulsed" him, and he was so weak that he had to lie in bed nearly all day. To walk fifty yards or more required the assistance of both his son and his grandson. Worse, he had begun spitting up phlegm, which he examined with almost scientific detachment and then diagnosed as revealing "pulmonary consumption." He disliked the idea of dying from a lingering disease like this that had "unpleasant symptoms." His one consolation was that his diarrhea was so severe that he figured it would probably kill him first. If this wasn't bad enough, he had an embarrassing urinary disorder and frequently soiled his clothes. He complained in his diary of "continual pain," and on May 9, he doubted he could survive "another week of torture." [30]

It was in this wretched state that he began writing "My Last Directions," his personal funeral instructions. He had barely put down his pen when a letter arrived that made his own sufferings seem inconsequential: Julian Ruffin was dead, killed in battle on May 16, near Drewry's Bluff. Stunned, heartbroken, the father poured out his grief in his diary: "My mind cannot take in the momentous fact, nor my perceptions approach to the measure of the reality." The loss of his son hurt so much that he wanted to cry, to sob aloud. Yet "I have not shed a tear," he wrote in amazement, and he worried once more whether "age & decay have withered & dried up my affections . . . & hardened my heart." But he could still feel some emotions—pride, for example—and he was happy when Julian's commanding officer relayed the details of his death. Julian had died while facing the enemy. Having just fired off a cannon, he had stepped forward to admire the effect of his handiwork when a Yankee minnie ball hit him squarely between the eyes. "I thank God," wrote his proud father, "that his death happened on the battle ground."[31]

7

There seemed to be no end to the losses and humiliation Ruffin suffered at the hands of the enemy. Having robbed him of a son, the Yankees struck again at Marlbourne that spring, stealing what was left of the food and farm animals, burning down the garden fences and the lovely forest trees, filling Ruffin's carefully dug drainage ditches with dirt and mud. Before the Union raiders moved on, a wartime correspondent for the New York *Herald* stopped to praise the beauty of the Marlbourne plantation and to compliment the owner on the "remains" of a once obviously well-stocked library. "When these marauding scoundrels leave," Ruffin commented sarcastically, "I do not suppose there will be any 'remains' of books, or anything else for the next comers to destroy."[32]

Meanwhile, Yankee troops had invaded the Ruthven neighborhood, forcing Lottie and her children to crowd into Redmoor. This time, before the enemy moved out, a Union newsman devoted an entire column to Ruffin alone. Entitled "A Notorious Rebel," the article reported that in Prince George County, the place where Ruffin was born and raised, he was "noted as being one of the most vile and degenerate of men." According to neighbors who allegedly knew him well, Ruffin was frequently in and out of jail "for cruelly beating his wife," and once "he was taken prisoner to Petersburg for having flayed alive two of his negro women whom he had stripped naked and tied up by the thumbs, while he administered the blows with his own hand." "Let the world know, therefore," thundered the Yankee writer, "that the man who volunteered to fire the first gun upon the flag of the United States was Edmund Ruffin, Sr., a jailbird and a wife-beater."[33]

When Ruffin read this article a few months later—his grandson Thomas, now a prisoner of war in a Northern camp, had sent him a copy —he was furious. Southerners would never believe such outrageous drivel, he felt sure, but Northerners were just stupid and credulous enough to swallow these lies. Previously, Ruffin had rather enjoyed being the target of Yankee insults, threats, and denunciations; they proved he was a figure to be reckoned with, someone not to be lightly dismissed. It flattered him to think that there was no one else "in all the Southern Confederacy, whose capture would afford so much triumph to the Yankees." But being called a wife-beater and a jailbird was not the sort of attention he craved. This particular Yankee notice, he admitted, had "somewhat disturbed my equanimity."[34]

8

More disturbing to Ruffin's "equanimity" was the Confederate military situation. Reading about Union General William T. Sherman's triumphs in the West, he longed "for a Stonewall Jackson in command of our army." He kept up his own morale by constantly reminding himself of historical examples of underdog nations overcoming seemingly insurmountable odds to defeat a stronger opponent. Hadn't Xerxes and the mighty Persian army failed to conquer Greece? Wasn't Napoleon humbled when he invaded Spain and Russia?[35]

Despite the North's "stupendous efforts" to subjugate the South, Ruffin assured himself, the weaker side with its "superior" cause would win out in the end. On May 3, he sensed that the war was heading toward its final denouement. "There will no doubt be soon arrayed on both sides the most numerous armies, by far, that have ever been assembled in this country," he predicted somewhat nervously. "And the greatest & bloodiest battle will be fought—of which the result probably will decide the present war & the fate of the C. S. Sanguine as I am, I cannot look to such impending & momentous results without feelings of awe & dread."[36]

Even as he wrote, Sherman was leading the Northern Army of the West toward Atlanta, Georgia. At the same time, Grant—now General-in-Chief of all the Union forces—was accompanying the Army of the Potomac back into Virginia. His object: to destroy Lee's army and the Confederacy's ability to continue the war. For a month, Lee and Grant clashed spectacularly, first in the dense Virginia Wilderness, then at Spotsylvania Courthouse, and finally at a place called Cold Harbor. Each time, Lee managed to outfight and outmaneuver his opponent, causing a devastating number of Union casualties to boot.

At Redmoor, this unexpected string of Confederate victories thrilled Ruffin, whose own physical ailments seemed magically to disappear. His prophesies about ultimate Rebel success, he felt, were being vindicated. Perhaps David really would slay Goliath.

But Ruffin's optimism was again premature. Despite heavy Union losses—60,000 men killed in a single month—Grant would not retreat. Instead he pursued Lee with bulldog-like tenacity, willing to fight a merciless war of attrition, a war the badly outnumbered Confederates were bound to lose eventually.[37]

9

Perhaps Ruffin could sense what was coming. Anyway, that summer he began to hope that even if the South could not win its independence on the battlefield, it could be victorious on the Northern political front. 1864 was an election year, and Ruffin combed the newspapers for articles indicating that dissatisfied Northern voters, Copperhead peace Democrats, and even members of the Republican party might repudiate President Lincoln come November.

Lincoln's reelection prospects did indeed look gloomy. Three long years of fighting had exhausted Northern citizens both financially and emotionally, and with Grant stalled in front of Petersburg and Sherman before Atlanta, no end to the war seemed to be in sight. Nor had the draft or the emancipation proclamation added to the President's popularity. Many Northerners were ready to call it quits or at least change leaders. Lincoln himself thought it was "exceedingly probable" that he would lose the election.

Even members of the Republican party were beginning to doubt that Lincoln was the right man to sit in the White House. Although the President got the nod from party regulars at the Baltimore Convention that June, one faction of dissident Republicans—Ruffin labeled them "the more rabid wing of the abolitionists"—broke off and nominated John C. Fremont, while another group planned to convene at Cincinnati in September to choose still a different standard-bearer.[38]

This split within Republican ranks delighted Ruffin, for it made the election of a peace candidate more likely. He was even more optimistic in August when Copperhead Democrats took control of the party convention in Chicago and adopted a platform that pledged peace "at the earliest possible moment." He was less pleased with the party's candidate, George B. McClellan, who accepted the nomination but repudiated his party's platform. McClellan promised Northern voters that if elected, he would win the war and restore the Union just as it always had been—with Negro slavery intact. To a confirmed secessionist like Ruffin, McClellan's solution to the war was no more acceptable than the solution offered by "Black Republicans." But Ruffin figured that like all unscrupulous Northern politicians, McClellan was lying, mouthing ideals that he thought would win him votes. Once in office, Ruffin predicted, McClellan would change his tune, call a halt to further hostilities, and agree to let the South depart from the Union in peace.[39]

As September approached, Ruffin became uncomfortably aware of how the coming election results hinged on what happened now in the military arena. "If our armies should defeat those opposed, it will make the result certain," he declared confidently. Then Lincoln surely would lose. "But if Sherman or Grant should gain decisive victories & capture Atlanta or Richmond," he prophesied, "then I would expect that nearly every peace democrat will immediately return to his former support of 'a vigorous war,' & clamor for the subjugation of the South."[40]

10

On September 2, Atlanta surrendered to Sherman. Although, contrary to Ruffin's expectations, peace Democrats did not use this as an excuse to change their stripes and rally around the flag, Republicans did close ranks around the President. Fremont withdrew from the presidential race, and there was no more talk of a Cincinnati convention. Lincoln's reelection prospects suddenly looked bright.

Ruffin refused to believe that Atlanta had fallen. Scheming, lying Republicans, he insisted, had made up this Union military triumph in order to keep Lincoln in the White House. Ruffin's major worry, even as late as mid-October, was that the President would be reelected on the strength of such "false" victories.[41]

"False" victories or not, as election day drew closer, Ruffin had to admit that Lincoln was almost certain to be the winner. Deftly reversing his former position, Ruffin now argued that Lincoln's reelection would be the best thing that ever happened to the Confederacy, for the following reason: in order to defeat McClellan, Ruffin insisted, the President would have to use fraud and violence to crush free elections in states like West Virginia, Tennessee, Arkansas, and Louisiana. This would prove to Northerners that even a man "as low, stupid, & despicable as Lincoln" could make himself a permanent dictator. Peace Democrats "will be rendered desperate," Ruffin predicted, and in Indiana, Ohio, and Illinois, Copperheads would lead the entire Northwest out of the Union. Certainly, he felt, he could count on at least one state to revolt, and a single insurrection in the North, he contended, "would at once disable Yankeedom from carrying on the war."[42]

On election day, November 8, Lincoln won handily. Much to Ruffin's chagrin, the losers accepted defeat peacefully. Eight days later, though, he grew hopeful when he heard of newspaper speculation that Lincoln was about to send commissioners to Richmond to try to negotiate a treaty. But the alleged peace terms, reconstruction of the old Union and the abolition of slavery, enraged him. Did Northerners think that Lincoln's recent victory had scared Confederates so much that they would agree to rejoin the Union? he asked incredulously. If so, they were victims of a "delusion." "Every man in the South who understands & values free government," Ruffin insisted vehemently, "would prefer to the present government of the Northern people, to be extended over the South, not only a limited monarchy like England, but even a despotic one like France, or even Russia."[43]

On November 16, the same day Ruffin was rejecting hypothetical Northern peace overtures, Sherman moved his men out of Atlanta and began his famous march to the sea. On December 24, he "gave" Savannah to Lincoln as a Christmas present. This time Ruffin believed the Yankee dispatches, and he took the news of Savannah's surrender very hard. "In no previous disaster of this war," he wrote soon afterwards, "have I been so despondent & almost despairing."[44]

"Superfluous lags the veteran on the stage," Ruffin concluded dramatically on January 5, 1865, the occasion of his seventy-first birthday. If indeed the Confederate cause was lost, "I cannot die too soon." His dearest wish was "to be shot dead" while giving "feeble aid" to his country's defense. Alas, "so honorable a death" seemed unlikely. So Ruffin began hinting darkly of taking his own life, praying that a natural death "shall preclude me from the necessity of choosing my course, when such dreadful alternatives shall only be available."[45]

11

Although he might have been "entirely despairing" of Confederate victory that January, Ruffin still had an unconquerable spirit and was not "inclined to yield" one inch to the enemy. Anti-Yankee propaganda—much of which he had helped to create—had frightened him to such a hysterical pitch that he was willing to make any sacrifice, no matter how drastic, to stave off the inevitable Rebel defeat. Rather than submit to Northern domination, he would prefer to see "the speedy & bloody extermination of the whole southern people." Better to embrace some "able dictator & despot"—a Caesar, a Cromwell, or a Napoleon—than to accept the "popular" rule of "a series of Lincolns & Sewards." Better to seek "colonial vassalage" to some European country—Great Britain perhaps, or even Russia—than to rejoin the former Union. Better even to give up the most cherished institution of the South: Negro slavery. "The destruction of our negro slavery system would be a wound to our economical interests, to refinement of manners, & civilization, which would not be cured & recovered from in a century," Ruffin admitted sadly. "Yet even that I would not only accept, but deem immeasurably preferable to Yankee domination."[46]

In the South, the subject of abolition now revolved around the extremely controversial question of whether or not to put guns in the hands of slaves and enlist them as Confederate soldiers. There was no doubt that the Rebel army was sorely in need of men to replace the thousands of white soldiers who had deserted, had been wounded or killed, or were missing in action. Then, too, after Lincoln issued his emancipation proclamation in 1863, the South had found itself in the rather unique and unenviable position of supplying the enemy with new recruits. So, in the winter of 1865, as the Confederacy's chances of winning the war grew fainter and fainter, many men like Ruffin—though by no means the majority of Southerners—were ready to take this final desperate step.[47]

Ruffin had not come to this decision easily. After all, slavery was, in the words of Confederate Vice-President Alexander Stephens, the very "cornerstone of the Confederacy." Southerners had seceded, gone to war, fought, and died to preserve and defend their peculiar institution. As late as October 29, 1864, Ruffin was mightily against using blacks as soldiers, calling their recruitment "a last resort" and "a matter not to be talked aloud." Although he noted at the time that "there is a growing opinion in favor of enlisting our negro slaves as soldiers," he based his opposition to this "fatal policy" on three reservations. First, he questioned the value of slaves as fighting material. The Yankee experience of employing black troops, Ruffin contended, "proved what was believed by slave-holders in advance of the trial, that the constitutional & natural timidity of negroes causes them to be cowardly & untrustworthy as embodied soldiers." Second, he feared that few blacks would willingly serve "the country under whose laws they were held as slaves." "I should expect the greater number of such recruits to desert to the opposed Yankee forces on the first safe opportunity!" he exclaimed. Last and most important of all, Ruffin hated the very idea of employing black troops, because that would mean the extinction of slavery "& all the evil consequences of that change to these states, & to the present ruling class."[48]

But after Savannah capitulated to Sherman's army in late December, the fear of defeat and Yankee conquest overcame all of Ruffin's previous objections. "My views of the dreadful & ruinous consequences of our adopting this policy . . . are not in the least removed," he explained. But he was ready to heed the advice of the Richmond *Sentinel,* which asked Southerners to make "any sacrifice of opinion, any sacrifice of property, any surrender of prejudice" to avoid "Yankee subjugation."[49]

12

In February, 1865, as the war shuddered toward its conclusion, both the Confederate Congress and the Virginia Assembly debated bills which would authorize black conscription. By this time, Ruffin had become a thorough, even enthusiastic, supporter of the Negro soldier policy. Necessity being the mother of invention, he reversed his previous arguments, countering his own former objections point by point.

He now said that slaves would make splendid soldiers, because, despite their alleged innate cowardice, "when commanded & led by their masters, or by officers of the class whom they had obeyed & respected as superiors, they will fight better, than under their Yankee equals." Also, Ruffin predicted that slaves would gladly volunteer to fight for the Rebel cause. In fact, when fugitives who were presently fighting for the Union learned about the South's new policy, "they will desert to us in great numbers." For, besides gaining freedom, these blacks would be spared the awful necessity of moving North after the war to live in a harsh climate among "vile" Yankees. Finally, Ruffin argued that the use of black soldiers did not have to spell the end of slavery. While the South must agree to emancipate every slave who took up arms for the Confederacy—Ruffin was adamant on this point—he estimated that this number would not exceed two hundred thousand men. In about forty years, these freedmen would be dead, he figured. Then the South would contain about the same free black and slave population as in antebellum days. The Confederacy could, in other words, emerge from the Civil War victorious and with its "sacred" principles and institutions still intact.[50]

In March, President Davis signed the "Negro Soldier Law," and Ruffin sent his gold watch and his last few pennies into the Confederate treasury at Richmond. The Ruffin women contributed their jewelry and the family silverware. These actions were well-meaning but futile gestures of patriotism. Before the South could put a single black volunteer on the battlefield, the dying nation crumbled, its "noble cause" lost forever. On April 2, the ragged gray line defending Petersburg gave way. Richmond fell that night, and a week later, Lee surrendered to Grant at Appomattox Courthouse.[51]

The Confederacy's defeat broke Ruffin's heart but never his fighting spirit. When he learned that Jefferson Davis and his Cabinet had escaped from Richmond, he hoped the government and what was left of the army could regroup somewhere in the Southwest and then eventually "liberate" the Southeast. If he were younger and stronger, vowed the old fire-eater, there was nothing he would like better than to pack his musket and go west to fight Yankees.

But he was neither young nor strong, so he decided to stay put—at least for the present. "When the time shall come for this part of the country to be permanently occupied by the enemy, then a different course of procedure must be adopted," he told his diary. An attempted escape was out of the question now; it was too "undignified & humiliating." Continuing to "sponge" off his impoverished children was equally unattractive. But death

—natural or by design—was an alternative, "I must then act according as circumstances shall *compel,*" he finally decided, "& try so to time my action as [to] cause the least damage to my children."[52]

13

Ruffin did not learn of Lee's surrender at Appomattox until Tuesday, April 11. The next day was the fourth anniversary of the firing on Fort Sumter. It should have been a day of Confederate celebration, Ruffin protested bitterly, a day when his fellow Southerners lifted their glasses and toasted his name. Instead it was a day of Yankee rejoicing, and no one praised the name of Edmund Ruffin.[53]

Good Friday was the anniversary of the surrender of Sumter. Abraham Lincoln died this day, killed by an assassin's bullet. Ruffin noted the historical irony and then commented coldly that it was a pity and a shame that Seward was still alive. During the period of deep national mourning that followed the President's death, Ruffin scoffed at Republican attempts to portray Lincoln as a "martyr–hero." Why the man was a "laughing-stock" while he still breathed, he declared. Lincoln was "lucky" that an assassin had lifted him out of his deserved obscurity and elevated him to the undeserved fame that Ruffin secretly coveted for himself. Bitterly envious, Ruffin copied down every scurrilous and abusive remark, every gossipy racial slur that he could find concerning the slain President: accusations that Lincoln's mother had had intimate relations with black men, that Lincoln himself was black, that his first-term vice-president, Hannibal Hamlin, was a mulatto. He personally doubted that Lincoln himself was Negro, but he was positive that Hamlin had black blood. Still, he wrote contemptuously, "Nigger Hamlin" was the President's superior in every way.[54]

And yet after reading the last speech Lincoln made before he died, Ruffin confessed he was surprised that such a "low-minded" scoundrel as the late President had favored a reconstruction policy that was so "merciful." He had expected angry words, harsh and vindictive measures. Instead, there was no talk of punishment or revenge, no sweeping confiscation of Confederate property, no threats to hang Southern traitors. Even Yankee troops had begun to conduct themselves in a civilized fashion. Northern "roughs" ceased pillaging Southern farms and plantations and in general were showing what Ruffin considered an unyankeelike respect for private property. There were no more stories of rapes, murders, or other Northern "atrocities." Ruffin found it "remarkable" that even men like Horace Greeley and Gerrit Smith, "the most distinguished of the abolitionists," were publicly advocating a mild and conciliatory reconstruction program.[55]

He expected no such "mercy" from Lincoln's successor, "the low & vulgar & shameless drunken demagogue, Andrew Johnson of Ten." The humbly born Johnson was a self-made man, a prosperous tailor and Tennessee politician, who championed the cause of the common white man and never made a secret of his loathing for the South's "stuck-up aristocrats," who, he once said, "are not half as good as the man who earns his bread by the sweat of his brow." Although Johnson was a Southerner and had owned slaves himself, he had remained loyal to the Union. In Ruffin's estimation, this made him doubly "despicable." Now "the tailor king," as Ruffin scornfully referred to him, was President of the United States, and Ruffin was frightened that he would carry out his threats to topple the South's traditional ruling classes, destroy the economic, political, and social power of the planter aristocrats, and make the "poor white trash" masters of a "New South."[56]

But with Lincoln dead, Ruffin worried even more about what angry Republicans and "fanatical" abolitionists might do about Southern race relations. The war had barely ended, he complained, and already Yankee authorities were treating Southern "black laws" with "contempt." For example, he thought it was "ridiculous" to require planters who suspected their servants of theft to obtain legal warrants before conducting a search. "Another absurd change made by the new condition of emancipation," he added, forbid white employers to whip or otherwise physically chastise their hired Negro help. Now what possible harm could a few "stripes" do to misbehaving blacks? asked Ruffin in genuine bewilderment. He predicted that without corporal punishment, the Negro crime rate would increase "a hundredfold."[57]

It seemed clear to Ruffin that vengeance-seeking Northerners were deliberately pampering Southern Negroes and encouraging them to defy their former owners. For instance, when Lottie Ruffin returned to Ruthven, she found several of her ex-slaves living on the grounds. When she tried to order them off, they obstinately refused to leave. Blacks were learning this kind of impudence at Yankee schools for freedmen, frothed Ruffin. It was there, he claimed, that Northern teachers stirred up racial resentments and taught their pupils subversive hymns "in honor of John Brown."[58]

Someday, Ruffin predicted, there would be an all-out race war in the South, with the white gentry facing uppity blacks, no-account scalawags, and unscrupulous Northern carpetbaggers. Until that day of reckoning, there would be no justice in the reconstructed South. White men of breeding like himself would lie helpless at the feet of their former slaves and their social inferiors. Already, he complained, Northern authorities were accepting the word of any black man over the sworn testimony of white "gentlemen." And with this thought in mind, Ruffin was almost sorry that in the past, he had freely expressed his anti-Yankee opinions with such "virulence, & venom, & even exaggerated malediction" when his slaves were within hearing distance. He cursed his "usual heedlessness" and the tongue that always got him into trouble. What would happen now, he wondered, if "these ignorant listeners"—his own former bondsmen—decided to denounce him to the Yankees? Would he spend his last days on earth alone and reviled in some enemy jail cell?[59]

14

Ruffin never gave up the fear—it was a conceit really—that Yankees would eventually be coming for him and that, therefore, his presence at Redmoor endangered his entire family. By early June, though, it was apparent to the rest of the household that their eldest member was safe, and Ruffin's children began making preparations to move back to the family plantations: Lottie would go to Marlbourne, Edmund to Beechwood. Meanwhile Ruffin kept to his own room, where he spent hour after hour poring over the pages of his Bible. Again and again he read the Old Testament story of how God had sent Moses to deliver the enslaved Hebrews—His chosen people—from Egypt. One day, predicted the prophet without honor, God would send another Moses to the South to smite the power of the Northern Pharaohs and save His people from Yankee bondage.[60]

But Ruffin had no patience left to await the Confederacy's divine "deliverance." If he were younger, perhaps, he would bide his time and pretend to submit quietly to the Yankee "ruling despotism." Then when the North went to war with some foreign enemy or "better" yet, was "exposed to a powerful invader," Ruffin would reveal his true colors, urge his fellow Confederates to take up their arms for the "lost cause," and the South would rise again. But he was too old to wait out this dream. Besides, he had made up his mind to die.

Throughout the four years of civil war, Ruffin's only reason for living was to witness a Confederate victory. When Richmond fell, something inside him shriveled up and died. Since then, every night before he went to sleep, he got down on his knees and prayed with all his might that he would not wake up the next morning. "It is my earnest wish," he would tell the Lord, "that I may not live another day."

Ruffin, though, was in excellent health lately. The previous symptoms that he had supposed fatal were gone: no more trouble with diarrhea, no more consumptive "hawking." Unless he took matters into his own hands, Ruffin concluded gloomily, unless he seized control over his own death, he might live on for many more years.[61]

15

Suicide was the logical solution to Ruffin's dilemma, but he did not act immediately. Held back by concern for the pain he knew he would cause his children and his fear of offending God, he agonized for weeks over his decision. But in the end, his resolve stiffened. He could wait no longer. Death was too appealing as a "refuge" for the tired old Southerner, a "release from the pains of life."

Besides, his family would grieve not so much over his dying as over the manner of his death. And this grief, Ruffin reasoned, would rest on a false and erroneous interpretation of the Bible which contended that suicide was a sin, a violation of God's sacred laws. But he had conducted his own painstaking study of the holy Scriptures and had come to the conclusion that when God commanded man, "Thou shalt not kill," He only meant to forbid murder, not suicide.

"If a man by throwing off the painful burden of life leaves unperformed important duties to his family, or his country," Ruffin declared, "his committing suicide would be cowardly & base, as well as criminal." But if a man had done right by his kin and country, then suicide "should not be deemed criminal, or as disobedience to God." Furthermore, he was certain there were some instances "where the death of an individual would not only produce no damage, but would remove incumbrances, lessen evils, or ward off dangers to others." "In such cases," insisted Ruffin, "the act by his own hand would not only be venial, or innocent, but commendable." Suicide could be an affair of honor.

He sincerely believed that he met all of these criteria and could therefore face his Maker without fear. He was not perfect, he admitted humbly, but he had done a great deal both for family and country. As a parent, Ruffin reminded the Lord, he had been more than generous, twice dividing his estate among his children. As a patriot, he had pioneered Southern agricultural reform, toiled to promote secession, and fought as hard as he could for Confederate independence. He could do no more, now that the South's "noble cause" had been "trampled in the dust." "I can do no good in any way," he explained regretfully just a few days before he died. "I am now merely a cumberer of the earth, & a useless consumer of its fruits."[62]

But underneath Ruffin's apparently selfless facade, there were darker, hidden motives for contemplating suicide. Anger drove him to take his own life: anger at a world that failed to give him the love, attention, and respect he hungered for, a world that refused to make room for his intellectual genius, his talent for leadership, a world that denied him his rightful place, that isolated and rejected him. Death was his means of ultimate withdrawal, the revenge and punishment he would inflict on an unappreciative, ungrateful public. He hoped that death would elevate his earthly reputation, as it had enhanced the stature of the ancient biblical prophets. Hence his appeal to "future generations," to posterity, to remember and revere him.

Equally important, by dying now he would avoid the stigma of having been wrong—a false prophet about secession, civil war, the North. He could escape this painful humiliation with one last defiant gesture. He had come to view himself as the personification of the Old South. With his death, they could both perish dramatically and undefeated.

16

On Saturday morning, June 17, Ruffin got up and went downstairs for breakfast with his family. This would be his last meal on earth, and he seemed to enjoy it. No one noticed anything odd about his behavior, and Edmund, who had been worrying lately about his father's moodiness, was pleased to see him looking so cheerful.

After eating, Ruffin returned to his room. The others assumed that, as usual, he was writing in his diary, and they were correct. Ruffin was, in fact, making his last diary entry, explaining the reasons for his actions, begging his children to forgive him, absolving himself of all guilt. Then, after leaving detailed funeral instructions, he penned what he thought would be his very last words:

> I hereby declare my unmitigated hatred to Yankee rule—to all political, social, & business connection with Yankees—& to the Yankee race. Would that I could impress these sentiments, in their full force, on every living southerner, & bequeath them to everyone yet to be born! May such sentiments be held universally in the outraged & down-trodden South, although in silence & stillness, until the now far-distant day shall arrive for just retribution for Yankee usurpation, oppression, & atrocious outrages—& for deliverance & vengeance for the now ruined, subjugated, & enslaved Southern States!

Ruffin had no worldly goods to pass on, so this was his legacy to present and future generations of Southerners: undying hatred for Northerners and unquenchable thirst for revenge. He would die unrepentant and unreconstructed, a fire-eater to the very end, still hoping that some day, like the fabled Phoenix, the South would rise again from its own ashes.

At ten o'clock that morning, he finished his diary, signed and dated his "will," and wrote "The End." But "the end" was not quite there. Three neighbors who paid an unexpected visit to Redmoor were keeping the old man waiting. He was anxious that only family members should find his mangled body.

Finally at 12:15 P.M., the guests drove off, and Ruffin put his carefully worked-out plan into action. For his weapon, he chose a handsome silver-mounted rifle that his son always kept loaded in order to chase away horse thieves and "bummers." Taking hold of the gun, he sat down in a chair, a large trunk at his feet. Mouth wide open, he placed the rifle muzzle inside and rested the butt on the trunk. Then, bracing himself, he picked up a forked stick and pulled the trigger.

There was a loud concussion, but the cap merely exploded. Jane Ruffin, who was sitting on the front porch at the time, heard the noise and ran to get her husband. But by the time they reached Ruffin, the determined old man had managed to fire off another shot. This one was fatal. Edmund and Jane found him, still sitting up ramrod straight, a lifeless corpse. Next to him on his desk, his diary lay open. Edmund read his father's final words:

> And now, with my latest writing & utterance, & with what will be near to my latest breath, I hereby repeat & would willingly proclaim my unmitigated hatred to Yankee rule—to all political, social, & business connection with Yankees, & to the perfidious, malignant, & vile Yankee race.

Two days later, Edmund wrote a letter to his sons. "The Yankees," he said simply, have "killed your Grandfather."[63]

NOTES

Preface

1. Paul Murray Kendall, *The Art of Biography* (New York: W. W. Norton & Company, Inc., 1965), p. 28.

1. The Prophet of Marl

1. Edmund Ruffin Diary, October 4, 1859, Library of Congress; Ruffin Diary, August 30, 1859; Julian Calx Ruffin to Edmund Ruffin, October 8, 1852, Ruffin Papers, Virginia Historical Society; Ruffin Diary, September 30 and 22, 1859.
2. Ruffin Diary, October 4, 1859.
3. Ibid., June 4, 1864, and October 18, 1859.
4. Stephen B. Oates, *To Purge This Land With Blood: A Biography of John Brown* (New York: Harper & Row, 1970), pp. 290–306; Betty L. Mitchell, "Massachusetts Reacts to John Brown's Raid," *Civil War History,* 19 (March, 1973), 65.
5. Oates, pp. 320–24; Betty L. Mitchell, "Realities Not Shadows: Franklin Benjamin Sanborn, The Early Years," *Civil War History,* 20 (June, 1974), 109.
6. Ruffin Diary, October 19, 1859.
7. Edmund Lorraine Ruffin, "Descendants of Edmund Ruffin, The Great Agriculturalist and Author, Who Fired the First Gun at Fort Sumter in the War Between the States," *Tyler's Quarterly Historical and Genealogical Magazine,* 22 (April, 1941), 250–51; United States, Bureau of the Census, *Census of Virginia: 1810. Prince George County.*
8. Ruffin Diary, March 17, 1863.
9. E. L. Ruffin, pp. 252–55; Edmund Ruffin, "The Blackwater Guerilla," Ruffin Papers.
10. Robert McColley, *Slavery and Jeffersonian Virginia* (Urbana, Illinois: University of Illinois Press, 1964), pp. 43–44; "Edwin Ruffin, of Virginia, Agriculturalist, Embracing a View of Agricultural Progress in Virginia for the Last Thirty Years," *DeBow's Review,* 11 (October, 1851), 431; Henry G. Ellis, "Edmund Ruffin: His Life and Times," *The John P. Branch Historical Papers of Randolph-Macon College,* 3 (June, 1910), 101.
11. Edmund Ruffin to [?], June 1, 1857, Ruffin Papers; Thomas Nelson Page, *Social Life in Old Virginia Before the War* (Freeport, New York: Books for Libraries Press, 1897), p. 65; McColley, p. 40; Edmund Ruffin to [?], June 1, 1857, Ruffin Papers.

12. Avery Odelle Craven, *Edmund Ruffin, Southerner: A Study in Secession* (New York: D. Appleton and Company, 1932), pp. 3–4; E. L. Ruffin, p. 255.

13. "Edwin Ruffin," p. 431; Ellis, p. 101; W. P. Cutter, "A Pioneer in Agricultural Science," *Yearbook of the United States Department of Agriculture, 1895* (Washington, D.C.: Government Printing Office, 1896), p. 494; *American Farmer,* VII (December 23, 1825), 293.

14. "Edwin Ruffin," p. 431; Ruffin Diary, March 1, 1857.

15. "Edwin Ruffin," p. 432; Craven, pp. 52–53; United States, *Annals of Congress,* Sixteenth Congress, First Session, II, 1392; *Lynchburg Virginian,* July 4, 1833, in Charles Henry Ambler, *Sectionalism in Virginia from 1776 to 1861* (Chicago: University of Chicago Press, 1910), pp. 110–11; McColley, p. 3.

16. Johann David Schopf, *Travels in the Confederation, 1783–1784* (Philadelphia: W. J. Campbell, 1911), II, 32; *Farmers' Register,* I (1833), 150.

17. Ellis, pp. 103–04; Clement Eaton, *The Growth of Southern Civilization, 1790–1860* (New York: Harper & Row, 1961), p. 5; *American Farmer,* IV (March 29, 1822), 41; Richard B. Davis, *Francis Walker Gilmer: Life and Learning in Jefferson's Virginia* (Richmond: The Dietz Press, 1939), p. 115; Ambler, pp. 111–12; Eaton, pp. 15–16; Winfield Hazlitt Collins, *The Domestic Slave Trade of the Southern States* (Port Washington, New York: Kennikat Press, 1904), p. 26.

18. Davis, p. 115; Eaton, p. 4; McColley, pp. 16–17.

19. Eaton, p. 4; "Edwin Ruffin," pp. 431–32.

20. United States, *Annals of Congress,* Sixteenth Congress, First Session, II, 1392; *Lynchburg Virginian,* July 4, 1833, in Ambler, pp. 110–11.

21. Ruffin Diary, January 10, 1857, and June 2, 1863.

22. Cutter, p. 496.

23. Ambler, pp. 113–14; *Farmers' Register,* I (1833), 111; Edmund Ruffin, "Address to the Agricultural Society of the Rappahannock," Rappahannock, Virginia, 1833, Ruffin Papers.

24. John Taylor, *Arator; Being a Series of Agricultural Essays, Practical and Political: In Sixty-Four Numbers* (Petersburg, Virginia: Whitworth & Yancey, 1818), p. 190.

25. Ruffin Diary, October 28, 1858; Taylor, pp. 48, 94–95, 53.

26. Edmund Ruffin, "Incidents of My Life, 1851," II, 14–30, Ruffin Papers; Cutter, p. 497; "Edwin Ruffin," p. 432.

27. "Edwin Ruffin," p. 432.

28. Ibid., p. 433; Craven, p. 54.

29. Cutter, p. 497; "Edwin Ruffin," p. 433.

30. "Edwin Ruffin," p. 433; Cutter, pp. 498–99; *American Farmer,* III, (December 28, 1821), 313–19.

31. Avery Odelle Craven, *Soil Exhaustion as a Factor in the Agricultural History of Virginia and Maryland, 1606–1860* (Urbana, Illinois: University of Illinois Press, 1925), p. 136; Eaton, p. 179; Ruffin, "Incidents of My Life," II, 7; Edmund Ruffin, *An Essay on Calcareous Manures* (Petersburg, Virginia: J. W. Campbell, 1832), pp. 29–30; Craven, *Soil Exhaustion,* p. 138.

32. Craven, *Edmund Ruffin,* pp. 58–59; Cutter, pp. 498–99.

2. Dogma and Demagogues

1. Ruffin Diary, June 1, 1859, and June 18, 1863.

2. Ibid., June 18, 1863.

3. Ibid., January 18, 1859.
4. Ibid., February 24, 1864; June 30, 1857; May 17, 1857; and April 18, 1858.
5. Ibid., March 1, 1858; February 24, 1864; and September 29, 1859.
6. Ibid., August 9, 1863.
7. Ibid., August 9, 1863, and February 24, 1864. Ruffin's attitude toward religion may have been influenced by John Taylor of Caroline, who wrote, "At the awful day of judgment, the discrimination of the good from the wicked, is not made by the criterion of sects or of dogmas, but by one which constitutes the daily employment and the great end of agriculture. The judge upon this occasion has . . . pronounced, that to feed the hungry, clothe the naked, and give drink to the thirsty, are the passports to future happiness" (*Arator*, p. 189).
8. Ruffin Diary, February 25, 1864, and June 1, 1859.
9. Ibid., June 1, 1859.
10. Ibid., February 25, 1864.
11. Ibid.
12. Ibid., February 25, 1864, and July 8, 1859.
13. George Fitzhugh, *Sociology for the South; or, The Failure of Free Society* (Richmond: A. Morris, 1854), p. 156; E. L. Ruffin, pp. 250–51; United States, Bureau of the Census, *Census of Virginia: 1820. Prince George County.*
14. Richmond *Enquirer*, June 23, 1823.
15. George Dangerfield, *The Era of Good Feelings* (New York: Harcourt, Brace & World, Inc., 1952), p. 190.
16. Craven, *Soil Exhaustion*, pp. 116–17; Taylor, p. 159.
17. Ellis, pp. 103–04; "Edwin Ruffin," pp. 434–35.
18. Richmond *Enquirer*, June 23, 1823.
19. Ibid.
20. Ibid., Dangerfield, pp. 219–19.
21. *American Farmer*, III (December 28, 1821), 313.
22. Ruffin, "Incidents of My Life," II, 9.
23. Ruffin Diary, May 14, 1863, and January 20, 1864.
24. Ellis, pp. 104–05.
25. Ruffin Diary, "Conversations with John Tyler," November, 1857; see also *The Diary of Edmund Ruffin,* ed. William Kauffman Scarborough (Baton Rouge: Louisiana State University Press, 1972), I, 619–20.
26. Ruffin Diary, January 20, 1863, and October 22, 1858.
27. Ibid., January 20, 1863.
28. Ibid.
29. Ibid.

3. Prophet without Honor

1. Ruffin Diary, "Conversations with John Tyler," November, 1857.
2. Ruffin, "Incidents of My Life," II, 2–3. For more about the attitudes of Southern intellectuals toward plantation life, see Drew Gilpin Faust, *A Sacred Circle: The Dilemma of the Intellectual in the Old South* (Baltimore: Johns Hopkins University Press, 1977), pp. 7–14.
3. Ruffin, "Incidents of My Life," II, 4.
4. Ibid., 4–5.
5. Ibid., 7.
6. Ibid., 2.

7. Ibid., 10.

8. Ibid., 2–3, 10–11.

9. Stephen B. Oates, *The Fires of Jubilee: Nat Turner's Fierce Rebellion* (New York: Harper & Row, 1975), pp. 78–103, 112–14; Joseph Clarke Robert, *The Road from Monticello: A Study of the Virginia Slavery Debate of 1832* (Durham, North Carolina: Duke University Press, 1941), pp. 3–4.

10. Ulrich Bonnell Phillips, *The Course of the South to Secession* (New York: D. Appleton-Century Company, Inc., 1939), p. 106; Robert, p. 5; Oates, *Fires of Jubilee*, pp. 123–24; Robert, pp. 7–8.

11. Ruffin Diary, January 4, 1862.

12. Ibid.

13. Ibid.

14. *Farmers' Register*, II (1834), 632; III (1835), 717–21; IV (1836), pp. 95–104; Ruffin Diary, "Conversations with John Tyler," November, 1857.

15. Ruffin, "Incidents of My Life," II, 12, 13.

16. "Farmers' Register: A Proposal for Publishing by Subscription, a Periodical Work," in Earl G. Swem, "An Analysis of Ruffin's Farmers' Register, With a Bibliography of Edmund Ruffin," *Bulletin of the Virginia State Library*, 11 (July, October, 1918), 41–144; Cutter, p. 500.

17. *Farmers' Register*, I (1833), Frontispiece; Ruffin, "Incidents of My Life," II, 13; *Farmers' Register*, V (1837), 34–35; Richmond *Enquirer*, June 18, 1833; August 2, 1833 and November 11, 1834; Craven, *Edmund Ruffin*, p. 61; Craven, *Soil Exhaustion*, pp. 138–39.

18. Cutter, pp. 500–01; Sterling P. Anderson, Jr., "Edmund Ruffin, Editor and Publisher," *Virginia Cavalcade*, 17 (Summer, 1967), 35.

19. Ruffin, "Incidents of My Life," II, 35–37; "Writers of Anonymous Articles in the Farmers' Register," *Journal of Southern History*, 23 (February, 1957), 90–102.

20. Ruffin, "Incidents of My Life," II, 38; Anderson, p. 35.

21. Ruffin, "Incidents of My Life," II, 38–39.

22. Ruffin, "Statement of the Closing Scenes of the Life of Thomas Cocke, February 25, 1840," Ruffin Papers; Ruffin "Incidents of My Life," II, 10–11; Ruffin, "Thomas Cocke."

23. Ruffin, "Thomas Cocke."

24. Ibid.

25. Ibid.

26. Ibid.

27. Ibid.

28. Ruffin, "Incidents of My Life," II, 38.

29. Ibid., 41, 43.

30. Ibid., 45.

31. Ibid., 46.

32. Ibid., 58, 45. For a more detailed explanation of the causes of the Panic of 1837 and the ensuing Panic of 1839, see Peter Temin, *The Jacksonian Economy* (New York: W. W. Norton & Company, Inc., 1969), pp. 113–71.

33. Ruffin, "Incidents of My Life," II, 43, 50–53. Ruffin, like many of his contemporaries and most traditional historians, blamed the banks and/or President Andrew Jackson's policies for the inflation and subsequent depression of the 1830s. Recent studies, however, show that this interpretation is mistaken. The feverish American inflation was the result of complex changes in Oriental trade, the high

price of cotton, and huge capital imports from England. The financial crises of 1837 and 1839 were triggered not by Jackson's policies or irresponsible banking practices but by a chain of external circumstances that neither the President nor the banks were in any position to control. For more on this situation, see Temin. For a good general treatment of the subject, see Leonard L. Richards, *The Advent of American Democracy* (Glenview, Illinois: Scott, Foresman and Company, 1977), pp. 138–42.

34. Edmund Ruffin to James Henry Hammond, September 7, 1845, Hammond Papers, Library of Congress.

35. Ibid.; Edmund Ruffin to James Henry Hammond, October 24, 1845, Hammond Papers.

36. Ibid., September 7, 1845.

37. Ruffin, "Incidents of My Life," II, 52–53; Eaton, p. 213. Virginia banks were, for the most part, conservative, responsible, and very sound. In fact, after the Panic of 1837, when banks in other states were failing, the Virginia banks all survived. For more information on the banks in Virginia and the politics involved between soft-money and hard-money advocates, see James Roger Sharp, *The Jacksonians Versus the Banks: Politics in the States After the Panic of 1837* (New York: Columbia University Press, 1970), pp. 215–73; see also John M. McFaul, *The Politics of Jacksonian Finance* (Ithaca, New York: Cornell University Press, 1972), pp. 198–201.

38. *Bank Reformer,* III (November 1, 1841), 37; Ruffin, "Incidents of My Life," II, 53–54.

39. Ibid.

40. Ibid., 50; *Bank Reformer,* III (November 1, 1841), 35.

41. Anderson, p. 35; Ruffin, "Incidents of My Life," II, 53–54.

42. *Farmers' Register,* X (1842).

43. Ruffin, "Incidents of My Life," II, 38.

44. James Henry Hammond to Edmund Ruffin, December 18, 1842, Ruffin Papers; Edmund Ruffin, Diary as South Carolina Agricultural Surveyor, 1843, Ruffin Papers; Matthew, 13:57.

4. Master of Marlbourne

1. James Henry Hammond to Edmund Ruffin, February 5, 1845, Ruffin Papers.

2. Ruffin, "Incidents of My Life," II, 59; *Farmers' Register,* VIII (1840), 244.

3. Ruffin, Diary as South Carolina Agricultural Surveyor, 1843, Ruffin Papers; Ruffin, "Incidents of My Life," II, 60.

4. James Henry Hammond to Edmund Ruffin, October 10, 1845, Ruffin Papers; Clement Eaton, *The Mind of the Old South* (Baton Rouge: Louisiana State University Press, 1967), p. 40; Elizabeth Merritt, *James Henry Hammond, 1807–1864* (Baltimore: Johns Hopkins Press, 1923), pp. 61–62. According to Drew Gilpin Faust (*A Sacred Circle,* p. x), during the late 1830s and 1840s Edmund Ruffin and four other Southern intellectuals—James Henry Hammond, William Gilmore Simms, Nathaniel Beverley Tucker, and George Frederick Holmes—formed an intense personal friendship that evolved into a mutual support network. The basis for this friendship network was their common sense of alienation, of being both neglected prophets and the rightful stewards of Southern society; and their desire "to reform the South to make a place for their particular talents." Faust's analysis is insightful and at times brilliant, but she exaggerates the intensity of this friendship

in Ruffin's case. While he was always attracted to men who felt their superior talents had not been justly rewarded—men who also included Thomas Cocke, John Tyler, Robert Barnwell Rhett, and William Lowndes Yancey—his naturally suspicious nature made him essentially a loner even among other disaffected Southern intellectuals. Only in Hammond's case is there a good deal of evidence—in the form of exchanged letters and visits—of a close, mutually supportive friendship.

5. Eaton, *The Mind of the Old South,* pp. 37–39; Eaton, *The Growth of Southern Civilization,* p. 308.

6. Eaton, *The Mind of the Old South,* p. 25.

7. Merritt, pp. 34–37.

8. James Henry Hammond, "Address Delivered Before the South Carolina Institute, at Its First Annual Fair, On the 20th November, 1840," Hammond Papers.

9. James Henry Hammond to Edmund Ruffin, February 14, 1844, and December 21, 1846, Ruffin Papers.

10. William W. Freehling, *Prelude to Civil War: The Nullification Controversy in South Carolina, 1816–1836* (New York: Harper & Row, 1965), pp. 19–20.

11. Richmond *Examiner,* [?], 1853, appended to Edmund Ruffin, "Incidents of My Life," III, Ruffin Papers.

12. Ruffin, "Incidents of My Life," II, 60; James Henry Hammond to Edmund Ruffin, March 10, 1844, Ruffin Papers.

13. Ruffin, "Incidents of My Life," II, 60.

14. Ibid., 61.

15. Charleston *Mercury,* [?], and the Petersburg *Republican,* [?], attached to Ruffin, "Incidents of My Life," II; Ruffin, "Incidents of My Life," II, 60–62.

16. Ibid., 62.

17. Ibid.

18. Ibid.

19. Edmund Ruffin, Marlbourne Farm Journal, Ruffin Papers.

20. Ruffin, "Incidents of My Life," II, 61, 63–67.

21. Ibid., 60, 82.

22. Ellis, pp. 111–12; Ruffin, Marlbourne Farm Journal.

23. Ruffin, "Incidents of My Life," II, 67–68; Ellis, p. 113.

24. Ruffin, Marlbourne Farm Journal.

25. Ruffin, Marlbourne Farm Journal; Edmund Ruffin, Jr. to Edmund Ruffin, October 13, 1847, Ruffin Papers; Ruffin Diary, February 20, 1859.

26. Oates, *Fires of Jubilee,* pp. 3–4; Tombstone of Lucy Lockett, Born: February 15, 1774. Died: January 29, 1836. Blanford Cemetery, Petersburg, Virginia.

27. Ruffin, "Incidents of My Life," II, 30–33, 87–88. Even though overseers' contracts stipulated humane slave treatment, many of these men felt they could not live up to a planter's expectations of high crop yields without driving the slaves mercilessly.

Although black foremen were generally used on plantations that did not employ white overseers, Ruffin referred to Jem Sykes both as his foreman and as his "negro overseer." Ruffin seemed to use the two terms interchangeably, without drawing distinctions between the duties and responsibilities attached to either job title. See William Kauffman Scarborough, *The Overseer: Plantation Management in the Old South* (Baton Rouge: Louisiana State University Press, 1966), pp. 16–19, and Ruffin, "Incidents of My Life," II, 227–28.

The amount of trust Ruffin placed in Sykes was unusual and elicited comment among fellow Virginia planters. In August, 1848, for example, Ruffin took his daughters on a two-month vacation to White Sulphur Springs and left Sykes in charge of thrashing the wheat and delivering it to market. In "Incidents of My Life," II, pp. 227–28, Ruffin notes: "The facts of this crop being left to be thrashed & delivered, under the sole care & charge of my negro overseer, & that I could leave the farm without other superintendence for a visit to the Springs caused nearly as much remark as did the amount of the crop of wheat then made."

28. Ruffin, Marlbourne Farm Journal; Ruffin, "Incidents of My Life," II, 71–86, 91–113.

29. Ruffin Diary, May 2, 1857.

30. *Farmers' Register,* II (1834), 95–96.

31. Ruffin, "Incidents of My Life," II, 69–70.

32. Edmund Ruffin, "Farming Profits in Eastern Virginia: The Value of Marl," *American Farmer* (July, 1849), pp. 1–10.

33. Ruffin, "Incidents of My Life," II, 223–24.

34. Edmund Ruffin to James Henry Hammond, May 17, 1845, Hammond Papers.

5. The Mad Dog Cry of Disunion

1. James Henry Hammond to Edmund Ruffin, June 20, 1845, Ruffin Papers; Edmund Ruffin, Jr. to Edmund Ruffin, August 1, 1845, Ruffin Papers.

2. Ruffin, "Incidents of My Life," II, 82–83.

3. Ibid., 117–19.

4. Edmund Ruffin, Jr. to Edmund Ruffin, August 1, 1845, Ruffin Papers; Julian Calx Ruffin to Edmund Ruffin, March 24, 1848, Ruffin Papers.

5. James Henry Hammond to Edmund Ruffin, July 22, 1856 and August 26, 1846, Ruffin Papers; Edmund Ruffin to James Henry Hammond, May 17, 1845, Hammond Papers.

6. Merritt, pp. 66–67; Eaton, *The Mind of the Old South,* pp. 26–27; Ruffin Diary, January 20, 1863.

7. Ruffin Diary, November 14, 1857.

8. Edmund Ruffin to President John Tyler, June 29, 1841, inserted into the Ruffin Diary.

9. Ruffin, "Incidents of My Life," II, 49–50; *Southern Magazine and Monthly Review,* I (January, 1841), Frontispiece.

10. *Southern Magazine and Monthly Review,* I (January, 1841), Preface.

11. Mrs. Kirkland Ruffin, ed., "School-Boy Letters of Edmund Ruffin, Jr.," *North Carolina Historical Review,* 10 (October, 1933), 287; Edmund Ruffin, Jr. to Susan Ruffin, September 6, 1828, in Mrs. Kirkland Ruffin, "School-Boy Letters," p. 228.

12. Edmund Ruffin, Jr. to Susan Ruffin, November 6, 1828, in Mrs. Kirkland Ruffin, "School-Boy Letters," pp. 301–03; Edmund Ruffin, Jr. to Edmund Ruffin, March 28, 1829, in Mrs. Kirkland Ruffin, "School-Boy Letters," p. 318.

13. Edmund Ruffin to James Henry Hammond, July 6, 1845, Hammond Papers.

14. Edmund Ruffin, *African Colonization Unveiled* (Washington, D.C.: Lemuel Towers, [1859]), pp. 2–3.

15. Oates, *Fires of Jubilee,* pp. 159–61.

16. Charleston *Courier,* November 28, 1829; United States, *Congressional Globe,* Twenty-Fifth Congress, Second Session, January 10, 1838, Appendix, pp. 61–62; William Sumner Jenkins, *Pro-Slavery Thought in the Old South* (Chapel Hill: University of North Carolina Press, 1935), pp. 65–90; Oates, *Fires of Jubilee,* p. 163.

17. *Farmers' Register,* I (1833), 36.

18. Ibid., 405, 185–90; III (1835), 429–30; IV (1836), 4. Volumes V through X of the *Farmers' Register* (1837–1842) contain few articles on slavery and no mention of abolitionism.

19. Ibid., III (September, 1835), 287–89; Leonard L. Richards, *Gentlemen of Property and Standing: Anti-Abolition Mobs in Jacksonian America* (New York: Oxford University Press, 1970), pp. 49–62; Bertram Wyatt-Brown, "The Abolitionists' Postal Campaign of 1835," *Journal of Negro History,* 50 (October, 1965), 227–38; Edwin A. Miles, "The Mississippi Slave Insurrection Scare of 1835," *Journal of Negro History,* 42 (January, 1957), 48–60; W. Sherman Savage, *Controversy Over the Distribution of Abolition Literature* (The Association for the Study of Negro Life and History, Inc., 1938), pp. 1–42; Russell B. Nye, *Fettered Freedom: Civil Liberties and the Slavery Controversy, 1830–1860* (East Lansing, Michigan: Michigan State College Press, 1949), pp. 54–69. See *Niles' Register,* July–November, 1835, for numerous examples of the intense Southern Great Reaction to the antislavery mail campaign of 1835. The *Register* itself, though opposed to slavery, deplored the fact that a few "miserable fanatics . . . who manufacture abolition journals, have flooded the mails with them to the just exasperation of the south." *Niles' Register,* 12 (August 8, 1835), 402. For a discussion of the reasons why Southerners reacted so vehemently, see Richards, *Gentlemen of Property and Standing,* pp. 52–58.

20. Edmund Ruffin to James Henry Hammond, September 7, 1845, Hammond Papers.

21. James Henry Hammond to Edmund Ruffin, March 26, 1847, Ruffin Papers; Richmond *Enquirer,* December 25, 1848.

22. John C. Calhoun to John H. Means, April 13, 1849, in "The Correspondence of John C. Calhoun," *Annual Report of the American Historical Association for the Year 1899,* ed. J. Franklin Jameson (2 vols.; Washington, D.C.: Government Printing Office, 1900), II, 764–66.

23. James Henry Hammond to Edmund Ruffin, January 12, 1850, Ruffin Papers.

24. Ibid., February 8, 1850, Ruffin Papers. In 1833, British abolitionists had pushed an emancipation bill through Parliament freeing all the slaves in the British West Indies, which included Jamaica. Only two years earlier, in 1831, almost fifty thousand blacks in Jamaica had risen up in revolt. The population in Jamaica was 90% black, and in Jamaica, as opposed to the southern United States, there was no legal prohibition against sexual relations between whites and blacks. In fact, a law passed in 1733 made all third-generation mulattoes who professed to be Christians legally white. White Southerners like Hammond and Ruffin were horrified by this example of what they called the "Africanization" of the white race.

25. Edmund Ruffin to M. R. H. Garnett, April 22, 1850, Chisholm Papers, Virginia Historical Society.

26. Guadeloupe blacks were freed by the French in 1848. Ruffin and other Southerners were horrified not only by the poor economic conditions in countries like Jamaica and Guadeloupe but also by the absence of miscegenation laws.

27. Richmond *Enquirer,* March, 1850, a series of three articles, the last dated March 28, 1850 and signed "A Virginian"; William L. Barney, *The Road to Secession: A New Perspective on the Old South* (New York: Praeger Publishers, 1972), pp. 199–202. Ironically, Ruffin took the quote "Concession to fanatics never satisfies fanaticism" from a speech made by Senator Nathan Hale of Vermont, who was to be the presidential candidate of the Free Soil party in 1852.

28. *Leesburg Washingtonian,* quoted in the *National Intelligencer,* March 2, 1850; Richmond *Enquirer,* April 17, 1850.

29. James Henry Hammond to Edmund Ruffin, April [?], 1850 and May 17, 1850, Ruffin Papers.

30. *Acts of the General Assembly of Virginia, 1850–1851,* p. 201; Richmond *Enquirer,* March 27, 1851; Richmond *Whig,* July 26, 1850.

31. James Henry Hammond to Edmund Ruffin, February 7, 1851, Ruffin Papers.

32. Ibid., July 20, 1851.

33. Richmond *Enquirer,* November 7, 1851; Richmond *Examiner,* November 7, 1851.

34. Charleston *Mercury,* November 11 and 13, 1851, Hammond Papers.

35. Ibid., November 7, 1851.

36. Ibid., May 2, 1851.

37. Ibid., November 7, 1851.

38. Ruffin, "Incidents of My Life," III, 254.

39. James Henry Hammond to Edmund Ruffin, September 30, 1851, Ruffin Papers.

40. Merritt, p. 109; James Henry Hammond to Edmund Ruffin, July 7, 1844 and November 9, 1849, Ruffin Papers; James Henry Hammond to William Gilmore Simms, December [?], 1851, in Merritt, pp. 109–10.

41. Edmund Ruffin to James Henry Hammond, July 6, 1845, Hammond Papers.

6. A Time of Triumph

1. Edmund Ruffin to James Henry Hammond, December 3, 1853, Hammond Papers.

2. Ibid., May 17, 1845, Hammond Papers; Ruffin, "Farming Profits in Eastern Virginia," pp. 1–10; Ruffin "Incidents of My Life," II, 88–89; III, 227.

3. Ibid., 224.

4. Ibid., 226.

5. Ibid., 224–25, 228.

6. Ibid., 239, 244, 229.

7. *National Intelligencer,* [?], 1853; Richmond *Whig,* [?], 1852.

8. Richmond *Whig,* [?], 1852; Petersburg *Southside Democrat,* [?], 1852; Extract from ex-President John Tyler's Valedictory Speech to the Virginia State Agricultural Society, December, 1852, in Ruffin, "Incidents of My Life," III, n. pag.

9. "Edwin Ruffin," p. 435; Richmond *Whig,* [?], 1852.

10. Petersburg *Southside Democrat,* [?], 1852.

11. Ruffin, "Incidents of My Life," III, 237–39.

12. Ibid., 221–23.

13. Ibid., 225, 230.

14. Ibid., 230.

15. Ibid., 244; Ruffin, "Address to the Agricultural Society of the Rappahannock," Ruffin Papers; Ruffin, "Incidents of My Life," III, 231–33.

16. Edmund Ruffin, *An Address on the Opposite Results of Exhausting and Fertilizing Systems of Agriculture,* Read Before the South Carolina Institute; At Its Fourth Annual Fair, November 18, 1852 (Charleston: Press of Walker and James, 1853), pp. 12–13, 386.

17. Ibid., pp. 6–7; Ruffin, "Address to the Agricultural Society of the Rappahannock," p. 2, Ruffin Papers.

18. Edmund Ruffin, *The Influence of Slavery, or of its Absence on Manners, Morals, and Intellect,* Read Before the South Carolina Institute at Its Fourth Annual Fair, November 18, 1852 (Charleston: Steam Power Press of Walker and James, 1853), pp. 7–8.

19. Ibid., pp. 9–10; Eaton, *Growth of Southern Civilization,* p. 98; Kenneth M. Stampp, *The Peculiar Institution: Slavery in the Ante-Bellum South* (New York: Alfred A. Knopf, Inc., 1956), pp. 29–30.

20. Ruffin, *Influence of Slavery on Manners, Morals, and Intellect,* pp. 16–17, 10; Ruffin, *African Colonization Unveiled,* p. 2.

21. Ruffin, "Incidents of My Life," III, p. 247; Ruffin, *Address on the Opposite Results of Exhausting and Fertilizing Systems of Agriculture,* p. 386.

22. Ruffin, "Incidents of My Life," III, 245–46; Ruffin, *Address on the Opposite Results of Exhausting and Fertilizing Systems of Agriculture,* p. 4; Ruffin, "Address to the Agricultural Society of the Rappahannock," p. 1, Ruffin Papers.

23. Ruffin, "Incidents of My Life," III, 229, 246–47.

24. Fredericksburg *News,* December [?], 1852.

25. Ibid.

26. Extract from Tyler's Valedictory Speech, in Ruffin, "Incidents of My Life," III; *Extract from the Report of the Committee on Honorary Testimonials of the Virginia State Agricultural Society, 1852,* in Ruffin, "Incidents of My Life," III.

27. Ruffin, "Incidents of My Life," III, 234–37.

28. Edmund Ruffin to James Henry Hammond, December 3, 1853, Hammond Papers.

29. James Henry Hammond to William Gilmore Simms, July 8, 1853, Hammond Papers; Merritt, p. 109; Williamsburg *Weekly Gazette,* April 24, 1856.

30. Ruffin, "Incidents of My Life," III, 255–56.

31. Ruffin Diary, "Introduction to the Attempt," 1856.

32. Ibid., June 4, 1864.

33. Ibid., June 4, 1864, and "Introduction," 1856.

34. Edmund Ruffin, "In Memoriam, 1855," Ruffin Papers.

35. Julian Ruffin to Edmund Ruffin, [March 1823], Ruffin Papers; Edmund Ruffin to his stepmother, Elizabeth Cocke Ruffin, March 23, 1823, Ruffin Papers; Edmund Ruffin to Juliana Ruffin Coupland, November 23 and January 12, 1832, Ruffin Papers; Juliana Ruffin Coupland to Edmund Ruffin, December 14, 1833, Ruffin Papers; Agnes Ruffin Beckwith to Edmund Ruffin, January 9, 1863, Ruffin Papers; Ruffin Diary, March 10, 1857; Julian Calx Ruffin to Edmund Ruffin, March 14, 1855, Ruffin Papers; Ruffin Diary, May 31, 1857; Agnes Ruffin Beckwith to Edmund Ruffin, November 14, 1847, Ruffin Papers; Ruffin, "Incidents of My Life," III, 255.

36. Elizabeth Ruffin Sayre to Edmund Ruffin, July 14, 1860, Ruffin Papers: Ruffin Diary, October 18, 1859; Edmund Ruffin to Charles Lorraine Ruffin, October 19, 1857, Ruffin Papers; Ruffin, "Incidents of My Life," III, 255.

37. Ruffin Diary, January 23, 1863; June 4, 1864; and "Introduction," 1856.

38. Ibid., "Introduction," 1856.

39. Ibid., June 4, 1864.

40. Ibid., "Introduction," 1856; January 23, 1856; and January 4, 1864. See Eugene Genovese, *The Political Economy of Slavery* (New York: Random House, 1967), pp. 221–35, for a discussion of how Ruffin and a few other prominent

Southerners argued that slavery had a positive effect on the Southern white work force because it discouraged the influx of European immigrants and thus prevented the growth of "radical" foreign ideas.

41. Ruffin Diary, "Introduction," 1856.

7. Missionary of Disunion

1. Ruffin Diary, "Introduction," 1856.

2. United States, *Congressional Globe,* Thirty-third Congress, First Session, p. 281.

3. Stephen B. Oates, *With Malice Toward None: The Life of Abraham Lincoln* (New York: Harper & Row, 1977), pp. 111–13.

4. Charleston *Mercury,* May 13, 1857; Edmund Ruffin, "Cassandra's Warnings," Charleston *Mercury,* July 21, 1859, and May 13, 1857. Ruffin's fear of abolitionist penetration of the Old Southwest after repeal of the Missouri Compromise seems irrational. The southern half of the Louisiana Purchase was already organized into slave states. But at one time, Ruffin had expected that Congress would extend the Missouri line to the Pacific. He had assumed that the southern half of the continental United States belonged to slaveowners. The Kansas bill destroyed that assumption and made him fearful that slaveowners might have to compete with Northerners and abolitionists for the remaining southwestern territories.

5. Oates, *To Purge This Land With Blood,* pp. 238–39.

6. Ruffin Diary, "Introduction," 1856.

7. Henry A. Wise, Jr. to Edward Everett, September 17, 1856, Everett Papers, in Roy Franklin Nichols, *The Disruption of American Democracy* (New York: The Free Press, 1968), p. 57.

8. Edmund Ruffin, "Consequences of Abolitionist Agitation," *DeBow's Review,* 22 (June, 1857), 586. Installments of this article appeared in the Richmond *Enquirer,* beginning on December 19, 1856. Ruffin submitted the last part on December 28, 1856. See also *DeBow's Review,* 23 (September–December, 1857), 266–72, 385–90, 546–52, 596–607.

9. Ruffin, "Consequences of Abolitionist Agitation," *DeBow's Review,* 22 (June, 1857), 583–93. Ruffin's insistence that the majority of newly arrived Europeans in northeastern cities joined the Republican party was inaccurate. As Republicans themselves noted, the large Irish immigrant urban population usually voted Democratic.

10. Ruffin Diary, February 19 and January 10, 1857.

11. Ibid., February 14 and 16, 1857.

12. Ibid., January 22 and February 20, 1858.

13. Ibid., February 17, 1857; April 25, 1859; and February 17, 1857.

14. Ibid., February 22 and 20, 1857.

15. Charleston *Mercury,* May 13, 1857; Ruffin Diary, May 11, 1857.

16. Ruffin Diary, May 13, 1857.

17. Ibid., January 30 and May 13, 1857.

18. Ibid., May 19, 1857.

19. Edmund Ruffin to James Henry Hammond, July 4, 1857, Hammond Papers.

20. Henry T. Shanks, *The Secession Movement in Virginia, 1847–1861* (New York: DaCapo Press, 1934), pp. 83–84; Herbert Wender, *Southern Commercial*

Conventions, 1837–1859 (Baltimore: Johns Hopkins Press, 1930), p. 10; Ronald T. Takaki, *A Pro-Slavery Crusade; The Agitation to Reopen the African Slave Trade* (New York: Free Press, 1971), pp. 148–51; Edmund Ruffin to James Henry Hammond, July 4, 1857, Hammond Papers.

21. James Henry Hammond to Edmund Ruffin, July 24, 1857, Ruffin Papers.
22. Ruffin Diary, January 1 and June 8, 1857.
23. Ibid., August 9, 1857.
24. Ibid., August 31 and September 21, 1857.
25. Ibid., September 26, 1857.
26. Ibid., October 6, 1857.
27. Ibid., October 11, 1857; November 20, 1858; and October 11, 1857.
28. Ibid., November 30, 1857.

8. The Divine Institution

1. Ruffin, *African Colonization Unveiled,* p. 3; spoken by James Henry Hammond, October 29, 1858, in Freehling, p. 299. Historian Charles Grier Sellers, Jr. argues that while Southerners publicly appeared to be unanimous in their acceptance of slavery as a positive good, privately they often held very different views. In "The Travail of Slavery," in *The Southerner as American,* ed. Charles Grier Sellers, Jr. (Chapel Hill: University of North Carolina Press, 1960), pp. 62–63, Sellers quotes a Southern Congressman who in 1848 confided in a letter to his wife: "To expect men to agree that Slavery is a blessing, social, moral, and political, when many of those who have been accustomed to it . . . believe exactly the reverse, is absurd."

There is a debate among historians about what motivated proslavery apologists like Ruffin to defend slavery. Sellers, in "The Travail of Slavery," pp. 40–71, believes that the deep-seated guilt Southerners felt about the presence of slavery in a democratic society impelled them to defend their peculiar social system all the more ardently. Among other historians who agree with this interpretation are Ralph E. Morrow, "The Proslavery Argument Revisited," *Mississippi Valley Historical Review,* 47 (June, 1961), 79–94, and Freehling. William B. Hesseltine, in "Some New Aspects of the Pro-Slavery Argument," *Journal of Negro History,* 21 (January, 1936), 1–15, feels that the proslavery defense represents an attempt by the planter elite to win over nonslaveholding whites as allies against Northern abolitionism. David Donald, in "The Proslavery Argument Reconsidered," *Journal of Southern History,* 37 (February, 1971), 3–18, contends that slavery apologists directed their writings at fellow Southerners and were motivated by status anxieties and a desire to return to some imagined utopian past. Drew Gilpin Faust, in "A Sacred Duty: The Proslavery Argument," in her *A Sacred Circle,* 112–31, rejects the guilt, class, and status anxiety interpretations. She believes that Ruffin and other proslavery writers suffered from tensions and anxieties having nothing to do with guilt or status. Their goal, she argues, was to carve out an important place for themselves as intellectuals in Southern society and "to provide the region as a whole with a conventionalized formula of self-affirmation."

2. From the extensive list of proslavery writings, see James Henry Hammond, et al., *The Proslavery Argument* (Philadelphia: Lippincott, Grambo, & Company, 1853); Thornton Stringfellow, *Slavery, Its Origin, Nature and History* (Alexandria, Virginia: Virginia Sentinel Office, 1860) and *Scriptural and Statistical Views in Favor*

of Slavery (Richmond: J. W. Randolph, 1856); Josiah C. Nott and George R. Gliddon, *Types of Mankind* (Boston: Crocker and Brewster, 1856); John Fletcher, *Studies on Slavery, In Easy Lessons* (Natchez: J. Warner, 1852); Albert T. Bledsoe, *Liberty and Slavery* (Philadelphia: Lippincott, 1856); Edward Brown, *Notes on the Origin and Necessity of Slavery* (Charleston: A. E. Miller, 1826); George D. Armstrong, *The Christian Doctrine of Slavery* (New York: C. Scribner, 1857); Thomas Cooper, *On the Constitution of the United States, and Questions That Have Arisen Under It* (Columbia, South Carolina: D. & J. M. Faust, 1826); Edwin C. Holland, *A Refutation of the Calumnies Circulated Against the Southern and Western States Respecting the Institution and Existence of Slavery Among Them* (Charleston: A. E. Miller, 1822).

3. Edmund Ruffin, "Slavery and Free Labor Described and Compared" (n. p., [1860]), pp. 1–2; see also Edmund Ruffin, "Slavery and Free Labor Described and Compared," *Southern Planter,* 19 (December, 1859), 723–41, and 20 (January, 1860), 1–10; Edmund Ruffin, *The Political Economy of Slavery; or, The Institution Considered in Regard to Its Influence on Public Wealth and the General Welfare* (Washington, D.C.: Lemuel Towers, [1858]), pp. 5–6; Ruffin, *Influence of Slavery on Manners, Morals, and Intellect,* p. 18–19.

4. Ruffin, *African Colonization Unveiled,* p. 2; Ruffin Diary, June 20, 1858.

5. Ruffin, *Political Economy of Slavery,* p. 20; Ruffin Diary, June 20, 1858.

6. Ruffin, *Political Economy of Slavery,* p. 20.

7. Ruffin, *African Colonization Unveiled,* p. 2. The African Colonization Society was the target of criticism both from proslavery people, who considered it antislavery, and from blacks and abolitionists, who considered it anti-Negro.

8. Phillips, *The Course of the South to Secession,* pp. 93–94; Eaton, *The Growth of Southern Civilization,* pp. 94–96; McColley, p. 110; Ruffin, *African Colonization Unveiled,* p. 3.

9. Ruffin, *African Colonization Unveiled,* p. 9.

10. Ibid., pp. 2–3.

11. Phillips, *The Course of the South to Secession,* pp. 93–94; Eaton, *The Growth of Southern Civilization,* p. 95; Ruffin, *African Colonization Unveiled,* pp. 9–12, 25; Ruffin Diary, September 10, 1857, and January 20, 1858.

12. Ruffin Diary, September 10, 1857; Ruffin, Unpublished Appendix to *African Colonization Unveiled,* Ruffin Papers.

13. Ruffin, *African Colonization Unveiled,* pp. 14–21, 32.

14. Ruffin Diary, February 1, 1859; July 4, 1857; and February 6, 1862; "Blind Tom," *Atlantic Monthly,* 10 (November, 1862), 580–85.

15. Ruffin, *Political Economy of Slavery,* pp. 15–16.

16. Leon F. Litwack, *North of Slavery* (Chicago: University of Chicago Press, 1961), pp. 113–52; Ruffin *Political Economy of Slavery,* pp. 15, 22.

17. Thornton Stringfellow, *Scriptural and Statistical Views in Favor of Slavery* (Richmond: J. W. Randolph, 1856), pp. 6–54, passim, in *Slavery Defended: The Views of the Old South,* ed. Eric L. McKitrick (Englewood Cliffs, New Jersey: Prentice-Hall, 1963), pp. 86–87.

18. Ruffin Diary, June 2, 1859.

19. Clement Eaton, *The Freedom-of-Thought Struggle in the Old South* (New York: Harper & Row, 1964), pp. 308–10; Ruffin Diary, January 10, 1864. For a detailed study of the development of scientific racism, see William R. Stanton, *The Leopard's Spots: Scientific Attitudes Toward Race in America, 1815–1860* (Chicago: University of Chicago Press, 1960).

20. Ruffin Diary, September 11, 1858; Ruffin, *The Influence of Slavery on Manners, Morals, and Intellect,* pp. 18–20.

21. Ruffin, *African Colonization Unveiled,* p. 21; Ruffin Diary, December 10, 1857; February 3, 1858; and August 28, 1860.

22. Ruffin, "Slavery and Free Labor Compared," p. 9; Ruffin Diary, August 28, 1860.

23. Ruffin Diary, June 13, 1857; Ruffin, *African Colonization Unveiled,* pp. 6–7; Holland, p. 68, in Phillips, *The Course of the South to Secession,* p. 102; Ruffin, *Political Economy of Slavery,* p. 19; Ruffin Diary, June 15, 1857.

24. Ruffin, *African Colonization Unveiled,* pp. 7, 13.

25. Edmund Ruffin, "The Free Negro Nuisance and How to Abate It," *The South,* July 2, 1858, in Scarborough, *Diary of Edmund Ruffin,* Appendix C, I, 612–26; Ira Berlin, *Slaves Without Masters* (New York: Random House, 1974), pp. 348–49; George Fitzhugh, "What Shall Be Done With the Free Negroes?" Appended to his *Sociology for the South; or The Failure of Free Society* (Richmond: A. Morris, 1854), pp. 259–306; Litwack, pp. 66–74.

26. Ruffin, "The Free Negro Nuisance," p. 625.

27. Ruffin, "Slavery and Free Labor Compared," pp. 2, 6.

28. Ruffin, *Political Economy of Slavery,* p. 20.

29. Ibid., pp. 20–22; Ruffin, "Slavery and Free Labor Compared," pp. 3, 7.

30. Ruffin, *Political Economy of Slavery,* pp. 20–22.

31. Ibid., pp. 9–10; Fitzhugh, "Slavery Justified," Appended to his *Sociology for the South,* pp. 244–45.

32. Ruffin, *Political Economy of Slavery,* pp. 3–4; James Henry Hammond, " 'Mud-sill' speech," in McKitrick, pp. 121–25. In Lowell, Massachusetts, a Mr. Jonathan Doolittle liked Hammond's speech so much that in April, 1858, he began publishing a newspaper called *The Spindle City Idea,* which proposed that Northern factory operatives save themselves from wage slavery by volunteering for domestic servitude. Despite workers' complaints that they were virtually slaves to their employers, *The Spindle City Idea* did not catch on. The paper folded after only two issues, Ruffin noted sadly, for want of sufficient public support. See Ruffin Diary, April 17 and 25, 1853.

33. Ruffin Diary, October 26, 1858.

34. Ruffin, *Political Economy of Slavery,* p. 4; Ruffin Diary, February 23, 1859.

35. Ruffin, "Slavery and Free Labor Compared," pp. 9–16, 23–28.

36. Ibid., p. 27; Stampp, *The Peculiar Institution,* p. 351; Mary Boykin Chesnut, *A Diary From Dixie,* ed. Ben Ames Williams (Boston: Houghton Mifflin Company, 1961), pp. 21–22. The figures on the South's mulatto population come from the 1860 federal census. They must be read with caution, since census takers had no clear criteria for distinguishing mulattoes from blacks or even whites.

For a dissenting view about miscegenation, see Robert William Fogel and Stanley L. Engerman, *Time on the Cross; The Economics of American Negro Slavery* (Boston: Little, Brown and Company, 1974), pp. 130–36. They argue that the sexual exploitation of black women by white men was rare, and they hypothesize that the large number of mulattoes in the South were mostly the result of sexual unions between mulattoes or between mulattoes and blacks, not between blacks and whites. Most historians, though, insist that a high incidence of miscegenation existed in the South, and the testimonies of former slaves, visitors to the antebellum South, Southern women, and even Southern men support their conclusions. For example, see Solomon Northup, *Narrative of Solomon Northup, Twelve Years a Slave* (Auburn,

New York: Derby and Miller, 1853), pp. 188–90, 198, 256–59; Sarah M. Grimke, *Letters on the Equality of the Sexes and the Condition of Women* (Boston: Isaac Knapp, 1838), pp. 46–54; Angelina Grimke, *Appeal to the Christian Women of the South* (New York: American Anti-Slavery Society, 1836); Launcelot Minor Blackford, *Mine Eyes Have Seen the Glory; The Story of a Virginia Lady, Mary Berkeley Minor Blackford, 1802–1896, Who Taught Her Sons to Hate Slavery and to Love the Union* (Cambridge, Massachusetts: Harvard University Press, 1954), p. 47; Rebecca Latimer Felton, *Country Life in Georgia in the Days of My Youth* (Atlanta: Index Printing Company, 1919), p. 79; Chancellor Harper, "Memoir on Slavery," *Southern Literary Journal* (February, 1838), p. 1; also see Herbert S. Gutman, *Slavery and the Numbers Game: A Critique of Time on the Cross* (Urbana, Illinois: University of Illinois Press, 1975) for a critique of the methods Fogel and Engerman used in their study.

37. Ruffin Diary, November 7, 1857.

38. Ruffin, *Political Economy of Slavery,* p. 23; Ruffin, "Slavery and Free Labor Compared," pp. 9–28.

39. Ruffin, "Slavery and Free Labor Compared," pp. 8–9; see Eugene D. Genovese, *The World the Slaveholders Made: Two Essays in Interpretation* (New York: Random House, 1969), pp. 217–34, for a discussion of George Fitzhugh, in which Genovese compares Ruffin and Fitzhugh's views on slavery.

40. Ruffin, *Political Economy of Slavery,* p. 6; Ruffin, "Slavery and Free Labor Compared," p. 9; Ruffin, *The Influence of Slavery on Manners, Morals, and Intellect,* pp. 14, 16.

41. Ruffin, *The Influence of Slavery on Manners, Morals, and Intellect,* p. 15; see Richard Hofstadter, "John C. Calhoun: the Marx of the Master Class," in his *The American Political Tradition* (New York: Random House, 1948), pp. 68–92, for a detailed and provocative essay on Calhoun's appeal to slaveholders in the South and capitalists in the North to unite on a class basis in defense of property.

During the Panic of 1857, Ruffin read about the bread riots in New York City, where thousands of unemployed workers had marched on City Hall, demanding jobs and food. The men had threatened to take what they needed by force if their demands were not met. Ruffin predicted that after the South left the Union, these desperate "villains" would sack and destroy Northern cities, murdering the inhabitants. See Ruffin Diary, November 9 and 13, 1857.

42. Ruffin Diary, March 21 and November 20, 1858.

9. Cassandra's Warnings

1. Ruffin Diary, March 13, 1858.

2. Ibid., April 15 and 16, 1858.

3. Oates, *To Purge This Land With Blood,* pp. 226–37; Avery Odelle Craven, *The Coming of the Civil War* (New York: C. Scribner's Sons, 1950), pp. 387–89.

4. Ruffin Diary, January 5 and 22, 1858.

5. Ibid., January 22, 1858.

6. Ibid., February 9, 1858.

7. Ibid., April 17 and 24, 1858. Ruffin never really changed his anti-Lecompton feelings. When the House of Representatives voted to reject the Lecompton Bill in April, 1858, Ruffin was not disapppointed. He was, he said, "perfectly satisfied to be defeated." And when the House passed a compromise measure known as the

English Bill, which tried to bribe Kansas into ratifying a proslavery constitution, Ruffin accurately predicted that this was only "a nominal victory for the South" that would "soon be converted to a defeat & a loss." See Ruffin Diary, April 6 and May 5, 1858.

8. Ibid., May 1, 1858; Takaki, pp. 157–58.

9. Ruffin Diary, May 5, 1858.

10. Ibid., May 8–11 and 16, 1858.

11. Wender, pp. 208–10.

12. Ruffin Diary, May 11, 1858; Marshall J. Rachleff, "Racial Fear and Political Factionalism; A Study of the Secession Movement in Alabama, 1819–1861," (unpublished Ph.D. dissertation, University of Massachusetts, Amherst, 1974), pp. 254–55; James DeBow to Edmund Ruffin, June 29, 1859, Ruffin Papers.

13. Ruffin Diary, May 15, 1857; Ruffin, *Political Economy of Slavery*, p. 11.

14. Ruffin Diary, April. 26, 1859.

15. Ibid., May 15, 1857; Ruffin, *Political Economy of Slavery*, p. 11.

16. Ruffin Diary, May 11, 1858; Wender, p. 221; Ruffin, *Essay on Calcareous Manures*, pp. 162–64; Edmund Ruffin, "The Effects of High Prices of Slaves; Considered in Reference to the Interests of Agriculture, of Individuals, and of the Commonwealth of Virginia," *DeBow's Review,* 26 (June, 1859), 647–57. Ironically, one year earlier in 1857, Pryor's newspaper, the Richmond *South,* had favored renewal of the slave trade from Africa. But Pryor was an ardent supporter of Senator Robert M. T. Hunter, who had presidential aspirations for 1860. So, in 1858, Hunter directed his wing of the state Democratic party to tone down divisive sectional issues like the African slave trade. See Shanks, pp. 62–63.

Many scholars question whether Virginia and the states of the Upper South in general practiced slave-breeding. Recently Fogel and Engerman, pp. 5, 78–86, argued that there is no substantial evidence to document abolitionist charges of slave-breeding in the South. Gutman, *Slavery and the Numbers Game,* pp. 96–98, and *The Black Family in Slavery and Freedom, 1750–1925* (New York: Vintage Books, 1976), pp. 75–79, refutes their arguments and presents evidence from slave-owners themselves—not abolitionists—that Southerners bred slaves for profit. "Really," said one Georgia planter, "the leading industry of the South was slave-rearing." Stampp, in *The Peculiar Institution,* pp. 245–51, admits that evidence of systematic and deliberate "slave-breeding" is scanty, but he argues that masters still encouraged what he calls "slave-rearing" by offering female slaves positive incentives to reproduce. Frederick Law Olmsted, a Northerner who visited the slave states in antebellum times, received a letter from one slaveowner who accused his fellow Southerners of widespread slave-breeding. "In the States of Maryland, Virginia, North Carolina, Kentucky, Tennessee and Missouri," the man wrote, "as much attention is paid to the breeding and growth of negroes as to that of horses and mules." See Frederick Law Olmsted, *The Slave States,* ed. Harvey Wish (New York: Capricorn Books, 1959), pp. 48–49. Although planters were reluctant to admit they reared slaves for sale, Olmsted commented, "that a slave woman is commonly esteemed least for her labouring qualities, most for those qualities which give value to a brood-mare is also ccnstantly made apparent." See also "Narrative of Martha Jackson, b. 1850," *Alabama Narratives,* Federal Works Project, W. P. A. for the State of Alabama, 1939, in *Black Women in White America,* ed. Gerda Lerner (New York: Vintage Books, 1973), pp. 47–48.

17. Ruffin Diary, May 10, 1858; Richmond *South,* May 24, 1858; Takaki, pp. 27–29; Ruffin Diary, May 15 and 14, 1857.

18. Ibid., May 8, 10, 15, and 16, 1858.

19. John Witherspoon DuBose, *The Life and Times of William Lowndes Yancey* (Birmingham, Alabama: Roberts & Son, 1892), pp. 190–91, 318, 351; Richard O. Boyer, *The Legend of John Brown* (New York: Alfred A. Knopf, 1973), p. 538; Ruffin Diary, May 11 and 13, 1858.

20. Ruffin Diary, May 26 and 27, 1858; Wender, pp. 209–10; Rachleff, pp. 256–57.

21. Ruffin Diary, May 27, 1858; William Lowndes Yancey to James H. Slaughter, June 15, 1858, in the *Montgomery Advertiser and State Gazette,* June 25, 1858, and in the Richmond *Whig,* July 21, 1860.

22. Ruffin Diary, May 27, 1858.

23. Ibid., May 30, 1858, and November 11, 1857.

24. Ibid., May 31, 1858.

25. Rachleff, pp. 302–03; Laura A. White, *Robert Barnwell Rhett: Father of Secession* (New York: The Century Company, 1931), pp. 146–47; Ruffin Diary, July 3 and 6, 1858.

26. Shanks, pp. 62–63; Richmond *South,* July 31, 1858; Ruffin Diary, August 11, 1858.

27. Ruffin Diary, August 16, 1858; James Henry Hammond to Edmund Ruffin, August 17, 1858, Ruffin Papers.

28. Ruffin Diary, August 14, 16, and 28, 1858.

29. Ibid., August 14 and 16, 1858.

30. Ibid., August 18, September 12, and November 30, 1858; January 5, 1859.

31. Ibid., "Introduction," 1856.

32. Ibid., May 22, 1860; August 19, 1864; November 26, 1860; and April 9, 1857.

33. Ibid., April 22, 1859, and March 14, 1858.

34. Ibid., February 1 and 18, 1859.

35. Ibid., September 7, 1857, and January 6, 1858.

36. Ibid., August 27, 1859.

37. Ibid., June 20 and January 18, 1859; March 27, 1857; June 24, 1864; June 20, 1858. Drew Gilpin Faust found that Ruffin's admiration for a man like Italy's freedom fighter, Giuseppe Garibaldi, was characteristic of all the members of the "sacred circle." "The members of the network seem to have had a peculiar interest in the figure of the partisan, the individual able to use his distance and isolation from society to make a significant impact upon it," Faust noted. "Perhaps the partisan appeared as a kind of military analogue of the role they themselves hoped to play." See Faust, p. 76.

38. Ruffin Diary, August 13, 1857; October 3 and 20, 1858; May 14, 1863; and March 4, 1864.

39. Ibid., November 11, 1857; see also Scarborough, *Diary of Edmund Ruffin,* I, Apendix B.

40. Ruffin Diary, January 4, 1859.

41. Ibid., January 15 and 16, 1859, and November 14, 1857.

42. Ibid., January 16, 1859; Stephen A. Channing, *Crisis of Fear: Secession in South Carolina* (New York: Simon and Schuster, 1970), p. 150; Ruffin Diary, April 26, 1859.

43. Ruffin Diary, December 27 and February 13, 1858, and January 29, 1859.

44. Ibid., January 8, 1858; January 19, 1860; and March 11, 1858.

45. Ibid., March 3, 1860, and August 5, 1858.

46. Ibid., May 27, 1859.

47. Ibid., May 28, 1859; Shanks, p. 66.

48. Edmund Ruffin, "Cassandra's Warnings," Charleston *Mercury*, July 21, 1859.

49. Ruffin Diary, August 22 and 29, 1859, and July 30, 1850.

10. The Approaching Storm

1. Ruffin Diary, October 19, 1859.

2. Charleston *Mercury*, November 3, 1859; Richmond *Enquirer*, October 25, 1859.

3. Oates, *To Purge This Land With Blood*, pp. 320–21; Shanks, pp. 86–89.

4. Oates, *To Purge This Land With Blood*, pp. 321–23; Craven, *Edmund Ruffin*, pp. 180–81.

5. Ruffin Diary, December 23, 1859; Richmond *Enquirer*, December 26, 9, 20, and 23, 1859; Richmond *Whig*, November 22 and December 16, 1859.

6. Oswald Garrison Villard, *John Brown, 1800–1859: A Biography Fifty Years After* (New York, 1943), pp. 566–67, in Oates, *To Purge This Land With Blood*, p. 323; Portsmouth *Transcript*, quoted in the Richmond *Whig*, November 22, 1859; John Tyler, *Letters and Times of John Tyler*, II, 55, in Shanks, p. 89; Richmond *Whig*, December 10, 1859.

7. Ruffin Diary, October 26, 1859.

8. Mitchell, "Massachusetts Reacts to John Brown's Raid," pp. 65–79.

9. Ruffin Diary, October 24 and November 10, 1859; Charleston *Mercury*, November 5, 1859; Ruffin Diary, November 27, 1859. Five months after Brown's execution, Ruffin was still searching newspapers and journals for evidence of Northern approval of the Harper's Ferry invasion. On May 15, 1860, he read the proceedings of several antislavery societies and was certain that he had found "direct recommendations of negro insurrection, and approval of John Brown's attempt." See Ruffin Diary, May 15, 1860. It is likely, though, that Ruffin confused abolitionist sympathy and admiration for Brown's noble antislavery ideals with approval of his violent tactics. For more on this, see Mitchell, "Massachusetts Reacts to John Brown's Raid," pp. 65–79.

10. Mitchell, "Massachusetts Reacts to John Brown's Raid," pp. 65–66; Shanks, p. 88; Ruffin Diary, October 26, 1859.

11. Ruffin Diary, November 10, 16, and 18, 1859.

12. Channing, pp. 20–23, 38; Ruffin Diary, October 26, 1859; January 12, 1850; and November 13 and 21, 1859. The fire broke out at Charles Ruffin's Prince George plantation. Again the circumstances were suspicious. This was the fifth fire to occur in a family plantation in as many years. After this, Ruffin stopped denying the probable guilt of his slaves but pointed out that there had been no such "accidents" in the forty-four years he ran a plantation. See Ruffin Diary, November 13, 1859.

13. Ruffin Diary, November 19, 24, and 25, 1859.

14. Ibid., November 24, 1859.

15. Ibid., November 16, 1859.

16. Ibid., November 27 and December 17, 1859.

17. Ibid., December 1 and 17, 1859.

18. Ibid., December 1, 1859; New York *Herald*, December 6, 1859; Ruffin Diary, December 6 and 9, 1859.

19. Ruffin Diary, November 27, 1859.

20. Nichols, p. 267; Ruffin Diary, November 27 and 29, 1859.

21. Ruffin Diary, November 30 and December 1, 1859.

22. Ibid., November 27, 1859.

23. Ibid., November 28 and 30 and December 1, 1859.

24. Ibid., December 2, 1859; Virginia Military Institute Cadets to Edmund Ruffin, January 18, 1860, Ruffin Papers; W. G. Paxton to Edmund Ruffin, January 30, 1860, Ruffin Papers. Ruffin accepted his honorary Virginia Military Institute membership and sent the cadets two of his agricultural essays and a personal photograph to show his appreciation.

25. Ruffin Diary, December 2 and 7, 1859.

26. Oates, *To Purge This Land With Blood,* p. 359; Ruffin Diary, December 7, 1859.

27. Ruffin Diary, December 8 and 9, 1859; Oates, *To Purge This Land With Blood,* p. 359; Ruffin Diary, December 17, 1859.

28. Ruffin Diary, December 8 and 31, 1859.

29. Richmond *Enquirer,* December 4, 1859.

30. Ruffin Diary, December 10, 1859; Richmond *Enquirer,* December 4, 1859; Edmund Ruffin to William H. Gist, Governor of South Carolina, December 16, 1859, in Ruffin Diary.

31. Ruffin Diary, December 11 and 21, 1859; Edmund Ruffin, "Subversion of Negro Slavery, or the Dissolution of the Present Union, the Only Alternatives for the South," Virginia *Index,* January, 1860, appended to Ruffin Diary.

32. Ruffin Diary, December 31, 1859; January 5, 1860; December 17 and 10, 1859.

33. Ibid., December 16 and 21, 1859.

34. Ibid., December 31, 1859.

35. Channing, pp. 117–20, 17–18; Ruffin Diary, January 13, 1860. Ruffin called on the commissioner from South Carolina, Christopher G. Memminger, at his Richmond hotel in February, 1860. He advised Memminger that although he personally was a "political outlaw" whose opinions "were worth but little," he believed that Virginia would secede from the Union if only another state—like South Carolina—would lead the way.

36. John Bachman to Edmund Ruffin, January 18, 1860, Ruffin Papers.

37. Nichols, pp. 279–80; Craven, *The Coming of the Civil War,* pp. 413–15.

38. Ruffin Diary, January 21, 1860 and February 14 and 17, 1860.

39. Ibid., February 29, 1860.

40. Edmund Ruffin, *Anticipations of the Future to Serve as Lessons for the Present Time* (Richmond: J. W. Randolph, 1860), pp. 1, 6–7. When Ruffin learned of Lincoln's nomination, he altered his story to conform with the new facts: Lincoln would be the victor in November, 1860, and Seward would follow him in 1864. In the Preface, Ruffin explained that his main propositions would hold true, no matter if "the wily, able and prominent Seward, or the obscure and coarse Lincoln" were the first or second Republican President.

41. Ibid., pp. 37–39.

42. Ibid., pp. 55–56.

43. Ibid., pp. 53, 82–85.

44. Ibid., pp. 242–51.

45. Ibid., pp. 251, 267.

46. Ruffin Diary, January 19 and 21, 1861.

47. Bruce Catton, *The Coming Fury* (New York: Doubleday, 1961), pp. 34–35; Ruffin Diary, May 2 and 4, 1860. On May 11, 1860, Ruffin learned that a new political party—made up mostly of die-hard Whigs from the border states and calling itself the Constitutional Union Party—had met in Baltimore and nominated John Bell of Tennessee for President. The new party had no substantial platform beyond what its name implied.

For a detailed account of Yancey's role at the Charleston Democratic Convention of 1860, see Rachleff, p. 296–311. In the fall of 1860, Yancey toured the North and the South, denying that he personally was a disunionist and speaking in favor of Breckinridge for President. Ruffin was peeved at Yancey's moderate rhetoric, and this prompted the letter begging Yancey to become a Patrick Henry for secession. See Rachleff, p. 325.

48. Ruffin Diary, May 21, 1860; John Bachman to Edmund Ruffin, May 23, 1860, Ruffin Papers.

49. Ruffin Diary, May 29 and 30, 1860.

50. Ibid., May 31, 1860.

51. Ibid., June 12 and 13, 1860. While he was in Washington, D. C., Ruffin picked up the fifteen John Brown pikes he had ordered from Harper's Ferry. The weapons came to the home of Alabama Senator Clement C. Clay, who kept them in his parlor. Mrs. Clay thought they were meant for some "decorative purpose." See *A Belle of the Fifties: Memoirs of Mrs. Clay of Alabama*, ed. Ada Sterling (New York: Doubleday, Page & Company, 1905), pp. 145–46. Ruffin collected his spears and handed them out to Southern delegates who were headed for the convention in Baltimore. He instructed the delegates to carry them back to their respective state legislatures. At the last minute, he withheld the Delaware pike, because he "doubted whether the gift would be appreciated." Instead he presented the pike to his host, Senator Clay, as a personal gift. See Ruffin Diary, June 25, 1860.

52. Ruffin Diary, June 19 and June 22, 1860.

53. Ibid., July 17, 1860; September 30, 1859; and June 8, 1863. Mildred's baby died less than a month after its birth.

54. Ibid., August 12, 16, and 25, 1860.

55. Ibid., August 29, 1860.

56. Channing, pp. 236–37; Oates, *With Malice Toward None,* pp. 187–88.

57. Ruffin Diary, August 17, 1860, and October 27, 1860.

58. Ibid., September 5 and 11, 1860.

59. Ibid., September 6, 1860.

60. Ibid., September 7, 1860.

61. Ibid., September 13, 1860.

62. Richmond *Whig,* October 18 and October 19, 1860.

63. Ruffin Diary, October 24, 1860; Edmund Ruffin, "The Sinews of War," Charleston *Mercury,* October [?], 1860, appended to Ruffin Diary; Edmund Ruffin, "What South Carolina Should Do Now," Charleston *Mercury,* October, [?], 1860, appended to Ruffin Diary.

64. Robert Barnwell Rhett to Edmund Ruffin, October 20, 1860, Ruffin Papers; Ruffin Diary, October 17, 1860.

65. Ruffin Diary, October 29, 1860; Edmund Ruffin to William Lowndes Yancey, October 29, 1860, appended to Ruffin Diary.

66. Ruffin Diary, November 2, 1860; Edmund Ruffin to William Lowndes Yancey, October 29, 1860, appended to Ruffin Diary; Ruffin Diary, November 1, 1860. At first, Ruffin did not intend to vote at all in the 1860 election, because Brecken-

ridge did not come up to his standard of what a Southern candidate should be. He changed his mind and voted, in order, he said, to avoid the "disgrace" of Virginia's giving a plurality to John Bell. Bell received the plurality anyway.

67. Ruffin Diary, October 26 and 31, 1860.
68. Ibid., November 3, 1860.
69. Ibid., November 5, 1860.

11. Striking the First Blow

1. Ruffin Diary, November 6, 1860.
2. Ibid., November 7, 1860. During his train ride to South Carolina, Ruffin handed out more than two hundred copies of a pamphlet entitled "The South Alone Should Govern the South and African Slavery Should be Controlled by Those Only Who are Friendly to It."
3. Ruffin Diary, November 7, 1860, Library of Congress; W. A. Swanberg, *First Blood: The Story of Fort Sumter* (New York: Charles Scribner's Sons, 1957), p. 16.
4. Ruffin Diary, November 7, 1860; Charleston *Mercury,* November [7], 1860; Charleston *Courier,* November [7], 1860; Edmund Ruffin to Edmund Ruffin, Jr. and Julian C. Ruffin, November 11, 1860, Ruffin Papers; Edmund Ruffin, "What Would a Seceding Southern State Suffer From Northern Invasion and Open Warfare?" Charleston *Mercury,* November 6, 1860; Edmund Ruffin, "The Consequences of the Blockade of a Seceded State," Charleston *Mercury,* November 7, 1860.
5. White, p. 177.
6. Ruffin Diary, November 17 and 18, 1860; *Chicago Democrat,* November [?], 1860, in Ruffin Diary.
7. Ruffin Diary, November 12 and 8, 1860; Kate L. Bachman to Edmund Ruffin, April 18, 1861, in Ruffin Diary.
8. Ruffin Diary, November 8–10, 1860.
9. Ibid., November 10, 1860; White, pp. 101, 133, 135, 181.
10. Edmund Ruffin to Edmund Ruffin, Jr. and Julian C. Ruffin, November 11, 1860, Ruffin Papers; Edmund Ruffin, Jr. to Edmund Ruffin, November 16, 1860, Ruffin Papers.
11. Ruffin Diary, November 14 and 15, 1860.
12. Ibid., November 16, 1860; Edmund Ruffin, Speech in front of a Charleston crowd, November 16, 1860.
13. Ruffin Diary, November 11, 1860.
14. Ibid., November 21, 1860; Edmund Ruffin to Edmund Ruffin, Jr. and Julian C. Ruffin, November 11, 1860, Ruffin Papers.
15. Ruffin Diary, November 22, 27, and 30.
16. Shanks, pp. 120–26, 245–46; Richmond *Enquirer,* November 10, 1860; Ruffin Diary, December 2, 1860; W. H. I'Anson to Edmund Ruffin, November 28, 1860, Ruffin Papers.
17. W. H. I'Anson to Edmund Ruffin, November 28, 1860, Ruffin Papers; Ruffin Diary, December 14, 1860.
18. Swanberg, p. 78; *Journal of the Convention of the People of South Carolina, Held in 1860–1861,* pp. 3–5.
19. Ruffin Diary, December 18–20, 1860; Catton, *The Coming Fury,* p. 132; *A History of South Carolina,* ed. Yates Snowden (New York, 1933), pp. 663–64, in Swanberg, p. 80.

20. Ruffin Diary, December 20, 1860; Swanberg, pp. 78–80; Catton, *The Coming Fury,* pp. 132–36; John G. Nicolay and John Hay, *Abraham Lincoln: A History,* ed. Paul M. Angle (1890; rpt. Chicago: University of Chicago Press, 1966), pp. 41–42. Not every South Carolinian rejoiced at the news of secession. Prominent Charleston lawyer and judge James L. Petigru was a staunch unionist. "South Carolina is too small for a republic," he once said, "and too big for a lunatic asylum." See Abner Doubleday, *Reminiscences of Forts Sumter and Moultrie in 1860–61* (New York: Harper & Brothers, 1876), p. 56, in Swanberg, p. 80.

21. *Frank Leslie's Illustrated Newspaper,* February 2, 1861.

22. Catton, *The Coming Fury,* pp. 156–66; Swanberg, pp. 83, 94–95.

23. Ruffin Diary, December 27, 1860, and January 2, 1861.

24. Ibid., January 13, 1861; Swanberg, pp. 134, 203.

25. Ruffin Diary, January 31, 1861; December 13, 1860; February 25, 1861.

26. Ibid., January 17 and February 4, 1861; Shanks, pp. 153–56; Ruffin Diary, February 8 and 12, 1861.

27. Ruffin Diary, February 4, 8, and 18, 1861. After three weeks of meetings, the Peace Congress finally agreed on a watered-down version of the Crittenden Compromise, a plan that had already failed in the Senate. The essential outlines of the proposal called for a more stringent fugitive slave code, a thirteenth amendment to the Constitution forbidding federal interference with slavery in the states where it existed, and an extension of the old Missouri Compromise line from ocean to ocean. Lincoln was willing to bend on the first two items but instructed Republicans in Congress not to give an inch on the last. Many Southerners also found the compromise terms unacceptable.

28. Ibid., February 15, 13, and 15, 1861; Shanks, pp. 142–45; Ruffin Diary, February 27, 1861.

29. Ruffin Diary, March 4, 1861; Oates, *With Malice Toward None,* pp. 218–19; Ruffin Diary, March 4, 1861. Neither the Senate, the House of Representatives, nor the Peace Congress, which met unofficially in Washington, could come up with acceptable peace terms. Lincoln was willing to offer some concessions to the South: he publicly endorsed an unamendable amendment to the Constitution which would have protected slavery forever in the states where it already existed. But he would not compromise on slavery's expansion into federal territories. "Let there be no compromise on the question of extending slavery," he instructed Republican congressmen.

30. Mildred Ruffin Sayre to Edmund Ruffin, January 21, 1861, Ruffin Papers; Ruffin Diary, April 2, 1861; Swanberg, p. 286.

31. Ruffin Diary, April 5–8, 1861; Charleston *Courier,* April 11, 1861.

32. Ruffin Diary, April 9–11, 1861.

33. Ibid., April 9 and 11, 1861; Swanberg, pp. 291–96.

34. Ruffin Diary, April 11, 1861. When Ruffin enlisted as a volunteer in the Palmetto Guards, he stipulated that he must be allowed to terminate his enlistment at his own discretion. He would set these same terms whenever he joined the Rebel army in the future. Since his value as a soldier was more symbolic than real, Confederate officers were glad to oblige him.

35. Ruffin Diary, April 12, 1861; *Battles and Leaders of the Civil War,* eds. Clarence C. Buel and Robert U. Johnson (4 vols.; New York: The Century Company, 1884–1887), I, 76; Charleston *Courier,* April 15, 1861.

36. Ruffin Diary, April 12, 1861; Doubleday, pp. 143–44.

37. Ruffin Diary, April 12, 1861.

38. Ibid., April 13 and 16, 1861; *Frank Leslie's Illustrated Newspaper,* April 27, 1861.

39. Ruffin Diary, April 14, 1861; Swanberg, pp. 326–32.

40. Ruffin Diary, April 15, 1861; General Stephen D. Lee and Julian M. Ruffin, "The First Gun at Fort Sumter," *Southern Historical Society Papers,* 24 (Richmond, 1896), 114; Charleston *Courier,* April 13, 1861.

41. Craven, *Edmund Ruffin,* p. 218; Ruffin Diary, May 3, 1861; New York *Post,* April [?], 1861, in Ruffin Diary; Ruffin Diary, April 28, 1861.

42. Ruffin Diary, May 13, 1861; Jefferson Davis to Edmund Ruffin, April 22, 1861, in Ruffin Diary.

43. E. H. Tracy to Edmund Ruffin, April 15, 1861, in Ruffin Diary.

44. Lee and Ruffin, "The First Gun," p. 114.

45. Edmund Ruffin, Jr. to Edmund Ruffin, April 18, 1861, Ruffin Papers.

46. Ruffin Diary, April 15, 18, and 19, 1861.

12. Once More into the Fray

1. Ruffin Diary, April 22, 23, 25, and 26, 1861.

2. "Ruffin, the Secessionist," Unidentified Northern newspaper article, Ruffin Diary. Although this Northern newspaper article is not identified or dated, Ruffin copied it into his diary, immediately following a description of his role at Fort Sumter in April, 1861.

3. Ruffin Diary, May 4, 1861; Richmond *Examiner,* May 20, 1861, Library of Congress; Ruffin Diary, May 16, 1861 and February 6, 1862.

4. Ruffin Diary, May 4, 1861.

5. Ibid., May 4 and 24, 1861.

6. Ibid., May 9, 11, 3, 4, and 15, 1861.

7. Ibid., May 20, 22, 9, and 17, 1861.

8. Elizabeth Ruffin Sayre to Edmund Ruffin, July 14, 1860, Ruffin Papers; Edmund Ruffin to Elizabeth Ruffin Sayre, July 20, 1861, Ruffin Papers; Charles Ruffin to Edmund Ruffin, February 17, 1861, Ruffin Papers; Ruffin Diary, May 29, 1861.

9. Ruffin Diary, May 28 and 30, 1861.

10. Edmund Ruffin, "Fidelity of Slaves to Their Masters," *DeBow's Review,* 3 (January, 1861), 118–20. For more information on the conduct of Virginians and the behavior of their slaves during the American Revolution and the War of 1812, see Herbert Aptheker, *American Negro Slave Revolts* (New York: International Publishers, 1963) and *The Negro in the American Revolution* (New York: International Publishers, 1940); Benjamin Quarles, *The Negro in the American Revolution* (Chapel Hill: University of North Carolina Press, 1961); and Robert McColley, *Slavery and Jeffersonian Virginia* (Urbana: University of Illinois Press, 1964).

11. Ruffin Diary, February 26, 1861. Even before the Nat Turner uprising, few Southerners relied on the loyalty of their slaves to hold the system intact. "Were *fidelity* the only security we enjoyed," said one slaveholder, "deplorable indeed would be our situation. The fear of punishment is the principle to which we must and do appeal, to keep them in awe and order." See the *Southern Patriot,* February 10, 1826, quoted in Freehling, p. 66.

12. Ruffin Diary, May 26, 1861.

13. Ibid., January 14, 1862; William L. Barney, *Flawed Victory: A New Perspective on the Civil War* (New York: Praeger, 1975), p. 86.

14. "Hellish Suggestions," *Westchester Democrat* (Pennsylvania), April [?], 1861, in Ruffin Diary.

15. "The Character of the Coming Campaign," New York *Herald,* May [?], 1861, in Ruffin Diary.

16. Ruffin Diary, June 16, 1861.

17. Catton, *The Coming Fury,* pp. 443–44; Ruffin Diary, May 27, 1861.

18. Ruffin Diary, May 31 and June 25, 1861.

19. Ibid., July 1–3, 1861.

20. Ibid., July 7 and 8, 1861.

21. Ibid., July 8, 1861.

22. Ibid., July 15 and 20, 1861.

23. Ibid., July 20, 1861.

24. Charleston *Mercury,* July [?], 1861, in Ruffin Diary.

25. Ruffin Diary, July 20, 1861; Catton, *The Coming Fury,* pp. 451–52.

26. Ruffin Diary, July 20 and 23, 1861.

27. Ibid., July 23, 1861; Catton, *The Coming Fury,* p. 463.

28. Ruffin Diary, July 23, 1861. Ruffin was not the only one that day to believe mistakenly that Confederate forces had been defeated. Both President Jefferson Davis, who had come up from Richmond, and Captain Edward Porter Alexander of the Confederate Corps of Engineers saw so many stragglers at the rear of the army that they also got the wrong impression. Alexander later wrote that he would have concluded that the Rebel army had lost the battle of Bull Run if he had not just seen them winning. See Catton, *The Coming Fury,* p. 243.

29. Ruffin Diary, July 23, 1861.

30. Mildred Ruffin Sayre to Edmund Ruffin, July 29, 1861, Ruffin Papers; Ruffin Diary, July 23, 1861; "The Battle of Manassas," Official Report of Colonel Kenshaw, Vienna, Virginia, July 26, 1861, quoted in Ruffin Diary; Catton, *The Coming Fury,* pp. 462–67; Bruce Catton, *The Civil War* (New York: American Heritage Press, 1971), pp. 46–48.

31. Ruffin Diary, July 23, 1861.

32. Ruffin Diary, July 23, 1861; Ruffin Diary, September 24, 1863 and February 16, 1864. As late as 1864, Ruffin was still trying to determine exactly how many Yankee deaths he had caused at the Confederate victory at the first Bull Run.

33. Ruffin Diary, July 24, 29–31, 1861.

13. Fight or Flee

1. Ruffin Diary, August 1 and 28, and September 8, 1861.

2. Ibid., August 1, 17, and 1, 1861.

3. Ibid., August 1 and 11, and December 12, 1861.

4. Ibid., August 1 and September 30, 1861.

5. Ibid., December 8, 1860; January 8 and February 26, 1861.

6. Ibid., September 30, 1861; October 16 and 30, 1861; Julian C. Ruffin to Edmund Ruffin, December 13, 1861, Ruffin Papers; Edmund Ruffin, Jr. to Edmund Ruffin, February 18, 1862, Ruffin Papers.

7. Ruffin Diary, October 7, 1861.

8. Bruce Catton, *Terrible Swift Sword* (New York: Pocket Books, 1970), pp. 102–10; Clement Eaton, *A History of the Southern Confederacy* (New York: The Free Press, 1954), p. 70; Clement Eaton, *Jefferson Davis* (New York: The Free Press, 1977), pp. 168–69; Ruffin Diary, November 21, 1861.

9. Ruffin Diary, January 2 and 3, 1862.

10. Ibid., May 16, June 3, and December, 1861, passim; February 8 and 19, 1862.

11. Ibid., December 23, 1861.

12. Barney, *Flawed Victory*, p. 75; Catton, *The Civil War*, pp. 30–31; Ruffin Diary, September 1, May 16, and June 21, 1861.

13. Ibid., May 16 and June 3, 1861.

14. Ibid., December 11, 1861.

15. Ibid., February 21 and March 8, 1861.

16. Richmond *Dispatch*, November 5, 1861; Richmond *Whig*, November 5, 1861; Ruffin Diary, November 5 and December 2, 1861; February 6, April 2, and May 25, 1862; White, pp. 208–11, 211–23; Ruffin Diary, May 19, 1862.

17. Ruffin Diary, March 10 and 8, 1862.

18. Ibid., March 10, 1862; Edmund Ruffin, Jr. to Edmund Ruffin, February 18, 1862, Ruffin Papers; Ruffin Diary, April 8 and February 21, 1862.

19. Julian C. Ruffin to Edmund Ruffin, February 24, 1862, Ruffin Papers; Charlotte Meade Ruffin to Edmund Ruffin, February 24, 1862, Ruffin Papers; Ruffin Diary, March 11, 1862.

20. Thomas Smith Ruffin to his sister Anne Ruffin, April 13, 1862, Ruffin Papers; Edmund Ruffin, Jr. to his daughter Anne Ruffin, April 25, 1862, Ruffin Papers.

21. Ruffin Diary, June 5, 1862; Julian C. Ruffin to Edmund Ruffin, April 26, 1862, Ruffin Papers.

22. Charles L. Ruffin to Edmund Ruffin, October 7, 1861, Ruffin Papers; Ruffin Diary, May 21, 1862.

23. Ruffin Diary, August 23 and 26, 1861; Edmund Ruffin to Jefferson Davis, August 27, 1861, Ruffin Papers; Ruffin Diary, May 21, 1862.

24. Ruffin Diary, May 21, 1861; Edmund Ruffin to Captain George B. Cuthbert, May 12, 1862, Ruffin Papers; Ruffin Diary, May 29, 1861. For more on Ruffin's opinion on how the Confederate government ought to treat deserters, see Ruffin Diary, December 12, 1863 and September 29, 1864.

25. Ruffin Diary, April 28 and 30, 1862.

26. Ibid., May 1, 1862.

27. Ibid.

28. Ibid., April 18 and May 7 and 12, 1862.

29. Ibid., April 18 and May 7, 10, and 11, 1862.

30. Ibid., May 3 and 13, April 13, and May 15, 1862.

31. Ibid., May 19, 22–24, and 28, 1862.

32. Ibid., May 31, 1862.

33. Ibid., June 1, 1862; Charleston *Courier*, June [?], 1862, quoted in Ruffin Diary, November 15, 1863. Ruffin's cursory body count at the battle of Seven Pines was incorrect. Actual figures showed that Confederate dead outnumbered Union dead. See Catton, *Terrible Swift Sword*, p. 297.

34. Ruffin Diary, June 1, 1862; January 20, 1863; and June 3, 1862.

35. Ibid., May 25, June 10 and 11, and July 4, 1862.

36. Ibid., May 26, 1862; Julian C. Ruffin to Edmund Ruffin, May 27, 1862, Ruffin Papers. Even with his slaves in "quiet rebellion," William Sayre was so scared of falling into Yankee hands himself that he abandoned Mrs. Lee and her daughters and fled the plantation, entrusting the keys to all the buildings to his rebellious blacks.

37. Ruffin Diary, May 20, 1862; Jane M. (Ruffin) Ruffin to Edmund Ruffin, May 24, 1862, Ruffin Papers; Ruffin Diary, May 29 and June 11, 1862.

38. Ibid., June 12, 23 and 18, 1862.

39. Ibid., June 30, 1862.

40. Ruffin Diary, July 4 and October 29, 1862.

41. Ibid., July 4 and 7, 1862 and November 29, 1862.

42. Ibid., July 1, 1862; Catton, *Terrible Swift Sword,* pp. 308–20.

43. Ruffin Diary, July 1, 1862.

44. Ibid., July 1–4, 1862.

45. Ibid., July 8 and 21, 1862.

46. Ibid., July 22 and 29, 1862.

47. Ibid., July 31, August 1–3, and September 16, 1862.

14. Warfare of Extermination

1. Unidentified Richmond newspaper, August [?], 1862, quoted in Ruffin Diary, August 22, 1862.

2. Letter found on the dead body of a Union soldier after the second battle of Bull Run, written to his brother and sister, August 11, 1862, in Ruffin Diary; letter taken from the haversack of another dead Union soldier after the second battle of Bull Run, to his sister Mollie, August 22, 1862, quoted in Ruffin Diary, February 12, 1863.

3. Ruffin Diary, August 17, 1862.

4. Ibid., August 17 and 20, 1862; Unidentified Richmond newspaper, August [?], 1862, quoted in Ruffin Diary, August 22, 1862; Ruffin Diary, August 17, 1862.

5. Ibid., August 18 and 22, 1862. The one hundred fifty thousand dollars represented losses from Beechwood, Marlbourne, and Evelynton combined.

6. Ibid., August 23, 1862.

7. Ibid., June 19, April 2, and July 21, 1862.

8. Ibid., June 12, July 21, and August 23, 1862. Ruffin urged that the Confederate raiders foment class revolution in each Northern city by sending out an advance proclamation that read: "Peace to friends, & to the poor—war and ruin to enemies, & especially to the wealthy." This by itself, predicted Ruffin, would be sufficient to start a servile rebellion in the North. He was certain that hundreds of destitute white free laborers would flock to join their slaveowning "liberators." Ruffin suggested that Confederates organize these Northern "fugitives" into raiding parties and then send them out with instructions to rob the rich and bring their plunder back to fill Southern coffers.

9. Catton, *The Civil War,* pp. 85–99.

10. Ruffin Diary, September 25 and November 6, 1862; March 30, 1863; and November 4, 1862.

11. Ibid., September 28, 1862; Oates, *With Malice Toward None,* p. 319.

12. Ruffin Diary, October 1, 1862; Barney, *Flawed Victory,* p. 87.

13. Ruffin Diary, August 14, 1861; April 11, July 28, and September 28, 1862. Only a few weeks after Fort Sumter, Ruffin read an article in *Harper's Weekly* that he took to be a statement of Northern intentions to free the slaves. "If the South expect that our gallant volunteers are going to hunt the slaves that may run away as they approach, they labor under a delusion," the magazine had warned. "Whatever may be the intentions of the government, the practical effect of a war in the Southern States, waged by Northern against Southern men, must be to liberate the slaves." See *Harper's Weekly* clipping in Ruffin Diary.

14. Ruffin Diary, October 14 and 1, 1862.

15. Ibid., October 1, 1862; Barney, *Flawed Victory*, p. 87. On January 7, 1863, after Ruffin read that Lincoln had, as promised, issued enancipation proclamation, he reiterated his belief that the document would have a salutary effect on the Confederacy. The Richmond *Examiner* and the Richmond *Whig* echoed similar sentiments, with the *Whig* referring disdainfully to the proclamation as Lincoln's "Latest 'Bull.' " See Ruffin Diary, January 7, 1863; Richmond *Examiner,* January 7, 1863; Richmond *Whig,* January 7, 1863.

Ruffin realized early in the war that there was a split in the Republican ranks over emancipation. Lincoln and those men Ruffin labeled "moderate" abolitionists favored *"union"* as the sole object and purpose of the Civil War. A minority of "rabid" abolitionists, Ruffin said, favored *"general emancipation"* of all the slaves. Ruffin hoped that the latter group would "carry the victory." In the long run, he figured that a harsh Northern emancipation policy would work to the Confederacy's advantage. See Ruffin Diary, December 16, 1861; January 15 and 16, and February 15, 1862.

16. Ibid., October 1, 1862; Oates, *With Malice Toward None,* pp. 320–21; Ruffin Diary, February 28, 1862. This letter, written in 1861, was from a Massachusetts soldier, who Ruffin thought was "doubtless" a "thorough abolitionist" before he came South. Ruffin predicted that thousands of Union soldiers would be similarly "cured" of this kind of hypothetical antislavery sentiment after they had come in actual contact with Southern slaves. Most Yankees would go home after the war, he said, hating the slaves, not the slaveowners. See Ruffin Diary, February 28 and March 27, 1863.

17. Ibid., October 16, 1862, and March 13 and 17, 1863.

18. New York *Evening Post,* in Ruffin Diary, December 3, 1862.

19. Ruffin Diary, October 16, 1862. On April 23, 1863, when Ruffin read that the Lincoln government had persuaded two boatloads of fugitive slaves to settle in Haiti, he insisted that the Yankee captains really intended to land in Cuba or Puerto Rico, where they would sell these would-be colonists back into bondage.

20. Ibid., October 28 and February 2, 1862.

21. Ibid., March 4, 1863; August 15, 1862; and February 28, 1863.

22. Ruffin Diary, March 4, 1863, and November 22, 1862.

23. Ibid., August 16 and 29, 1862; January 26 and April 24, 1863. Although Ruffin favored an offensive–defensive alliance with the Northwest, he would not have allowed any of those free states to join the Southern Confederacy until they adopted proslavery constitutions. He would not actually have required that the people of the Northwest own any slaves, just that their laws demonstrate that they were not abolitionists. Besides, Ruffin believed that blacks would make valuable fieldhands in the Southern portions of the Northwest and excellent domestic servants throughout the area. Once antislavery laws were off the books in these states, he predicted, slaves would be "sought for by the thousands."

Ruffin was also anxious to gain French recognition and support for the Confederacy. In exchange, he was willing to offer France free trade advantages with the Confederate nation and allow the French emperor Louis Napoleon to conquer Mexico. See Ruffin Diary, August 30, 1862, and July 18 and 21, 1863.

24. Ibid., November 8, 1862; January 1, 1863; and August 15, 1862.

25. Ibid., February 8, 1863.

26. Ibid., February 6, 1863, and September 2, 1862; Carl N. Degler, *The Other South* (New York: Harper & Row, 1974), pp. 143–46; Eaton, *Growth of Southern*

Civilization, p. 269. The right to free speech and free press was guaranteed under the Confederate Constitution. See Emory M. Thomas, *The Confederate Nation: 1861–1865* (New York: Harper & Row, 1979).

27. Ruffin Diary, January 1 and 26, 1863.

28. Ibid., January 5, 1863.

29. Ibid.

30. Ibid., January 6, 1863.

31. Agnes Ruffin Beckwith to Edmund Ruffin, January 9, 1863, Ruffin Papers; Agnes Ruffin Beckwith to Edmund Ruffin, January 21, 1863, Ruffin Papers; Edmund Ruffin to Agnes Ruffin Beckwith, January 26, 1863, Ruffin Papers; Ruffin Diary, January 29, 1863. Ruffin's curt reply is appended to his daughter Agnes's letter; Agnes Ruffin Beckwith to Edmund Ruffin, January 9, 1863, Ruffin Papers.

32. Ruffin Diary, January 20, 1863.

33. Ibid.

34. Ibid., March 20, 1863.

35. Ruffin Diary, March 9 and 25 and April 11, 1863.

36. Ibid., April 11, 1863, and October 23, 1862.

37. Ibid., January 23, 1863, and June 4, 1864. The original quotation reads: "It is contradictory to negro nature to be loyal to a copartnership of five individuals." Evidently Ruffin was referring to his original plan, which did not include his son-in-law William Sayre, whom he later made a full partner in Marlbourne along with his five children.

38. Ibid., January 23, 1863.

39. Ibid., April 11, 1863.

40. Ibid., May 4, 1863.

41. Ibid., May 5, 1863.

42. Ibid., May 8 and April 3, 1863.

43. Ibid., April 24 and June 5, 1863.

44. Ibid., November 6, 1862.

45. Eaton, *History of the Southern Confederacy,* pp. 191–93.

46. Ruffin Diary, June 5, 1863.

47. Ibid., July 6, 11, and 29, 1863.

48. Ibid., July 29, 1863; Barney, *Flawed Victory,* pp. 35–36; Ruffin Diary, June 4 and December 15, 1862; January 3, 1864; and December 31, 1863; Edmund Ruffin, Jr. to Edmund Ruffin, March 5, 1864, Ruffin Papers; Ruffin Diary, May 27, 1864.

49. James M. McPherson, *The Negro's Civil War* (New York: Vintage Books, 1965), p. 174; Benjamin Quarles, *The Negro in the Civil War* (Boston: Little, Brown and Company, 1953), pp. 206–07; Barney, *Flawed Victory,* pp. 88–89.

50. Ruffin Diary, September 26 and October 9, 1862; August 6, 1863; November 14, 1861; August 22, 1862; January 3 and 18, 1863; and February 11, 1864.

51. Ibid., May 30, 1863.

52. Quarles, *The Negro in the Civil War,* pp. 218–24, 3–21; McPherson, *The Negro's Civil War,* pp. 183–91; Ruffin Diary, June 12 and 17, 1863.

53. Ibid., August 1, 1863, and August 18, 1864.

54. McPherson, *The Negro's Civil War,* pp. 71–76; Ruffin Diary, July 18 and 20, 1863.

55. Ibid., July 20, 1863. Just one and a half years earlier, Ruffin had cut out an article quoting a sermon made by Northern evangelist and abolitionist George Barrell Cheever. Ruffin read the sermon and condemned Cheever for his supposed willingness to sacrifice human lives to the "Moloch of Anti-Slavery." "The slave-

owners being the prime movers in the rebellion, a price ought to have been set upon their heads," Cheever had said, "for if all the slaveowners were condemned to death, it was but carrying out what God had appointed to be done beforehand." See Ruffin Diary, January 9, 1862.

15. Superfluous Lags the Veteran on the Stage

1. Ruffin Diary, October 12, 1862.

2. Barney, *Flawed Victory,* pp. 108–11; Eaton, *A History of the Southern Confederacy,* pp. 224–34; Thomas H. O'Connor, *The Disunited States; The Era of Civil War and Reconstruction* (New York: Dodd, Mead & Company, 1973), pp. 185–86; Ruffin Diary, January 3 and 23 and February 28, 1862; March 17, 1863; February 8 and April 2, 1864; Catton, *The Civil War,* p. 182.

3. Ruffin Diary, April 2, 1863.

4. Ruffin Diary, April 2, 1863; October 14, 1862; and March 13, 1864.

5. Ibid., February 19, 1863.

6. Ibid., March 13 and October 27, 1864; Thomas Smith Ruffin to Edmund Ruffin, Jr., November 27, 1862, Ruffin Papers; Ruffin Diary, August 13, 1863.

7. Eaton, *A History of the Southern Confederacy,* p. 261; Ruffin Diary, September 29, 1864; May 19 and August 29, 1862; and April 11 and 17, 1863. In 1863, a Confederate soldier in Mississippi confessed, "I believe our troops are doing as much harm in this country as the Yankees would do with the exception of burning houses." In Barney, *Flawed Victory,* p. 41.

8. Ruffin Diary, October 1, 1862; February 19 and March 17, 1863; September 26, October 9, and December 12, 1862.

9. Ibid., July 16, 1863, and August 17, 1863.

10. Ibid., July 16 and August 22, 1863, and September 14, 1862.

11. Ibid., July and August, 1863, passim; September 14 and 18, 1863.

12. Ibid., September 23–25, 1863.

13. Ibid., September 29 and October 24, 1863.

14. Ibid., November 17, 1863.

15. Ibid., November 20, 1863, and December 10, 1863.

16. Ibid., December 31, 1863, and January 6, 1864.

17. Ibid., January 6, 1864, and March 31, 1864.

18. Ibid., March 31, February 4, and January 16, 1864.

19. Ibid., January 24, 1864; January 16, 1863; May 24 and January 17, 1864.

20. Sidney Kaplan, "The Miscegenation Issue in the Election of 1864," *Journal of Negro History,* 34 (July, 1949), pp. 284, 309; New Hampshire *Patriot,* quoted in Ruffin Diary, March 17, 1864; *New York Times,* quoted in Ruffin Diary, April 10, 1864.

21. Kaplan, "The Miscegenation Issue in the Election of 1864," pp. 274–373; Ruffin Diary, July 17, 1864.

22. Ruffin Diary, May 20, 1864.

23. Ibid., May 23, 1864.

24. Ibid., October 30 and July 20, 1864; Barney, *Flawed Victory,* pp. 136, 142–43.

25. Ruffin Diary, November 21, 1862.

26. Ibid., October 30, 1864.

27. Herbert G. Gutman, *The Black Family in Slavery and Freedom, 1750–1925,* pp. 267–69; Ruffin Diary, June 25, 1864; November 21, 1862; and October 30, 1864; Barney, *Flawed Victory,* pp. 147–50.

28. Ruffin Diary, April 21, 1864. See John Blassingame, *The Slave Community* (New York: Oxford University Press, 1972) for an excellent source on the slave family during antebellum times; also see Gutman, *The Black Family in Slavery and Freedom, 1750–1925.* Both these historians present convincing evidence of strong family ties among slaves.

29. Ruffin Diary, March 9 and April 14 and 19, 1864.

30. Ibid., April 21 and 27, 1864; August 15, 1863; June 8, 1864; and November 13, 1864.

31. Edmund Ruffin to Edmund Ruffin, Jr., May 17, 1864, in Ruffin Diary, May 17, 1864; Ruffin Diary, May 23, 24, and 26, 1864.

32. Ibid., May 27, 1864; New York *Herald,* May 31, 1864, in Ruffin Diary, June 15, 1864; Ruffin Diary, June 15, 1864.

33. Chicago *Commercial Times,* in Ruffin Diary, October 14, 1864.

34. Ruffin Diary, October 14, 1864.

35. Ibid., January 19 and February 25, 1864.

36. Ibid., May 3, 1864.

37. Catton, *The Civil War,* pp. 207–14; Eaton, *A History of the Southern Confederacy,* pp. 273–76; Bruce Catton, *A Stillness at Appomattox* (New York: Pocket Books, 1970), pp. 63–226.

38. Oates, *With Malice Toward None,* pp. 387–89, 394–95; Ruffin Diary, June 13, 1864.

39. Ruffin Diary, July 27 and September 3, 1864.

40. Ibid., July 27, 1864.

41. Ibid., October 14, 1864.

42. Ibid., October 11 and 31, 1864.

43. Ibid., November 16, 1864, and August 21, 1861.

44. Ibid., December 27, 1864.

45. Ibid., January 5, 1865.

46. Ibid., January 9, 1864, and February 23, 1865.

47. Barney, *Flawed Victory,* pp. 114–16; McPherson, *The Negro's Civil War,* pp. 241–44; Eaton, *A History of the Southern Confederacy,* pp. 264–65.

48. Ruffin Diary, October 29 and December 27, 1864.

49. Ibid., December 27, 1864; Richmond *Sentinel,* December [?], 1864, quoted in Barney, *Flawed Victory,* p. 117.

50. Ruffin Diary, February 13, 1865, and October 29 and February 18, 1864.

51. McPherson, *The Negro's Civil War,* p. 244; Eaton, *A History of the Southern Confederacy,* p. 265; Ruffin Diary, March 2, 1865. The "Negro Soldier Law" did not provide slave recruits with automatic emancipation after the war. Their freedom was conditional on the consent of their owners and of the states which furnished their services.

52. Ruffin Diary, April 3 and 17, 1865.

53. Ibid., April 12, 1865.

54. Ibid., April 18–20 and May 23, 1865.

55. Ibid., April 17 and 16, May 20, and June 16–18, 1865.

56. Ibid., April 20 and 25, 1865; Kenneth M. Stampp, *The Era of Reconstruction, 1865–1877* (New York: Vintage Books, 1965), pp. 54–59; Ruffin Diary, April 30 and June 5, 1865.

57. Ibid., May 6 and 19, 1865.

58. Ibid., March 10, June 5, and 16–18, and May 6, 1865.

59. Ibid., May 13, 1865.

60. Ibid., May and June, 1865, passim.
61. May 1, 9, 13, and 18, 1865.
62. Ibid., June 16–18, 1865.
63. Edmund Ruffin, Jr. to his sons, June 20, 1865, in "Death of Edmund Ruffin," *Tyler's Quarterly Historical and Genealogical Magazine,* 5 (January, 1924), 193; Ruffin Diary, June 16–18, 1865; Edmund Ruffin, Jr. to his sons, June 20, 1865, in "Death of Edmund Ruffin," p. 193–95. Ruffin's last diary entry reads June 18. But Ruffin died on a Saturday, according to his son Edmund, and the calendar of 1865 shows that June 17 was a Saturday. Evidently Ruffin had misdated his diary. He had complained once before that he was prone to make this kind of mistake.

According to Ellis, "Edmund Ruffin: His Life and Times," p. 122, Ruffin wrapped himself in the Confederate flag before he committed suicide. Phillips, in *The Course of the South to Secession,* p. 135, also makes this contention, probably on the basis of the Ellis article. But there is no evidence either in the Ruffin Diary or in the letter Edmund Ruffin, Jr., wrote to his sons describing Ruffin's death that the old man made this final dramatic gesture in behalf of the "lost cause."

SELECTED BIBLIOGRAPHY

PRIMARY SOURCES

Manuscripts

Campbell, David and Family. Papers. Duke University Library, Durham, North Carolina.

Chisolm, William Garnett. Papers. Virginia Historical Society. Richmond.

Cocke, Harrison Henry. Papers. University of North Carolina Library, Southern Historical Collection, Chapel Hill.

DeBow, James Dunwoody Brownson. Papers. Duke University Library, Durham, North Carolina.

Freeman, Mary Barry Martin. Papers. Tennessee State Library, Nashville.

Gooch Family. Papers. University of Virginia Library, Charlottesville.

Hammond, James Henry. Papers. Library of Congress, Washington, D.C.

Littleton Fitzgerald Papers. Virginia Historical Society, Richmond.

Marlbourne Farm Journal. Virginia State Library, Richmond.

Meade Family. Papers. University of North Carolina Library, Southern Historical Collection, Chapel Hill.

Perkins, John. Papers. University of North Carolina Library, Southern Historical Collection, Chapel Hill.

Ruffin, Edmund. Diary. Library of Congress, Washington, D.C.

_____. Papers. Virginia Historical Society, Richmond.

Tucker Family. Papers. Colonial Williamsburg Manuscript Collections, Williamsburg, Virginia.

Tucker–Coleman Papers. Colonial Williamsburg Manuscript Collections, Virginia State Library, Richmond.

Books

Armstrong, George D. *The Christian Doctrine of Slavery.* New York: C. Scribner, 1857.

Bledsoe, Albert T. *An Essay on Liberty and Slavery.* Philadelphia: Lippincott, 1856.

Brown, Edward. *Notes on the Origins and Necessity of Slavery.* Charleston: A. E. Miller, 1826.

Chesnut, Mary Boykin. *A Diary From Dixie.* Ed. Ben Ames Williams. Boston: Houghton Mifflin Company, 1961.

Cooper, Thomas. *On the Constitution of the United States, and Questions That Have Arisen Under It.* Columbia, South Carolina: D. & J. M. Faust, 1826.

Daniel, John Moncure. *The Richmond Examiner During the War; or, The Writings of John M. Daniel.* New York: Printed for John Moncure Daniel, 1868.

Dew, Thomas R. *Review of the Debate in the Virginia Legislature of 1831 and 1832.* Richmond: T. W. White, 1832.

Doubleday, Abner. *Reminiscences of Forts Sumter and Moultrie in 1860–'61.* New York: Harper & Brothers, 1876.

Felton, Rebecca Latimer. *Country Life in Georgia in the Days of My Youth.* Atlanta: Index Printing Company, 1919.

Fitzhugh, George. *Cannibals All! or Slaves Without Masters.* Richmond: A. Morris, 1857.

——————. *Sociology for the South; or, The Failure of Free Society.* Richmond: A. Morris, 1854.

Fletcher, John. *Studies on Slavery, in Easy Lessons.* Natchez, Mississippi: J. Warner, 1852.

Grimke, Angelina. *Appeal to the Christian Women of the South.* New York: American Anti-Slavery Society, 1836.

Grimke, Sarah M. *Letters on the Equality of the Sexes and the Condition of Women.* Boston: Isaac Knapp, 1838.

Helper, Hinton Rowan. *The Impending Crisis of the South; How to Meet It.* Ed. George M. Fredrickson. 1857; rpt. Cambridge, Mass.: Harvard University Press, 1968.

Hodgson, Joseph. *The Cradle of the Confederacy; or, The Times of Troup, Quitman, and Yancey.* Mobile: Register Publishing Office, 1876.

Holland, Edwin C. *A Refutation of the Calumnies Circulated Against the Southern and Western Slaves Respecting the Institution and Existence of Slavery Among Them.* Charleston: A. E. Miller, 1822.

Kettel, Thomas Prentice. *Southern Wealth and Northern Profits, As Exhibited in Statistical Facts and Official Figures: Showing the Necessity of Union to the Future Prosperity and Welfare of the Republic.* New York: G. W. & J. A. Wood, 1860.

Nicolay, John G. and John Hay. *Abraham Lincoln: A History.* Ed. Paul M. Angle. 1890; rpt. Chicago: University of Chicago, 1966.

Northup, Solomon. *Narrative of Solomon Northup, Twelve Years a Slave.* Auburn, New York: Derby and Miller, 1853.

Nott, Josiah C. and George R. Gliddon. *Types of Mankind.* London: Trubner and Company, 1854.

Nott, Samuel. *Slavery and the Remedy; or, Principles and Suggestions for a Remedial Code.* Boston: Crocker and Brewster, 1856.

Olmsted, Frederick Law. *The Cotton Kingdom: A Traveller's Observations on Cotton and Slavery in the American Slave States.* New York: Mason Brothers, 1861.

——————. *A Journey in the Seaboard Slave States.* New York: Mason Brothers, 1859.

——————. *The Slave States.* Ed. Harvey Wish. New York: Capricorn Books, 1959.

Priest, Josiah. *Bible Defence of Slavery; or the Origin, History, and Fortunes of the Negro Race.* Louisville, Kentucky: J. F. Brennan, 1851.

The Proslavery Argument; As Maintained by the Most Distinguished Writers of the Southern States: Containing the Several Essays, on the Subject, of Chancellor Harper, Governor Hammond, Dr. Simms, and Professor Dew. Philadelphia: Lippincott, Grambo, & Company, 1853.

Ruffin, Edmund. *Anticipations of the Future, to Serve as Lessons for the Present Time.* Richmond: J. W. Randolph, 1860.

_____. *An Essay on Calcareous Manures.* Petersburg, Virginia: J. W. Campbell, 1832.

_____. *Essays and Notes on Agriculture.* Richmond: J. W. Randolph, 1855.

_____. *Premium Essay on Agricultural Education.* 2nd ed. Richmond: J. W. Randolph, 1853.

Scarborough, William Kauffman (ed.). *The Diary of Edmund Ruffin.* Vol. I: *Toward Independence, October, 1856–April, 1861.* Baton Rouge: Louisiana State University Press, 1972.

Schopf, Johann David. *Travels in the Confederation, 1783–1784.* Philadelphia: W. J. Campbell, 1911.

Sterling, Ada (ed.). *A Belle of the Fifties: Memoirs of Mrs. Clay of Alabama.* New York: Doubleday, Page & Company, 1905.

Stringfellow, Thornton. *Scriptural and Statistical Views in Favor of Slavery.* Richmond: J. W. Randolph, 1856.

_____. *Slavery, Its Origin, Nature and History.* Alexandria, Virginia: Virginia Sentinel Office, 1860.

Taylor, John. *Arator; Being a Series of Agricultural Essays, Practical and Political: In Sixty-Four Numbers.* Petersburg, Virginia: Whitworth & Yancey, 1818.

Thornton, Reverend Thomas C. *An Inquiry Into the History of Slavery.* Washington, D.C.: W. M. Morrison, 1841.

Tucker, St. George. *A Dissertation on Slavery: With a Proposal for the Gradual Abolition of It in the State of Virginia.* Philadelphia: Printed for M. Carey, 1796.

Van Evrie, J. H. *Negroes and Negro 'Slavery': The First an Inferior Race, the Latter Its Normal Condition.* Washington, D.C.: C. Alexander, 1853.

_____. *White Supremacy and Negro Subordination; Or, Negroes as a Subordinate Race and (So Called) Slavery Its Normal Condition.* New York: Van Evrie, Horton & Company, 1861.

Government Documents: Federal and State

Reese, George H. (ed.). *Proceedings of the Virginia State Convention of 1861, February 13–May 1.* Richmond: Virginia State Library, 1965.

United States Bureau of Census. *Population Schedules of the Eighth Census of the United States, 1860: Virginia Slave Schedules.* Washington, D.C. The National Archives and Records Service General Services Administration, 1967.

United States Bureau of the Census. *Seventh Census of the United States: June 30, 1850.*

United States Bureau of the Census. *Census of Virginia: 1810.*

United States Bureau of the Census. *Census of Virginia: 1820.*

United States Congress. *Congressional Annals. The Debates and Proceedings in the Congress of the United States. Sixteenth Congress, First Session: December 6, 1819 to May 15, 1820.* Washington, D.C.: Gales and Seaton, 1855.

Collected Works

Ambler, Charles Henry (ed.). *Correspondence of Robert M. T. Hunter, 1826–1876.* New York: DeCapo Press, 1971.

Boucher, Chauncey S. and Robert P. Brooks (eds.). "Correspondence Addressed to John C. Calhoun, 1837–1849," *Annual Report of the American Historical Association for the Year 1929.* Washington, D.C.: Government Printing Office, 1930.

Carson, James Petigru. *Life, Letters and Speeches of James Louis Petigru, the Union Man of South Carolina.* Washington, D.C.: Lowdermilk & Company, 1920.

Hamilton, J. G. de Roulhac (ed.). *The Papers of Thomas Ruffin.* 4 vols. Raleigh, North Carolina: Raleigh, Edwards & Broughton Printing Company, State Printers, 1918–1920.

Jameson, J. Franklin (ed.). "The Correspondence of John C. Calhoun," *Annual Report of the American Historical Association for the Year 1899.* 2 vols. Washington, D.C.: Government Printing Office, 1900.

Lerner, Gerda (ed.). *Black Women in White America.* New York: Vintage Books, 1973.

McKitrick, Eric L. (ed.). *Slavery Defended: The Views of the Old South.* Englewood Cliffs, New Jersey: Prentice–Hall, 1963.

Osofsky, Gilbert. *Puttin' On Old Massa: The Slave Narratives of Henry Bibb, William Wells Brown, and Solomon Northup.* New York: Harper & Row, 1969.

Perkins, Howard Cecil (ed.). *Northern Editorials on Secession.* New York: D. Appleton–Century Company, Inc., 1942.

Phillips, Ulrich Bonnell (ed.). "The Correspondence of Robert Toombs, Alexander H. Stephens, and Howell Cobb," *Annual Report of the American Historical Association for the Year 1911.* 2 vols. Washington, D.C.: Government Printing Office, 1913.

Schwaab, Eugene L. (ed.). *Travels in the Old South.* Vol. 1. Lexington, Kentucky: University of Kentucky Press, 1973.

Yetman, Norman R. (ed.). *Life Under the Peculiar Institution: Selections From the Slave Narrative Collection.* New York: Holt, Rinehart and Company, 1970.

Newspapers

Charleston *Courier.*
Charleston *Daily Courier.*
Charleston *Mercury.*
Frank Leslie's *Illustrated Newspaper.*
Fredericksburg *News.*
Lynchburg *Republican.*
Lynchburg *Virginian.*
Montgomery *Advertiser.*

National Intelligencer.
New Orleans *Daily Crescent.*
Petersburg *Southside Democrat.*
Richmond *Dispatch.*
Richmond *Enquirer.*
Richmond *Examiner.*
Richmond *Whig.*
Williamsburg *Weekly Gazette.*

Periodicals

The African Repository.
The American Farmer.
The Bank Reformer.
DeBow's Review.
Farmers' Register.

Southern Literary Messenger.
Southern Magazine and Monthly Review.
Southern Planter.
Virginia Index.

Pamphlets and Articles

"Blind Tom," *Atlanta Monthly,* 10 (November, 1862), 580–85.

"Death of Edmund Ruffin," *Tyler's Quarterly Historical and Genealogical Magazine,* 5 (January, 1924), 193–95.

DeBow, James Dunwoody Brownson. *The Interest in Slavery of the Non-Slaveholder. The Right of Peaceful Secession. The Character and Influence of Abolitionism.* Charleston: Presses of Evans & Cogswell, 1860.

"Edwin Ruffin, of Virginia, Agriculturalist, Embracing a View of Agricultural Progress in Virginia for the Last Thirty Years," *DeBow's Review,* 11 (October, 1851), 431–36.

"Extracts From the Diary of Edmund Ruffin," *William and Mary College Quarterly,* 14 (January, 1906), 193–211; 20 (October, 1911), 69–101; 21 (January, 1913), 224–32; 22 (April, 1914), 258–62; 23 (July, 1914–April, 1915), 31–45, 154–71, 240–59.

Gaines, William H., Jr. *Biographical Register of Members, Virginia State Convention of 1861.* Richmond: Virginia State Library, 1969.

Harper, Chancellor. "Memoir on Slavery," *Southern Literary Journal* (February, 1838), pp. 1–97.

Lee, General Stephen D. and Julian M. Ruffin. "The First Gun at Fort Sumter— Who fired it?" *Southern Historical Society Papers,* 24 (Richmond, 1896), 111–15.

Ruffin, Edmund. *An Address on the Opposite Results of Exhausting and Fertilizing Systems of Agriculture.* Read Before the South Carolina Institute: At Its Fourth Annual Fair, November 18, 1852. Charleston: Press of Walker and James, 1853.

───────. *Address to the Virginia State Agricultural Society, On the Effects of Domestic Slavery on the Manners, Habits and Welfare of the Agricultural Population of the Southern States; And the Slavery of Class to Class in Northern States.* Read at the First Annual Meeting, in the Hall of the House of Delegates, December 16, 1852. Richmond: P. D. Bernard, Printer, 1853.

───────. *African Colonization Unveiled.* Washington, D.C.: Lemuel Towers, [1859].

───────. "On the Composition of Soils, and Their Improvement by Calcareous Manures," *American Farmer,* III, 313–20.

───────. "Consequences of Abolitionist Agitation," *DeBow's Review,* 22 (June, 1857), 583–93; 23 (September–December, 1857), 266–72, 385–90, 546–52, 596–607.

───────. "The Effects of High Prices of Slaves; Considered in Reference to the Interests of Agriculture, of Individuals, and of the Commonwealth of Virginia," *DeBow's Review,* 26 (June, 1859), 647–57.

───────. "Farming Profits in Eastern Virginia: The Value of Marl," *American Farmer* (July, 1849), pp. 1–10.

───────. "Fidelity of Slaves to Their Masters," *DeBow's Review,* 30 (January, 1861), 118–20.

───────. *The Influence of Slavery, or of Its Absence on Manners, Morals, and Intellect; An Address on the Opposite Results of Exhaustion and Fertilizing Systems of Agriculture.* Read Before the South Carolina Institute at Its Fourth Annual Fair, November 18, 1852. Charleston: Steam Power Press of Walker and James, 1853.

───────. "Liberia and the Colonization Society," *DeBow's Review,* 26 (April, 1859), 415–29; 27 (July–November, 1859), 55–73, 336–44, 392–402, 583–94.

───────. *The Political Economy of Slavery; or, The Institution Considered in Regard to Its Influence on Public Wealth and the General Welfare.* Washington, D.C.: Lemuel Towers, [1858].

───────. "A Reminiscence of the Time of Nullification," *Southern Literary Messenger,* 32 (April, 1861), 249–57.

───────. "Slavery and Free Labor Described and Compared," *Southern Planter,* 19 (December 1859), 723–41; 20 (January, 1860), 1–10.

_____. "Southern Agricultural Exhaustion, and Its Remedy," *Report of the Commission on Patents for the Year 1852.* Vol. 2. Washington, D.C.: Robert Armstrong, Printer, 1853.

Ruffin, Edmund Lorraine. "Descendants of Edmund Ruffin, The Great Agriculturalist and Author, Who Fired the First Gun at Fort Sumter in the War Between the States," *Tyler's Quarterly Historical and Genealogical Magazine,* 22 (April, 1941), 242–71.

_____. "Descendants of Edmund Ruffin, born 1794—died 1865, and Susan Hutchings Travis," Richmond: n. p., 1932. (Typewritten.)

Ruffin, Mrs. Kirkland (ed.). "School-Boy Letters of Edmund Ruffin, Jr.," *The North Carolina Historical Review,* 10 (October, 1933), 287–329.

Secondary Sources

Books

Ambler, Charles Henry. *Sectionalism in Virginia From 1776 to 1861.* Chicago: University of Chicago Press, 1910.

Aptheker, Herbert. *American Negro Slave Revolts.* New York: International Publishers, 1963.

_____. *The Negro in the American Revolution.* New York: International Publishers, 1940.

Bagley, William C. *Soil Exhaustion and the Civil War.* Washington, D.C.: American Council on Public Affairs, 1942.

Barney, William. *Flawed Victory: A New Perspective on the Civil War.* New York: Praeger, 1975.

_____. *The Road to Secession: A New Perspective on the Old South.* New York: Praeger Publishers, 1972.

_____. *The Secessionist Impulse: Alabama and Mississippi in 1860.* Princeton, New Jersey: Princeton University Press, 1974.

Beals, Carleton. *War Within a War; The Confederacy Against Itself.* Philadelphia: Chilton Books, 1965.

Berlin, Ira. *Slaves Without Masters.* New York: Random House, 1974.

Blackford, Launcelot Minor. *Mine Eyes Have Seen the Glory; The Story of a Virginia Lady, Mary Berkeley Minor Blackford, 1802–1896, Who Taught Her Sons to Hate Slavery and to Love the Union.* Cambridge, Massachusetts: Harvard University Press, 1954.

Blassingame, John. *The Slave Community.* New York: Oxford University Press, 1972.

Boney, F. N. *John Letcher of Virginia: The Story of Virginia's Civil War Governor.* University, Alabama: University of Alabama Press, 1966.

Boyer, Richard O. *The Legend of John Brown.* New York: Alfred A. Knopf, 1973.

Buel, Clarence C. and Robert U. Johnson (eds.). *Battles and Leaders of the Civil War.* 4 vols. New York: The Century Company, 1884–1887.

Cash, W. J. *The Mind of the South.* New York: Alfred A. Knopf, Inc., 1941.

Catton, Bruce. *The Civil War.* New York: American Heritage Press, 1971.

_____. *The Coming Fury.* New York: Doubleday, 1961.

_____. *This Hallowed Ground; The Story of the Union Side of the Civil War.* Garden City, New York: Doubleday, 1956.

_____. *A Stillness at Appomattox.* New York: Pocket Books, 1970.

_____. *Terrible Swift Sword.* New York: Pocket Books, 1970.

Catton, William and Bruce Catton. *Two Roads to Sumter.* New York: McGraw–Hill, 1963.

Channing, Stephen A. *Crisis of Fear: Secession in South Carolina.* New York: Simon and Schuster, 1970.

Coit, Margaret L. *John C. Calhoun: American Portrait.* Boston: Houghton Mifflin Company, 1950.

Collins, Winfield Hazlitt. *The Domestic Slave Trade of the Southern States.* Port Washington, New York: Kennikat Press, 1904.

Coulter, Ellis Merton. *The Confederate States of America, 1861–1865.* Baton Rouge: Louisiana State University Press, 1950.

Craven, Avery Odelle. *Civil War in the Making, 1815–1860.* Baton Rouge: Louisiana State University Press, 1959.

_____. *The Coming of the Civil War.* New York: C. Scribner's Sons, 1950.

_____. *Edmund Ruffin, Southerner: A Study in Secession.* New York: D. Appleton and Company, 1932.

_____. *The Growth of Southern Nationalism, 1848–1861.* Baton Rouge: Louisiana State University Press, 1953.

_____. *Soil Exhaustion as a Factor in the Agricultural History of Virginia and Maryland, 1606–1860.* Urbana, Illinois: University of Illinois Press, 1925.

Dangerfield, George. *The Era of Good Feelings.* New York: Harcourt, Brace & World, Inc., 1952.

Davis, Richard B. *Francis Walker Gilmer: Life and Learning in Jefferson's Virginia.* Richmond: The Dietz Press, 1939.

Degler, Carl N. *The Other South.* New York: Harper & Row, 1974.

Denman, Clarence Phillips. *The Secession Movement in Alabama.* 1933; rpt. Freeport, New York: Books for Libraries, 1971.

Dowdey, Clifford, *Experiment in Rebellion.* Garden City, New York: Doubleday & Company, Inc., 1946.

_____. *The Land They Fought For; The Story of the South as the Confederacy, 1823–1865.* Garden City, New York: Doubleday, 1955.

_____. *Lee's Last Campaign; The Story of Lee and His Men Against Grant–1864.* Boston: Little, Brown, 1960.

DuBose, John Witherspoon. *The Life and Times of William Lowndes Yancey.* Birmingham, Alabama: Roberts & Son, 1892.

Eaton, Clement. *The Civilization of the Old South; Writings of Clement Eaton.* Lexington, Kentucky: University of Kentucky Press, 1968.

_____. *Freedom of Thought in the Old South.* Durham, North Carolina: Duke University Press, 1946.

_____. *The Freedom-of-Thought Struggle in the Old South.* New York: Harper & Row, 1964.

_____. *The Growth of Southern Civilization, 1790–1860.* New York: Harper & Row, 1961.

_____. *A History of the Old South.* New York: Macmillan, 1949.

_____. *A History of the Southern Confederacy.* New York: Macmillan, 1954.

_____. *Jefferson Davis.* New York: The Free Press, 1977.

_____. *The Mind of the Old South.* Baton Rouge: Louisiana State University Press, 1967.

Faust, Drew Gilpin. *A Sacred Circle: The Dilemma of the Intellectual in the Old South.* Baltimore: Johns Hopkins University Press, 1977.

Fogel, Robert William and Stanley L. Engerman. *Time on the Cross; The Economics of American Negro Slavery.* Boston: Little, Brown, 1974.

Foner, Eric. *Free Soil, Free Labor, Free Men: The Ideology of the Republican Party Before the Civil War.* London: Oxford University Press, 1970.

Foote, Shelby. *The Civil War, A Narrative.* New York: Random House, 1958.

Franklin, John Hope. *The Militant South, 1800–1861.* Cambridge, Mass.: Belknap Press of Harvard University Press, 1956.

Freehling, William W. *Prelude to Civil War: The Nullification Controversy in South Carolina, 1816–1836.* New York: Harper & Row, 1965.

Gatell, Frank Otto. *Democracy and Union; The United States, 1815–1877.* New York: Holt, 1972.

Genovese, Eugene D. *The Political Economy of Slavery; Studies in the Economy and Society of the Slave South.* New York: Pantheon Books, 1967.

—————. *Roll Jordan Roll: The World the Slaves Made.* New York: Random House, 1972.

—————. *The World the Slaveholders Made: Two Essays in Interpretation.* New York: Random House, 1969.

Gerteis, Louis S. *From Contraband to Freedman: Federal Policy Toward Southern Blacks, 1861–1865.* Westport, Connecticut: Greenwood Press, 1973.

Gray, Lewis C. *History of Agriculture in the Southern United States to 1860.* Washington: The Carnegie Institution of Washington, 1933.

Gutman, Herbert G. *The Black Family in Slavery and Freedom, 1750–1925.* New York: Vintage Books, 1976.

—————. *Slavery and the Numbers Game: A Critique of Time on the Cross.* Urbana, Illinois: University of Illinois Press, 1975.

Hesseltine, William Best. *The South in American History.* New York: Prentice-Hall, Inc., 1943.

Hofstadter, Richard. *The American Political Tradition.* New York: Random House, 1948.

Hyman, Harold Melvin. *Era of the Oath; Northern Loyalty Tests During the Civil War and Reconstruction.* Philadelphia: University of Pennsylvania Press, 1954.

Jenkins, William Sumner. *Pro-Slavery Thought in the Old South.* Chapel Hill: University of North Carolina Press, 1935.

Jordan, Donaldson and Edwin J. Pratt. *Europe and the American Civil War.* New York: Houghton Mifflin Company, 1931.

Lerner, Gerda. *The Grimke Sisters of South Carolina.* New York: Schocken Books, 1971.

Litwak, Leon F. *North of Slavery.* Chicago: University of Chicago Press, 1961.

McColley, Robert. *Slavery and Jeffersonian Virginia.* Urbana, Illinois: University of Illinois Press, 1964.

McPherson, James M. *The Negro's Civil War: How American Negroes Felt and Acted During the War for the Union.* New York: Vintage Books, 1965.

—————. *The Struggle for Equality: Abolitionists and the Negro in the Civil War and Reconstruction.* Princeton: Princeton University Press, 1964.

Merritt, Elizabeth. *James Henry Hammond, 1806–1864.* Baltimore: Johns Hopkins Press, 1923.

Nevins, Allan. *Ordeal of the Union.* New York: Scribner's Sons, 1947.

Nichols, Roy Franklin. *The Disruption of American Democracy*. New York: The Free Press, 1968.

Oates, Stephen B. *The Fires of Jubilee: Nat Turner's Fierce Rebellion*. New York: Harper & Row, 1975.

——————. *To Purge This Land With Blood: A Biography of John Brown*. New York: Harper & Row, 1970.

——————. *With Malice Toward None: The Life of Abraham Lincoln*. New York: Harper & Row, 1977.

O'Connor, Thomas. *The Disunited States: The Era of Civil War and Reconstruction*. New York: Dodd, Mead & Company, 1973.

Osterweis, Rollin Gustav. *Romanticism and Nationalism in the Old South*. New Haven: Yale University Press, 1949.

Page, Thomas Nelson. *Social Life in Old Virginia Before the War*. Freeport, New York: Books for Libraries Press, 1897.

Phillips, Ulrich Bonnell. *The Course of the South to Secession*. New York: D. Appleton-Century Company, Inc., 1939.

Potter, David M. *The South and the Sectional Conflict*. Baton Rouge: Louisiana State University Press, 1968.

Quarles, Benjamin. *The Negro in the American Revolution*. Chapel Hill: University of North Carolina Press, 1961.

——————. *The Negro in the Civil War*. Boston: Little, Brown and Company, 1953.

Randall, J. G. and David Donald. *The Civil War and Reconstruction*. Lexington, Mass.: D. C. Heath and Company, 1969.

Reiners, Perceval. *The Springs of Virginia; Life, Love, and Death at the Waters, 1775–1900*. Chapel Hill: University of North Carolina Press, 1955.

Reynolds, Donald E. *Editors Make War; Southern Newspapers in the Secession Crisis*. Nashville: Vanderbilt University Press, 1970.

Roark, James L. *Masters Without Slaves: Southern Planters in the Civil War and Reconstruction*. New York: W. W. Norton & Company, 1977.

Robert, Joseph Clarke. *The Road From Monticello: A Study of the Virginia Slavery Debate of 1832*. Durham, North Carolina: Duke University Press, 1941.

Rose, Willie Lee. *Rehearsal for Reconstruction: The Port Royal Experiment*. New York: Random House, 1964.

Scarborough, William Kauffman. *The Overseer: Plantation Management in the Old South*. Baton Rouge: Louisiana State University Press, 1966.

Scott, Anne Firor. *The Southern Lady; From Pedestal to Politics, 1830–1930*. Chicago: University of Chicago Press, 1970.

Sellers, Charles G. (ed.). *The Southerner as American*. Chapel Hill: University of North Carolina Press, 1960.

Shanks, Henry T. *The Secession Movement in Virginia, 1847–1861*. New York: DaCapo Press, 1934.

Sitterson, Joseph Carlyle. *The Secession Movement in North Carolina*. Chapel Hill: University of North Carolina Press, 1939.

Skipper, Ottis C. *J. D. B. DeBow: Magazinist of the Old South*. Athens, Georgia: University of Georgia Press, 1958.

Stampp, Kenneth M. *And the War Came; The North and the Secession Crisis*. Baton Rouge: Louisiana State University, 1950.

——————. *The Era of Reconstruction, 1865–1877*. New York: Vintage Books, 1965.

──────────. *The Peculiar Institution: Slavery in the Ante-Bellum South.* New York: Alfred A. Knopf, Inc., 1956.

Stanton, William R. *The Leopard's Spots: Scientific Attitudes Toward Race in America, 1815–1860.* Chicago: University of Chicago Press, 1960.

Staudenraus, P. J. *The African Colonization Movement, 1816–1865.* New York: Columbia University Press, 1961.

Sydnor, Charles S. *The Development of Southern Sectionalism, 1819–1848.* Baton Rouge: Louisiana State University Press, 1948.

Takaki, Ronald T. *A Pro-Slavery Crusade; The Agitation to Reopen the African Slave Trade.* New York: Free Press, 1971.

Tatum, Georgia Lee. *Disloyalty in the Confederacy.* Chapel Hill: University of North Carolina Press, 1934.

Taylor, William R. *Cavalier & Yankee: The Old South and American National Character.* New York: Harper & Row, 1957.

Thomas, Emory M. *The Confederacy as a Revolutionary Experience.* Englewood Cliffs, New Jersey: Prentice-Hall, Inc., 1971.

──────────. *The Confederate Nation: 1861–1865.* New York: Harper & Row, 1979.

Trent, William P. *William Gilmore Simms.* 1892; rpt. New York: Greenwood Press, 1969.

Van Deusen, John George. *The Ante-Bellum Southern Commercial Conventions.* Durham, North Carolina: Duke University Press, 1926.

Wender, Herbert. *Southern Commercial Conventions, 1837–1859.* Baltimore: Johns Hopkins Press, 1930.

White, Laura A. *Robert Barnwell Rhett: Father of Secession.* New York: The Century Company, 1931.

Whitfield, Theodore Marshall. *Slavery Agitation in Virginia, 1829–1832.* 1930; rpt. New York: Negro Universities Press, 1969.

Williams, George Washington. *A History of the Negro Troops in the War of Rebellion, 1861–1865.* New York: Bergman Publishers, 1968.

Williams, T. Harry. *P. G. T. Beauregard: Napoleon in Gray.* Baton Rouge: Louisiana State University Press, 1955.

Wish, Harvey. *George Fitzhugh: Propagandist of the Old South.* Gloucester, Mass.: P. Smith, 1943.

Wooster, Ralph A. *The Secession Conventions of the South.* Princeton: Princeton University Press, 1962.

Articles

Adams, James Truslow. "The Dilemma of Edmund Ruffin," *The Virginia Quarterly Review,* 10 (July, 1934), 321–35.

Anderson, Sterling, P., Jr. "Edmund Ruffin, Editor and Publisher," *Virginia Cavalcade,* 17 (Summer, 1967), 32–38.

Bonner, James C. "Genesis of Agricultural Reform in the Cotton Belt," *Journal of Southern History,* 9 (November, 1943), 475–500.

Craven, Avery Odelle. "The South in American History," *Historical Outlook,* 21 (March, 1932), 105–09.

Cutter, W. P. "A Pioneer in Agricultural Science," *Yearbook of the United States Department of Agriculture, 1895* (Washington, D.C.: Government Printing Office, 1896), pp. 493–502.

Donald, David. "The Proslavery Argument Reconsidered," *Journal of Southern History,* 37 (February, 1971), 3–18.

Eaton, Clement. "Henry A. Wise and the Virginia Fire Eaters of 1856," *Mississippi Valley Historical Review,* 21 (March, 1935), 495–512.

Ellis, Henry G. "Edmund Ruffin: His Life and Times," *The John P. Branch Historical Papers of Randolph-Macon College,* 3 (June, 1910), 99–123.

Govan, Thomas P. "Was the Old South Different?" *Journal of Southern History,* 21 (November, 1955), 447–55.

Harrison, Lowell. "Thomas Roderick Dew: Philosopher of the Old South," *Virginia Magazine of History and Biography,* 57 (October, 1949), 390–404.

Hesseltine, William B. "Some New Aspects of the Pro-Slavery Argument," *Journal of Negro History,* 21 (January, 1936), 1–15.

Kaplan, Sidney, "The Miscegenation Issue in the Election of 1864," *Journal of Negro History,* 34 (July, 1949), 274–343.

Mitchell, Betty L. "Massachusetts Reacts to John Brown's Raid," *Civil War History,* 19 (March, 1973), 65–79.

_____. "Realities Not Shadows: Franklin Benjamin Sanborn, the Early Years," *Civil War History,* 20 (June, 1974), 101–17.

Morrison, Alfred J. "The Virginia Farmer," *William and Mary College Quarterly,* 23 (January, 1915), 172–73.

Morrow, Ralph E. "The Proslavery Argument Revisited," *Mississippi Valley Historical Review,* 47 (June, 1961), 79–94.

Phillips, Ulrich Bonnell. "The Central Theme of Southern History," *American Historical Review,* 34 (October, 1928), 30–43.

Russel, Robert R. "The General Effects of Slavery Upon Southern Economic Progress," *Journal of Southern History,* 4 (February, 1938), 34–56.

Smith, Kenneth L. "Edmund Ruffin and the Raid on Harper's Ferry," *Virginia Cavalcade,* 22 (Autumn, 1972), 28–37.

Stampp, Kenneth M. "An Analysis of T. R. Dew's Review of the Debates in the Virginia Legislature," *Journal of Negro History,* 27 (October, 1942), 380–87.

_____. "The Southern Refutation of the Proslavery Argument," *North Carolina Historical Review,* 21 (January, 1944), 35–45.

Steinberg, Alfred. "Edmund Ruffin: Fire-eating Farmer of the Confederacy," *American Heritage,* 9 (December, 1957), 22–25, 114–17.

Swem, Earl G. "An Analysis of Ruffin's Farmers' Register, With a Bibliography of Edmund Ruffin," *Bulletin of the Virginia State Library,* 11 (July, October, 1918), 41–144. Richmond: Davis Bottom, Superintendent of Public Printing, 1919.

Wish, Harvey. "The Slave Insurrectionary Panic of 1856," *Journal of Southern History,* 4 (May, 1939), 206–22.

Woodward, C. Vann. "The Irony of Southern History," *Journal of Southern History,* 19 (February, 1953), 3–19.

Wooster, Ralph A. "An Analysis of the Membership of the Secession Conventions in the Lower South," *Alabama Review,* 24 (August, 1958), 360–68.

"Writers of Anonymous Articles in the Farmers' Register," *Journal of Southern History,* 23 (February, 1957), 90–102.

Dissertations

Rachleff, Marshall J. "Racial Fear and Political Factionalism; A Study of the Secession Movement in Alabama, 1819–1861." Ph.D. dissertation, University of Massachusetts, Amherst, 1974.

INDEX

299